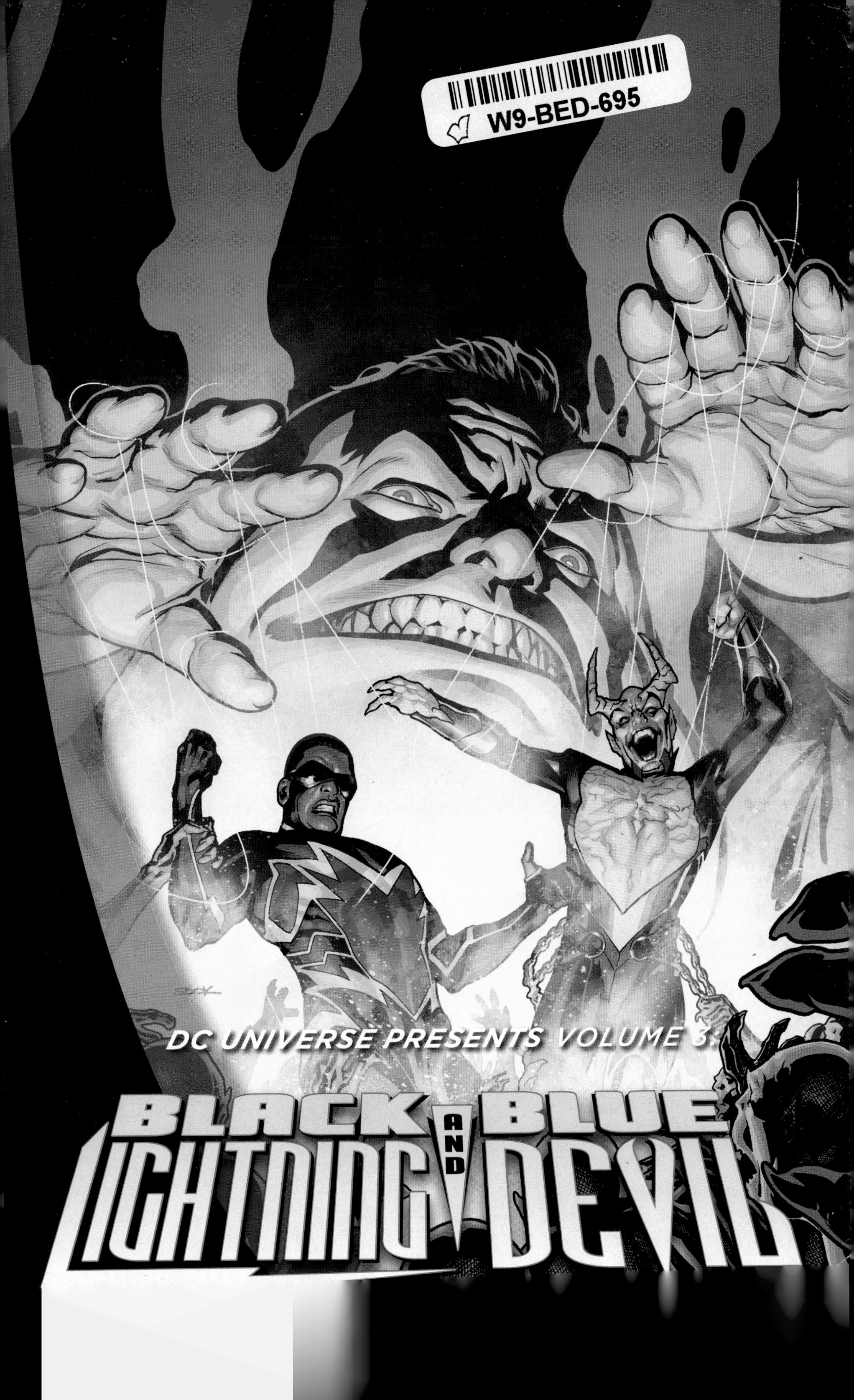
SOOK
DC UNIVERSE PRESENTS VOLUME 3:
BLACK LIGHTNING AND BLUE DEVIL

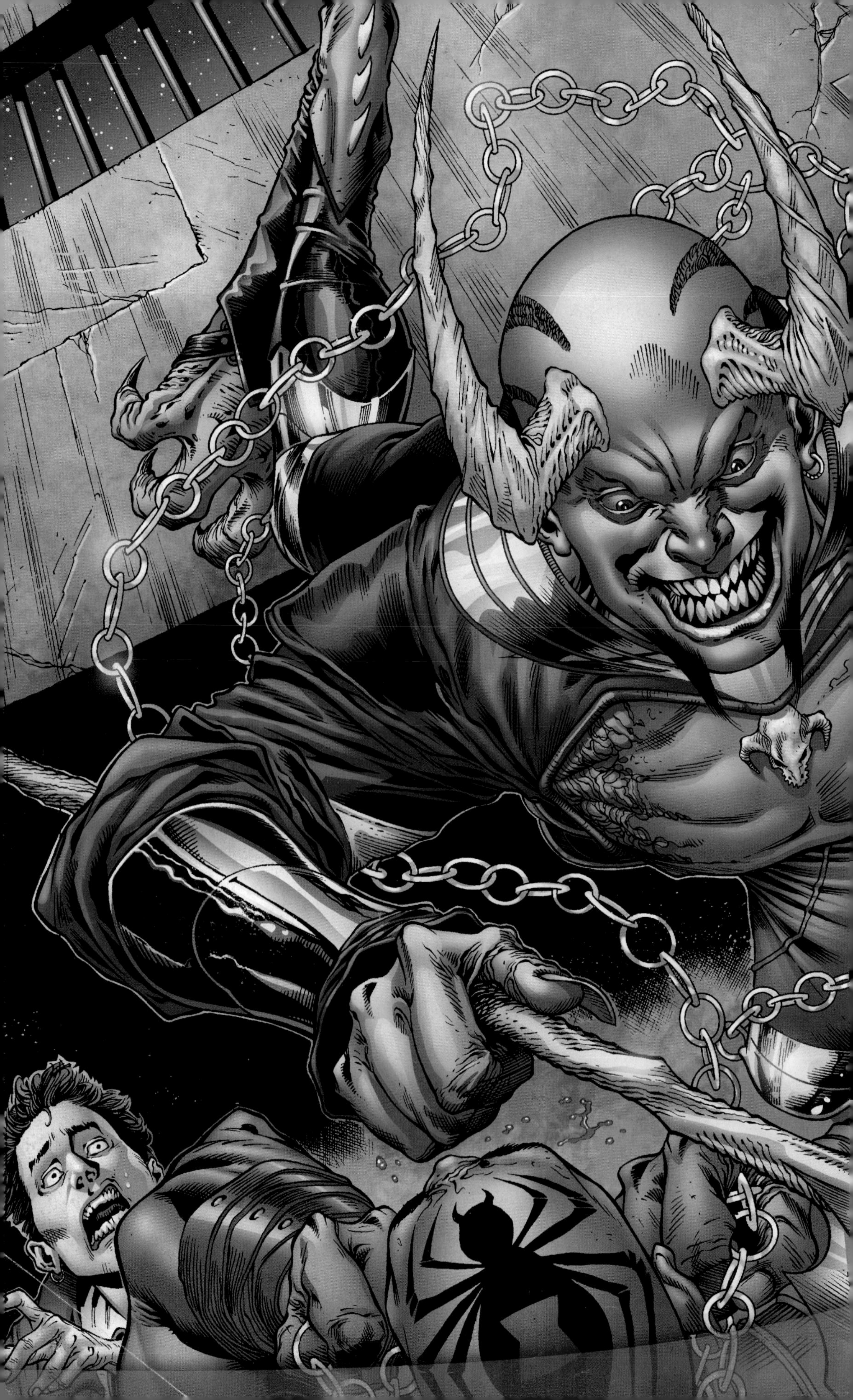

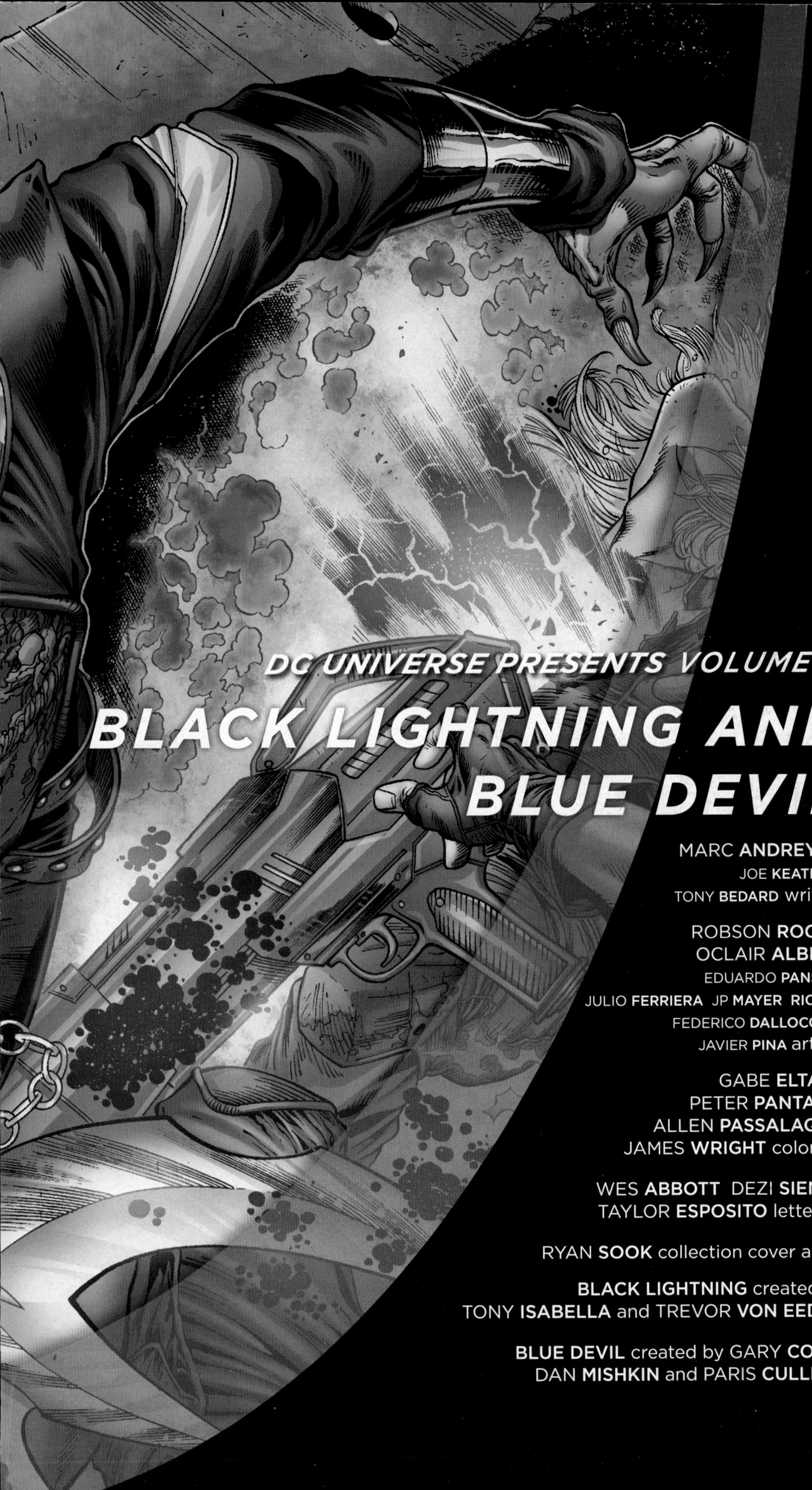

DC UNIVERSE PRESENTS VOLUME 3:

BLACK LIGHTNING AND BLUE DEVIL

MARC **ANDREYKO**
JOE **KEATINGE**
TONY **BEDARD** writers

ROBSON **ROCHA**
OCLAIR **ALBERT**
EDUARDO **PANSICA**
JULIO **FERRIERA** JP **MAYER** **RICKEN**
FEDERICO **DALLOCCHIO**
JAVIER **PINA** artists

GABE **ELTAEB**
PETER **PANTAZIS**
ALLEN **PASSALAQUA**
JAMES **WRIGHT** colorists

WES **ABBOTT** DEZI **SIENTY**
TAYLOR **ESPOSITO** letterers

RYAN **SOOK** collection cover artist

BLACK LIGHTNING created by
TONY **ISABELLA** and TREVOR **VON EEDEN**

BLUE DEVIL created by GARY **COHN**,
DAN **MISHKIN** and PARIS **CULLIINS**

EDDIE BERGANZA MIKE COTTON Editors – Original Series WIL MOSS Associate Editor – Original Series
DARREN SHAN ANTHONY MARQUES Assistant Editors – Original Series RACHEL PINNELAS Editor
ROBBIN BROSTERMAN Design Director – Books ROBBIE BIEDERMAN Publication Design

BOB HARRAS Senior VP – Editor-in-Chief, DC Comics

DIANE NELSON President DAN DIDIO and JIM LEE Co-Publishers
GEOFF JOHNS Chief Creative Officer
JOHN ROOD Executive VP – Sales, Marketing and Business Development
AMY GENKINS Senior VP – Business and Legal Affairs NAIRI GARDINER Senior VP – Finance
JEFF BOISON VP – Publishing Planning MARK CHIARELLO VP – Art Direction and Design
JOHN CUNNINGHAM VP – Marketing TERRI CUNNINGHAM VP – Editorial Administration
ALISON GILL Senior VP – Manufacturing and Operations HANK KANALZ Senior VP – Vertigo and Integrated Publishing
JAY KOGAN VP – Business and Legal Affairs, Publishing JACK MAHAN VP – Business Affairs, Talent
NICK NAPOLITANO VP – Manufacturing Administration SUE POHJA VP – Book Sales
COURTNEY SIMMONS Senior VP – Publicity BOB WAYNE Senior VP – Sales

DC UNIVERSE PRESENTS VOLUME 3: BLACK LIGHTNING AND BLUE DEVIL

Published by DC Comics. Copyright © 2014 DC Comics. All Rights Reserved.

Originally published in single magazine form in DC UNIVERSE PRESENTS 13-19. Copyright © 2012, 2013 DC Comics.
All Rights Reserved. All characters, their distinctive likenesses and related elements featured in this publication are
trademarks of DC Comics. The stories, characters and incidents featured in this publication are entirely fictional.
DC Comics does not read or accept unsolicited ideas, stories or artwork.

DC Comics, 1700 Broadway, New York, NY 10019
A Warner Bros. Entertainment Company.
Printed by RR Donnelley, Salem, VA, USA. 1/24/14. First Printing.
ISBN: 978-1-4012-4277-0

Library of Congress Cataloging-in-Publication Data

Andreyko, Marc, author.
DC Universe Presents. Volume 3, Black Lightning and Blue Devil / Marc Andreyko ; illustrated by Robson Rocha ;
illustrated by Oclair Albert.
pages cm. -- (The New 52!)
ISBN 978-1-4012-4277-0 (paperback)
1. Graphic novels. I. Rocha, Robson, illustrator. II. Albert, Oclair, illustrator. III. Title. IV. Title: Black Lightning and Blue
Devil.
PN6728.D35334A53 2014
741.5'973--dc23

2013049984

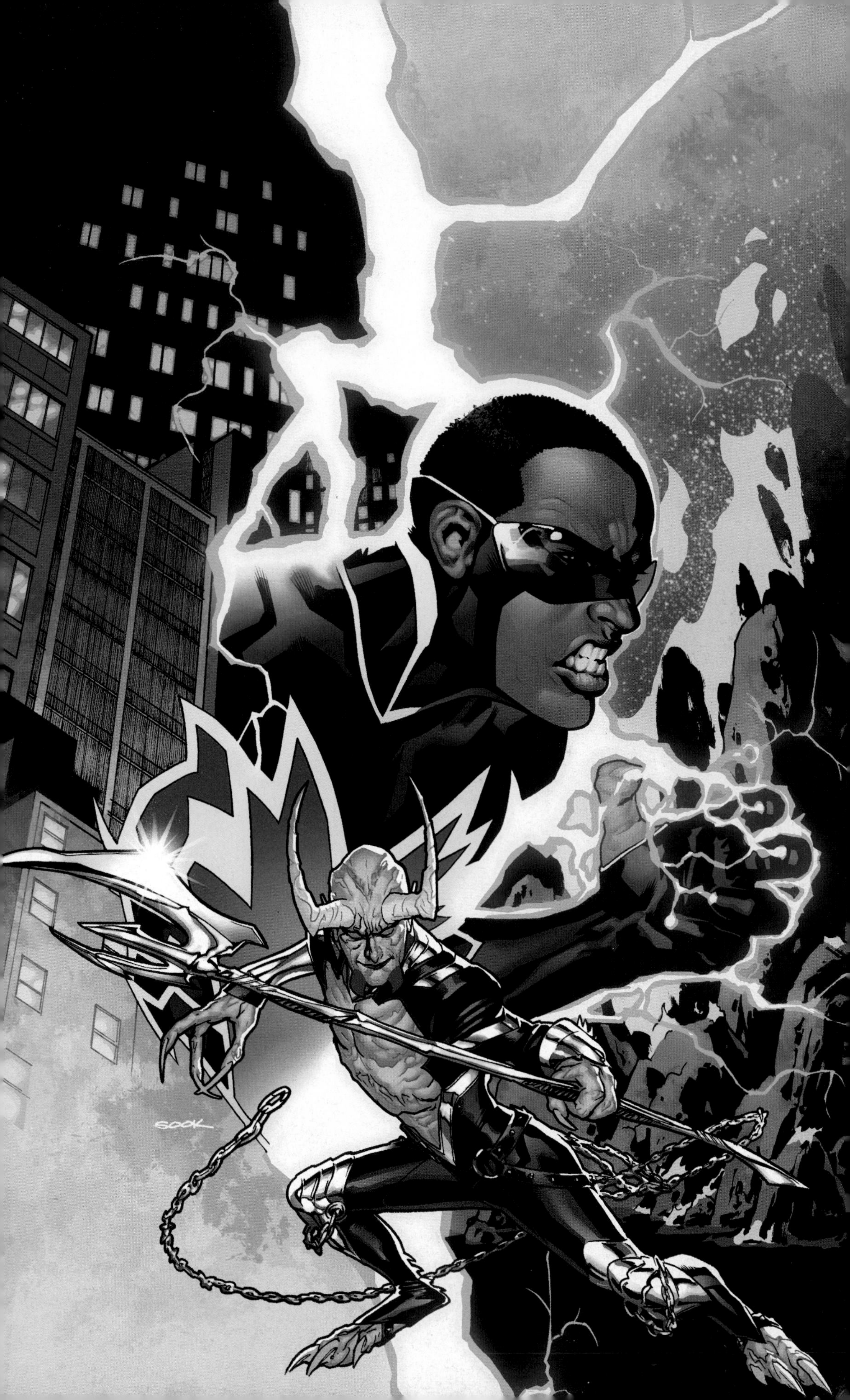
SOOK

THE DEVIL MADE ME DO IT

MARC ANDREYKO
writer

ROBSON ROCHA
penciller

OCLAIR ALBERT
inker

cover art by RYAN SOOK

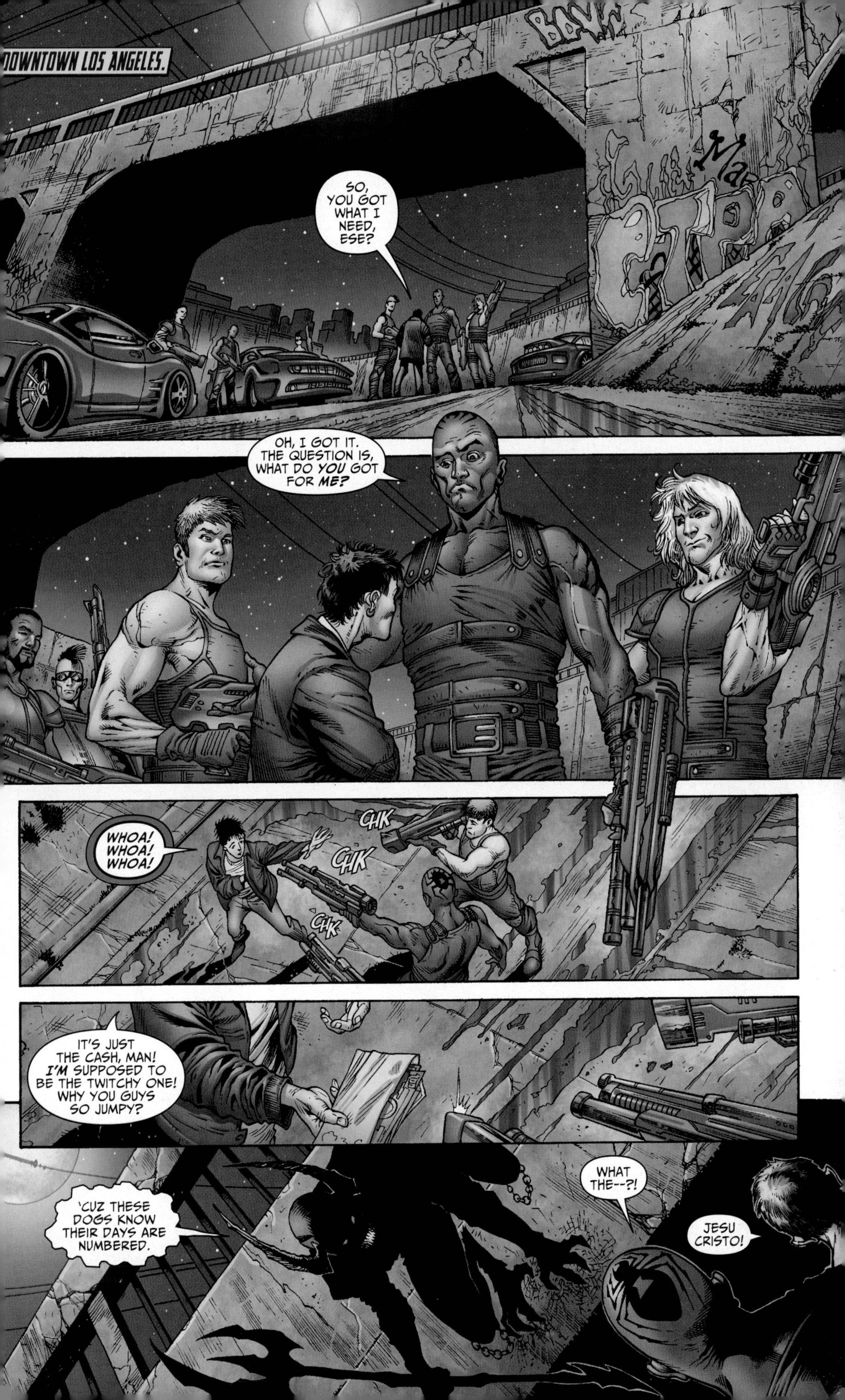
DOWNTOWN LOS ANGELES.
SO, YOU GOT WHAT I NEED, ESE?
OH, I GOT IT. THE QUESTION IS, WHAT DO *YOU* GOT FOR *ME?*
WHOA! WHOA! WHOA!
CHK
CHK
CHK
IT'S JUST THE CASH, MAN! *I'M* SUPPOSED TO BE THE TWITCHY ONE! WHY YOU GUYS SO JUMPY?
'CUZ THESE DOGS KNOW THEIR DAYS ARE NUMBERED.
WHAT THE--?!
JESU CRISTO!

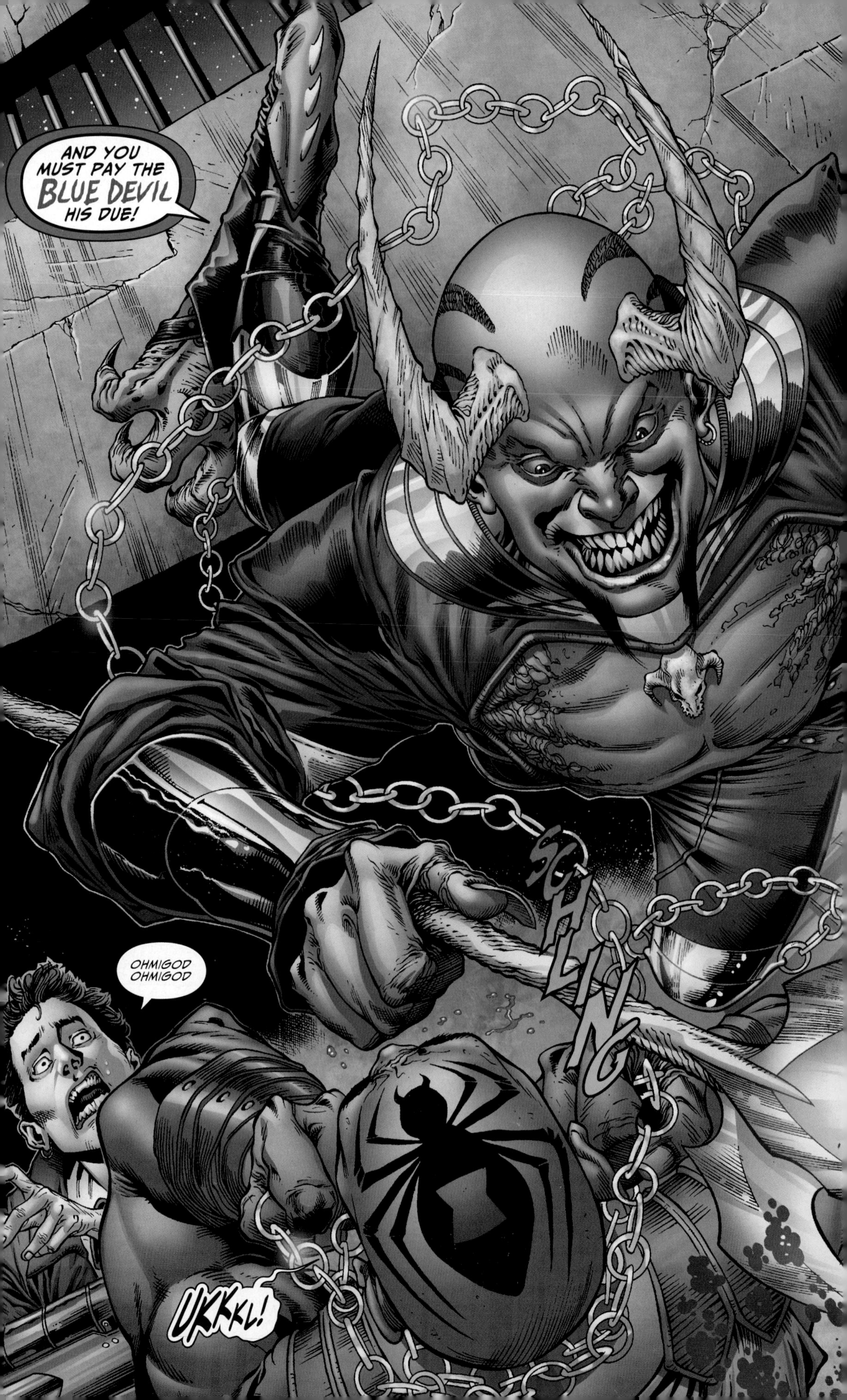
AND YOU MUST PAY THE BLUE DEVIL HIS DUE!
SCHLUNG
OHMIGOD OHMIGOD
UKKKL!

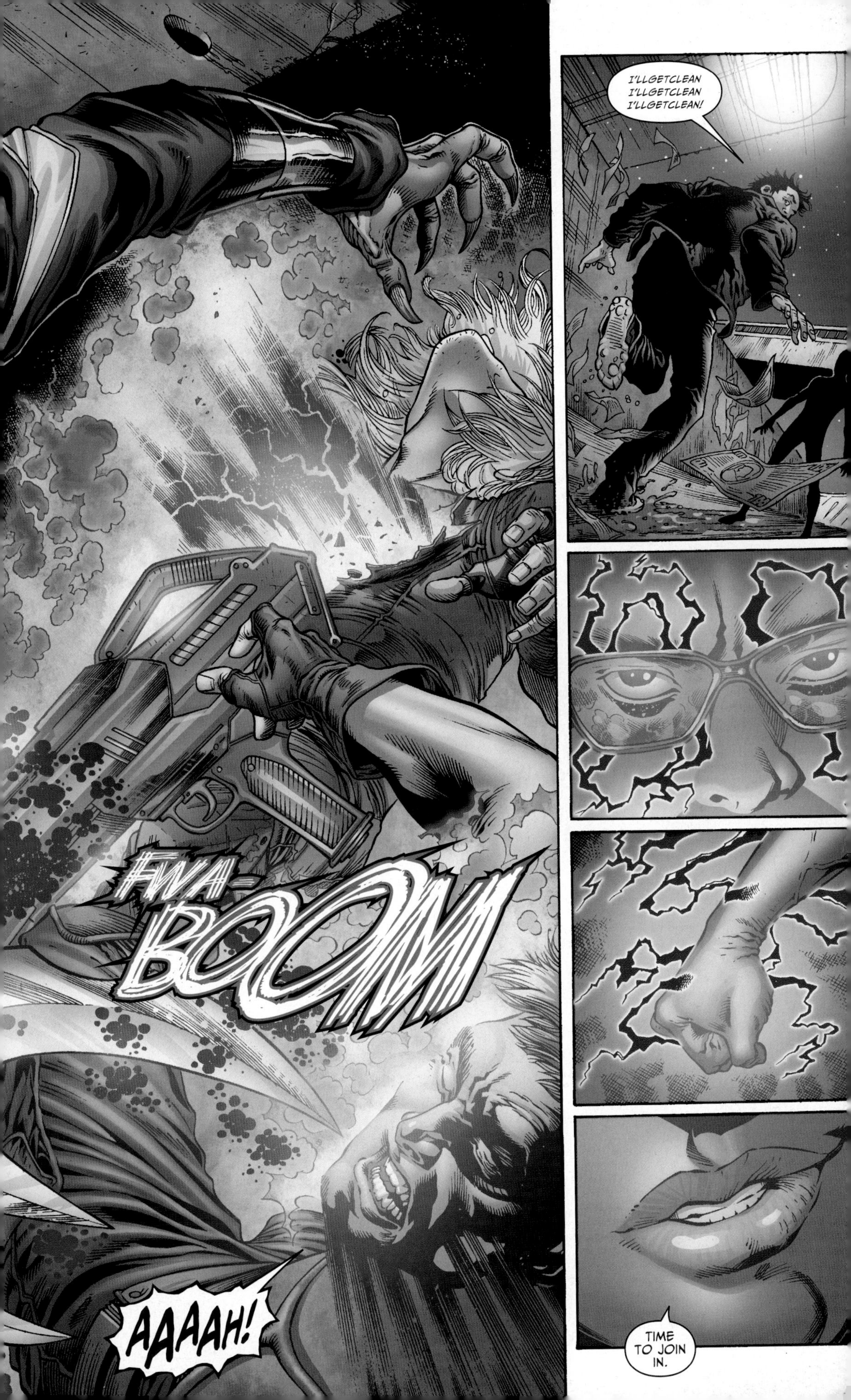
FWA-BOOM
AAAAH!
I'LLGETCLEAN I'LLGETCLEAN I'LLGETCLEAN!
TIME TO JOIN IN.

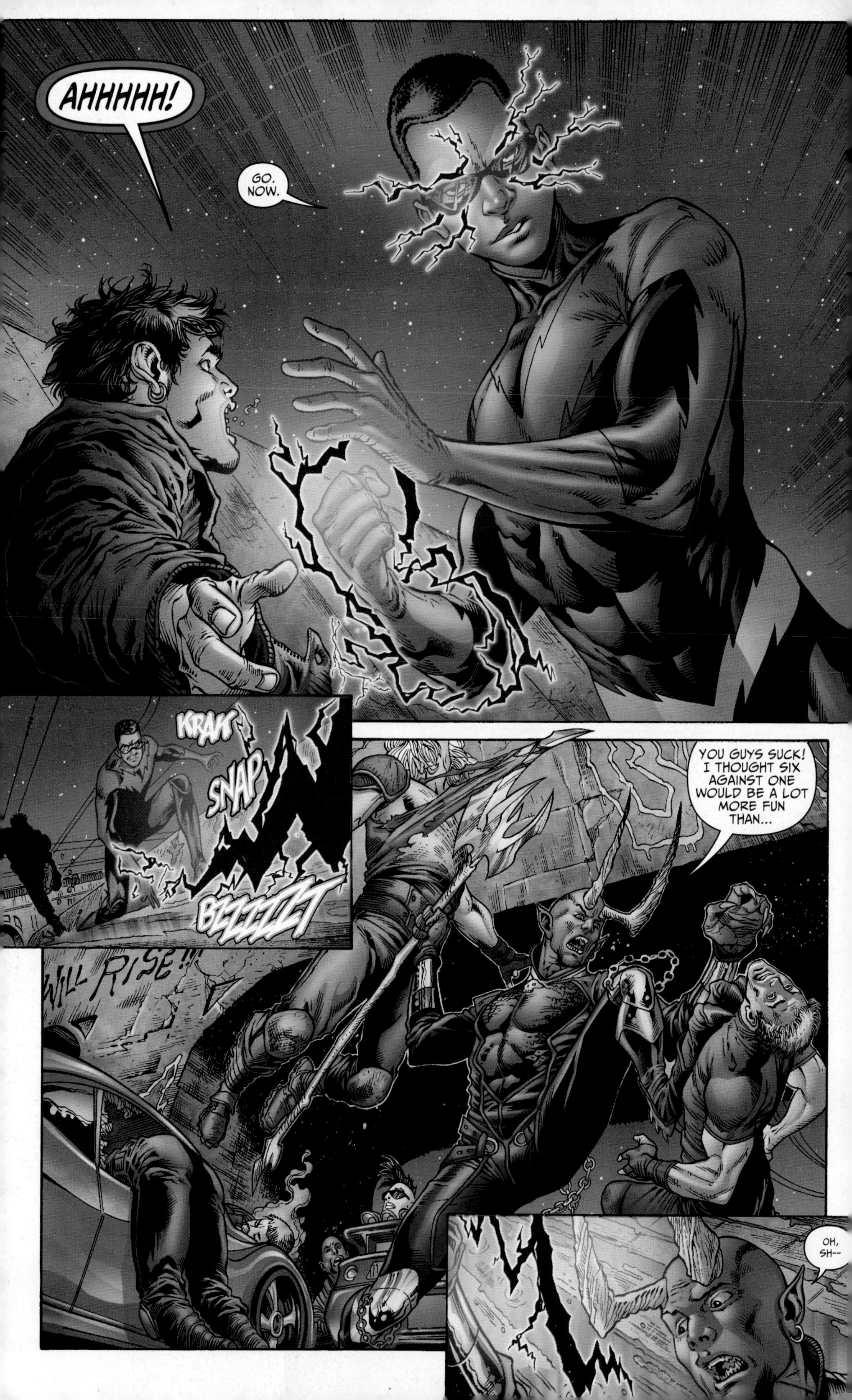
AHHHHH!
GO. NOW.
KRAK
SNAP
BZZZZZT
YOU GUYS SUCK! I THOUGHT SIX AGAINST ONE WOULD BE A LOT MORE FUN THAN...
WILL RISE!!!
OH, SH--

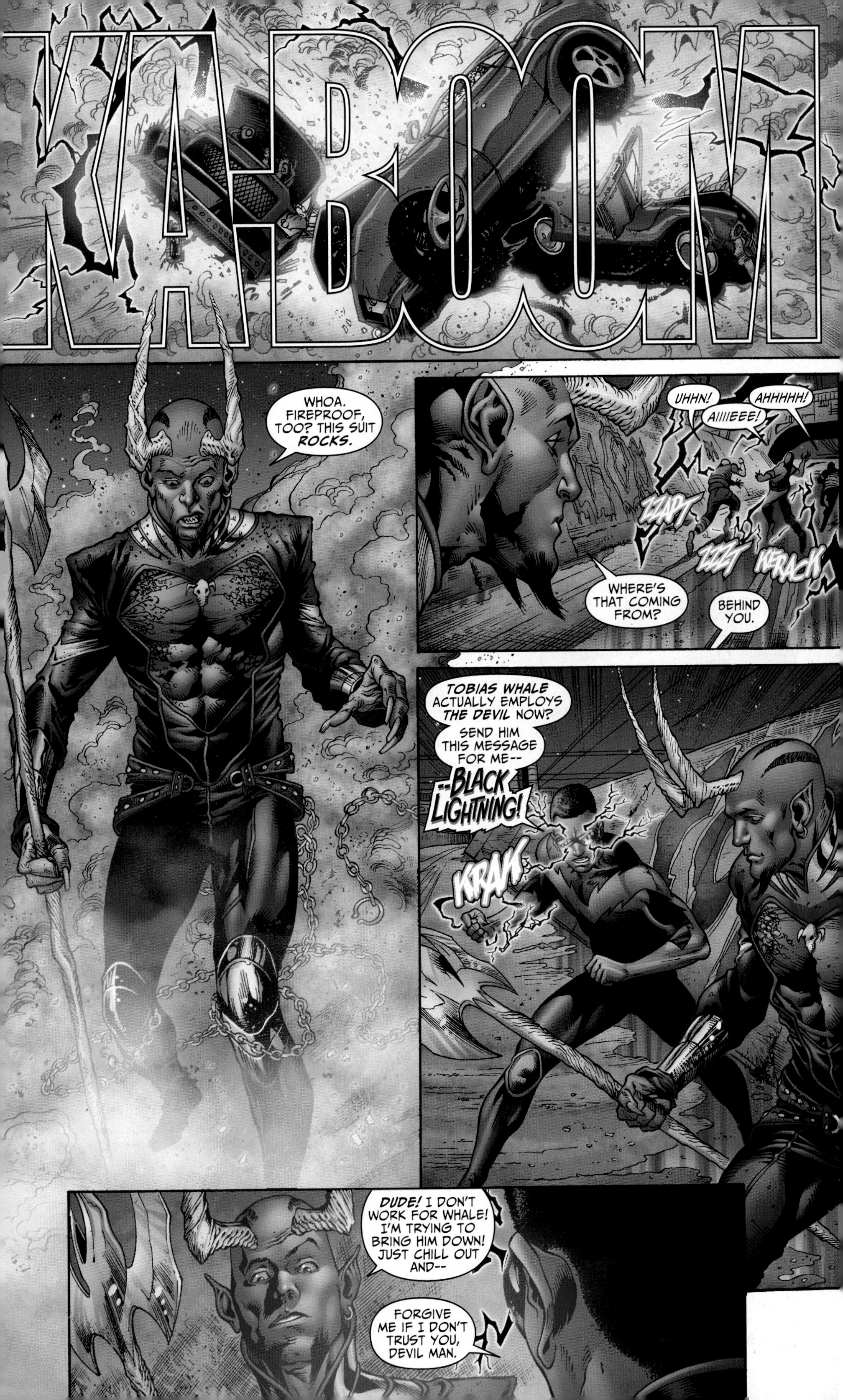
KA-BOOM
WHOA. FIREPROOF, TOO? THIS SUIT ROCKS.
UHHN!
AIIIEEE!
AHHHHH!
ZZAPT
ZZZT
KERACK
WHERE'S THAT COMING FROM?
BEHIND YOU.
TOBIAS WHALE ACTUALLY EMPLOYS THE DEVIL NOW?
SEND HIM THIS MESSAGE FOR ME--
--BLACK LIGHTNING!
KRAK
DUDE! I DON'T WORK FOR WHALE! I'M TRYING TO BRING HIM DOWN! JUST CHILL OUT AND--
FORGIVE ME IF I DON'T TRUST YOU, DEVIL MAN.

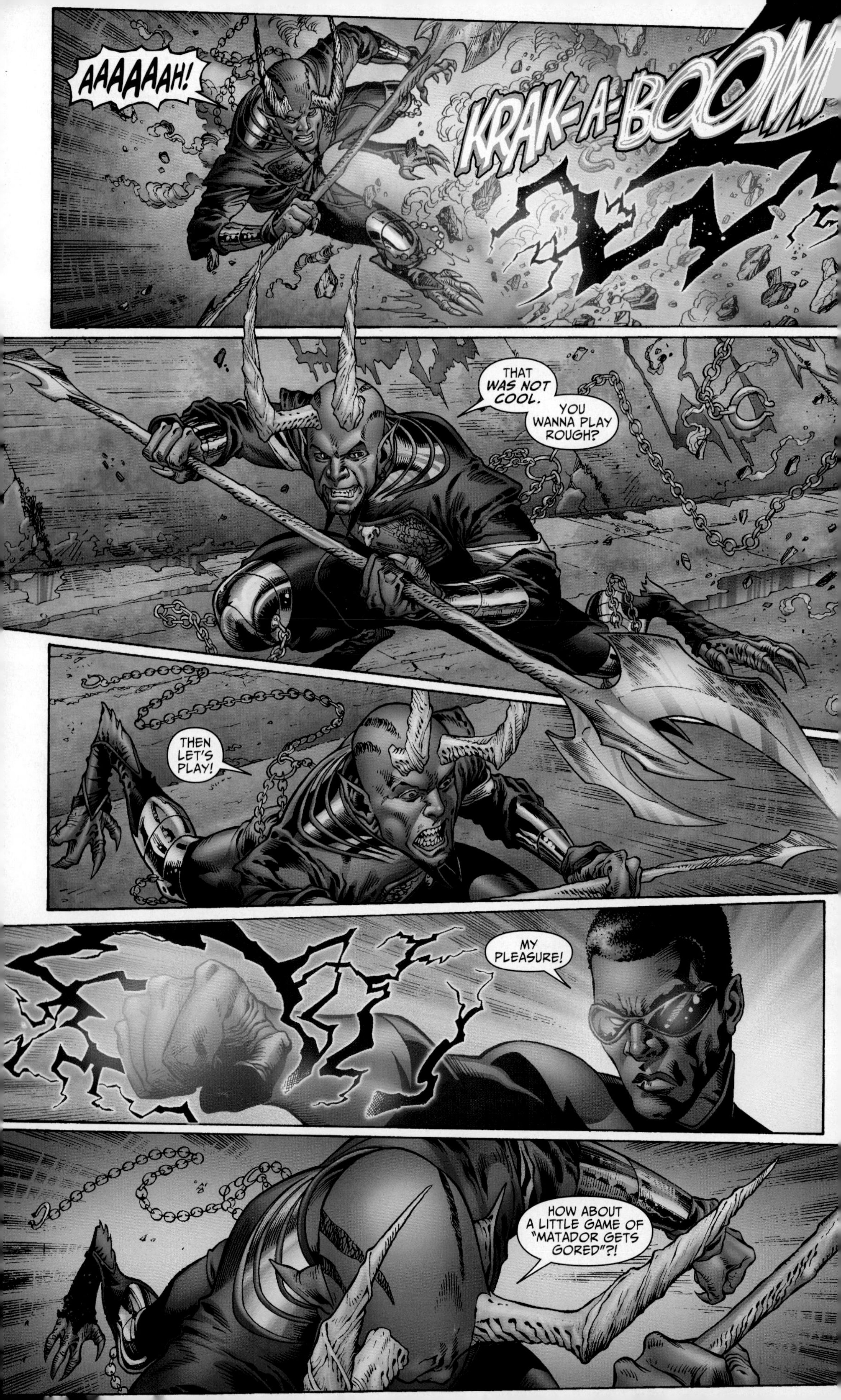
AAAAAAH!
KRAK-A-BOOM
THAT WAS NOT COOL.
YOU WANNA PLAY ROUGH?
THEN LET'S PLAY!
MY PLEASURE!
HOW ABOUT A LITTLE GAME OF "MATADOR GETS GORED"?!

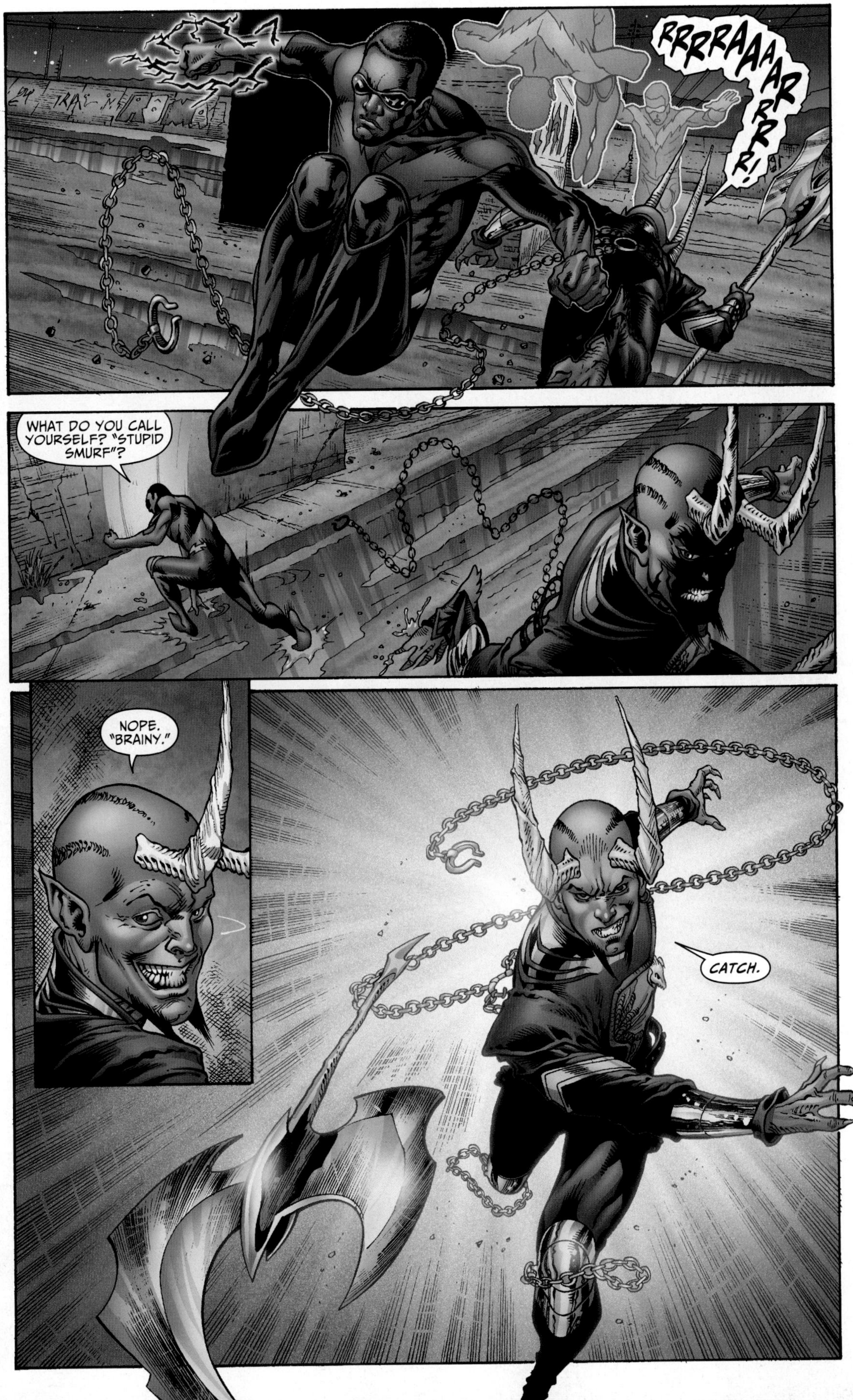

RRRRAAAARRRRR!
WHAT DO YOU CALL YOURSELF? "STUPID SMURF"?
NOPE. "BRAINY."
CATCH.

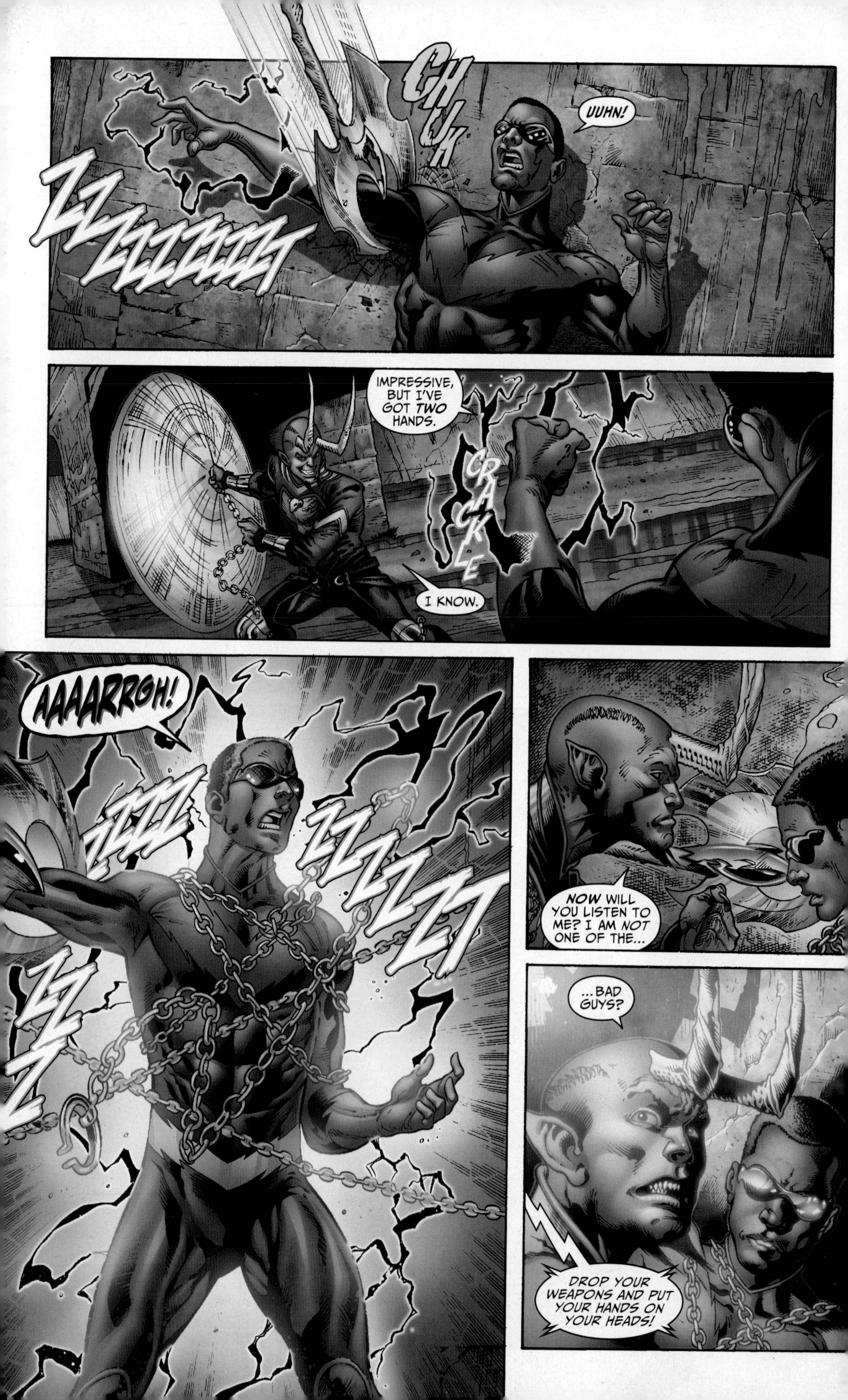
CHUK
UUHN!
ZZZZZZZZZZZT
IMPRESSIVE, BUT I'VE GOT TWO HANDS.
CRACKLE
I KNOW.
AAAARRGH!
ZZZZ
ZZZZZZT
ZZZZ
NOW WILL YOU LISTEN TO ME? I AM NOT ONE OF THE...
...BAD GUYS?
DROP YOUR WEAPONS AND PUT YOUR HANDS ON YOUR HEADS!

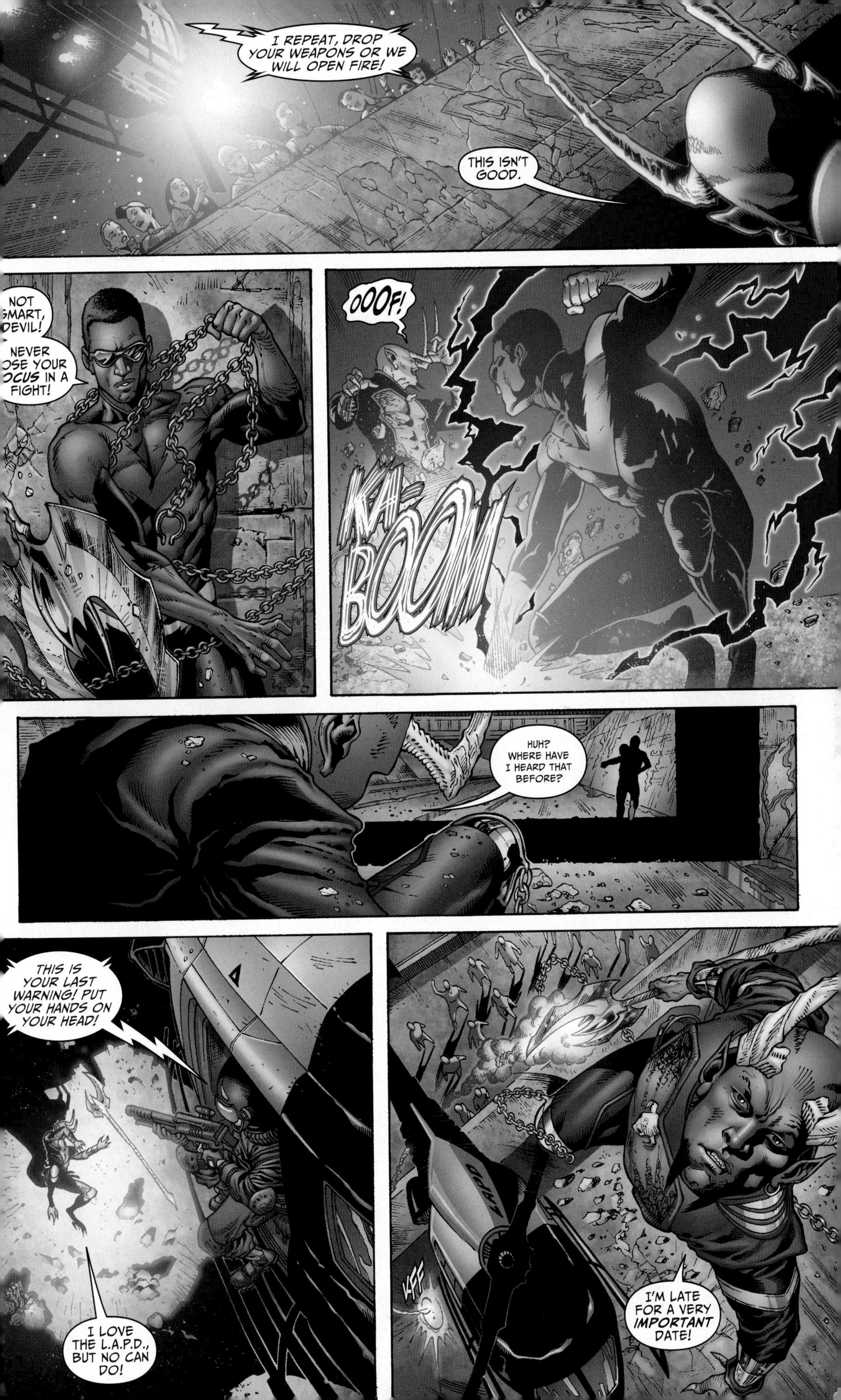

I REPEAT, DROP YOUR WEAPONS OR WE WILL OPEN FIRE!
THIS ISN'T GOOD.
NOT SMART, DEVIL!
NEVER OSE YOUR OCUS IN A FIGHT!
OOOF!
KA-BOOM
HUH? WHERE HAVE I HEARD THAT BEFORE?
THIS IS YOUR LAST WARNING! PUT YOUR HANDS ON YOUR HEAD!
I LOVE THE L.A.P.D., BUT NO CAN DO!
I'M LATE FOR A VERY IMPORTANT DATE!

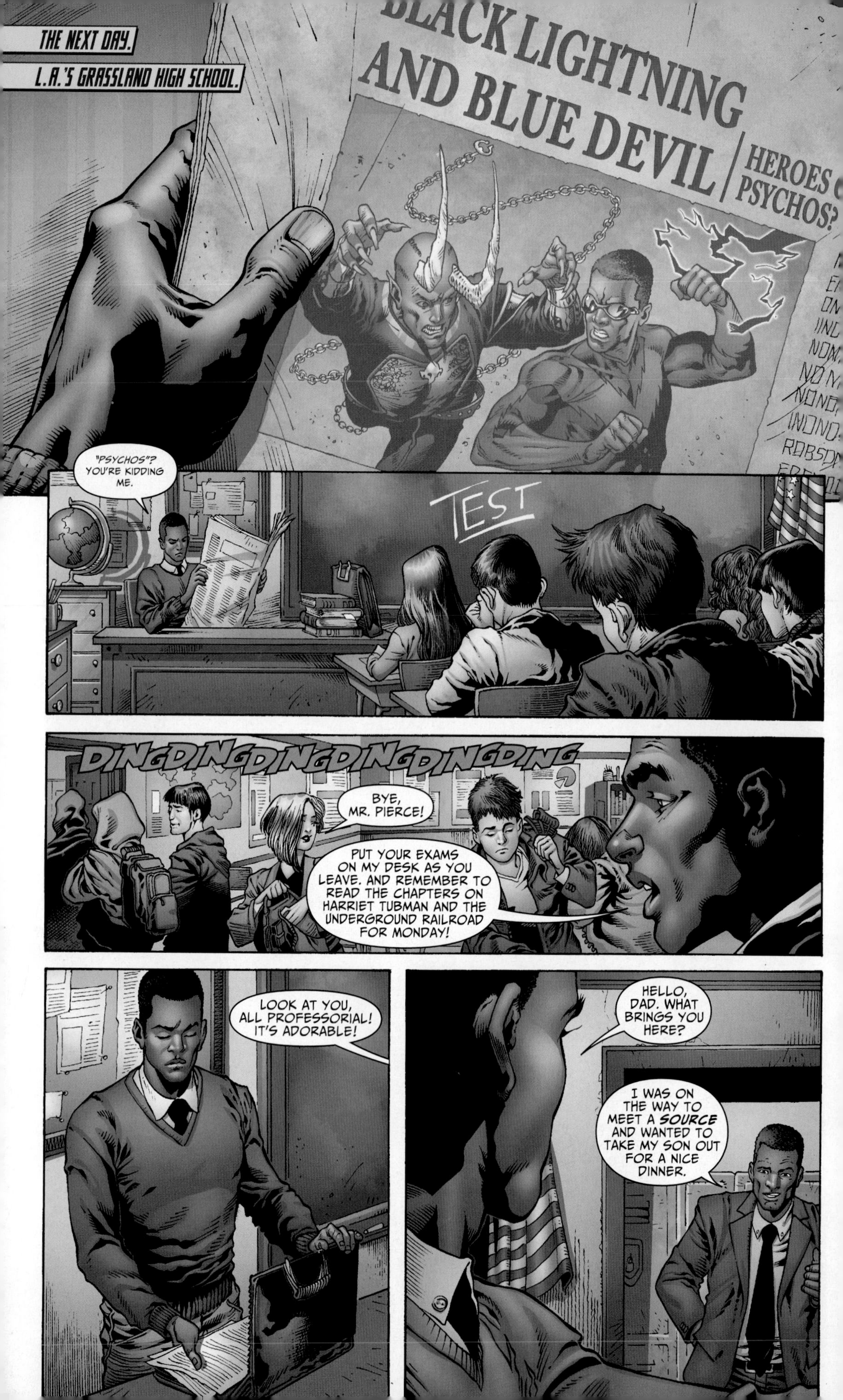

THE NEXT DAY.
L.A.'S GRASSLAND HIGH SCHOOL.
BLACK LIGHTNING AND BLUE DEVIL
HEROES OR PSYCHOS?
"PSYCHOS"? YOU'RE KIDDING ME.
TEST
DINGDINGDINGDINGDINGDING
BYE, MR. PIERCE!
PUT YOUR EXAMS ON MY DESK AS YOU LEAVE. AND REMEMBER TO READ THE CHAPTERS ON HARRIET TUBMAN AND THE UNDERGROUND RAILROAD FOR MONDAY!
LOOK AT YOU, ALL PROFESSORIAL! IT'S ADORABLE!
HELLO, DAD. WHAT BRINGS YOU HERE?
I WAS ON THE WAY TO MEET A SOURCE AND WANTED TO TAKE MY SON OUT FOR A NICE DINNER.

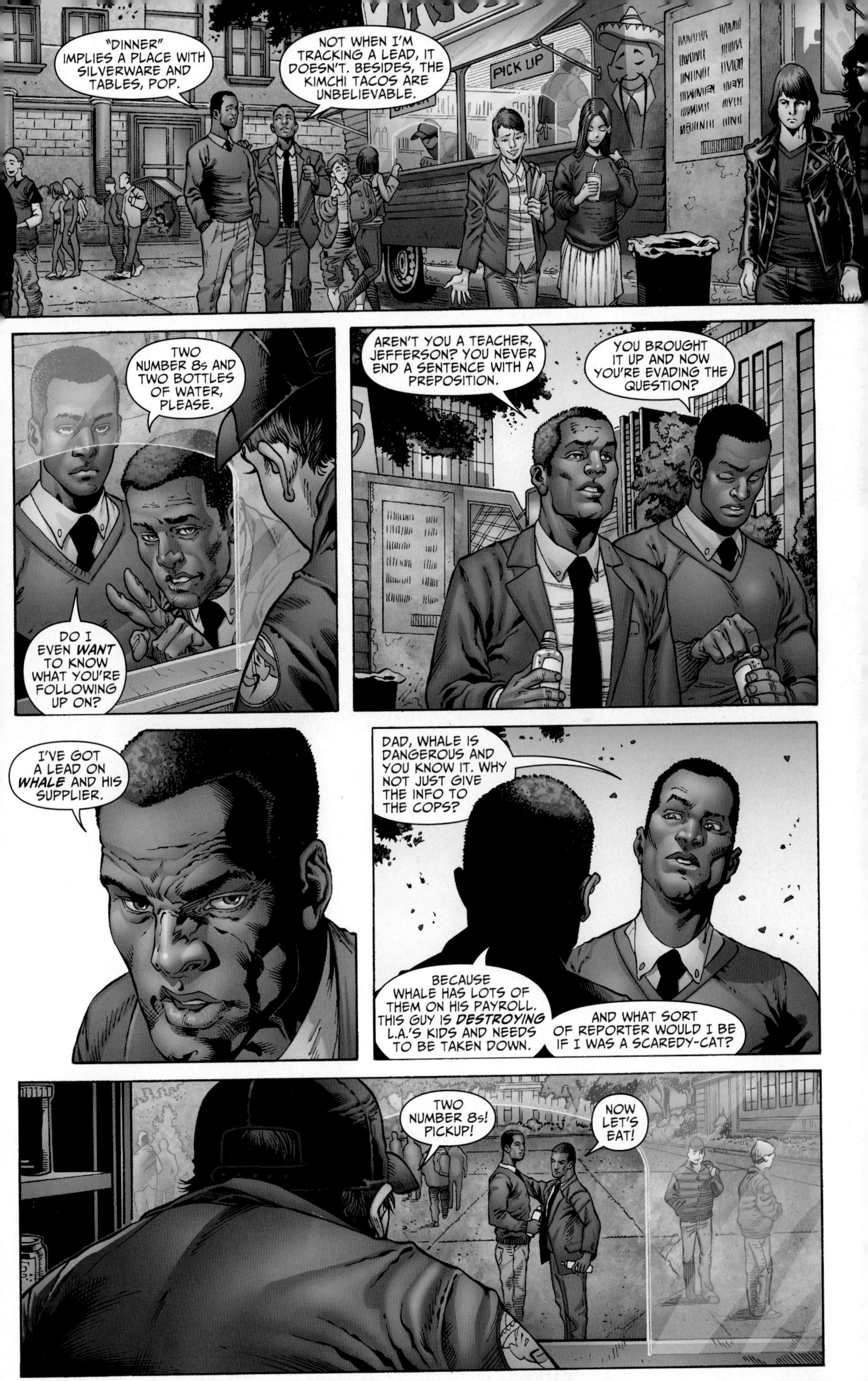
"DINNER" IMPLIES A PLACE WITH SILVERWARE AND TABLES, POP.
NOT WHEN I'M TRACKING A LEAD, IT DOESN'T. BESIDES, THE KIMCHI TACOS ARE UNBELIEVABLE.
PICK UP
TWO NUMBER 8s AND TWO BOTTLES OF WATER, PLEASE.
DO I EVEN WANT TO KNOW WHAT YOU'RE FOLLOWING UP ON?
AREN'T YOU A TEACHER, JEFFERSON? YOU NEVER END A SENTENCE WITH A PREPOSITION.
YOU BROUGHT IT UP AND NOW YOU'RE EVADING THE QUESTION?
I'VE GOT A LEAD ON WHALE AND HIS SUPPLIER.
DAD, WHALE IS DANGEROUS AND YOU KNOW IT. WHY NOT JUST GIVE THE INFO TO THE COPS?
BECAUSE WHALE HAS LOTS OF THEM ON HIS PAYROLL. THIS GUY IS DESTROYING L.A.'S KIDS AND NEEDS TO BE TAKEN DOWN.
AND WHAT SORT OF REPORTER WOULD I BE IF I WAS A SCAREDY-CAT?
TWO NUMBER 8s! PICKUP!
NOW LET'S EAT!

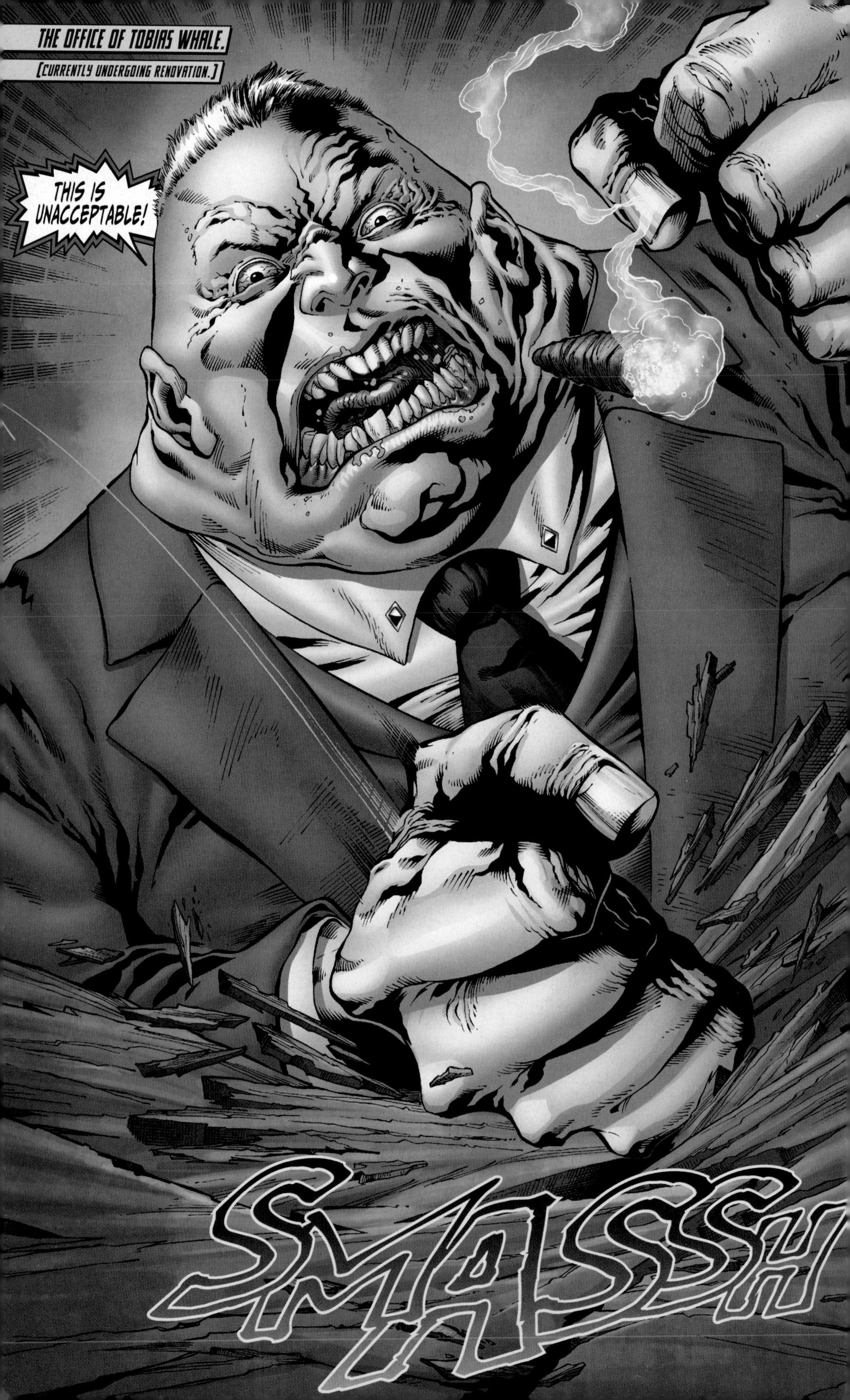
THE OFFICE OF TOBIAS WHALE.
[CURRENTLY UNDERGOING RENOVATION.]
THIS IS UNACCEPTABLE!
SMASSSH

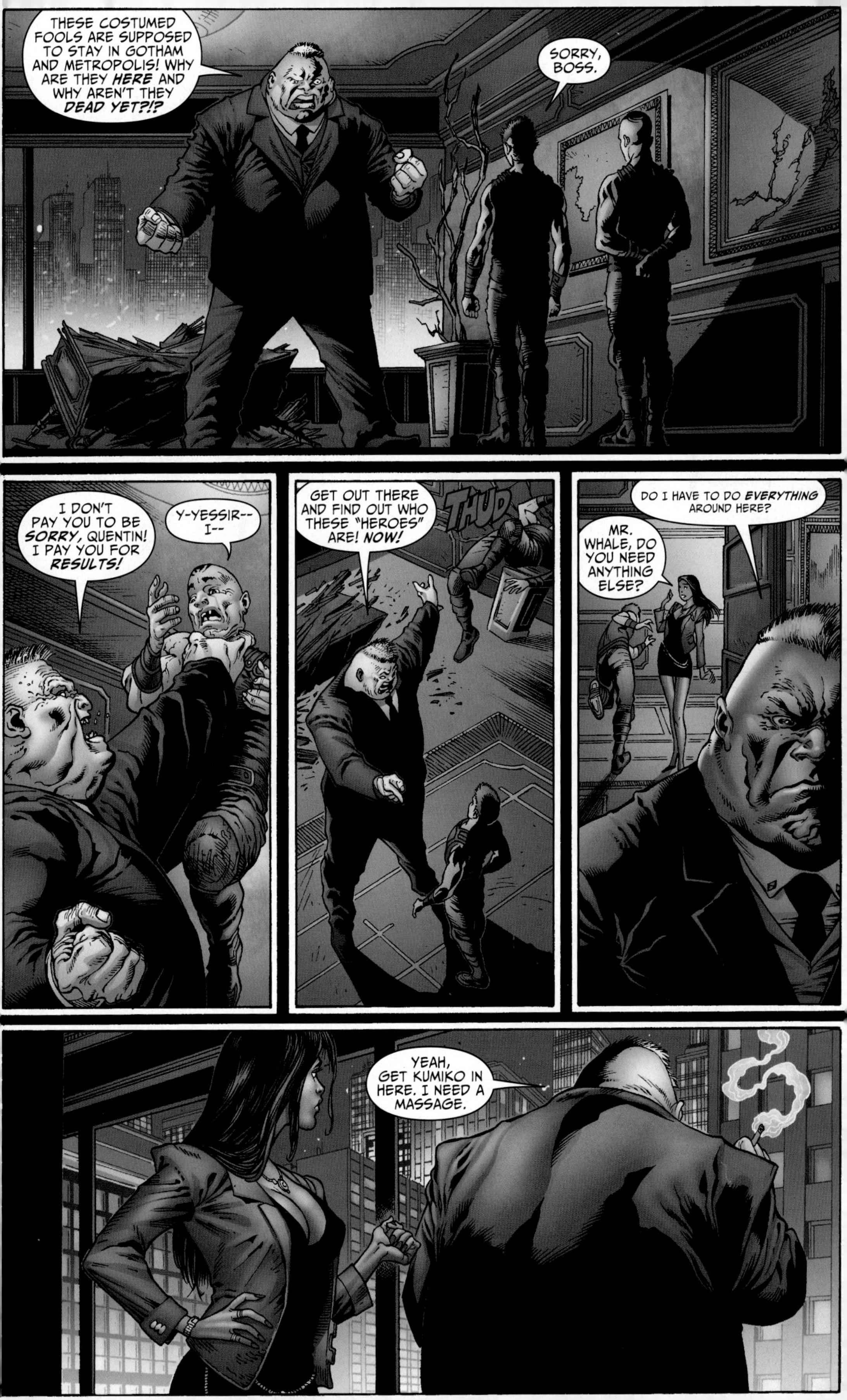
THESE COSTUMED FOOLS ARE SUPPOSED TO STAY IN GOTHAM AND METROPOLIS! WHY ARE THEY HERE AND WHY AREN'T THEY DEAD YET?!?
SORRY, BOSS.
I DON'T PAY YOU TO BE SORRY, QUENTIN! I PAY YOU FOR RESULTS!
Y-YESSIR-- I--
GET OUT THERE AND FIND OUT WHO THESE "HEROES" ARE! NOW!
THUD
DO I HAVE TO DO EVERYTHING AROUND HERE?
MR. WHALE, DO YOU NEED ANYTHING ELSE?
YEAH, GET KUMIKO IN HERE. I NEED A MASSAGE.

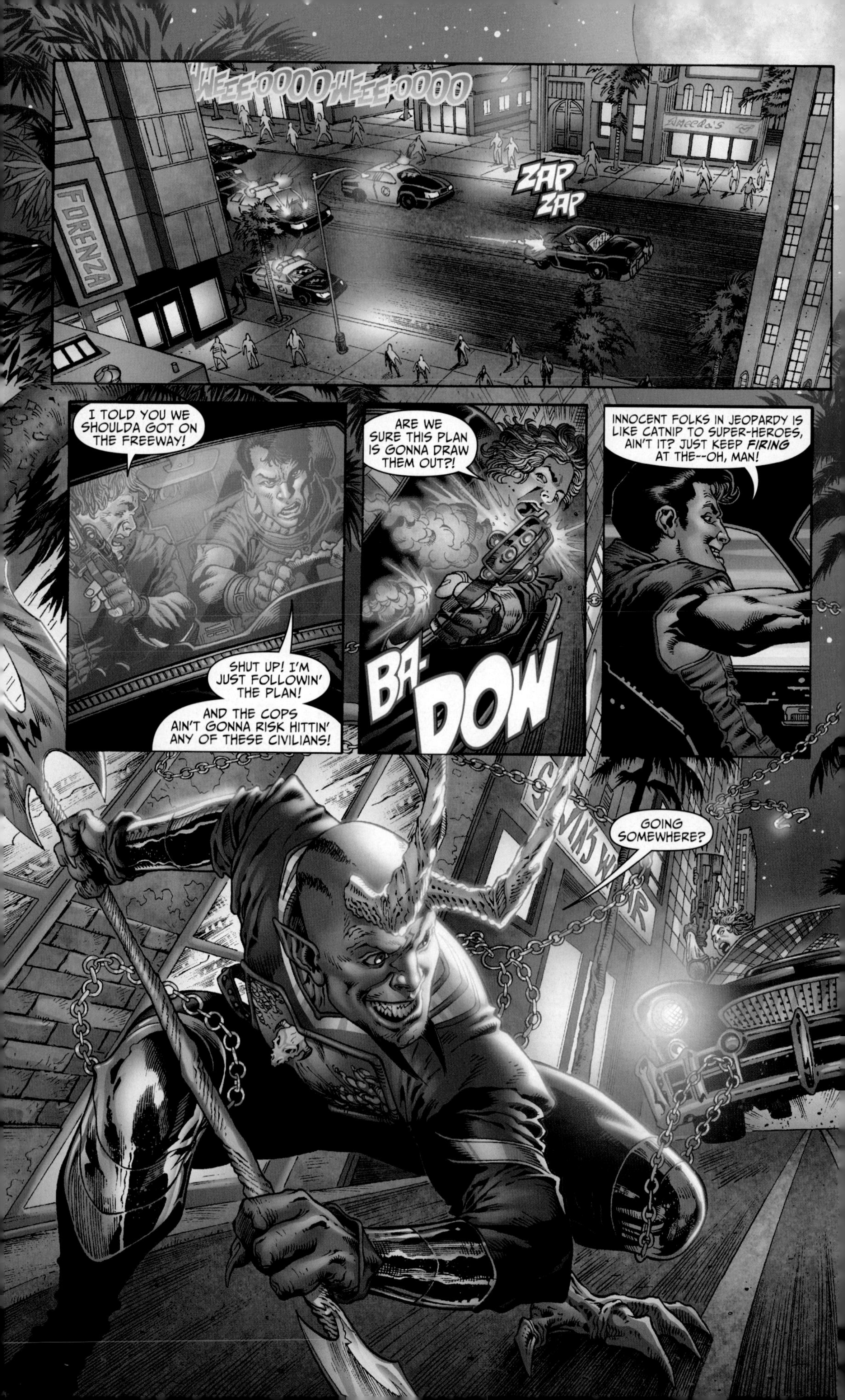
WEEE-OOOO WEEE-OOOO
FORENZA
ZAP ZAP
I TOLD YOU WE SHOULDA GOT ON THE FREEWAY!
SHUT UP! I'M JUST FOLLOWIN' THE PLAN!
AND THE COPS AIN'T GONNA RISK HITTIN' ANY OF THESE CIVILIANS!
ARE WE SURE THIS PLAN IS GONNA DRAW THEM OUT?!
BA-DOW
INNOCENT FOLKS IN JEOPARDY IS LIKE CATNIP TO SUPER-HEROES, AIN'T IT? JUST KEEP *FIRING* AT THE--OH, MAN!
GOING SOMEWHERE?

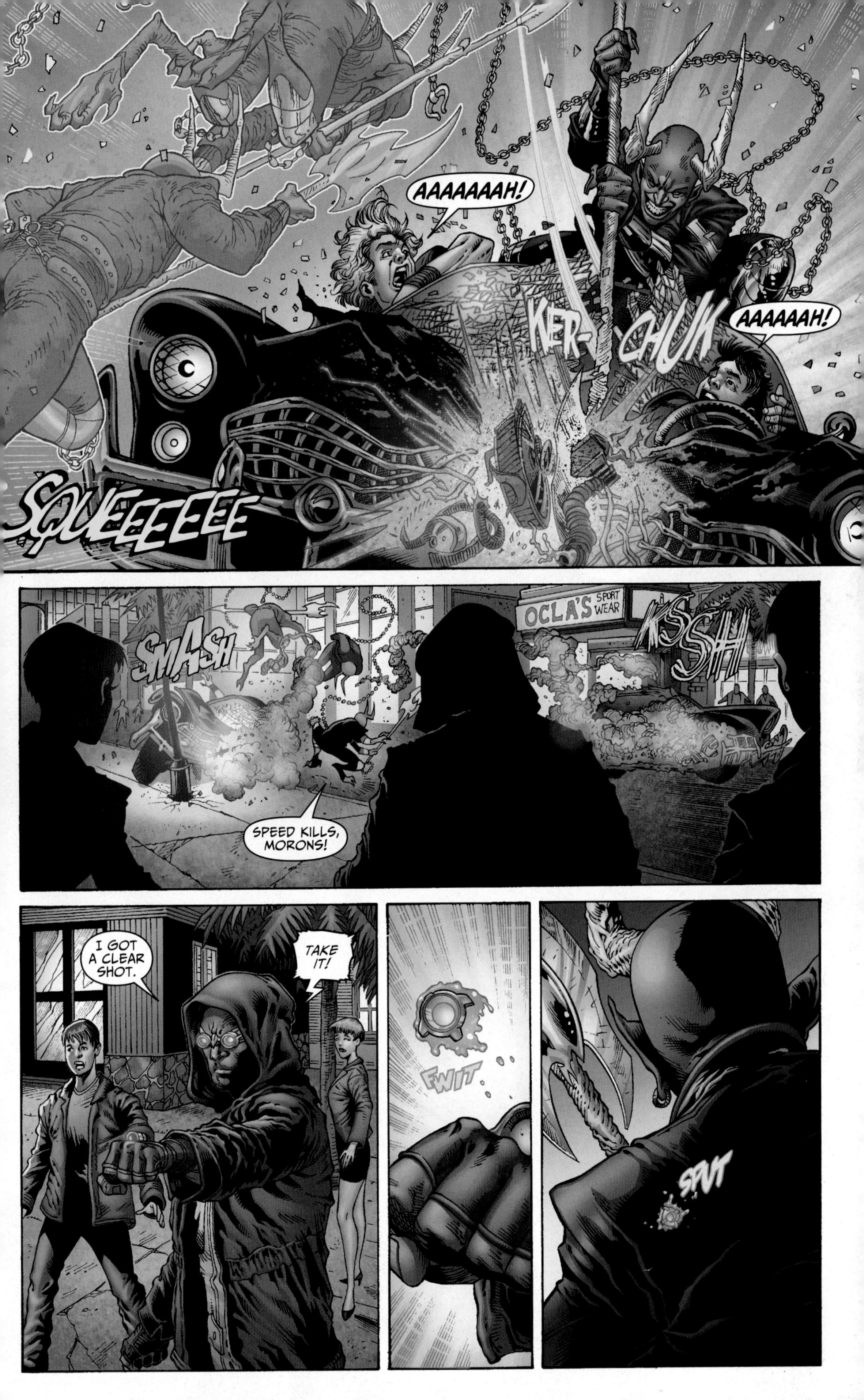
AAAAAAAH!
KER-CHUK
AAAAAAH!
SQUEEEEEEE
SMASH
OCLA'S SPORT WEAR
KSSH
SPEED KILLS, MORONS!
I GOT A CLEAR SHOT.
TAKE IT!
FWIT
SPUT

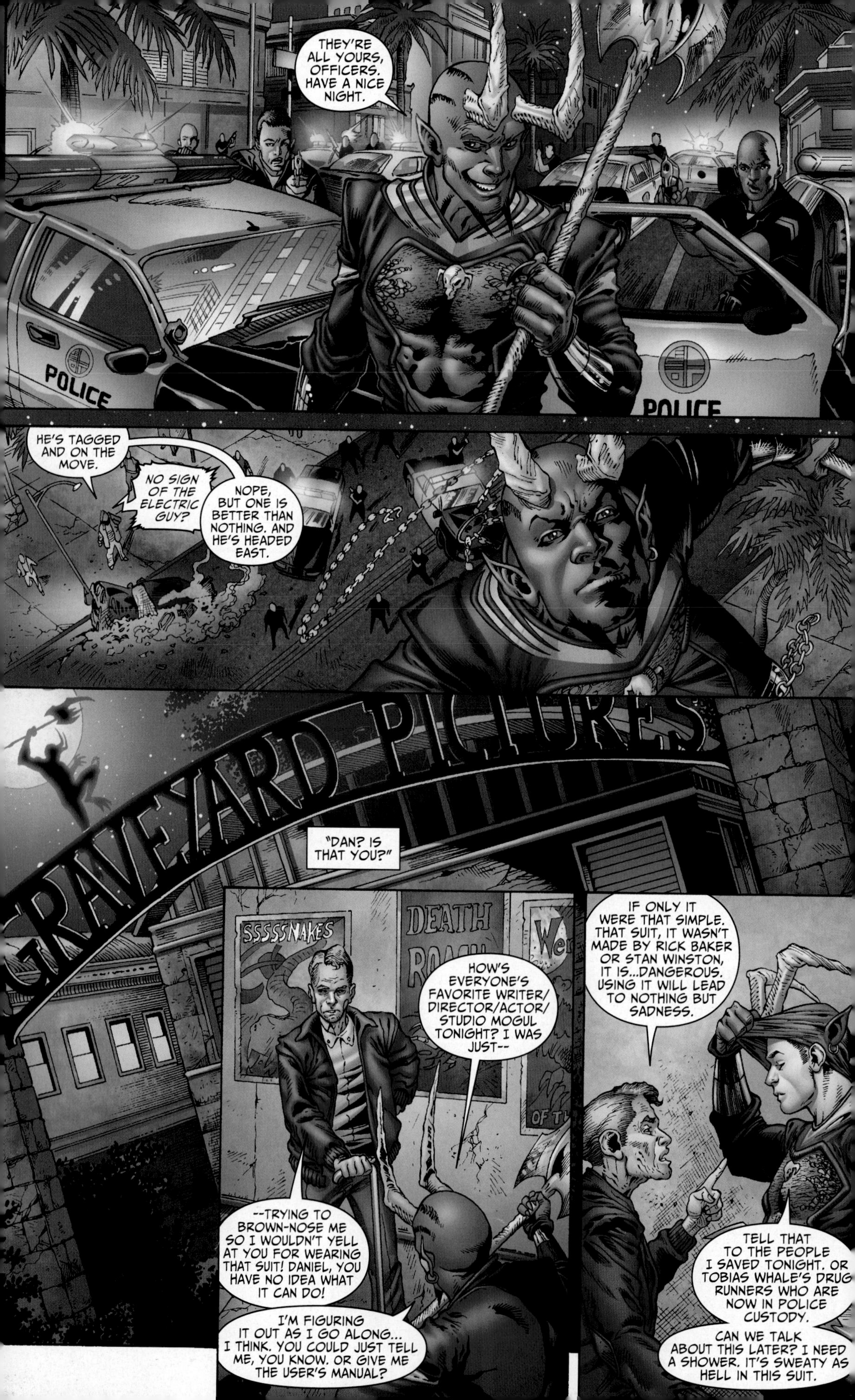
THEY'RE ALL YOURS, OFFICERS. HAVE A NICE NIGHT.
POLICE
POLICE
HE'S TAGGED AND ON THE MOVE.
NO SIGN OF THE ELECTRIC GUY?
NOPE, BUT ONE IS BETTER THAN NOTHING. AND HE'S HEADED EAST.
GRAVEYARD PICTURES
"DAN? IS THAT YOU?"
SSSSSNAKES
DEATH
HOW'S EVERYONE'S FAVORITE WRITER/DIRECTOR/ACTOR/STUDIO MOGUL TONIGHT? I WAS JUST--
--TRYING TO BROWN-NOSE ME SO I WOULDN'T YELL AT YOU FOR WEARING THAT SUIT! DANIEL, YOU HAVE NO IDEA WHAT IT CAN DO!
I'M FIGURING IT OUT AS I GO ALONG... I THINK. YOU COULD JUST TELL ME, YOU KNOW. OR GIVE ME THE USER'S MANUAL?
IF ONLY IT WERE THAT SIMPLE. THAT SUIT, IT WASN'T MADE BY RICK BAKER OR STAN WINSTON, IT IS...DANGEROUS. USING IT WILL LEAD TO NOTHING BUT SADNESS.
TELL THAT TO THE PEOPLE I SAVED TONIGHT. OR TOBIAS WHALE'S DRUG RUNNERS WHO ARE NOW IN POLICE CUSTODY.
CAN WE TALK ABOUT THIS LATER? I NEED A SHOWER. IT'S SWEATY AS HELL IN THIS SUIT.

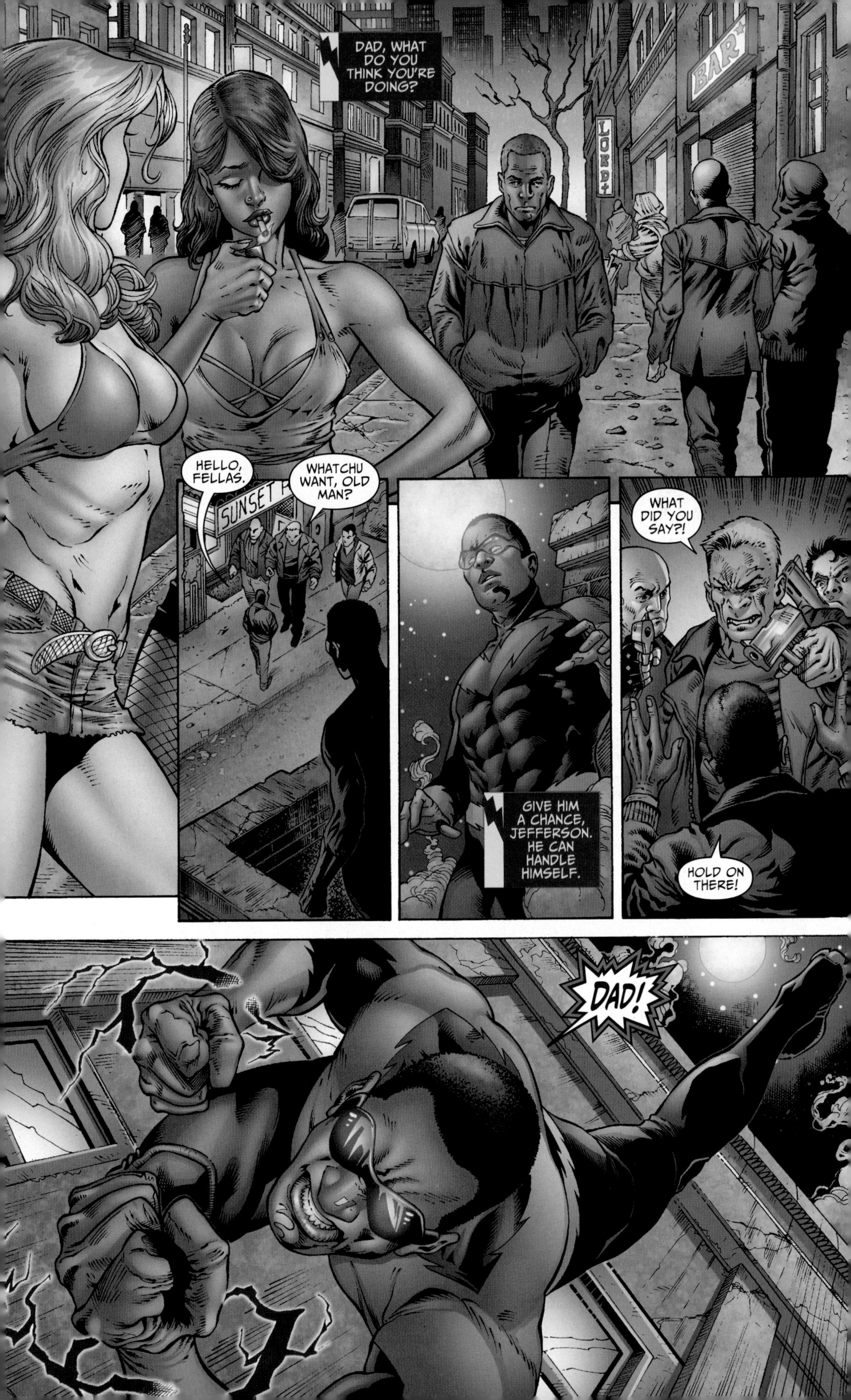
DAD, WHAT DO YOU THINK YOU'RE DOING?
BAR
LORD
HELLO, FELLAS.
WHATCHU WANT, OLD MAN?
GIVE HIM A CHANCE, JEFFERSON. HE CAN HANDLE HIMSELF.
WHAT DID YOU SAY?!
HOLD ON THERE!
DAD!

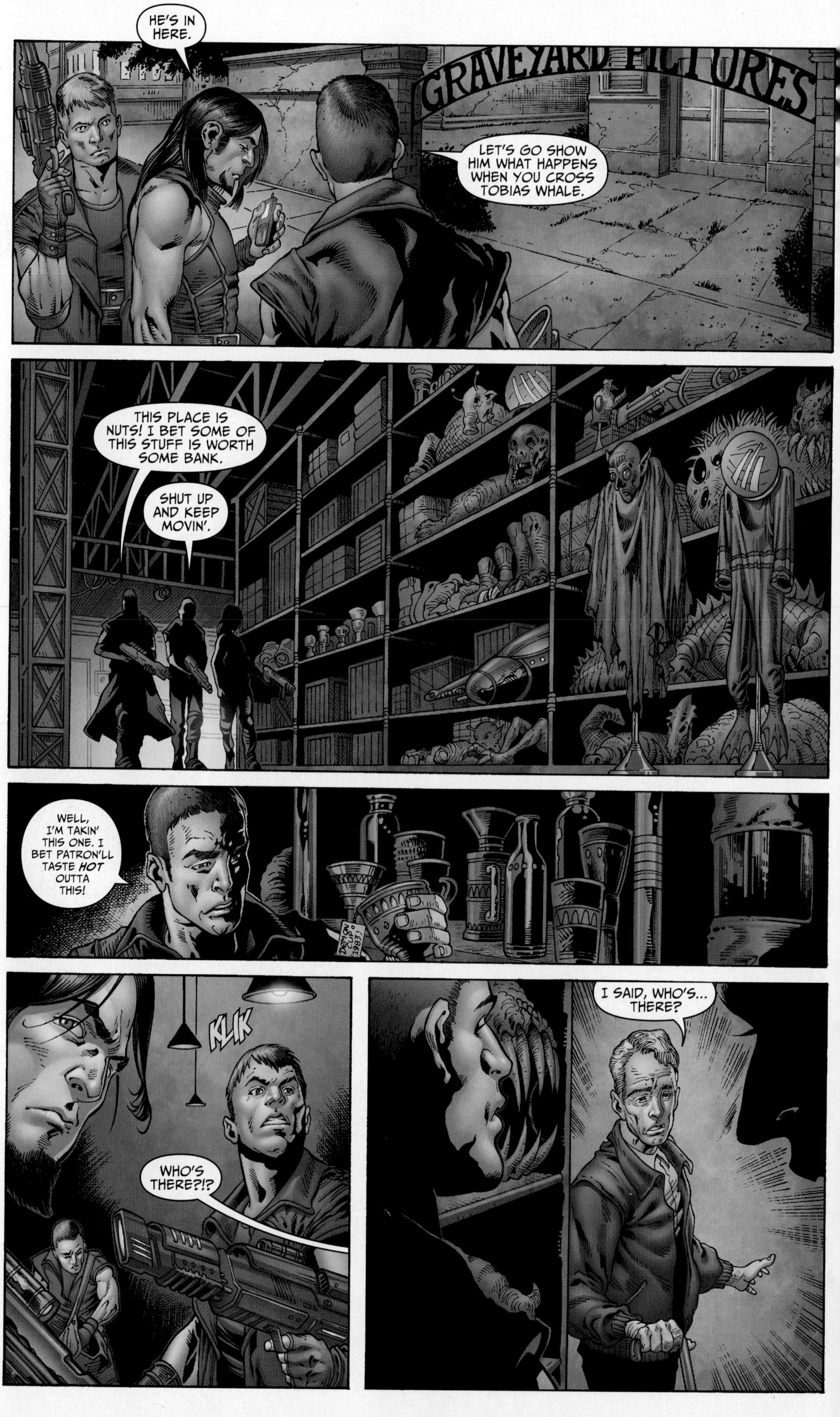
HE'S IN HERE.
GRAVEYARD PICTURES
LET'S GO SHOW HIM WHAT HAPPENS WHEN YOU CROSS TOBIAS WHALE.
THIS PLACE IS NUTS! I BET SOME OF THIS STUFF IS WORTH SOME BANK.
SHUT UP AND KEEP MOVIN'.
WELL, I'M TAKIN' THIS ONE. I BET PATRON'LL TASTE *HOT* OUTTA THIS!
KLIK
WHO'S THERE?!?
I SAID, WHO'S... THERE?

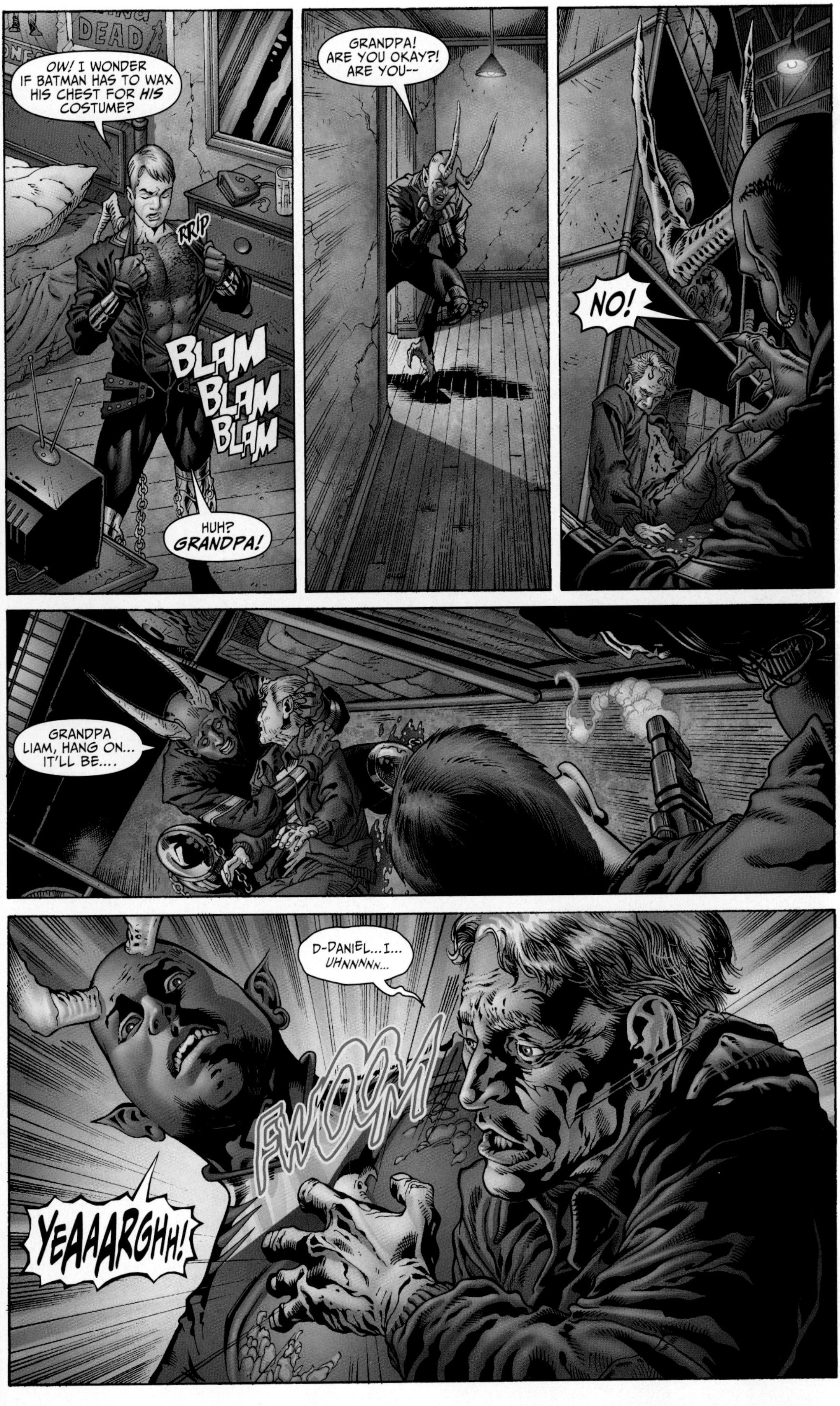

DEAD
OW! I WONDER IF BATMAN HAS TO WAX HIS CHEST FOR HIS COSTUME?
RRIP
BLAM BLAM BLAM
HUH? GRANDPA!
GRANDPA! ARE YOU OKAY?! ARE YOU--
NO!
GRANDPA LIAM, HANG ON... IT'LL BE....
D-DANIEL... I... UHNNNNN...
FWOOM
YEAAARGHH!

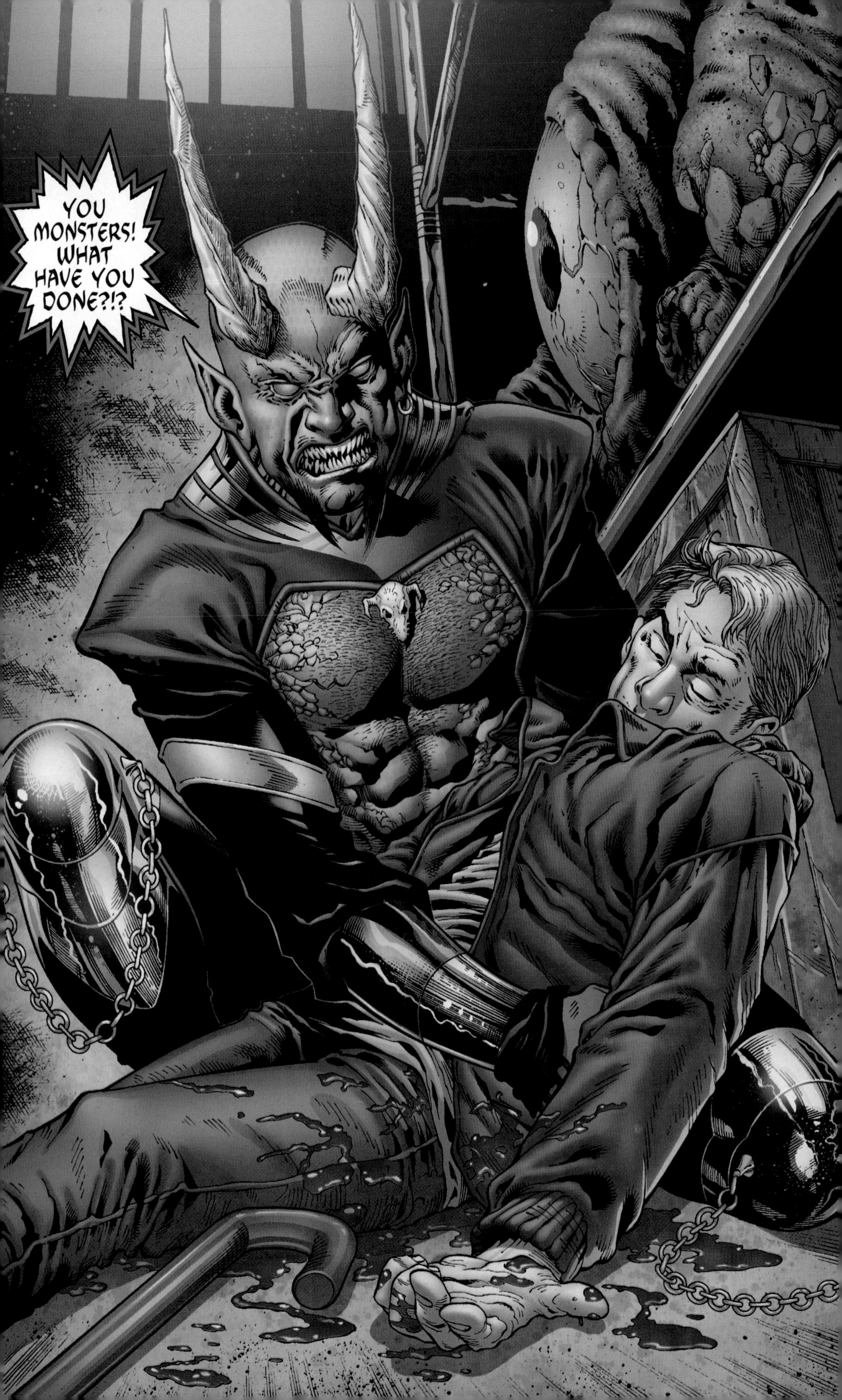

YOU MONSTERS! WHAT HAVE YOU DONE?!?

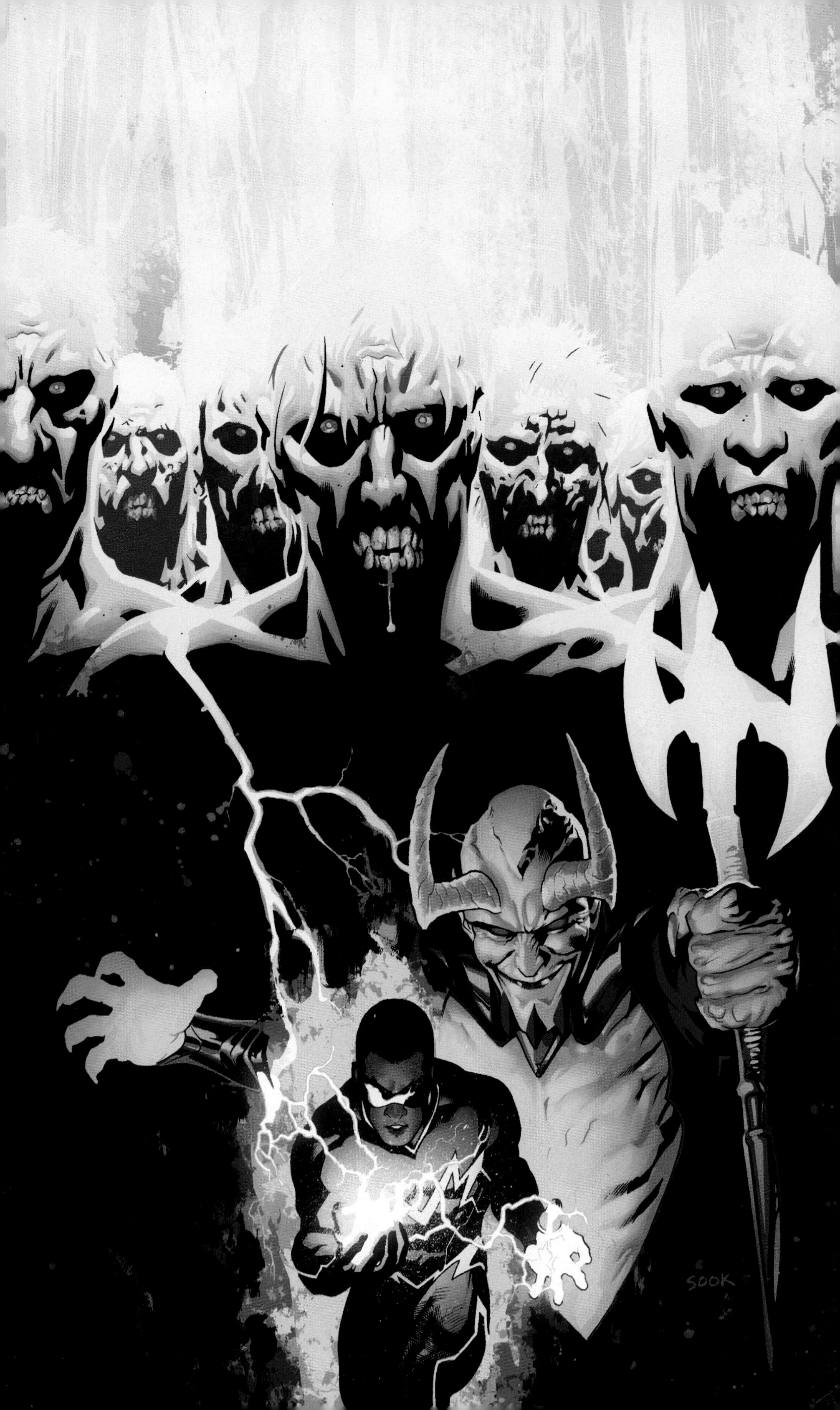
SOOK

GRAVE MATTERS

MARC ANDREYKO
writer

ROBSON ROCHA
penciller

OCLAIR ALBERT
inker

cover art by RYAN SOOK

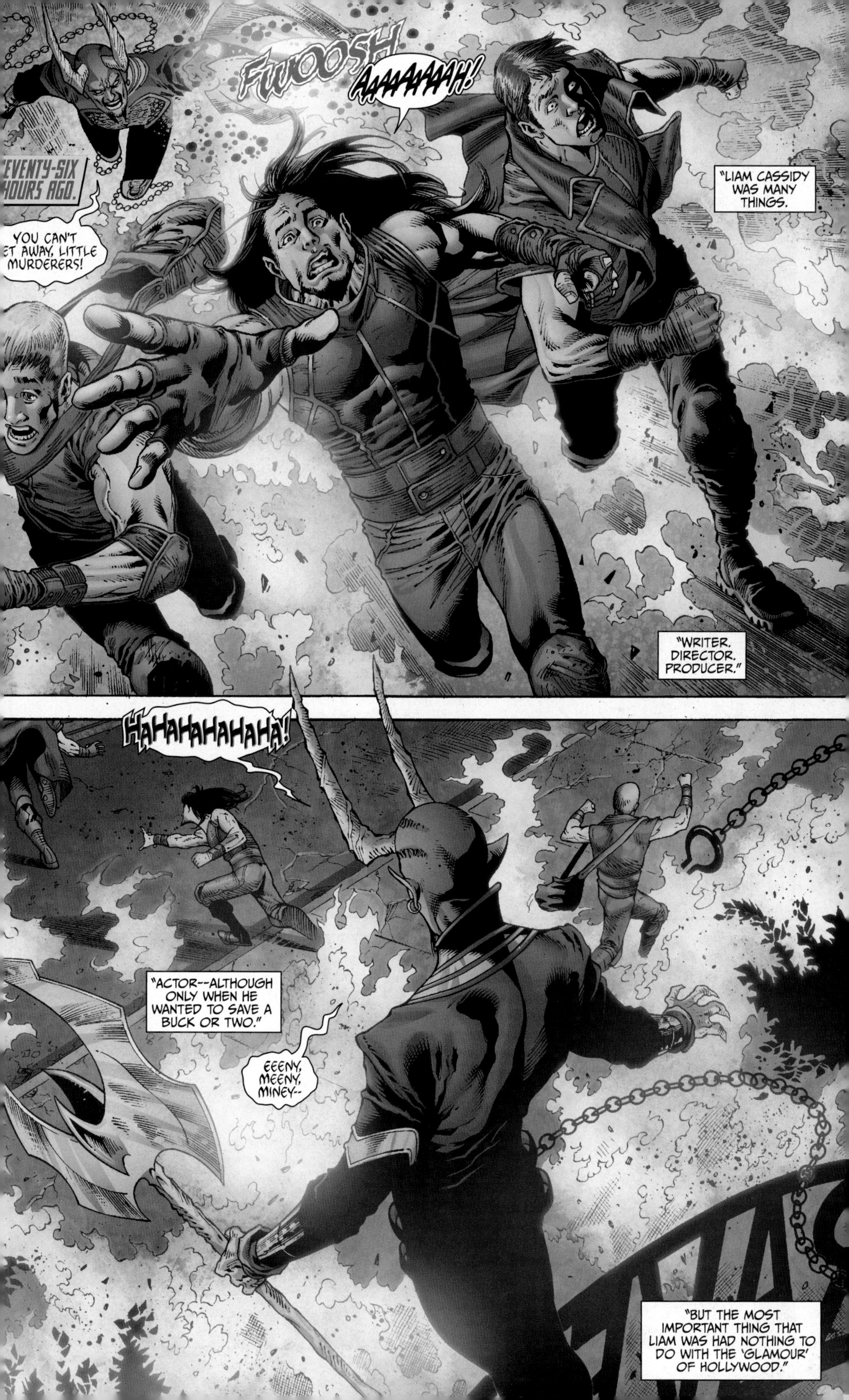
FWOOSH
AAAAAAAAH!
EVENTY-SIX HOURS AGO.
YOU CAN'T ET AWAY, LITTLE MURDERERS!
"LIAM CASSIDY WAS MANY THINGS.
"WRITER. DIRECTOR. PRODUCER."
HAHAHAHAHAHA!
"ACTOR--ALTHOUGH ONLY WHEN HE WANTED TO SAVE A BUCK OR TWO."
EEENY, MEENY, MINEY--
"BUT THE MOST IMPORTANT THING THAT LIAM WAS HAD NOTHING TO DO WITH THE 'GLAMOUR' OF HOLLYWOOD."

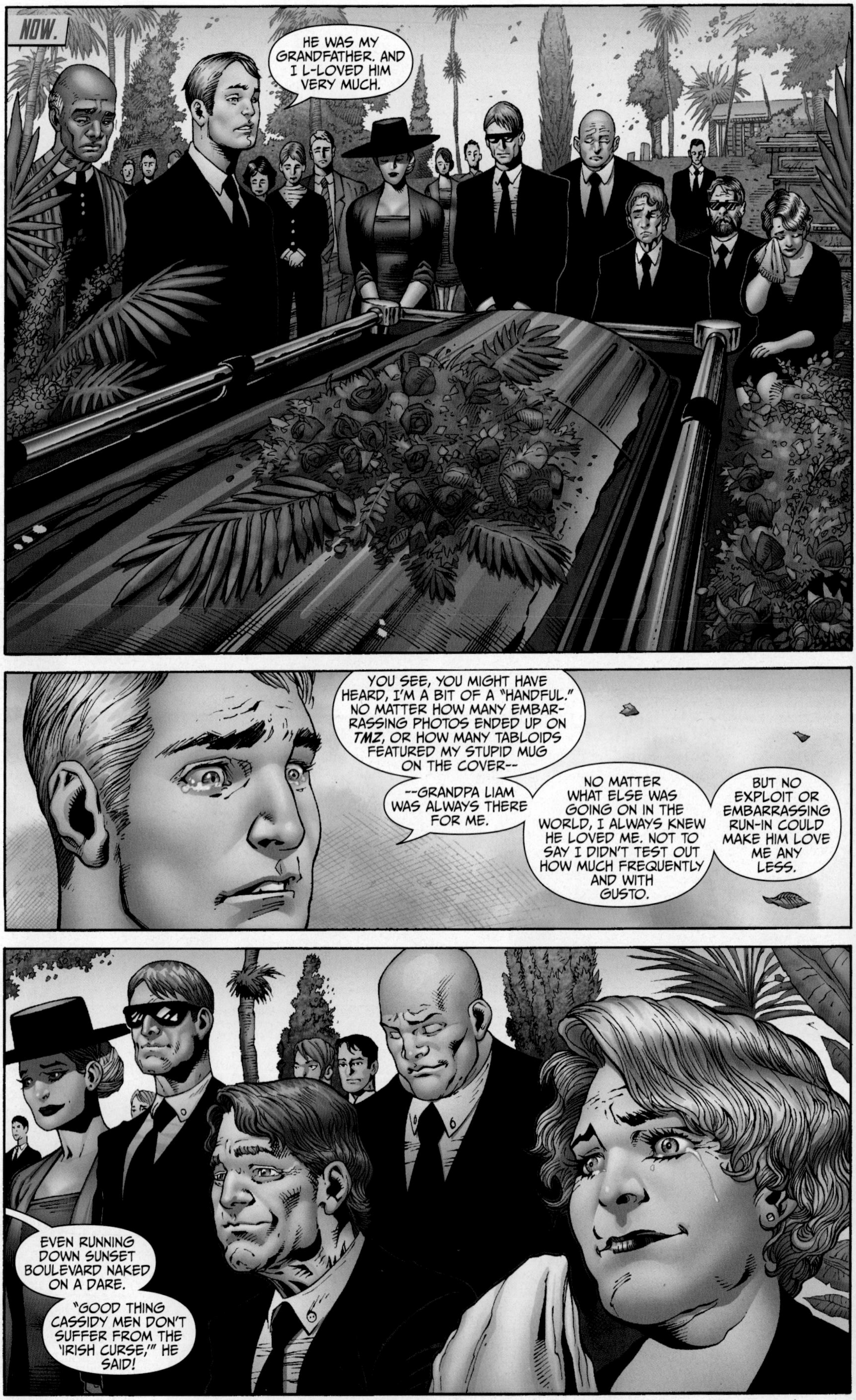
NOW.
HE WAS MY GRANDFATHER. AND I L-LOVED HIM VERY MUCH.
YOU SEE, YOU MIGHT HAVE HEARD, I'M A BIT OF A "HANDFUL." NO MATTER HOW MANY EMBARRASSING PHOTOS ENDED UP ON TMZ, OR HOW MANY TABLOIDS FEATURED MY STUPID MUG ON THE COVER--
--GRANDPA LIAM WAS ALWAYS THERE FOR ME.
NO MATTER WHAT ELSE WAS GOING ON IN THE WORLD, I ALWAYS KNEW HE LOVED ME. NOT TO SAY I DIDN'T TEST OUT HOW MUCH FREQUENTLY AND WITH GUSTO.
BUT NO EXPLOIT OR EMBARRASSING RUN-IN COULD MAKE HIM LOVE ME ANY LESS.
EVEN RUNNING DOWN SUNSET BOULEVARD NAKED ON A DARE.
"GOOD THING CASSIDY MEN DON'T SUFFER FROM THE 'IRISH CURSE,'" HE SAID!

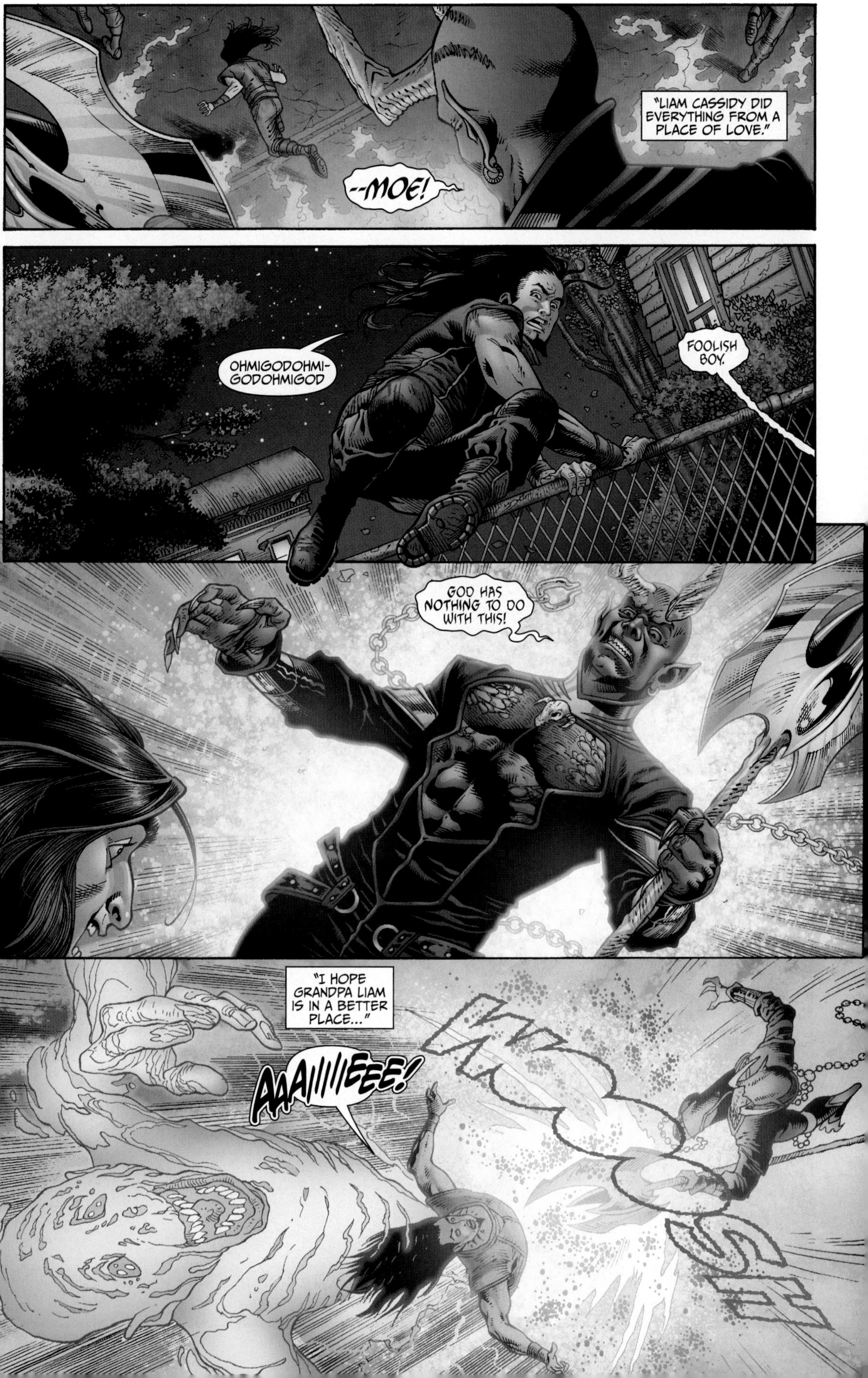
"LIAM CASSIDY DID EVERYTHING FROM A PLACE OF LOVE."
--MOE!
OHMIGODOHMI-GODOHMIGOD
FOOLISH BOY.
GOD HAS NOTHING TO DO WITH THIS!
"I HOPE GRANDPA LIAM IS IN A BETTER PLACE..."
AAAIIIIIIEEE!

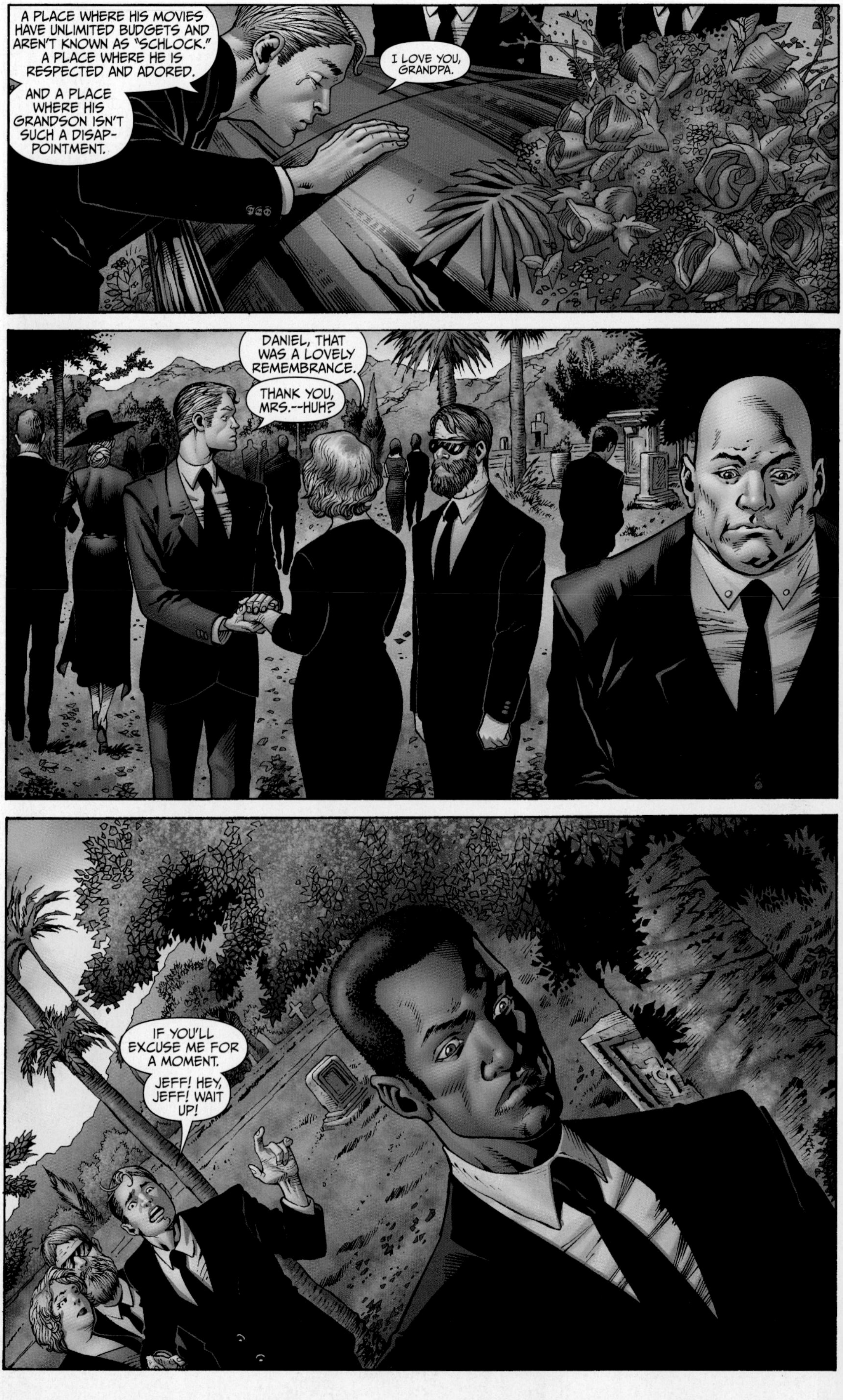
A PLACE WHERE HIS MOVIES HAVE UNLIMITED BUDGETS AND AREN'T KNOWN AS "SCHLOCK." A PLACE WHERE HE IS RESPECTED AND ADORED.
AND A PLACE WHERE HIS GRANDSON ISN'T SUCH A DISAP-POINTMENT.
I LOVE YOU, GRANDPA.
DANIEL, THAT WAS A LOVELY REMEMBRANCE.
THANK YOU, MRS.--HUH?
IF YOU'LL EXCUSE ME FOR A MOMENT.
JEFF! HEY, JEFF! WAIT UP!

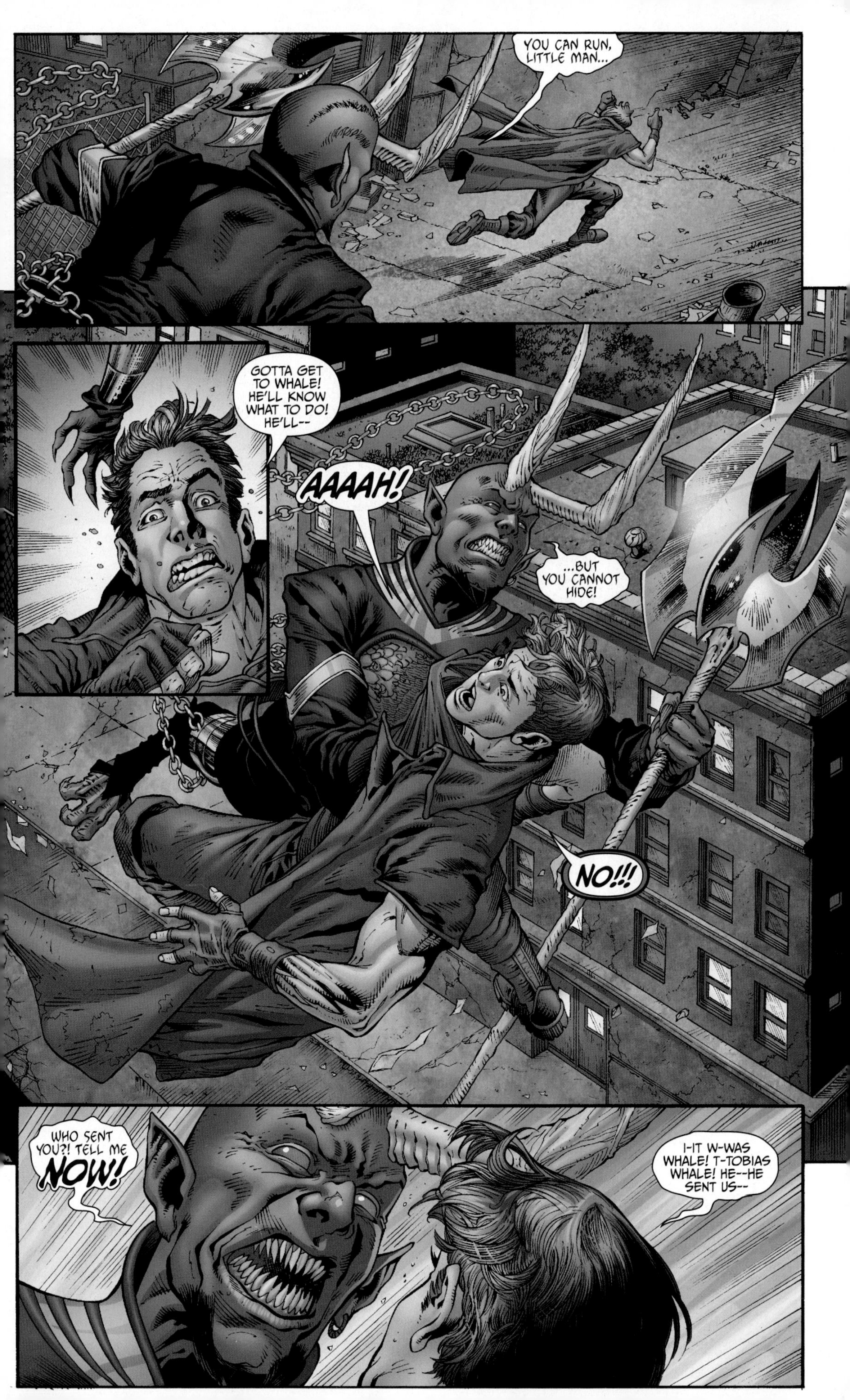
YOU CAN RUN, LITTLE MAN...
GOTTA GET TO WHALE! HE'LL KNOW WHAT TO DO! HE'LL--
AAAAH!
...BUT YOU CANNOT HIDE!
NO!!!
WHO SENT YOU?! TELL ME NOW!
I-IT W-WAS WHALE! T-TOBIAS WHALE! HE--HE SENT US--

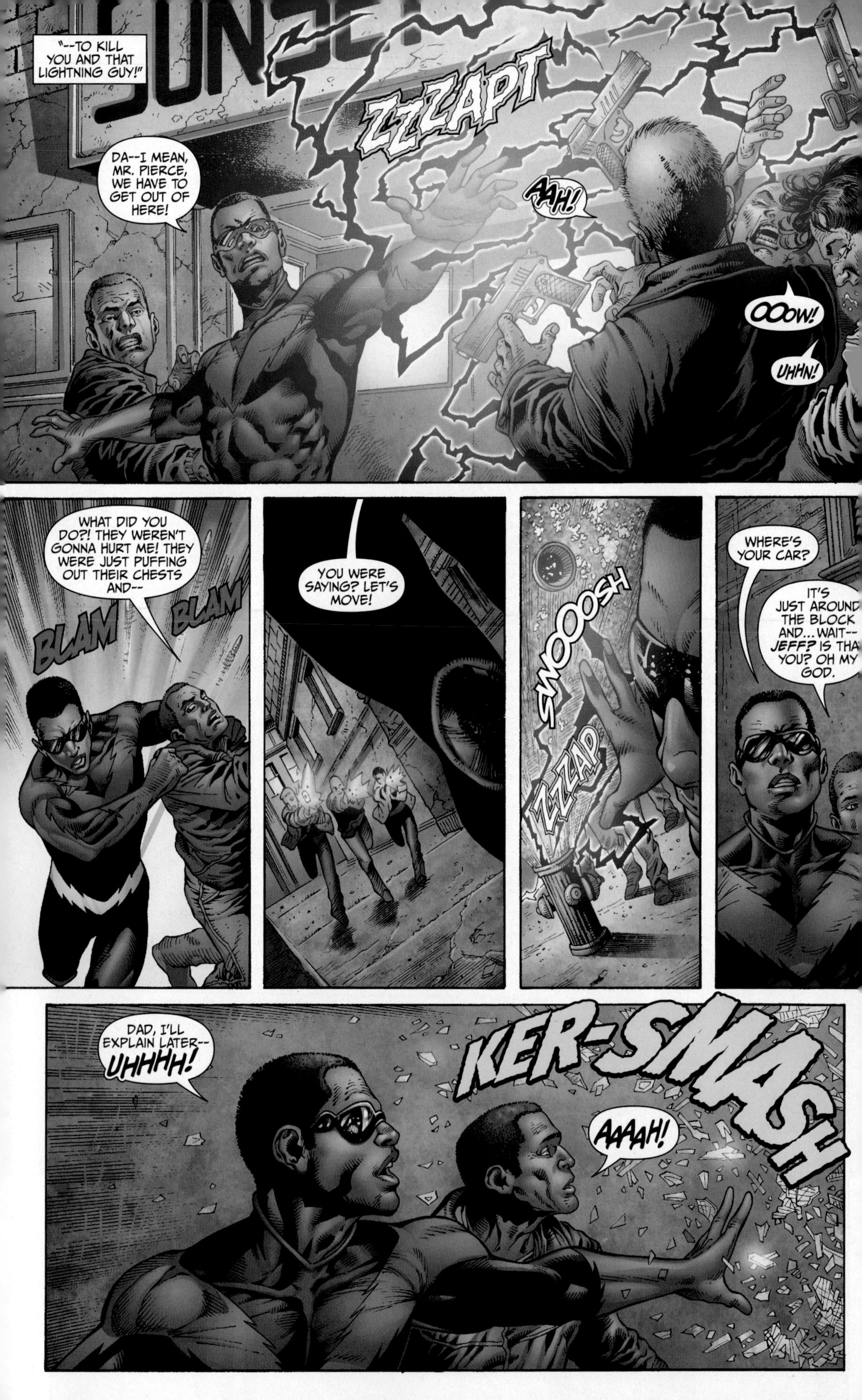
"--TO KILL YOU AND THAT LIGHTNING GUY!"
ZZZAPT
DA--I MEAN, MR. PIERCE, WE HAVE TO GET OUT OF HERE!
AAH!
OOOW!
UHHN!
WHAT DID YOU DO?! THEY WEREN'T GONNA HURT ME! THEY WERE JUST PUFFING OUT THEIR CHESTS AND--
BLAM
BLAM
YOU WERE SAYING? LET'S MOVE!
SWOOOSH
ZZZAP
WHERE'S YOUR CAR?
IT'S JUST AROUND THE BLOCK AND... WAIT-- JEFF? IS THAT YOU? OH MY GOD.
DAD, I'LL EXPLAIN LATER-- UHHHH!
KER-SMASH
AAAAH!

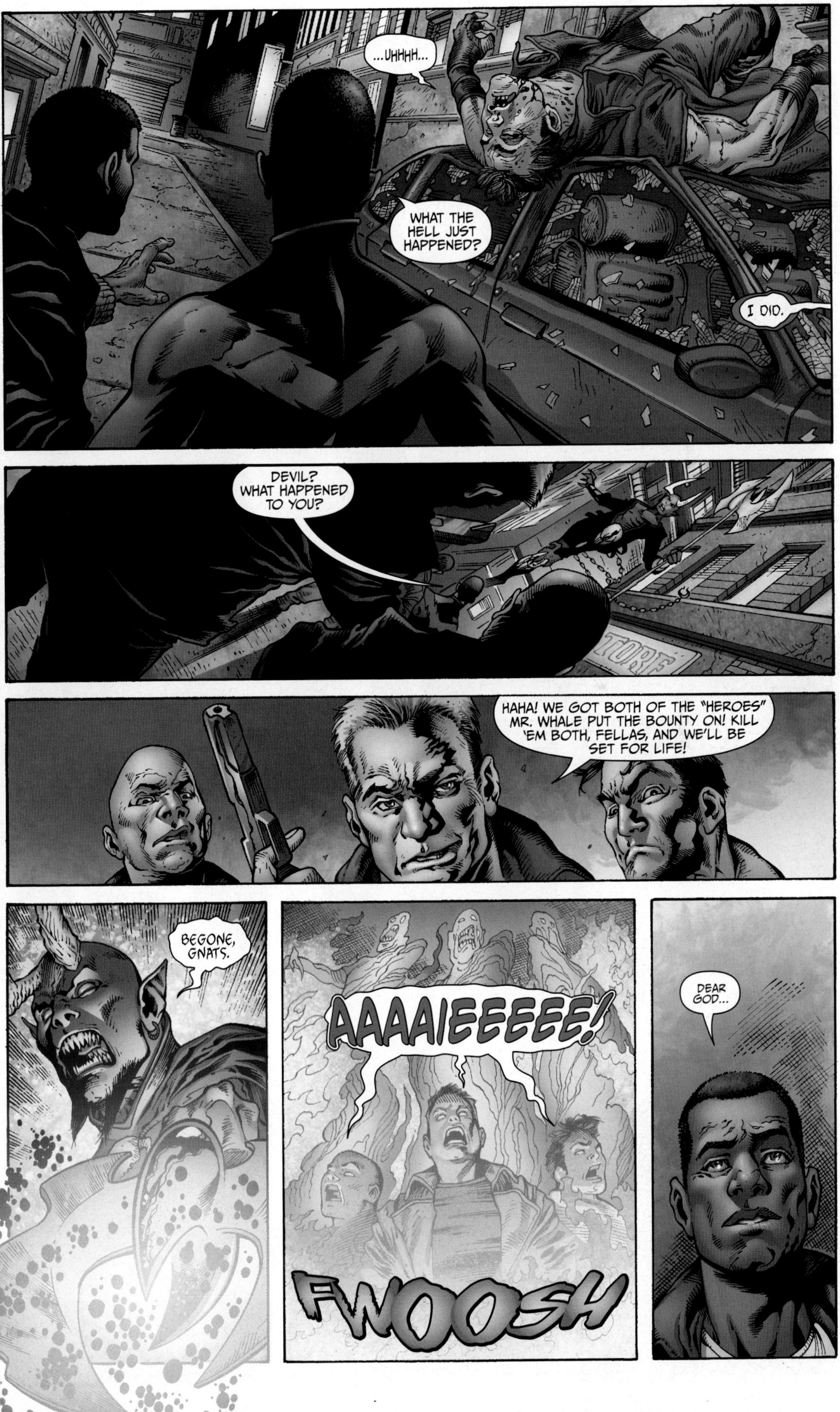
...UHHHH...
WHAT THE HELL JUST HAPPENED?
I DID.
DEVIL? WHAT HAPPENED TO YOU?
HAHA! WE GOT BOTH OF THE "HEROES" MR. WHALE PUT THE BOUNTY ON! KILL 'EM BOTH, FELLAS, AND WE'LL BE SET FOR LIFE!
BEGONE, GNATS.
AAAAIEEEEEE!
FWOOSH
DEAR GOD...

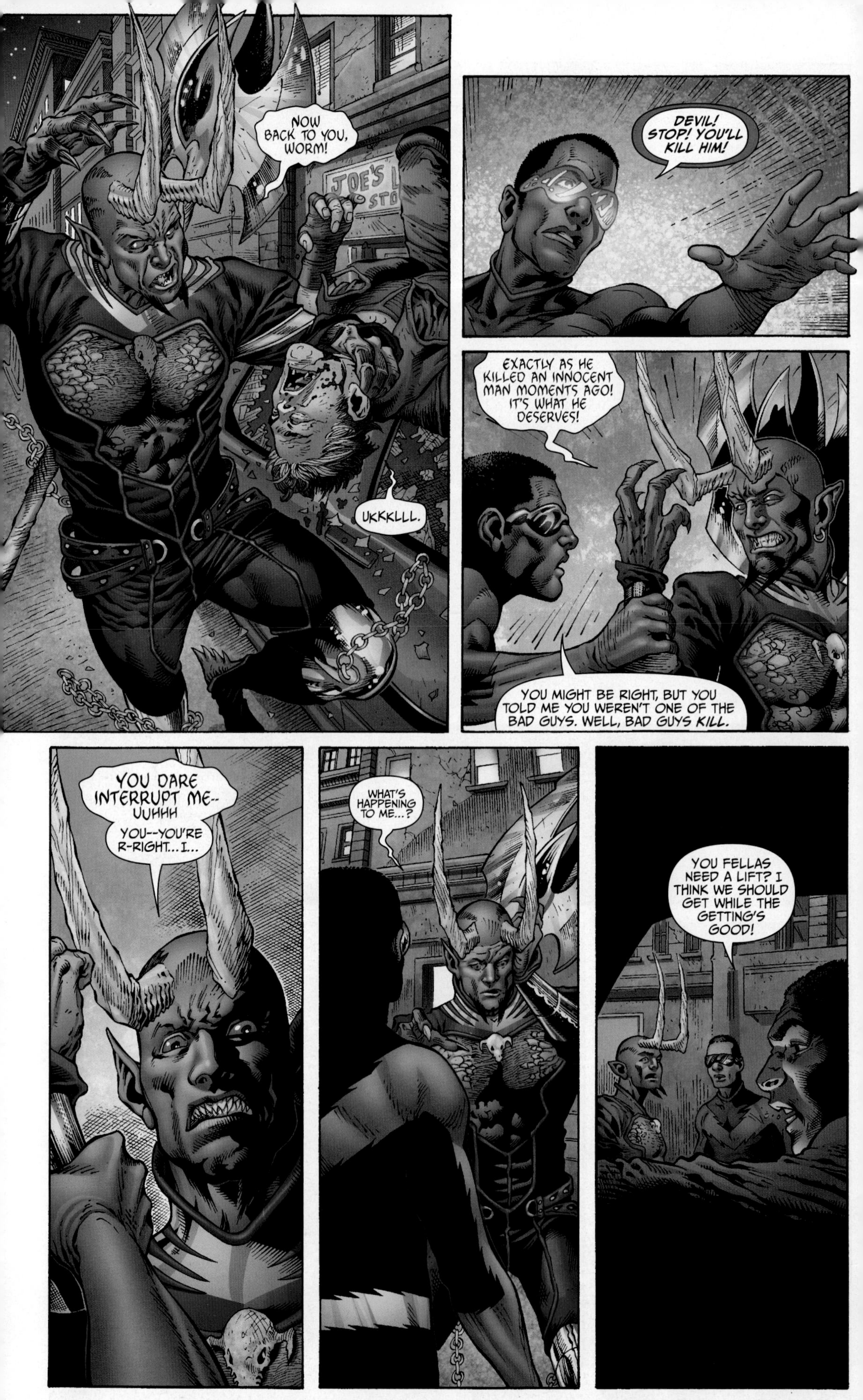
NOW BACK TO YOU, WORM!
JOE'S
UKKKLLL.
DEVIL! STOP! YOU'LL KILL HIM!
EXACTLY AS HE KILLED AN INNOCENT MAN MOMENTS AGO! IT'S WHAT HE DESERVES!
YOU MIGHT BE RIGHT, BUT YOU TOLD ME YOU WEREN'T ONE OF THE BAD GUYS. WELL, BAD GUYS KILL.
YOU DARE INTERRUPT ME-- UUHHH
YOU--YOU'RE R-RIGHT... I...
WHAT'S HAPPENING TO ME...?
YOU FELLAS NEED A LIFT? I THINK WE SHOULD GET WHILE THE GETTING'S GOOD!

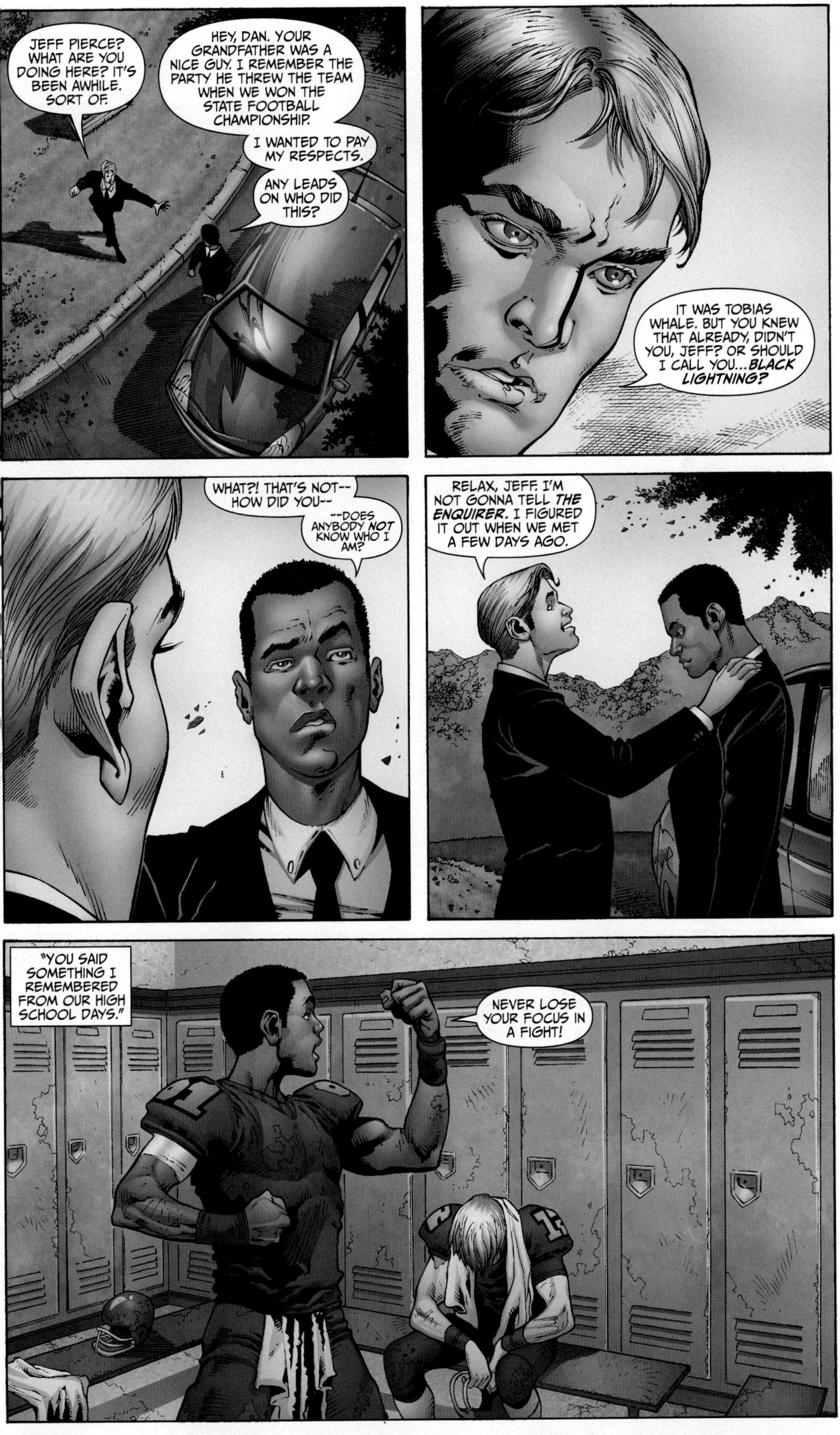
JEFF PIERCE? WHAT ARE YOU DOING HERE? IT'S BEEN AWHILE. SORT OF.
HEY, DAN. YOUR GRANDFATHER WAS A NICE GUY. I REMEMBER THE PARTY HE THREW THE TEAM WHEN WE WON THE STATE FOOTBALL CHAMPIONSHIP.
I WANTED TO PAY MY RESPECTS.
ANY LEADS ON WHO DID THIS?
IT WAS TOBIAS WHALE. BUT YOU KNEW THAT ALREADY, DIDN'T YOU, JEFF? OR SHOULD I CALL YOU...BLACK LIGHTNING?
WHAT?! THAT'S NOT-- HOW DID YOU--
--DOES ANYBODY NOT KNOW WHO I AM?
RELAX, JEFF. I'M NOT GONNA TELL THE ENQUIRER. I FIGURED IT OUT WHEN WE MET A FEW DAYS AGO.
"YOU SAID SOMETHING I REMEMBERED FROM OUR HIGH SCHOOL DAYS."
NEVER LOSE YOUR FOCUS IN A FIGHT!

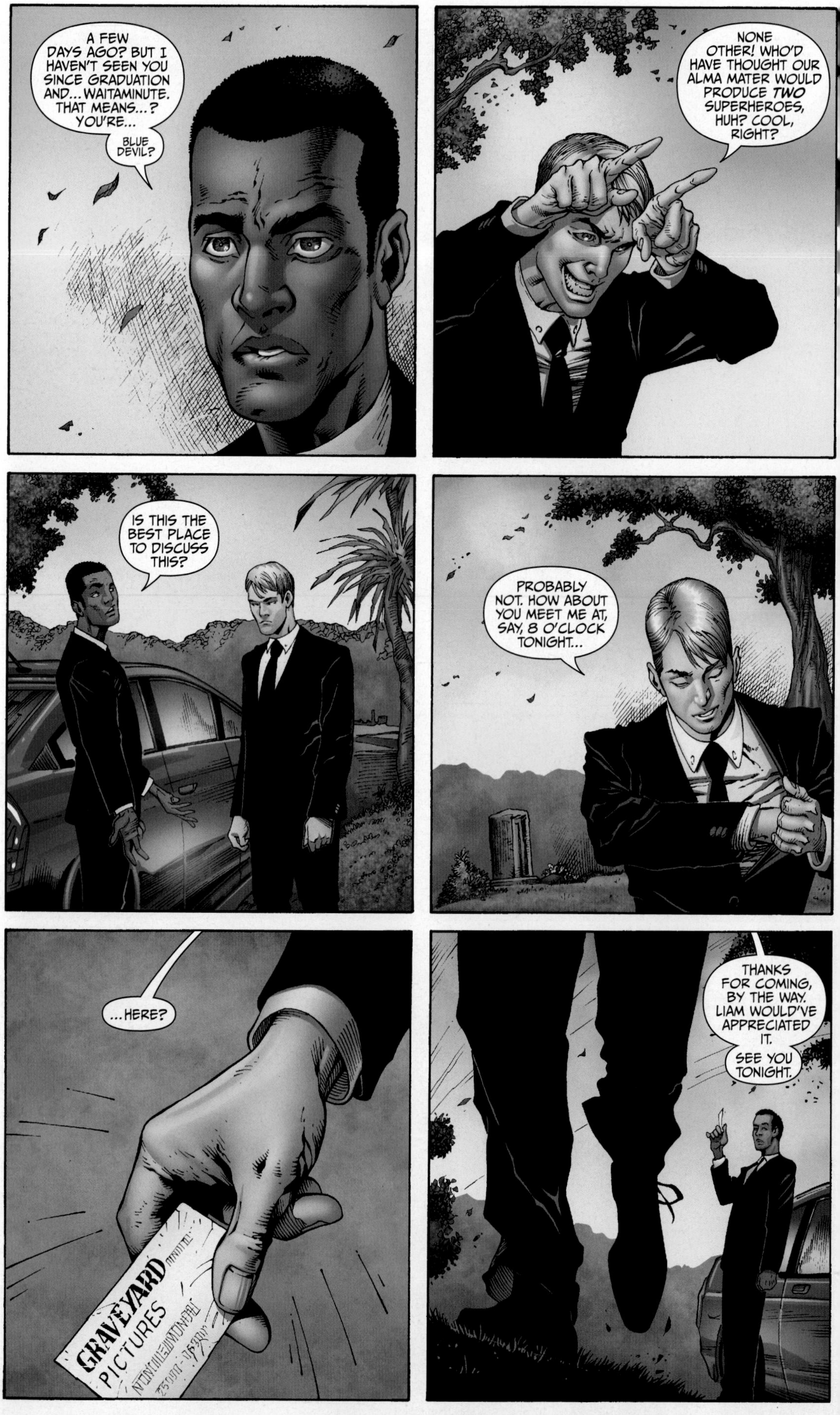
A FEW DAYS AGO? BUT I HAVEN'T SEEN YOU SINCE GRADUATION AND...WAITAMINUTE. THAT MEANS...? YOU'RE...
BLUE DEVIL?
NONE OTHER! WHO'D HAVE THOUGHT OUR ALMA MATER WOULD PRODUCE *TWO* SUPERHEROES, HUH? COOL, RIGHT?
IS THIS THE BEST PLACE TO DISCUSS THIS?
PROBABLY NOT. HOW ABOUT YOU MEET ME AT, SAY, 8 O'CLOCK TONIGHT...
...HERE?
GRAVEYARD PICTURES
THANKS FOR COMING, BY THE WAY. LIAM WOULD'VE APPRECIATED IT.
SEE YOU TONIGHT.

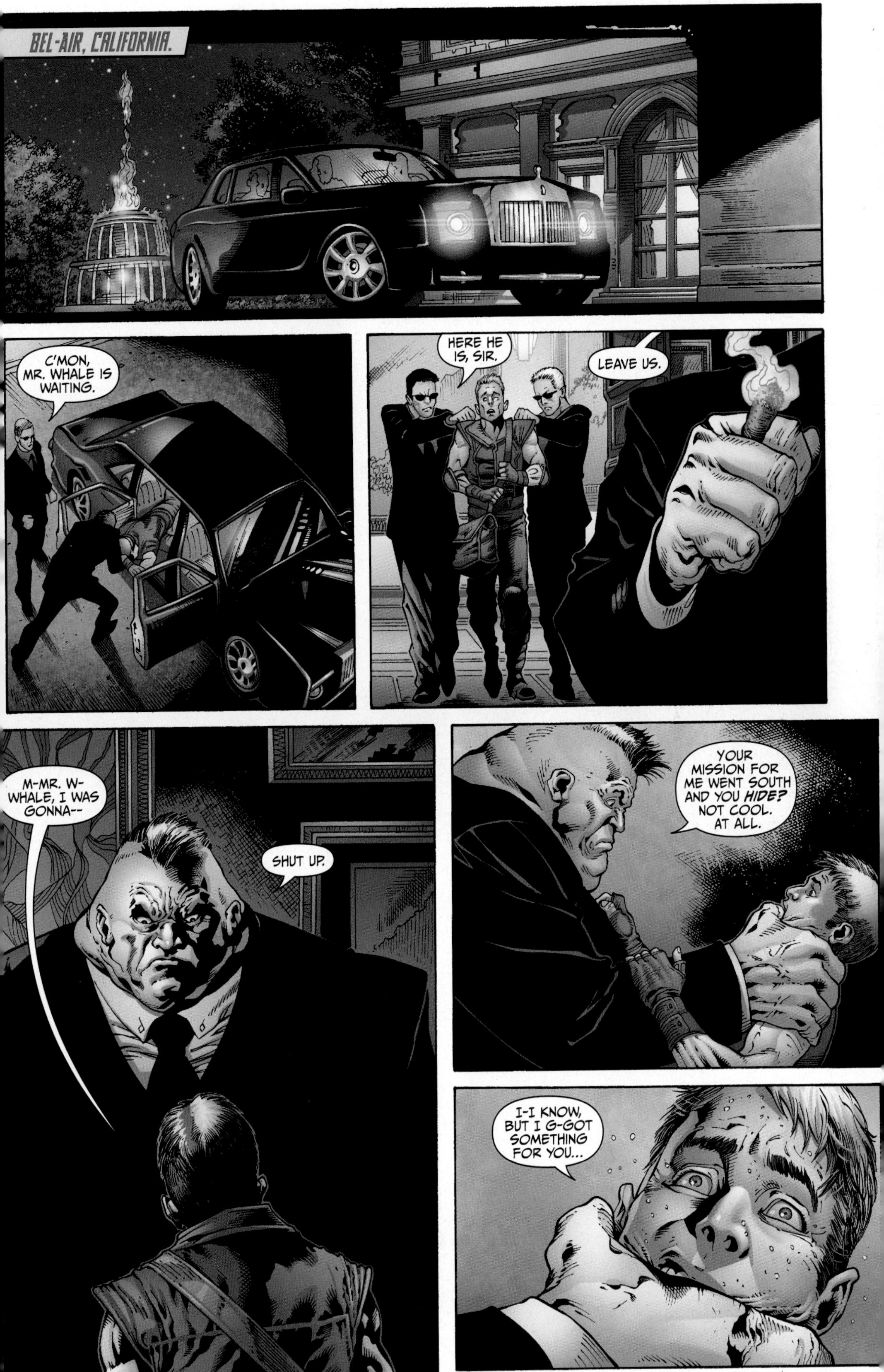
BEL-AIR, CALIFORNIA.
C'MON, MR. WHALE IS WAITING.
HERE HE IS, SIR.
LEAVE US.
M-MR. W-WHALE, I WAS GONNA--
SHUT UP.
YOUR MISSION FOR ME WENT SOUTH AND YOU HIDE? NOT COOL. AT ALL.
I-I KNOW, BUT I G-GOT SOMETHING FOR YOU...

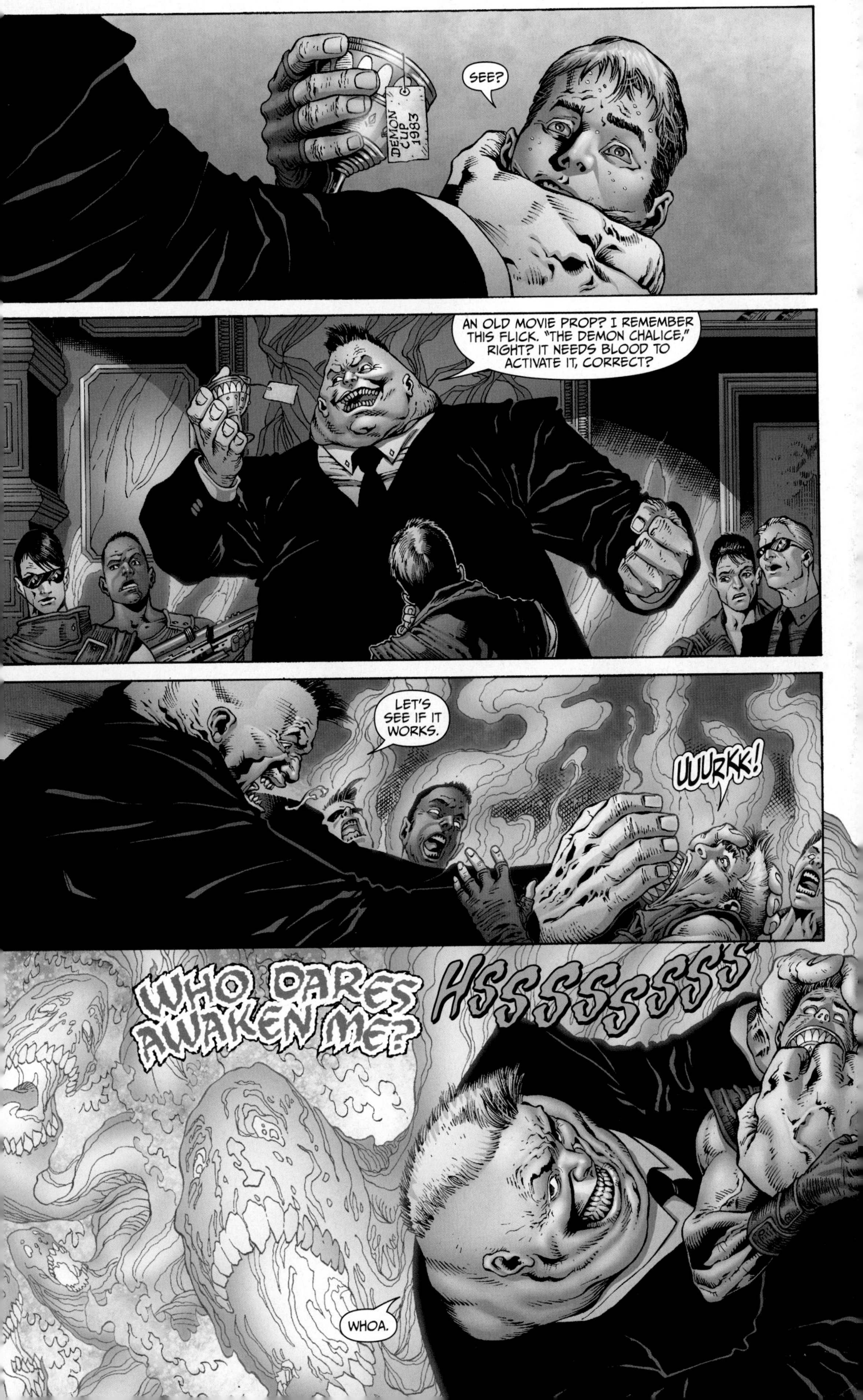
DEMON CUP 1983
SEE?
AN OLD MOVIE PROP? I REMEMBER THIS FLICK. "THE DEMON CHALICE," RIGHT? IT NEEDS BLOOD TO ACTIVATE IT, CORRECT?
LET'S SEE IF IT WORKS.
UUURKK!
WHO DARES AWAKEN ME?
HSSSSSSSS
WHOA.

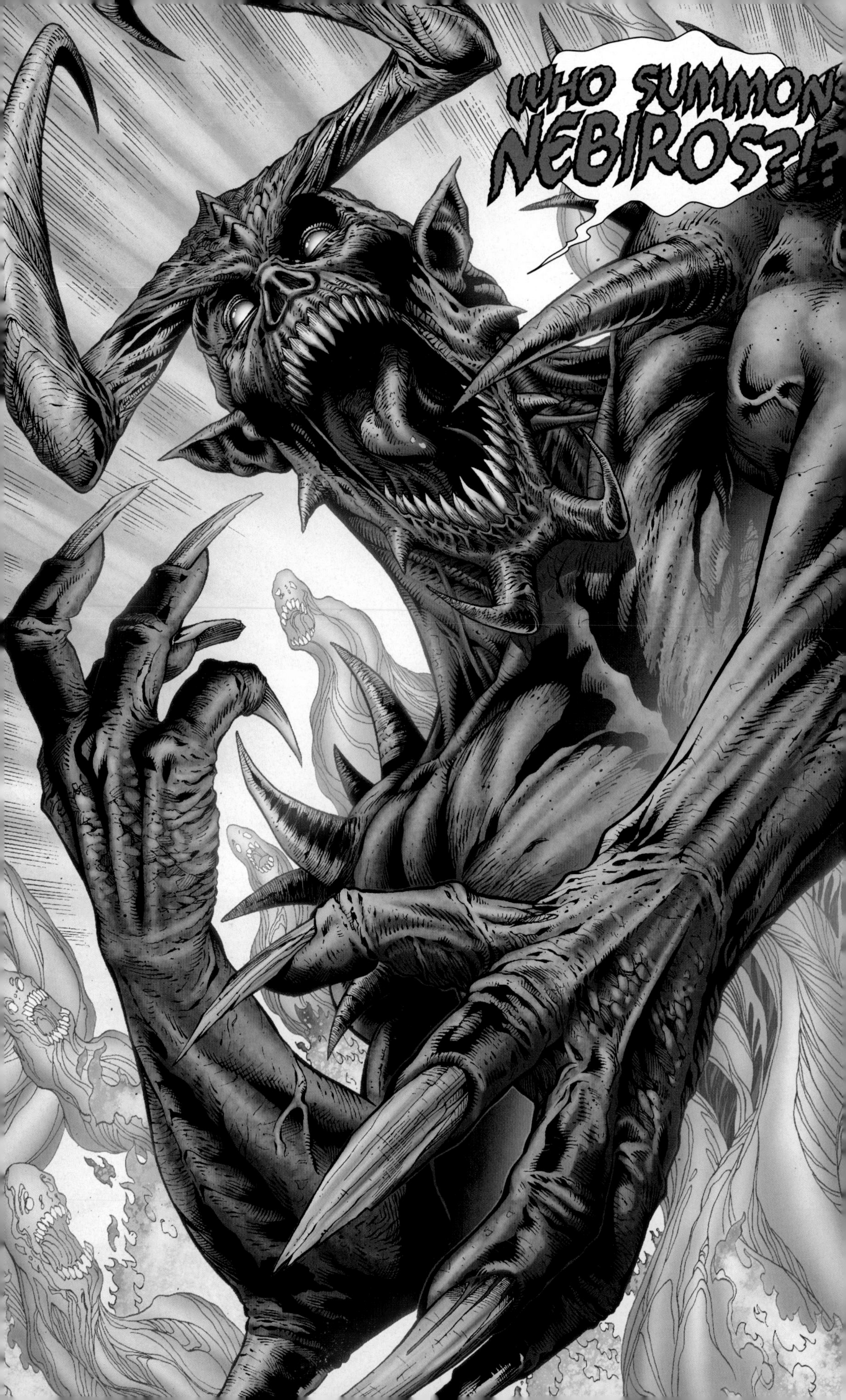
WHO SUMMONS
NEBIROS?!?

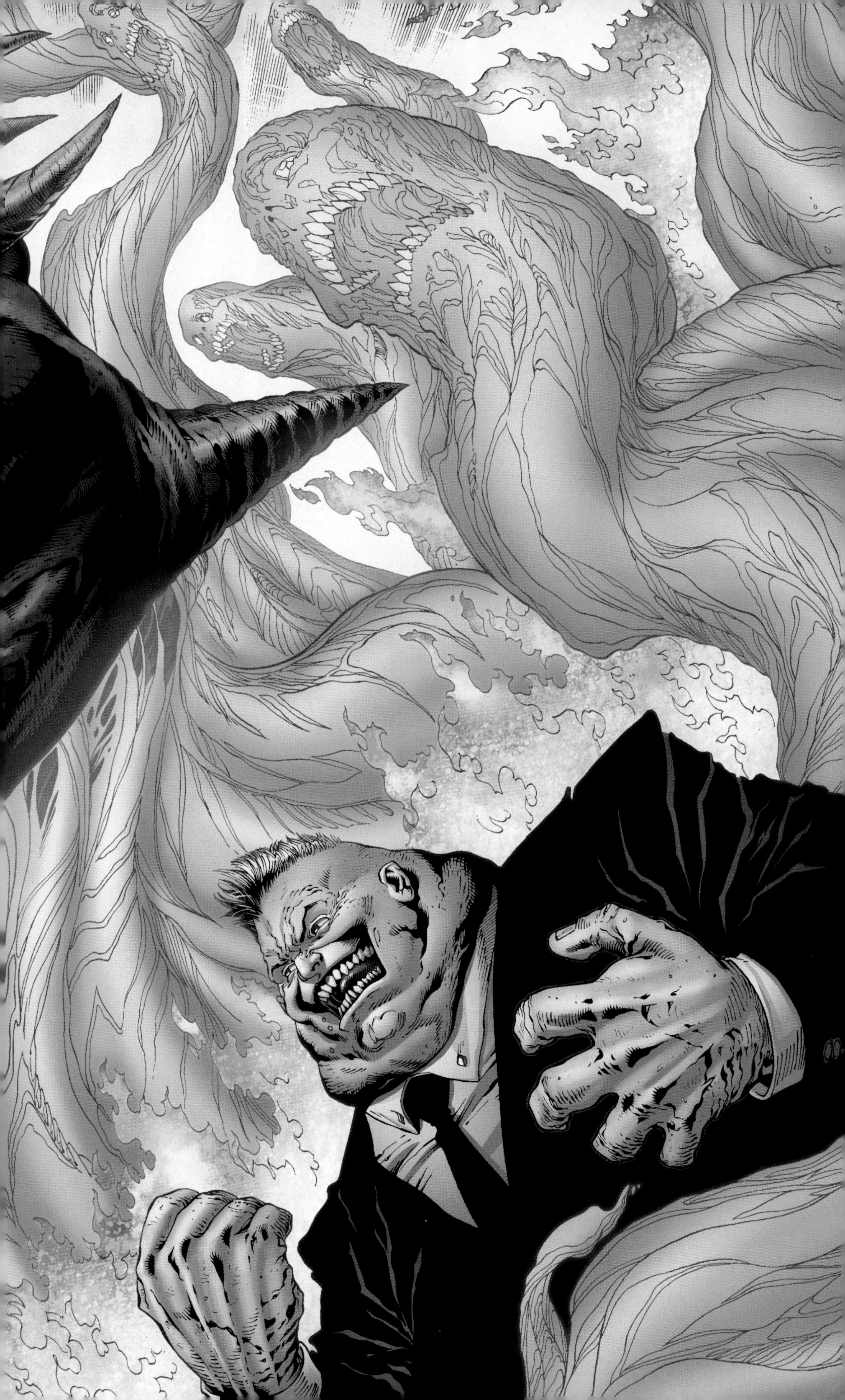

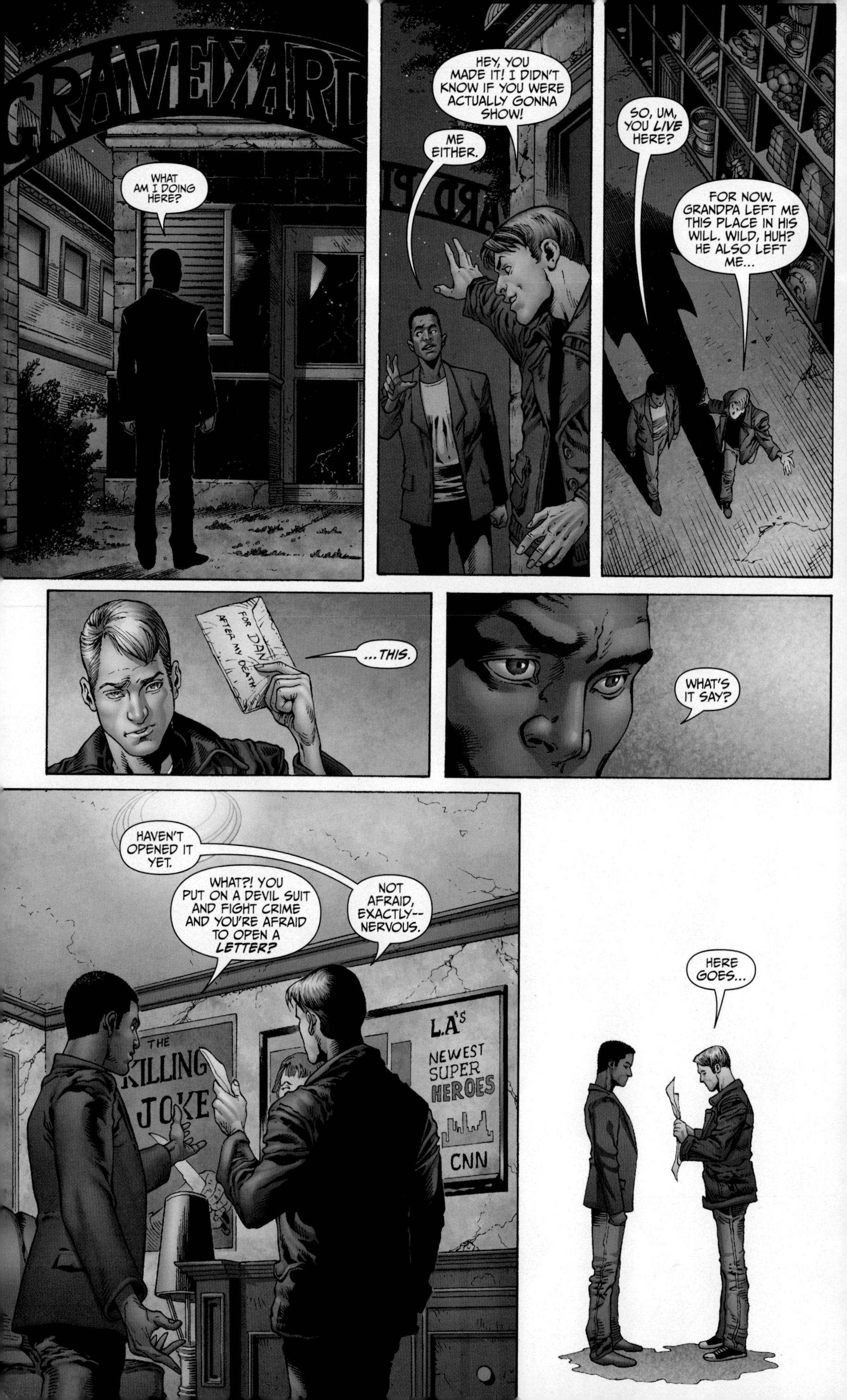
GRAVEYARD
WHAT AM I DOING HERE?
HEY, YOU MADE IT! I DIDN'T KNOW IF YOU WERE ACTUALLY GONNA SHOW!
ME EITHER.
SO, UM, YOU LIVE HERE?
FOR NOW. GRANDPA LEFT ME THIS PLACE IN HIS WILL. WILD, HUH? HE ALSO LEFT ME...
FOR DAN AFTER MY DEATH
...THIS.
WHAT'S IT SAY?
HAVEN'T OPENED IT YET.
WHAT?! YOU PUT ON A DEVIL SUIT AND FIGHT CRIME AND YOU'RE AFRAID TO OPEN A LETTER?
NOT AFRAID, EXACTLY-- NERVOUS.
THE KILLING JOKE
L.A's NEWEST SUPER HEROES
CNN
HERE GOES...

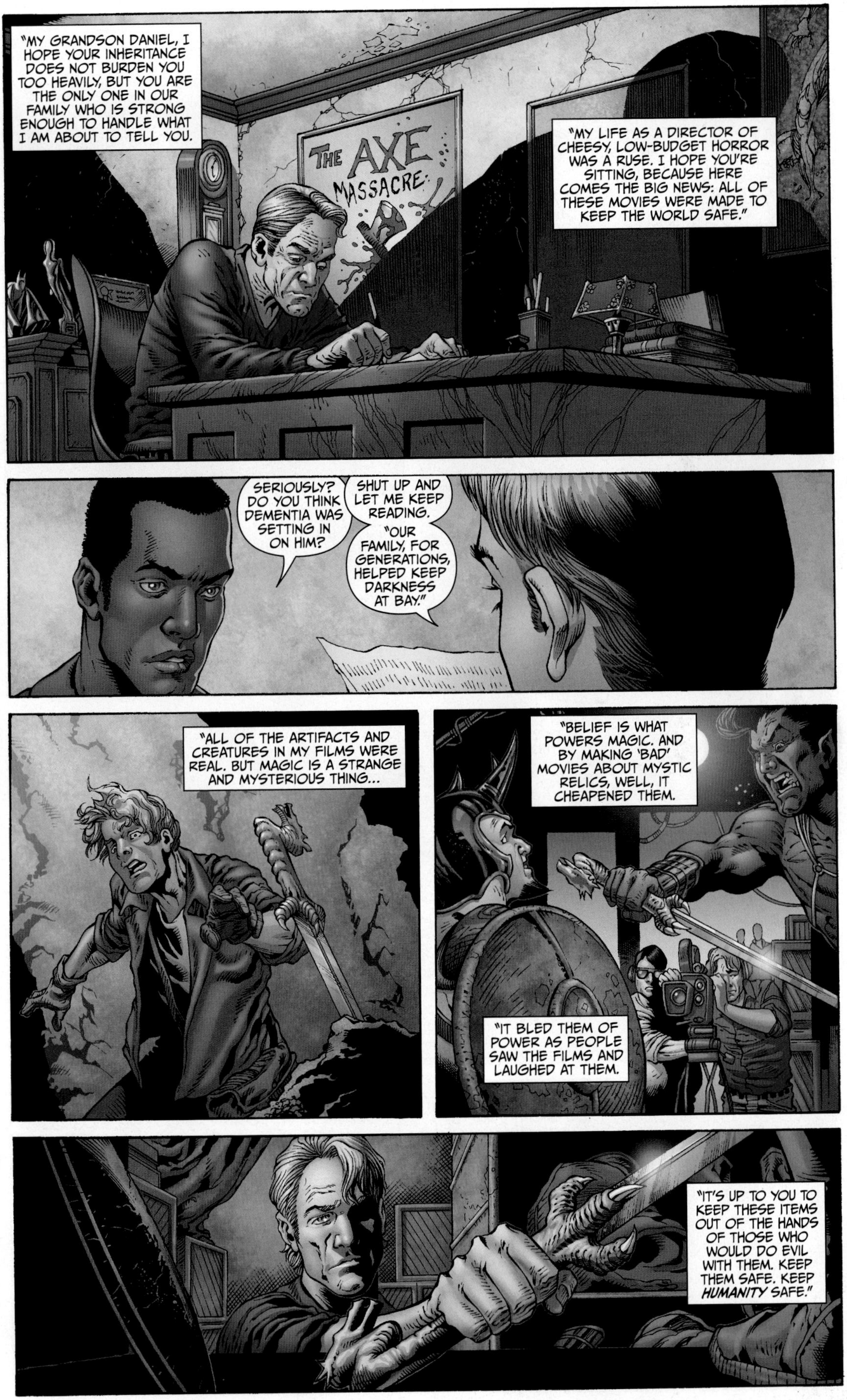
"MY GRANDSON DANIEL, I HOPE YOUR INHERITANCE DOES NOT BURDEN YOU TOO HEAVILY, BUT YOU ARE THE ONLY ONE IN OUR FAMILY WHO IS STRONG ENOUGH TO HANDLE WHAT I AM ABOUT TO TELL YOU.
THE AXE MASSACRE
"MY LIFE AS A DIRECTOR OF CHEESY, LOW-BUDGET HORROR WAS A RUSE. I HOPE YOU'RE SITTING, BECAUSE HERE COMES THE BIG NEWS: ALL OF THESE MOVIES WERE MADE TO KEEP THE WORLD SAFE."
SERIOUSLY? DO YOU THINK DEMENTIA WAS SETTING IN ON HIM?
SHUT UP AND LET ME KEEP READING.
"OUR FAMILY, FOR GENERATIONS, HELPED KEEP DARKNESS AT BAY."
"ALL OF THE ARTIFACTS AND CREATURES IN MY FILMS WERE REAL. BUT MAGIC IS A STRANGE AND MYSTERIOUS THING...
"BELIEF IS WHAT POWERS MAGIC. AND BY MAKING 'BAD' MOVIES ABOUT MYSTIC RELICS, WELL, IT CHEAPENED THEM.
"IT BLED THEM OF POWER AS PEOPLE SAW THE FILMS AND LAUGHED AT THEM.
"IT'S UP TO YOU TO KEEP THESE ITEMS OUT OF THE HANDS OF THOSE WHO WOULD DO EVIL WITH THEM. KEEP THEM SAFE. KEEP *HUMANITY* SAFE."

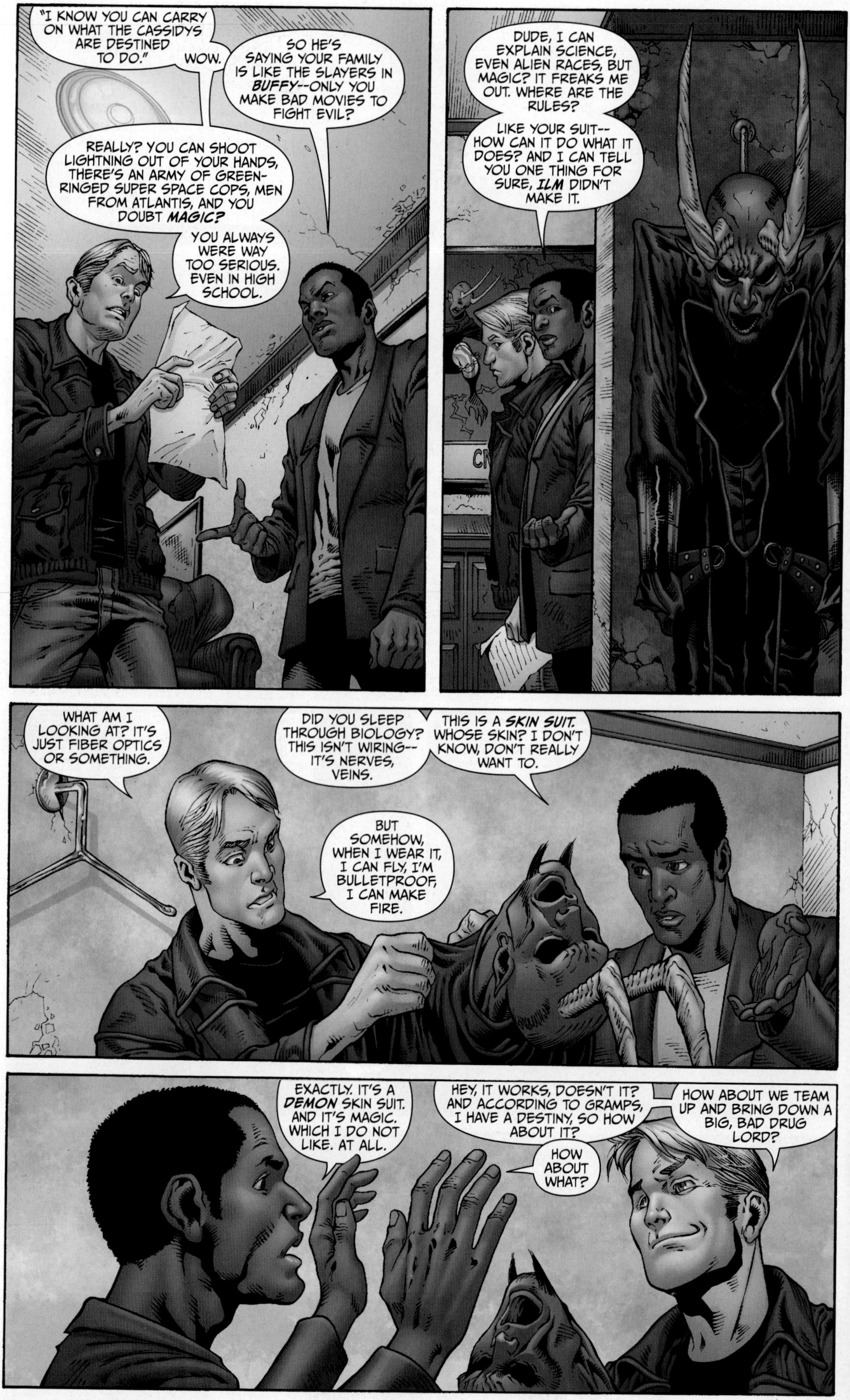
"I KNOW YOU CAN CARRY ON WHAT THE CASSIDYS ARE DESTINED TO DO."
WOW.
SO HE'S SAYING YOUR FAMILY IS LIKE THE SLAYERS IN BUFFY--ONLY YOU MAKE BAD MOVIES TO FIGHT EVIL?
REALLY? YOU CAN SHOOT LIGHTNING OUT OF YOUR HANDS, THERE'S AN ARMY OF GREEN-RINGED SUPER SPACE COPS, MEN FROM ATLANTIS, AND YOU DOUBT MAGIC?
YOU ALWAYS WERE WAY TOO SERIOUS. EVEN IN HIGH SCHOOL.
DUDE, I CAN EXPLAIN SCIENCE, EVEN ALIEN RACES, BUT MAGIC? IT FREAKS ME OUT. WHERE ARE THE RULES?
LIKE YOUR SUIT--HOW CAN IT DO WHAT IT DOES? AND I CAN TELL YOU ONE THING FOR SURE, ILM DIDN'T MAKE IT.
WHAT AM I LOOKING AT? IT'S JUST FIBER OPTICS OR SOMETHING.
DID YOU SLEEP THROUGH BIOLOGY? THIS ISN'T WIRING--IT'S NERVES, VEINS.
THIS IS A SKIN SUIT. WHOSE SKIN? I DON'T KNOW, DON'T REALLY WANT TO.
BUT SOMEHOW, WHEN I WEAR IT, I CAN FLY, I'M BULLETPROOF, I CAN MAKE FIRE.
EXACTLY. IT'S A DEMON SKIN SUIT. AND IT'S MAGIC. WHICH I DO NOT LIKE. AT ALL.
HEY, IT WORKS, DOESN'T IT? AND ACCORDING TO GRAMPS, I HAVE A DESTINY, SO HOW ABOUT IT?
HOW ABOUT WHAT?
HOW ABOUT WE TEAM UP AND BRING DOWN A BIG, BAD DRUG LORD?

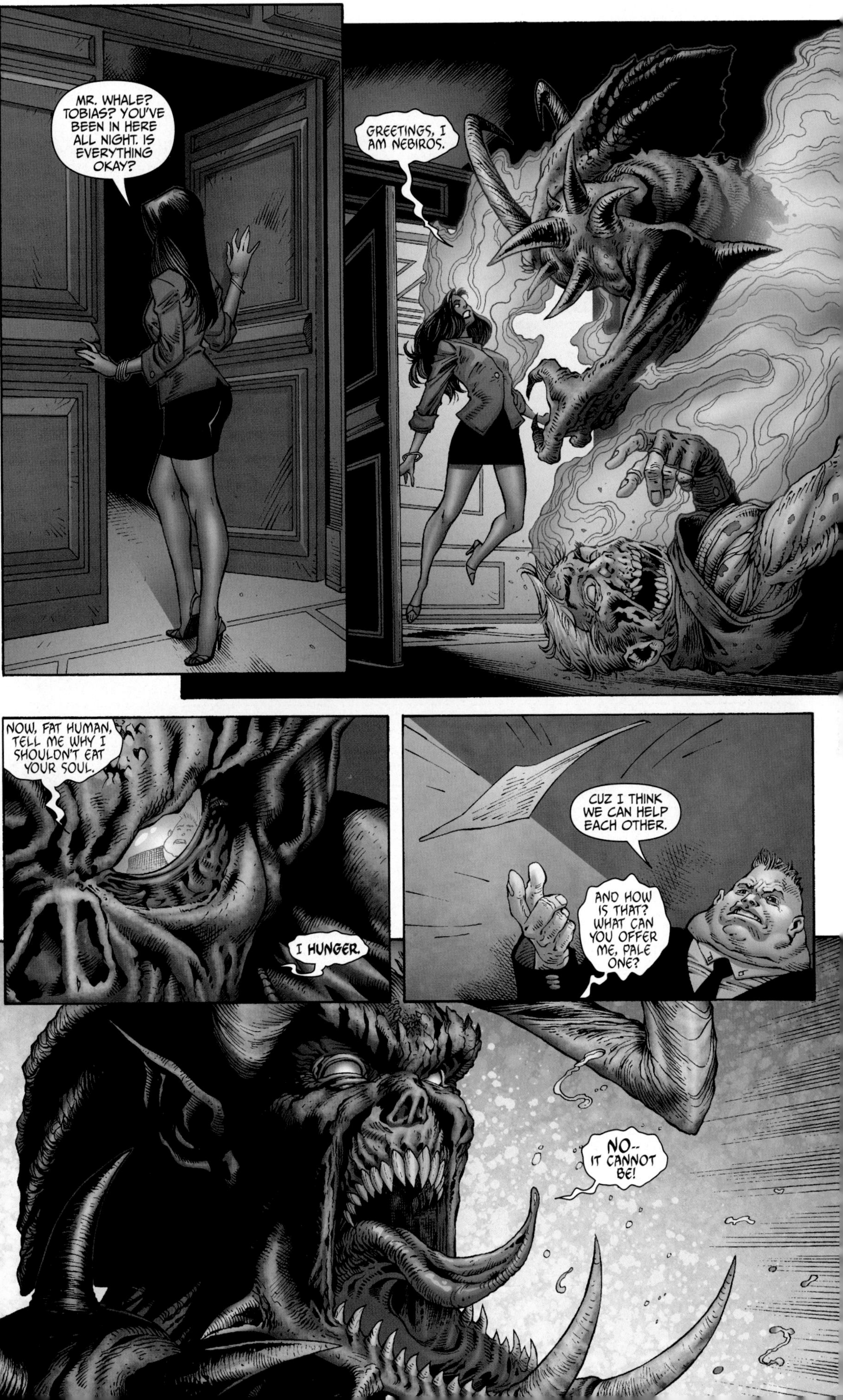
MR. WHALE? TOBIAS? YOU'VE BEEN IN HERE ALL NIGHT. IS EVERYTHING OKAY?
GREETINGS, I AM NEBIROS.
NOW, FAT HUMAN, TELL ME WHY I SHOULDN'T EAT YOUR SOUL.
I HUNGER.
CUZ I THINK WE CAN HELP EACH OTHER.
AND HOW IS THAT? WHAT CAN YOU OFFER ME, PALE ONE?
NO-- IT CANNOT BE!

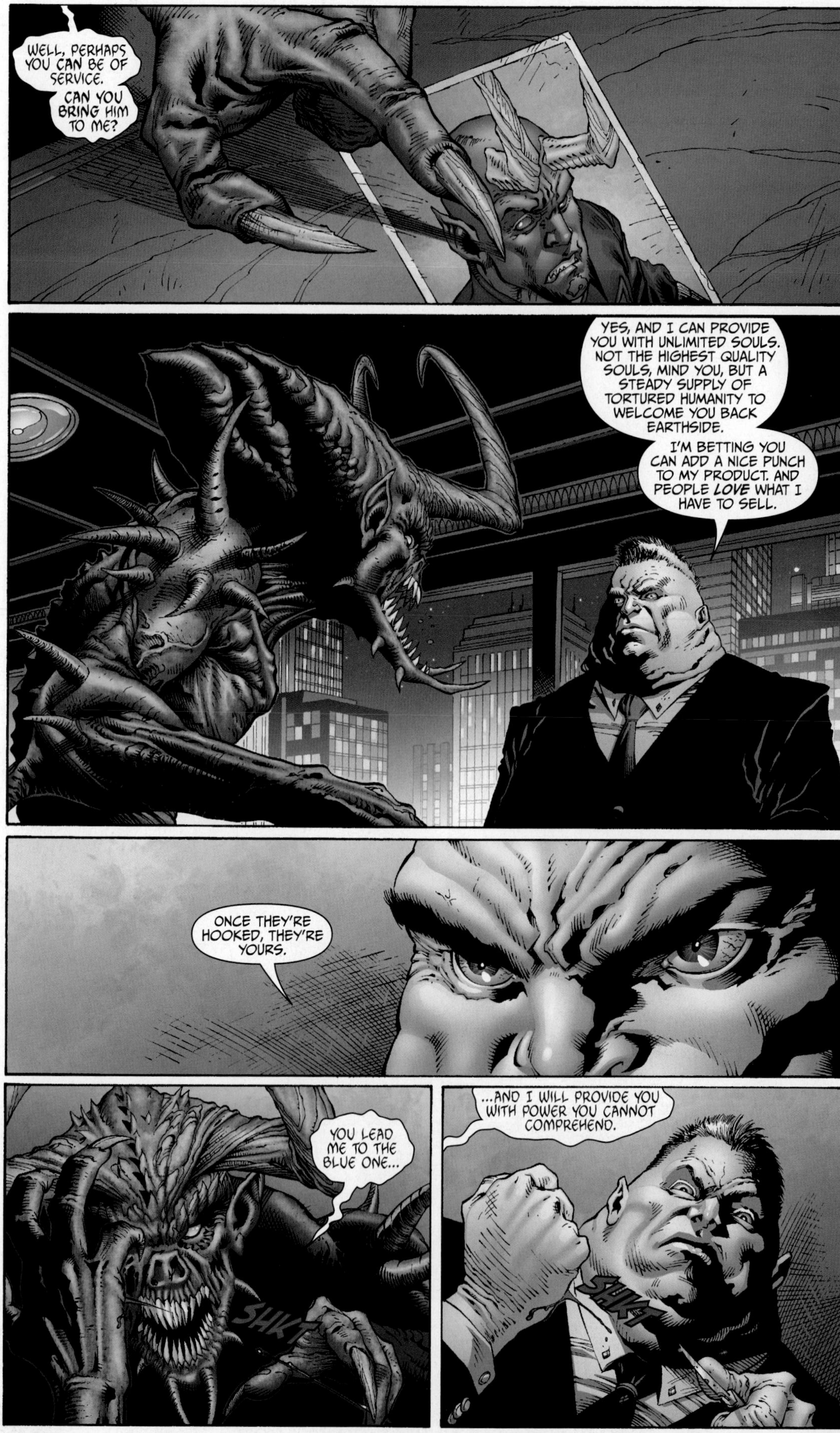
WELL, PERHAPS YOU CAN BE OF SERVICE.
CAN YOU BRING HIM TO ME?
YES, AND I CAN PROVIDE YOU WITH UNLIMITED SOULS. NOT THE HIGHEST QUALITY SOULS, MIND YOU, BUT A STEADY SUPPLY OF TORTURED HUMANITY TO WELCOME YOU BACK EARTHSIDE.
I'M BETTING YOU CAN ADD A NICE PUNCH TO MY PRODUCT. AND PEOPLE LOVE WHAT I HAVE TO SELL.
ONCE THEY'RE HOOKED, THEY'RE YOURS.
YOU LEAD ME TO THE BLUE ONE...
SHKT
...AND I WILL PROVIDE YOU WITH POWER YOU CANNOT COMPREHEND.
SHKT

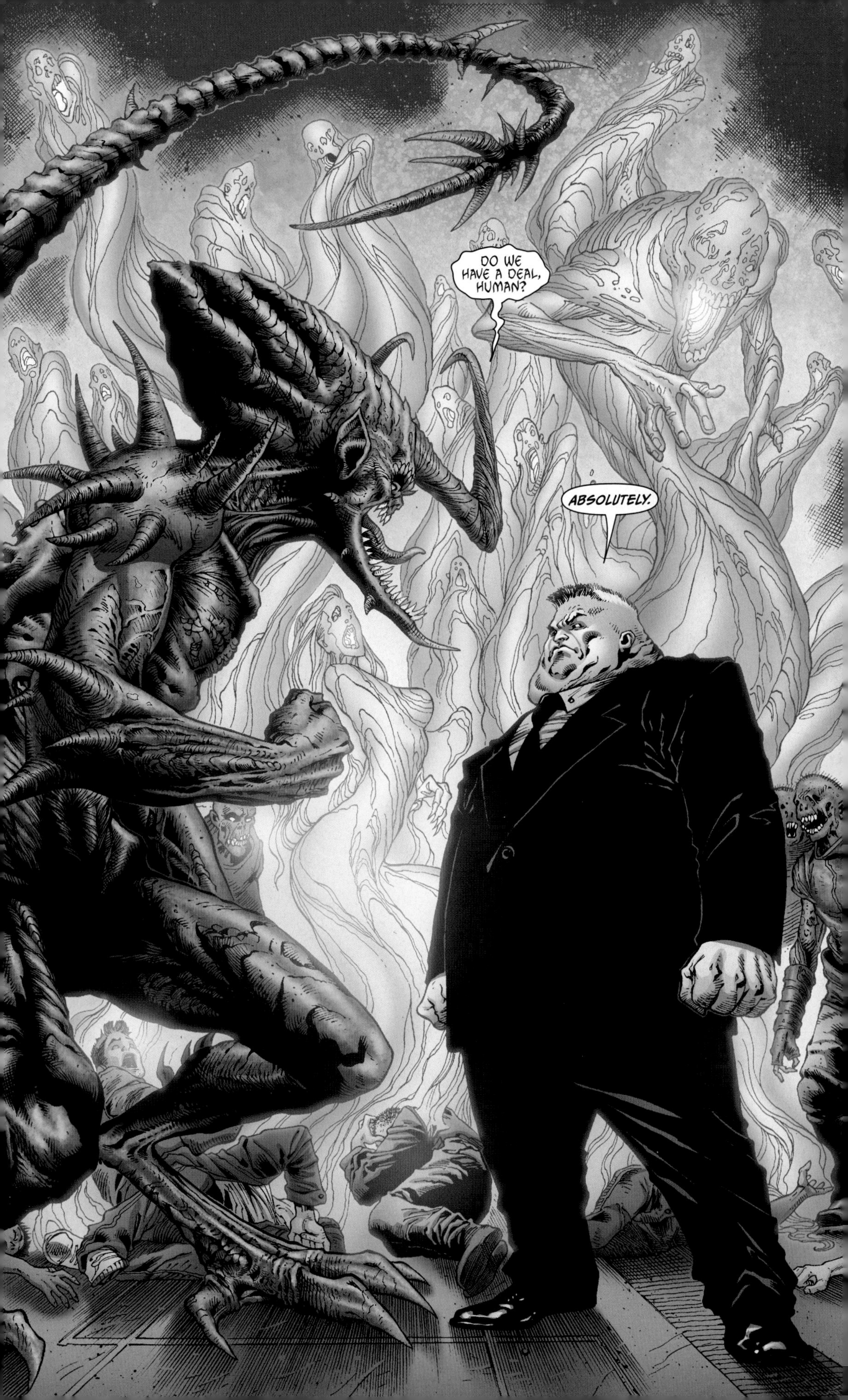
DO WE HAVE A DEAL, HUMAN?
ABSOLUTELY.

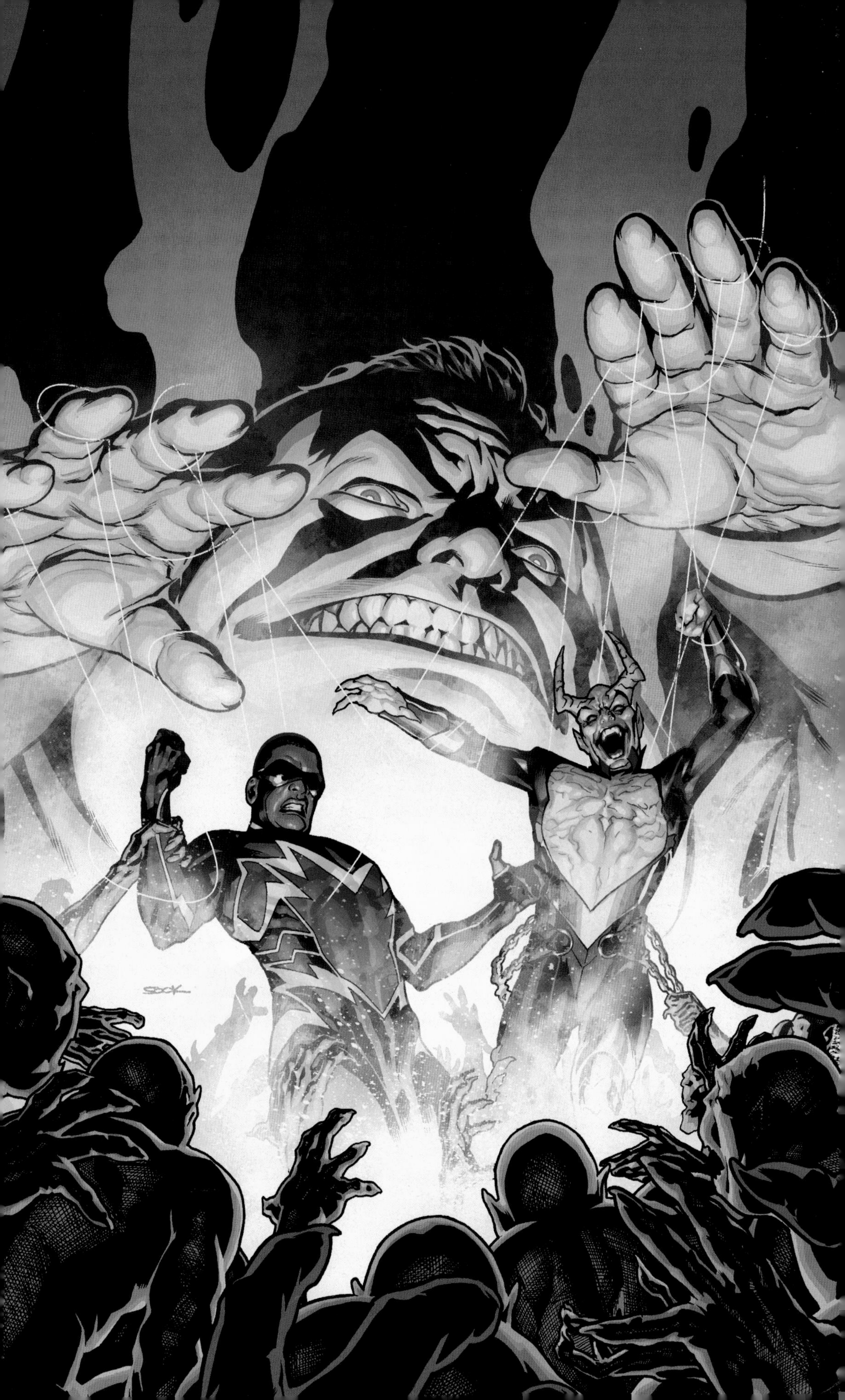

UNDER YOUR SKIN

MARC ANDREYKO
writer

ROBSON ROCHA with EDUARDO PANSICA
pencillers

OCLAIR ALBERT with JP MAYER
inkers

cover art by RYAN SOOK

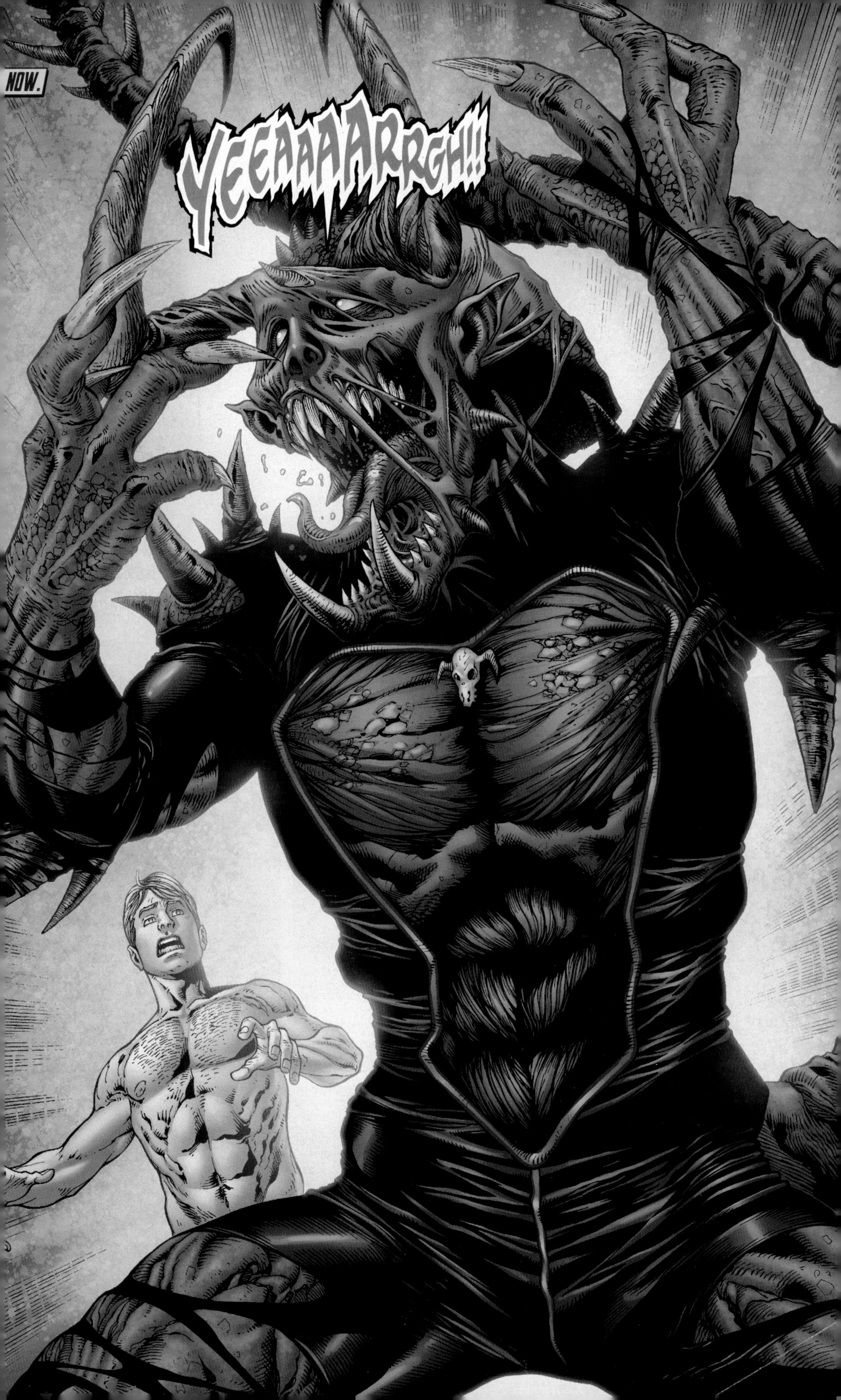
NOW.
YEEAAAARRRGH!!!

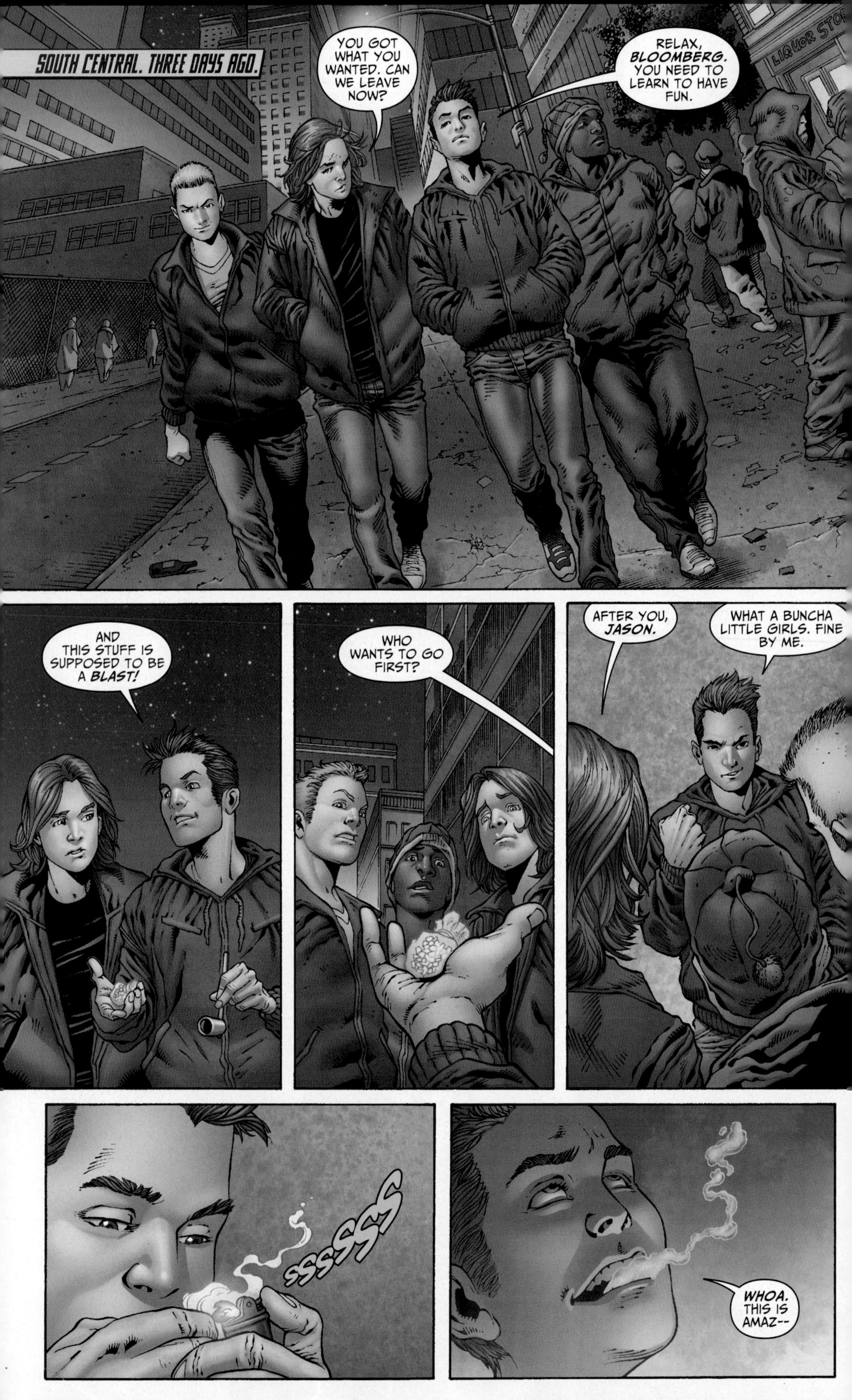
SOUTH CENTRAL. THREE DAYS AGO.
YOU GOT WHAT YOU WANTED. CAN WE LEAVE NOW?
RELAX, BLOOMBERG. YOU NEED TO LEARN TO HAVE FUN.
LIQUOR STO
AND THIS STUFF IS SUPPOSED TO BE A BLAST!
WHO WANTS TO GO FIRST?
AFTER YOU, JASON.
WHAT A BUNCHA LITTLE GIRLS. FINE BY ME.
SSSSSS
WHOA. THIS IS AMAZ--

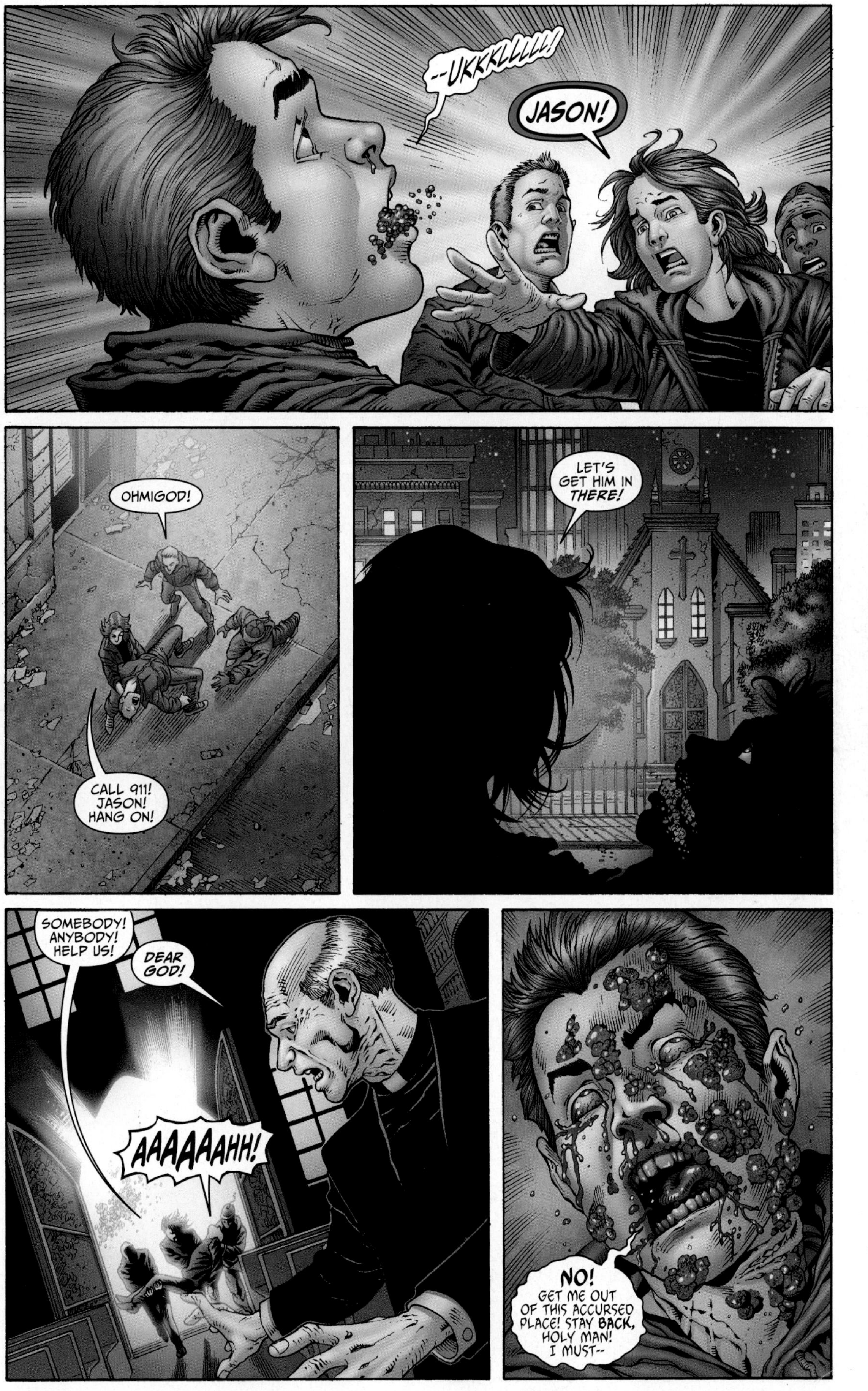
--UKKKLLLLL!
JASON!
OHMIGOD!
CALL 911! JASON! HANG ON!
LET'S GET HIM IN THERE!
SOMEBODY! ANYBODY! HELP US!
DEAR GOD!
AAAAAAHH!
NO! GET ME OUT OF THIS ACCURSED PLACE! STAY BACK, HOLY MAN! I MUST--

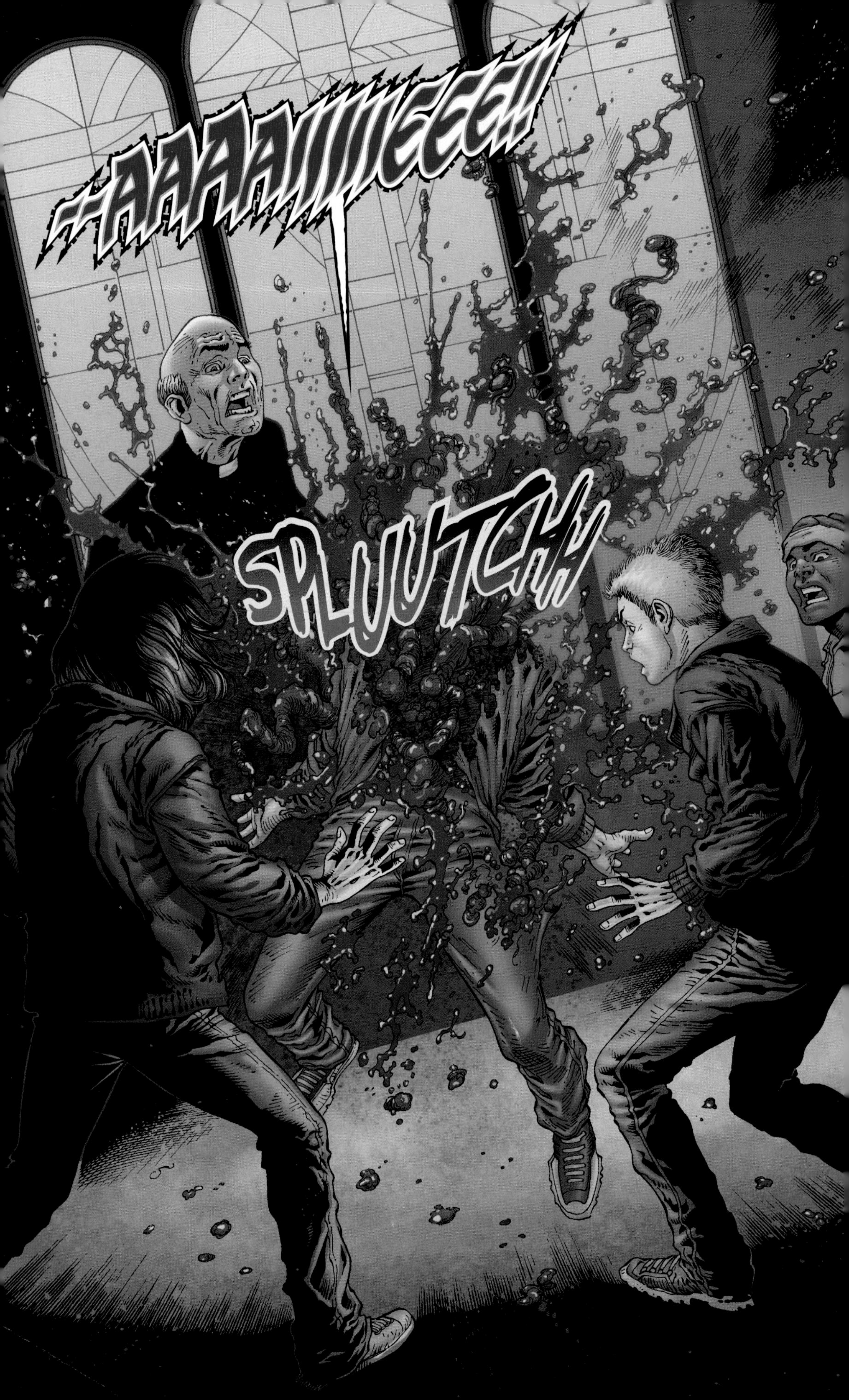
--AAAAIIIIIEEEE!!
SPLUUTCH

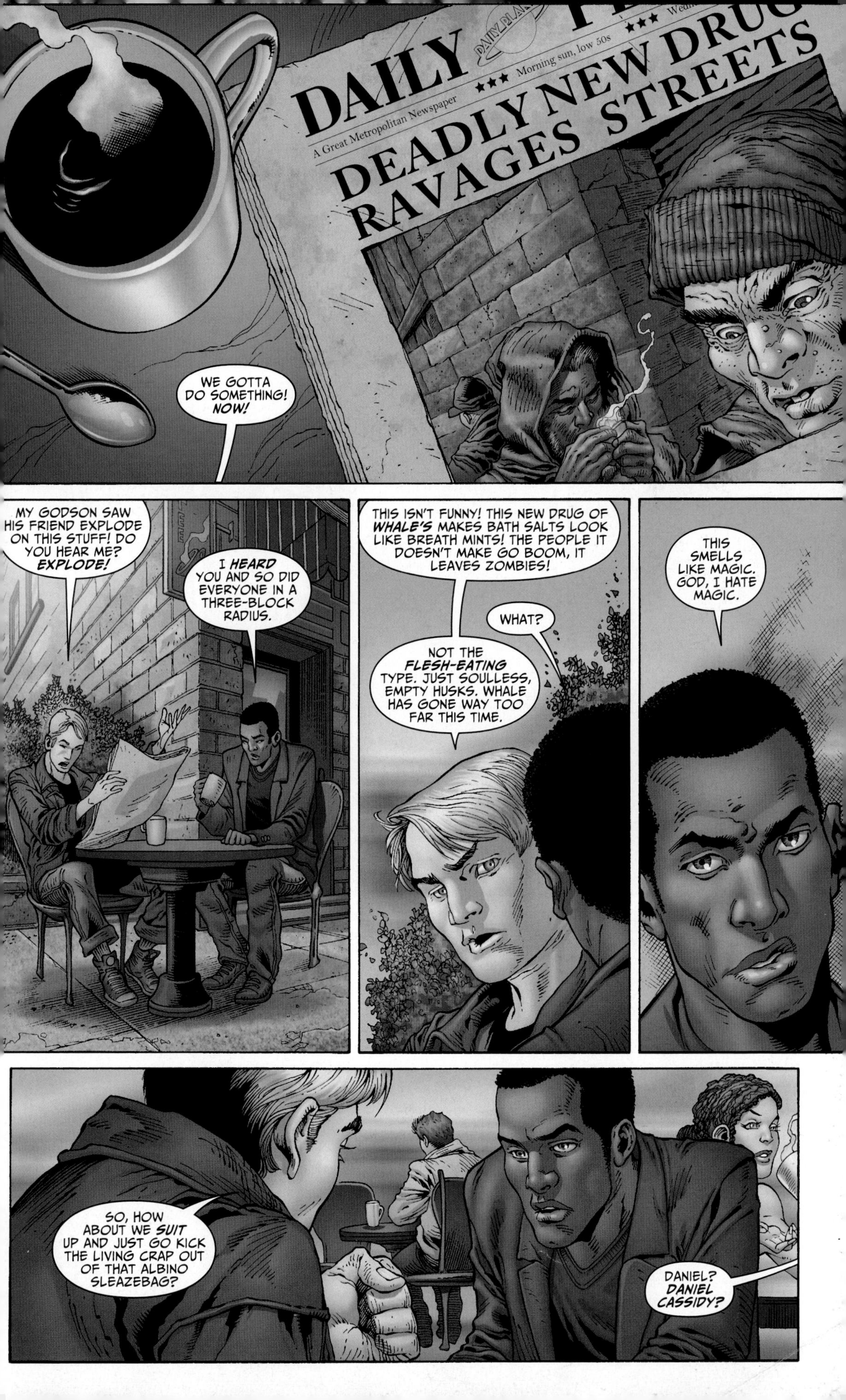
DAILY
A Great Metropolitan Newspaper
Morning sun, low 50s
DEADLY NEW DRUG
RAVAGES STREETS
WE GOTTA DO SOMETHING! NOW!
MY GODSON SAW HIS FRIEND EXPLODE ON THIS STUFF! DO YOU HEAR ME? EXPLODE!
I HEARD YOU AND SO DID EVERYONE IN A THREE-BLOCK RADIUS.
THIS ISN'T FUNNY! THIS NEW DRUG OF WHALE'S MAKES BATH SALTS LOOK LIKE BREATH MINTS! THE PEOPLE IT DOESN'T MAKE GO BOOM, IT LEAVES ZOMBIES!
WHAT?
NOT THE FLESH-EATING TYPE. JUST SOULLESS, EMPTY HUSKS. WHALE HAS GONE WAY TOO FAR THIS TIME.
THIS SMELLS LIKE MAGIC. GOD, I HATE MAGIC.
SO, HOW ABOUT WE SUIT UP AND JUST GO KICK THE LIVING CRAP OUT OF THAT ALBINO SLEAZEBAG?
DANIEL? DANIEL CASSIDY?

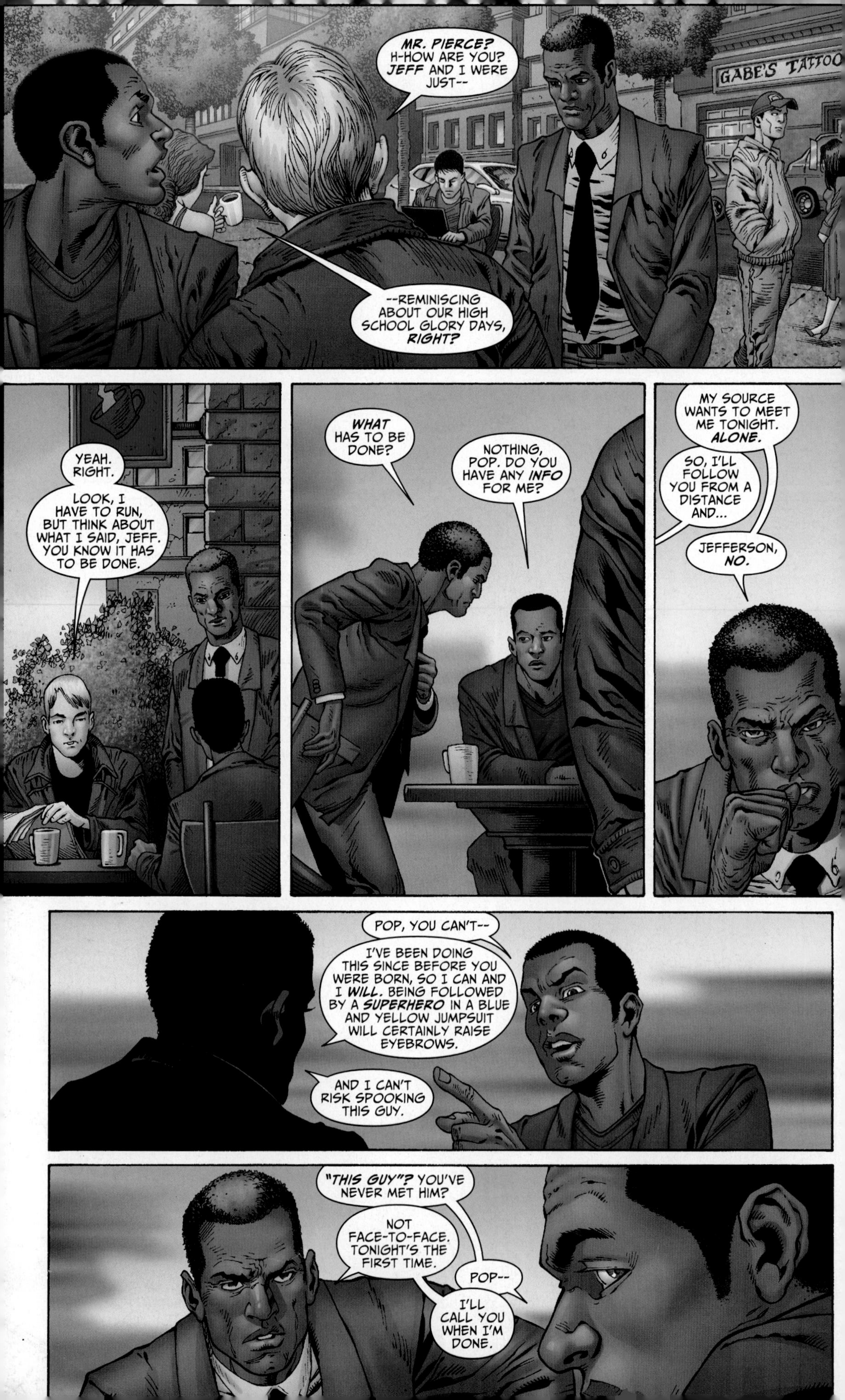

MR. PIERCE? H-HOW ARE YOU? JEFF AND I WERE JUST--
--REMINISCING ABOUT OUR HIGH SCHOOL GLORY DAYS, RIGHT?
GABE'S TATTOO
YEAH. RIGHT.
LOOK, I HAVE TO RUN, BUT THINK ABOUT WHAT I SAID, JEFF. YOU KNOW IT HAS TO BE DONE.
WHAT HAS TO BE DONE?
NOTHING, POP. DO YOU HAVE ANY INFO FOR ME?
MY SOURCE WANTS TO MEET ME TONIGHT. ALONE.
SO, I'LL FOLLOW YOU FROM A DISTANCE AND...
JEFFERSON, NO.
POP, YOU CAN'T--
I'VE BEEN DOING THIS SINCE BEFORE YOU WERE BORN, SO I CAN AND I WILL. BEING FOLLOWED BY A SUPERHERO IN A BLUE AND YELLOW JUMPSUIT WILL CERTAINLY RAISE EYEBROWS.
AND I CAN'T RISK SPOOKING THIS GUY.
"THIS GUY"? YOU'VE NEVER MET HIM?
NOT FACE-TO-FACE. TONIGHT'S THE FIRST TIME.
POP--
I'LL CALL YOU WHEN I'M DONE.

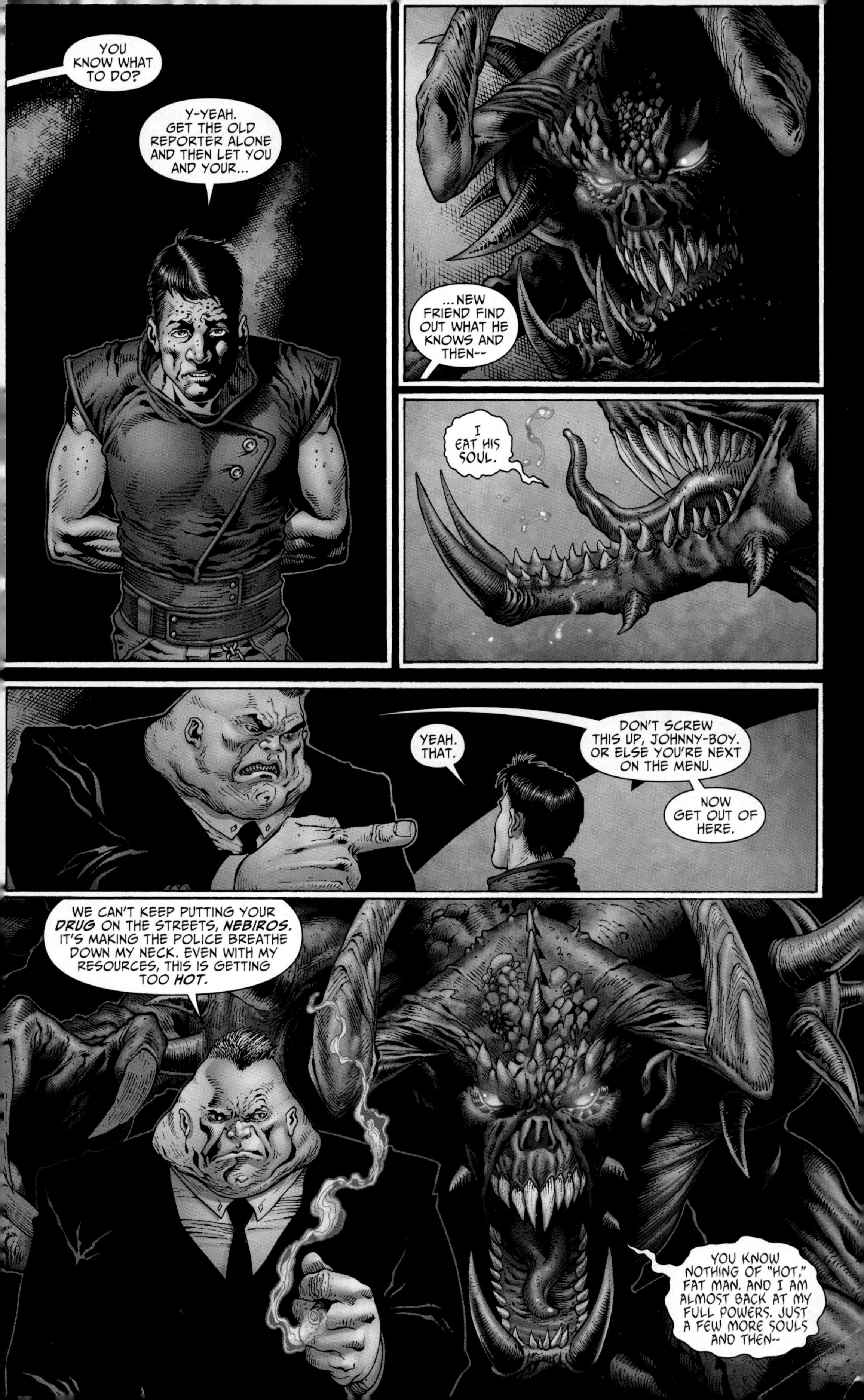
YOU KNOW WHAT TO DO?
Y-YEAH. GET THE OLD REPORTER ALONE AND THEN LET YOU AND YOUR...
...NEW FRIEND FIND OUT WHAT HE KNOWS AND THEN--
I EAT HIS SOUL.
YEAH. THAT.
DON'T SCREW THIS UP, JOHNNY-BOY. OR ELSE YOU'RE NEXT ON THE MENU.
NOW GET OUT OF HERE.
WE CAN'T KEEP PUTTING YOUR DRUG ON THE STREETS, NEBIROS. IT'S MAKING THE POLICE BREATHE DOWN MY NECK. EVEN WITH MY RESOURCES, THIS IS GETTING TOO HOT.
YOU KNOW NOTHING OF "HOT," FAT MAN. AND I AM ALMOST BACK AT MY FULL POWERS. JUST A FEW MORE SOULS AND THEN--

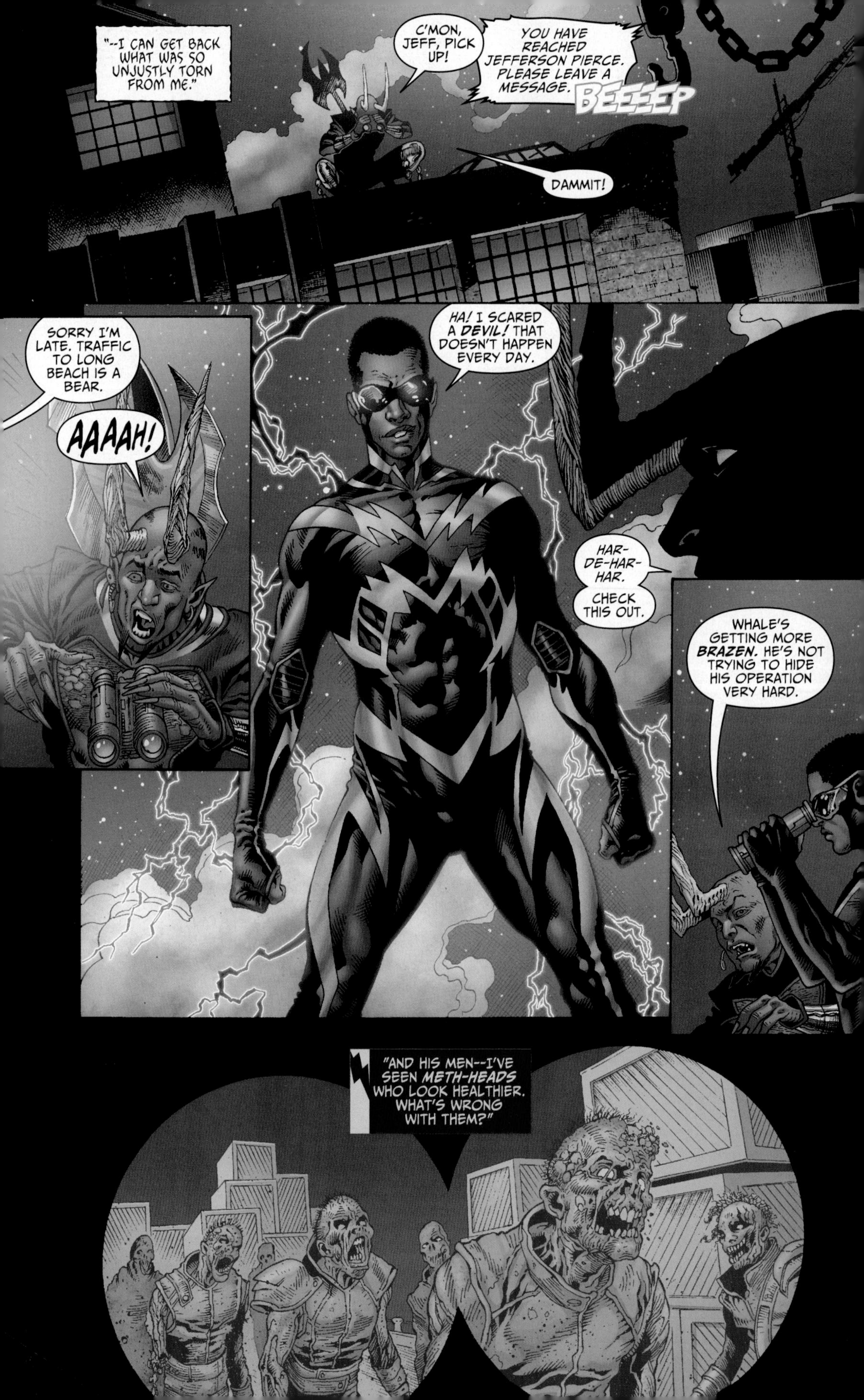
"--I CAN GET BACK WHAT WAS SO UNJUSTLY TORN FROM ME."
C'MON, JEFF, PICK UP!
YOU HAVE REACHED JEFFERSON PIERCE. PLEASE LEAVE A MESSAGE.
BEEEEP
DAMMIT!
SORRY I'M LATE. TRAFFIC TO LONG BEACH IS A BEAR.
AAAAH!
HA! I SCARED A DEVIL! THAT DOESN'T HAPPEN EVERY DAY.
HAR-DE-HAR-HAR.
CHECK THIS OUT.
WHALE'S GETTING MORE BRAZEN. HE'S NOT TRYING TO HIDE HIS OPERATION VERY HARD.
"AND HIS MEN--I'VE SEEN METH-HEADS WHO LOOK HEALTHIER. WHAT'S WRONG WITH THEM?"

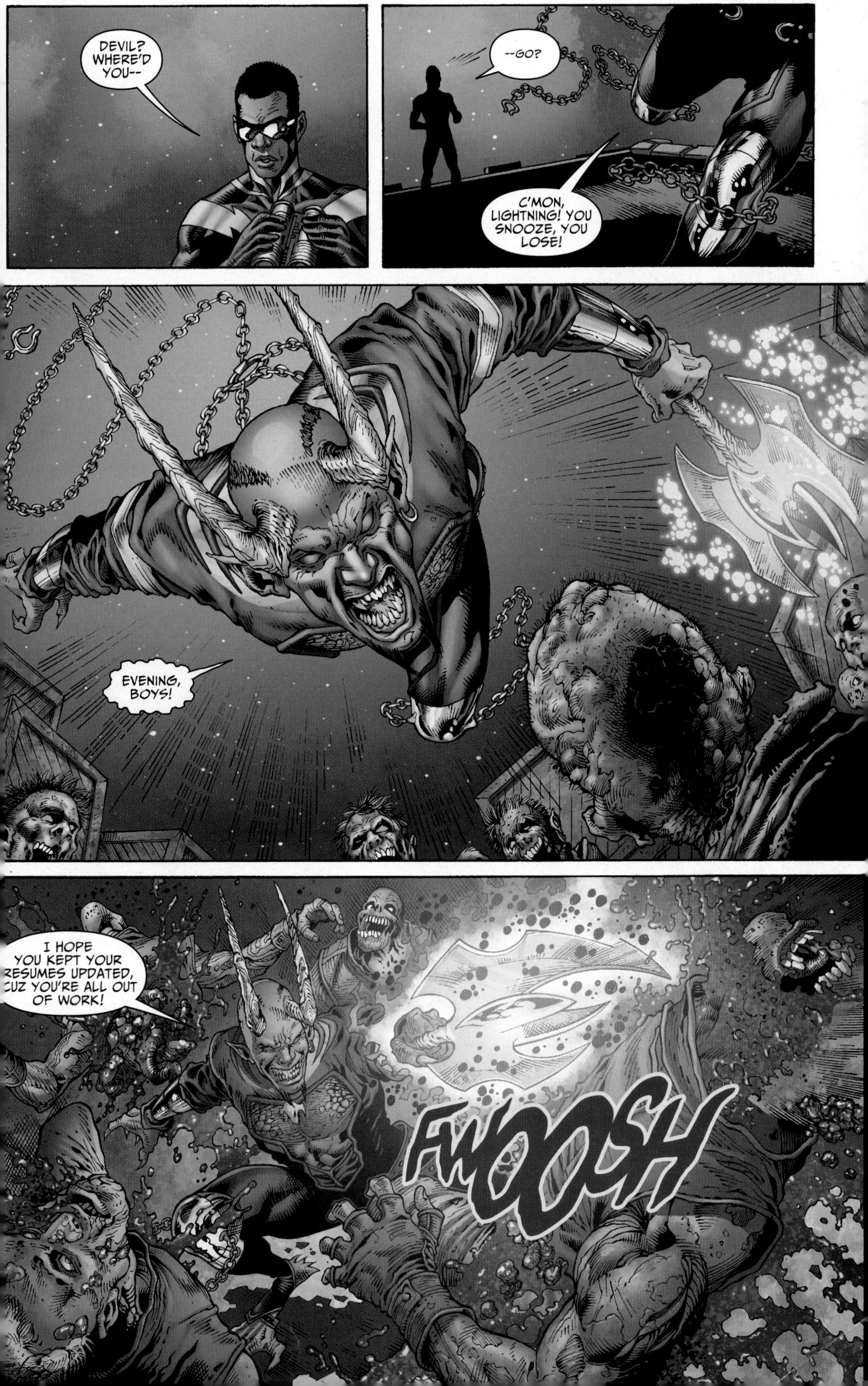
DEVIL? WHERE'D YOU--
--GO?
C'MON, LIGHTNING! YOU SNOOZE, YOU LOSE!
EVENING, BOYS!
I HOPE YOU KEPT YOUR RESUMES UPDATED, CUZ YOU'RE ALL OUT OF WORK!
FWOOSH

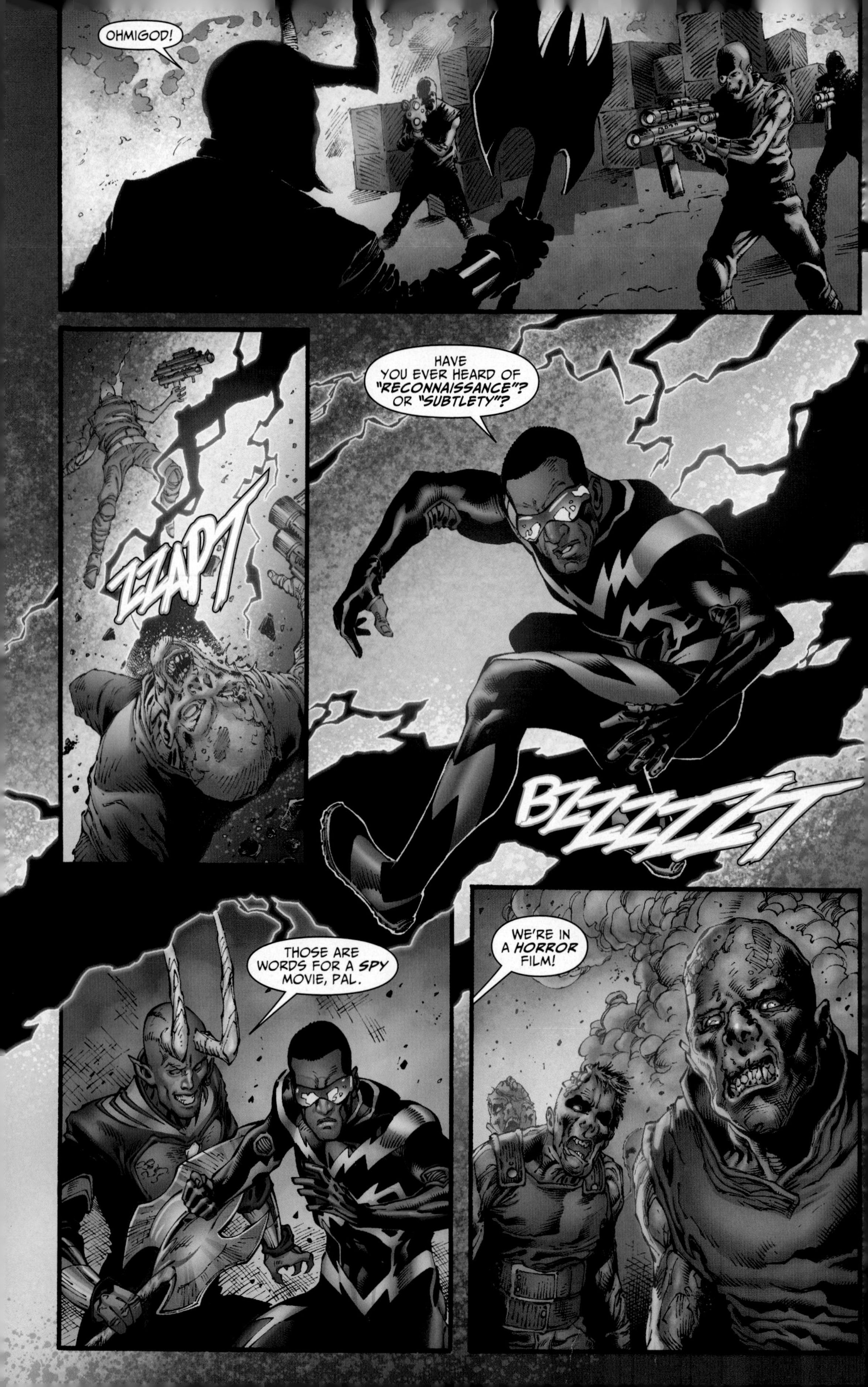
OHMIGOD!
ZZAPT
HAVE YOU EVER HEARD OF "RECONNAISSANCE"? OR "SUBTLETY"?
BZZZZZT
THOSE ARE WORDS FOR A SPY MOVIE, PAL.
WE'RE IN A HORROR FILM!

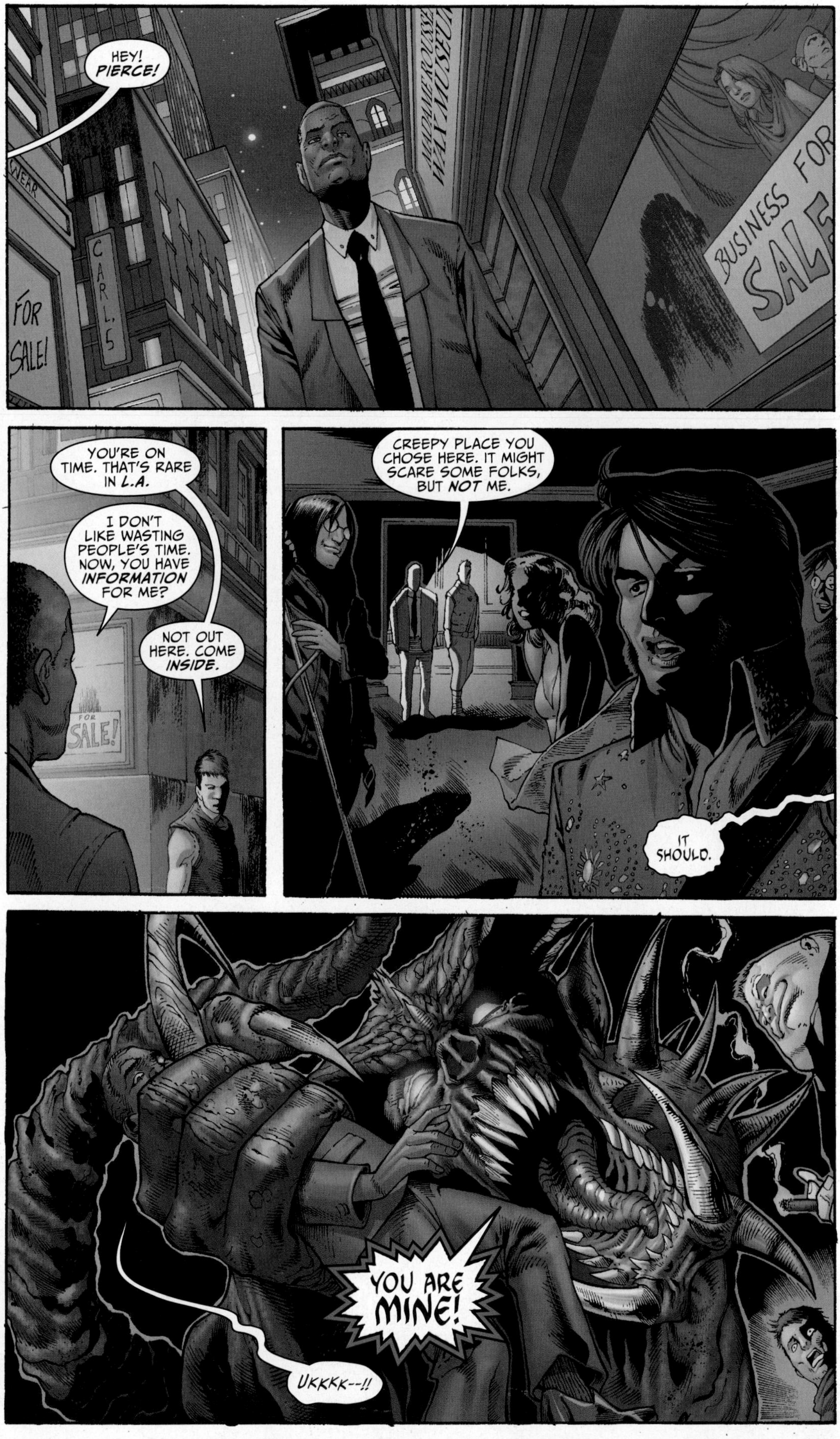
HEY! PIERCE!
WEAR
CARL'S
FOR SALE!
BUSINESS FOR SALE
YOU'RE ON TIME. THAT'S RARE IN L.A.
I DON'T LIKE WASTING PEOPLE'S TIME. NOW, YOU HAVE INFORMATION FOR ME?
NOT OUT HERE. COME INSIDE.
FOR SALE!
CREEPY PLACE YOU CHOSE HERE. IT MIGHT SCARE SOME FOLKS, BUT NOT ME.
IT SHOULD.
YOU ARE MINE!
UKKKK--!!

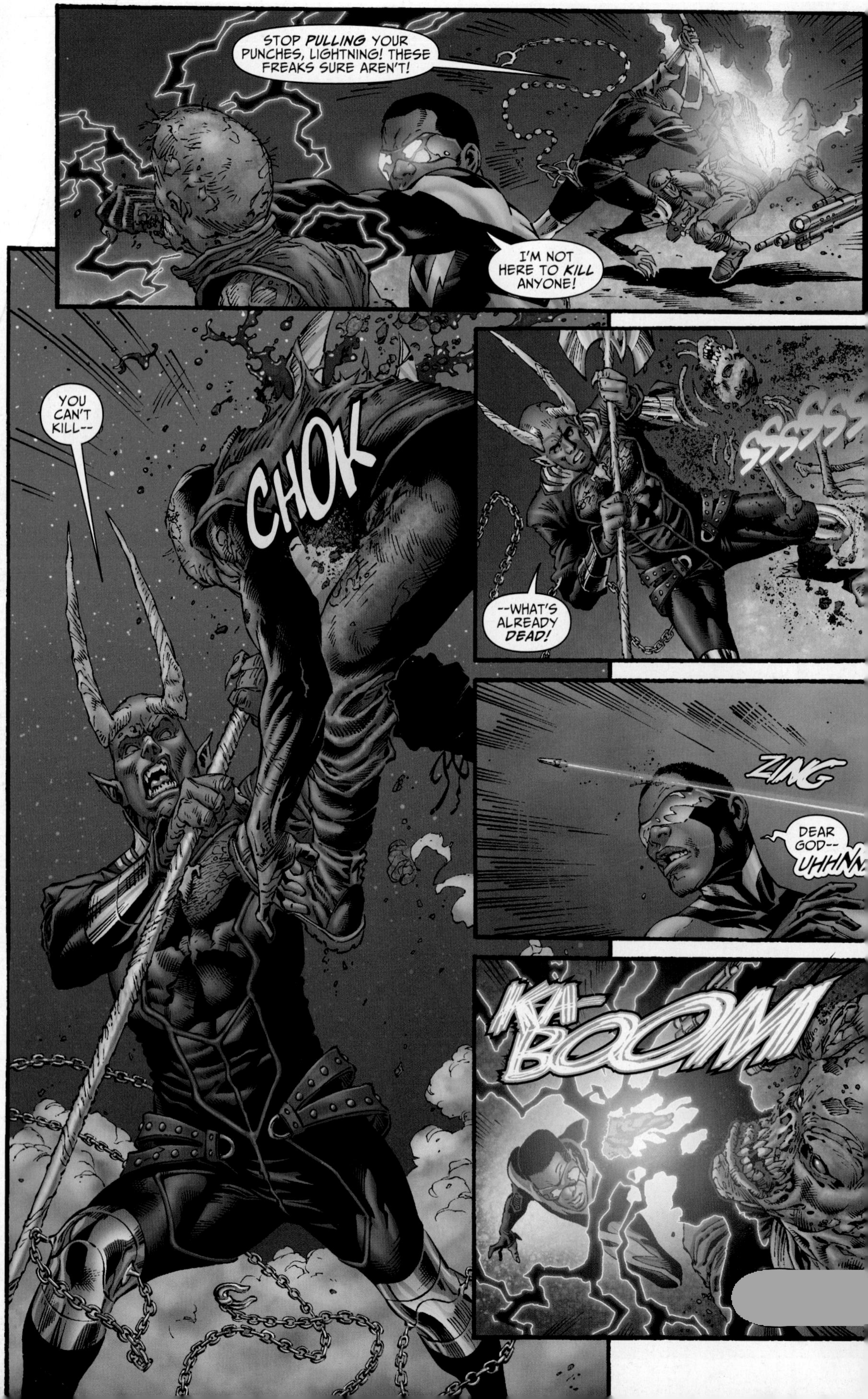
STOP PULLING YOUR PUNCHES, LIGHTNING! THESE FREAKS SURE AREN'T!
I'M NOT HERE TO KILL ANYONE!
YOU CAN'T KILL--
CHOK
--WHAT'S ALREADY DEAD!
SSSSSS
ZING
DEAR GOD-- UHHNN
KA-BOOM

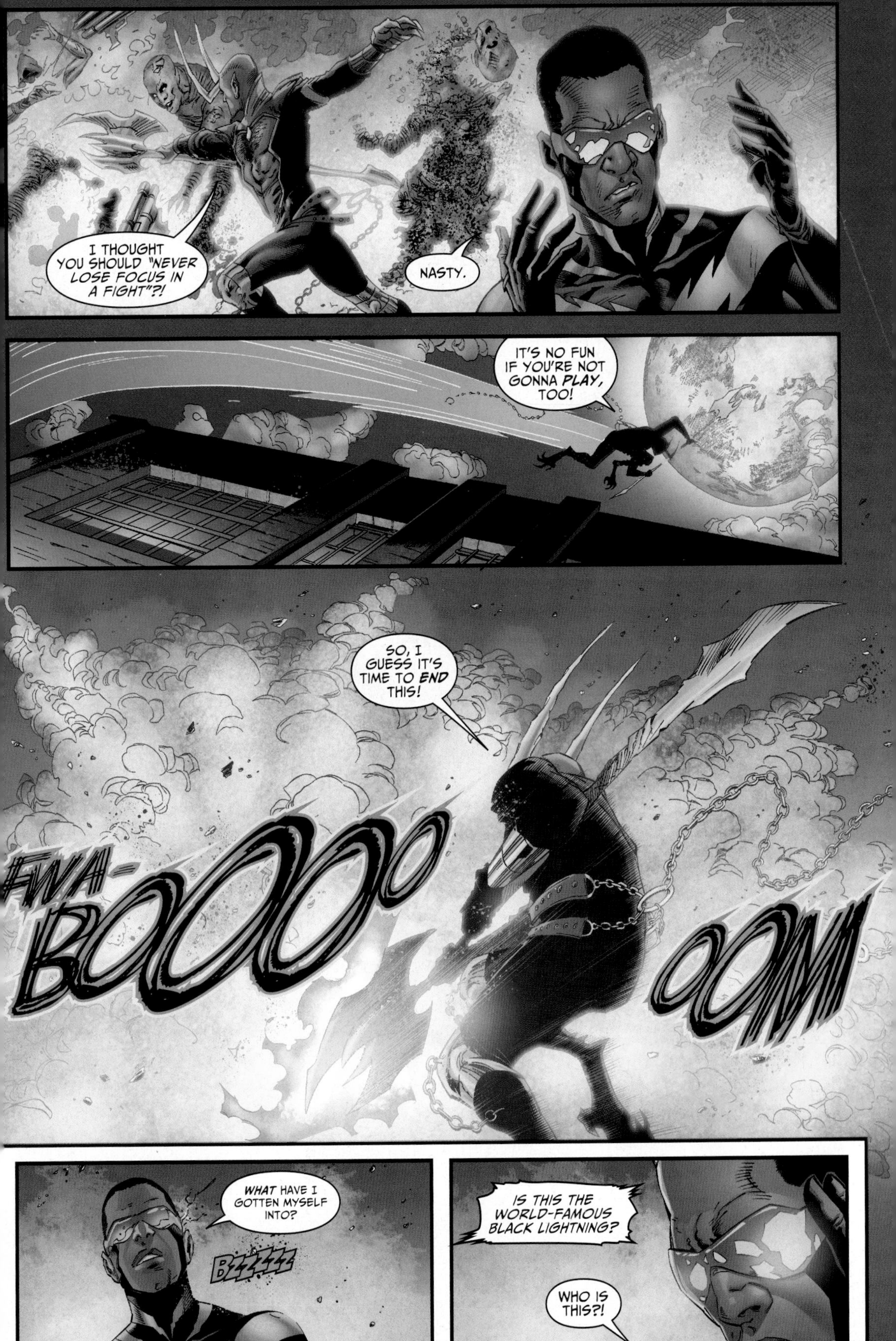

I THOUGHT YOU SHOULD "NEVER LOSE FOCUS IN A FIGHT"?!
NASTY.
IT'S NO FUN IF YOU'RE NOT GONNA PLAY, TOO!
SO, I GUESS IT'S TIME TO END THIS!
FWA-BOOOOOOOM
WHAT HAVE I GOTTEN MYSELF INTO?
BZZZZZ
IS THIS THE WORLD-FAMOUS BLACK LIGHTNING?
WHO IS THIS?!

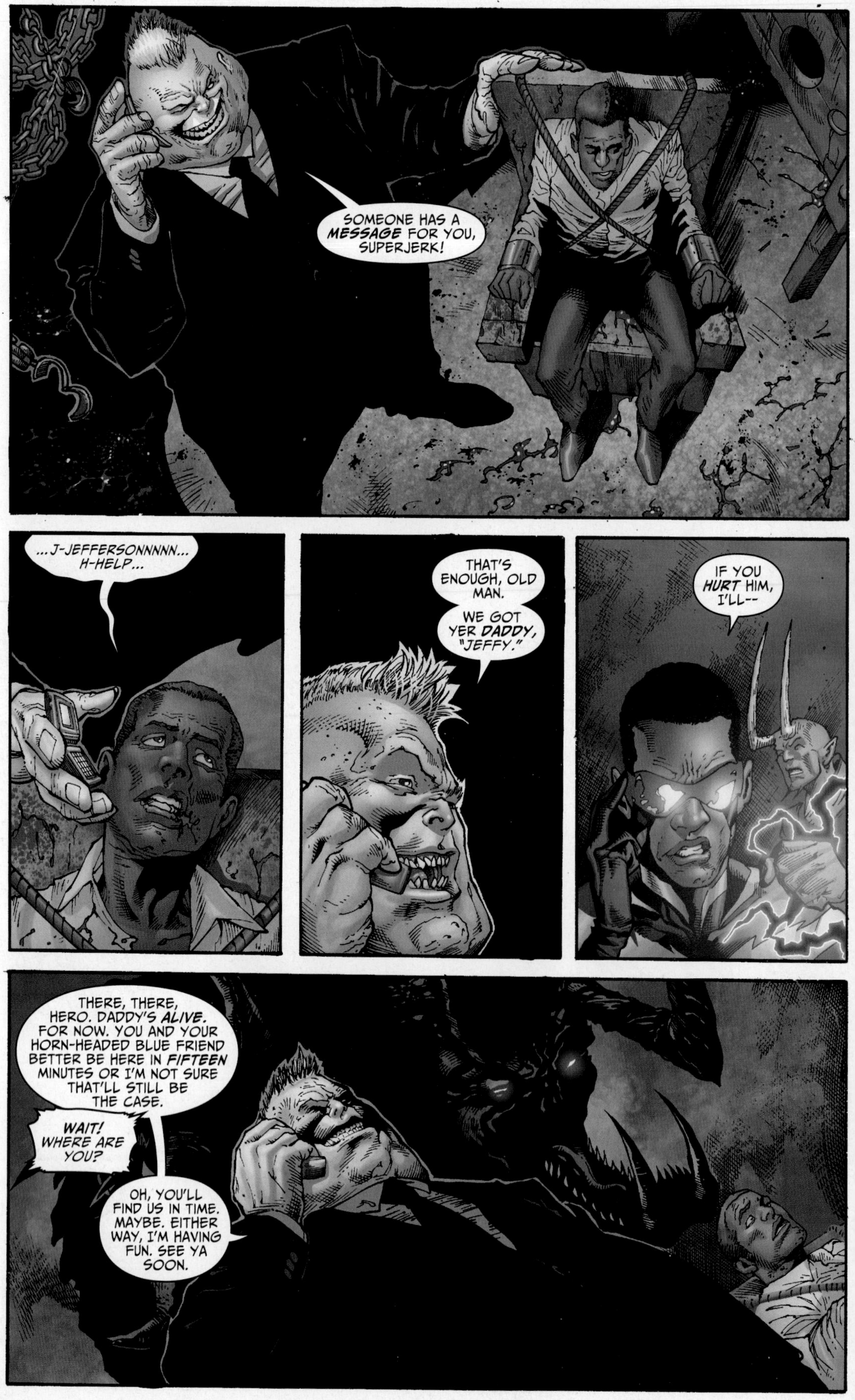
SOMEONE HAS A MESSAGE FOR YOU, SUPERJERK!
...J-JEFFERSONNNNN... H-HELP...
THAT'S ENOUGH, OLD MAN.
WE GOT YER DADDY, "JEFFY."
IF YOU HURT HIM, I'LL--
THERE, THERE, HERO. DADDY'S ALIVE. FOR NOW. YOU AND YOUR HORN-HEADED BLUE FRIEND BETTER BE HERE IN FIFTEEN MINUTES OR I'M NOT SURE THAT'LL STILL BE THE CASE.
WAIT! WHERE ARE YOU?
OH, YOU'LL FIND US IN TIME. MAYBE. EITHER WAY, I'M HAVING FUN. SEE YA SOON.

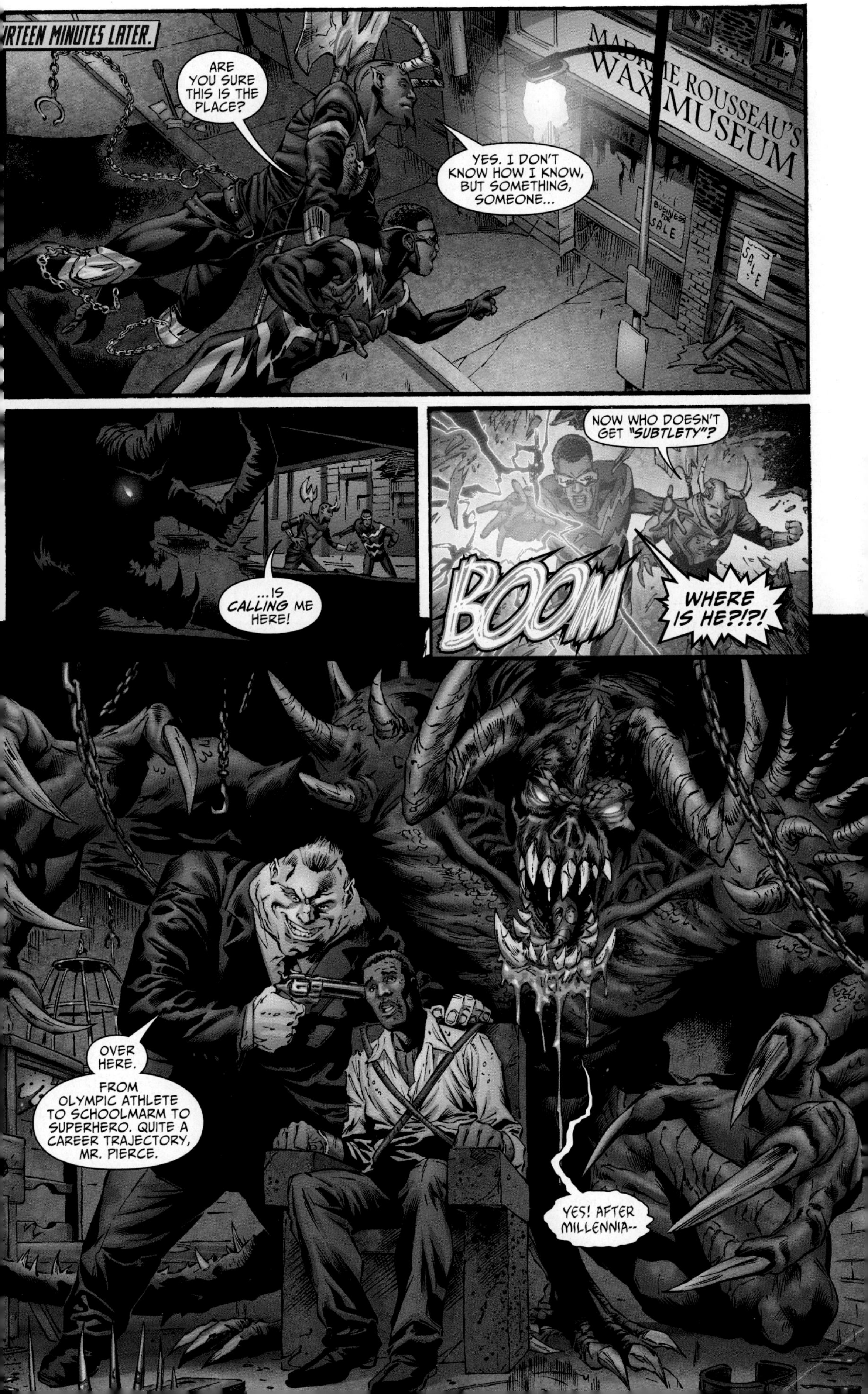

RTEEN MINUTES LATER.
ARE YOU SURE THIS IS THE PLACE?
MADAME ROUSSEAU'S WAX MUSEUM
YES. I DON'T KNOW HOW I KNOW, BUT SOMETHING, SOMEONE...
BUSINESS FOR SALE
...IS CALLING ME HERE!
NOW WHO DOESN'T GET "SUBTLETY"?
BOOM
WHERE IS HE?!?!
OVER HERE.
FROM OLYMPIC ATHLETE TO SCHOOLMARM TO SUPERHERO. QUITE A CAREER TRAJECTORY, MR. PIERCE.
YES! AFTER MILLENNIA--

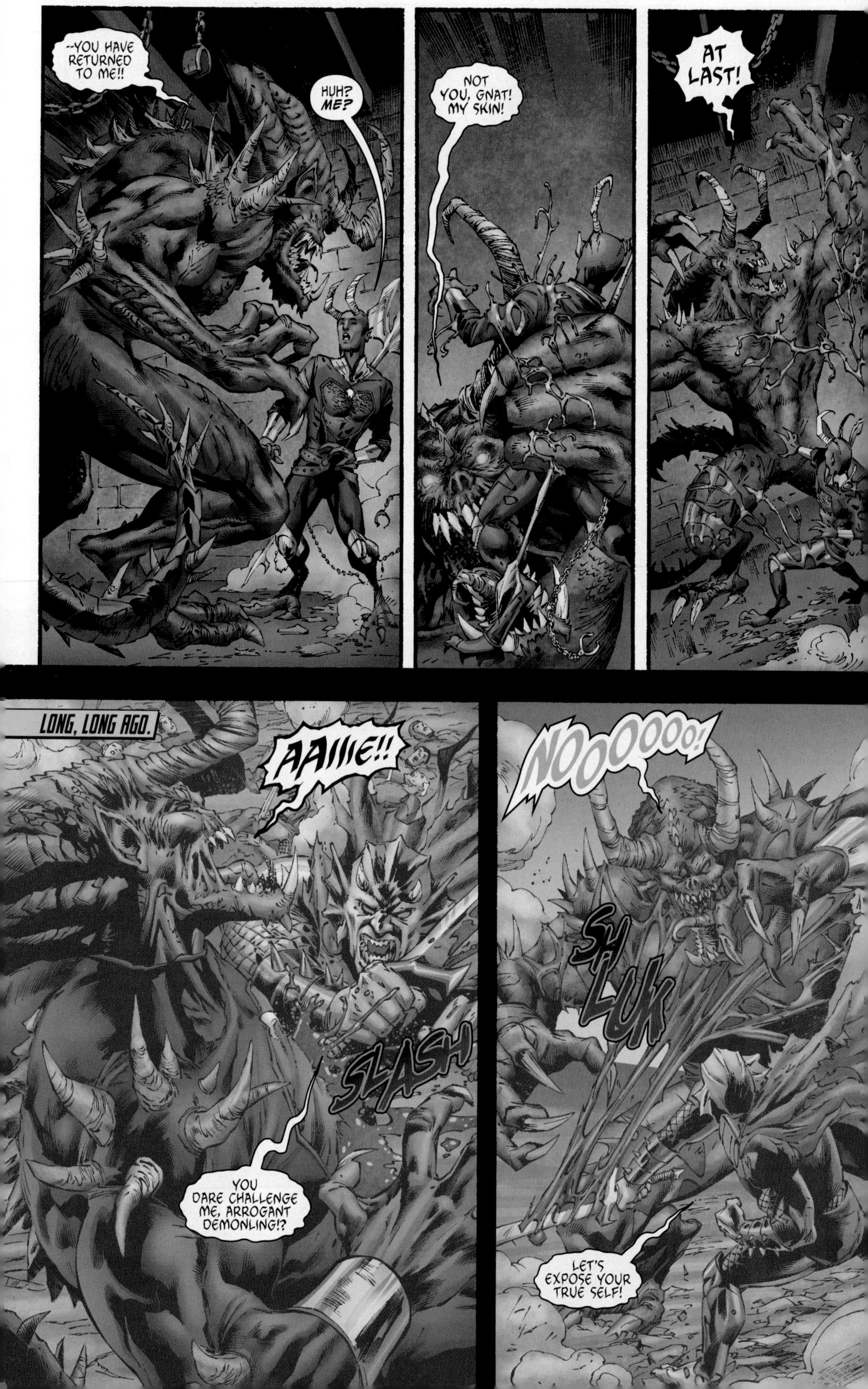
--YOU HAVE RETURNED TO ME!!
HUH? ME?
NOT YOU, GNAT! MY SKIN!
AT LAST!
LONG, LONG AGO.
AAIIIE!!
SLASH
YOU DARE CHALLENGE ME, ARROGANT DEMONLING!?
NOOOOOO!
SHLUK
LET'S EXPOSE YOUR TRUE SELF!

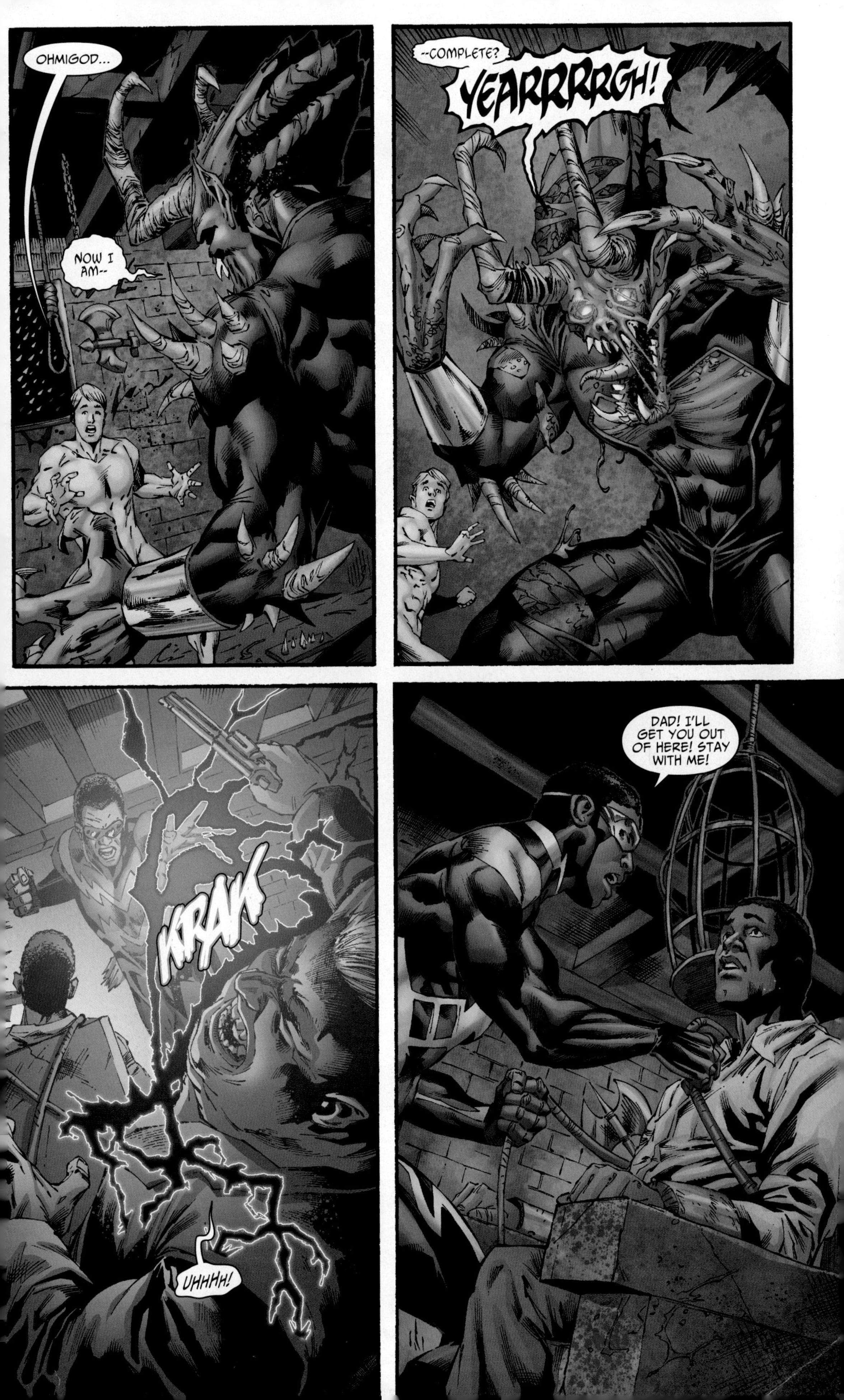
OHMIGOD...
NOW I AM--
--COMPLETE?
YEARRRRGH!
KRAK
UHHHH!
DAD! I'LL GET YOU OUT OF HERE! STAY WITH ME!

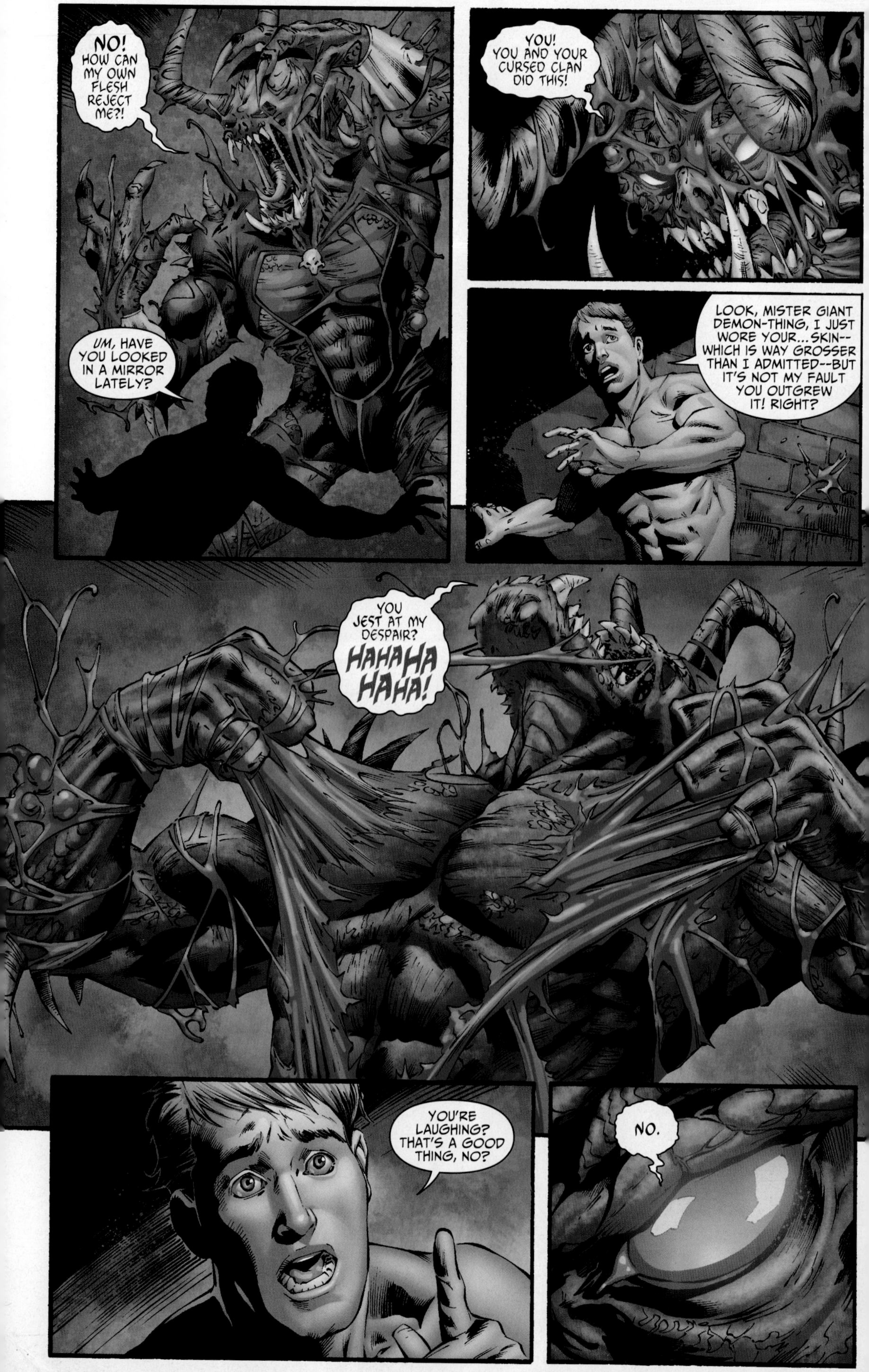
NO! HOW CAN MY OWN FLESH REJECT ME?!
UM, HAVE YOU LOOKED IN A MIRROR LATELY?
YOU! YOU AND YOUR CURSED CLAN DID THIS!
LOOK, MISTER GIANT DEMON-THING, I JUST WORE YOUR...SKIN-- WHICH IS WAY GROSSER THAN I ADMITTED--BUT IT'S NOT MY FAULT YOU OUTGREW IT! RIGHT?
YOU JEST AT MY DESPAIR? HAHAHA HAHA!
YOU'RE LAUGHING? THAT'S A GOOD THING, NO?
NO.

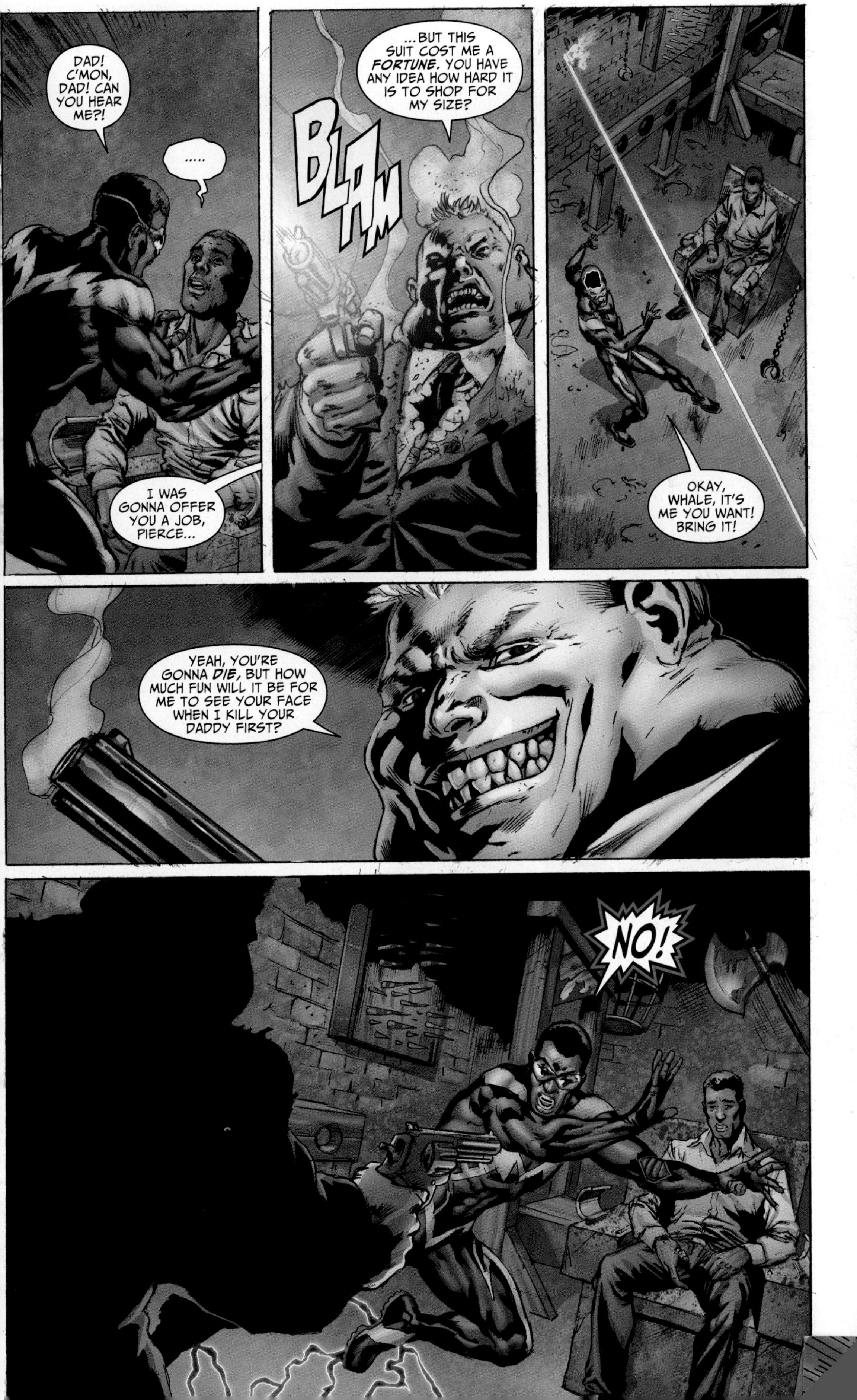
DAD! C'MON, DAD! CAN YOU HEAR ME?!
.....
I WAS GONNA OFFER YOU A JOB, PIERCE...
BLAM
...BUT THIS SUIT COST ME A FORTUNE. YOU HAVE ANY IDEA HOW HARD IT IS TO SHOP FOR MY SIZE?
OKAY, WHALE, IT'S ME YOU WANT! BRING IT!
YEAH, YOU'RE GONNA DIE, BUT HOW MUCH FUN WILL IT BE FOR ME TO SEE YOUR FACE WHEN I KILL YOUR DADDY FIRST?
NO!

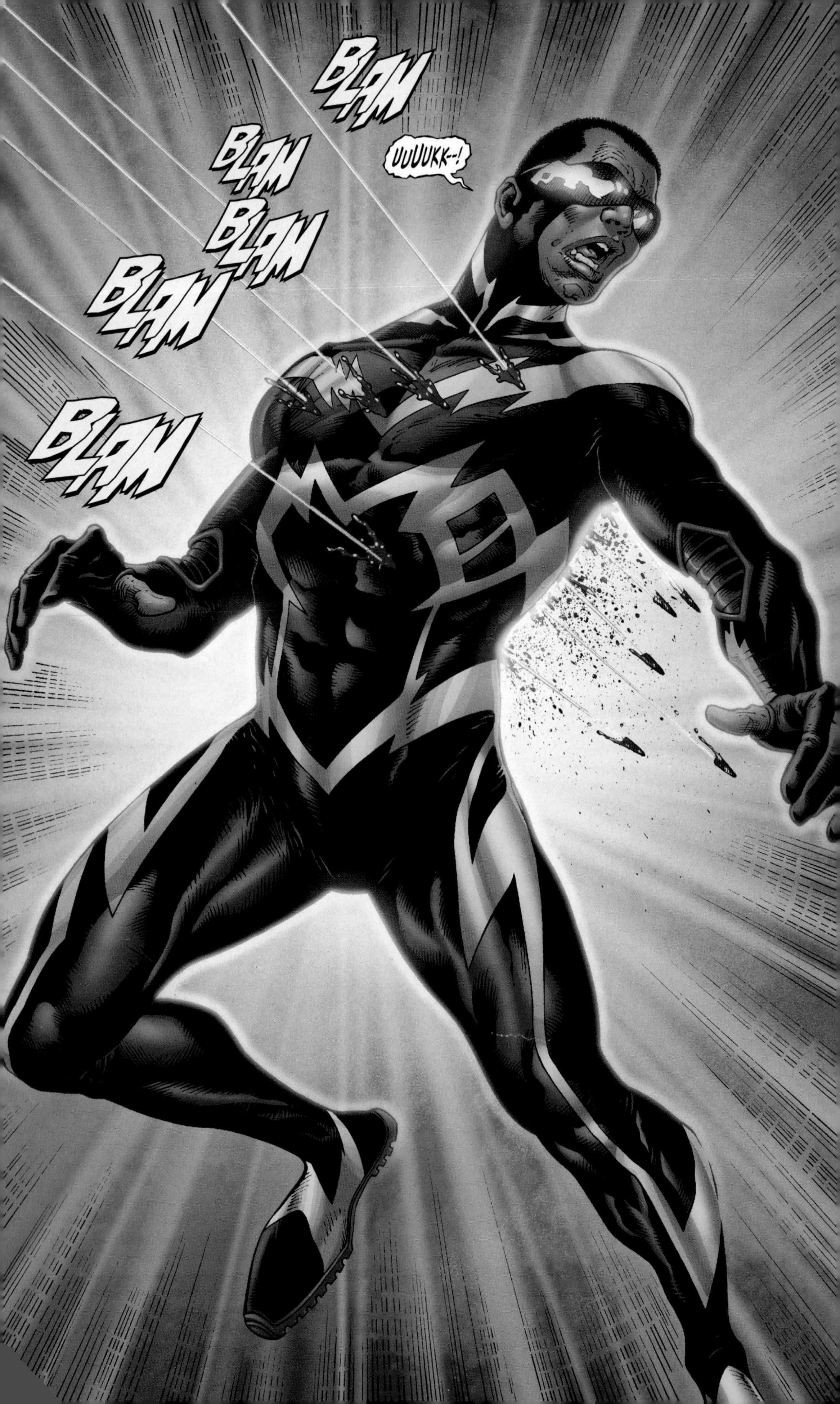
BLAM
UUUUKK--!
BLAM
BLAM
BLAM
BLAM

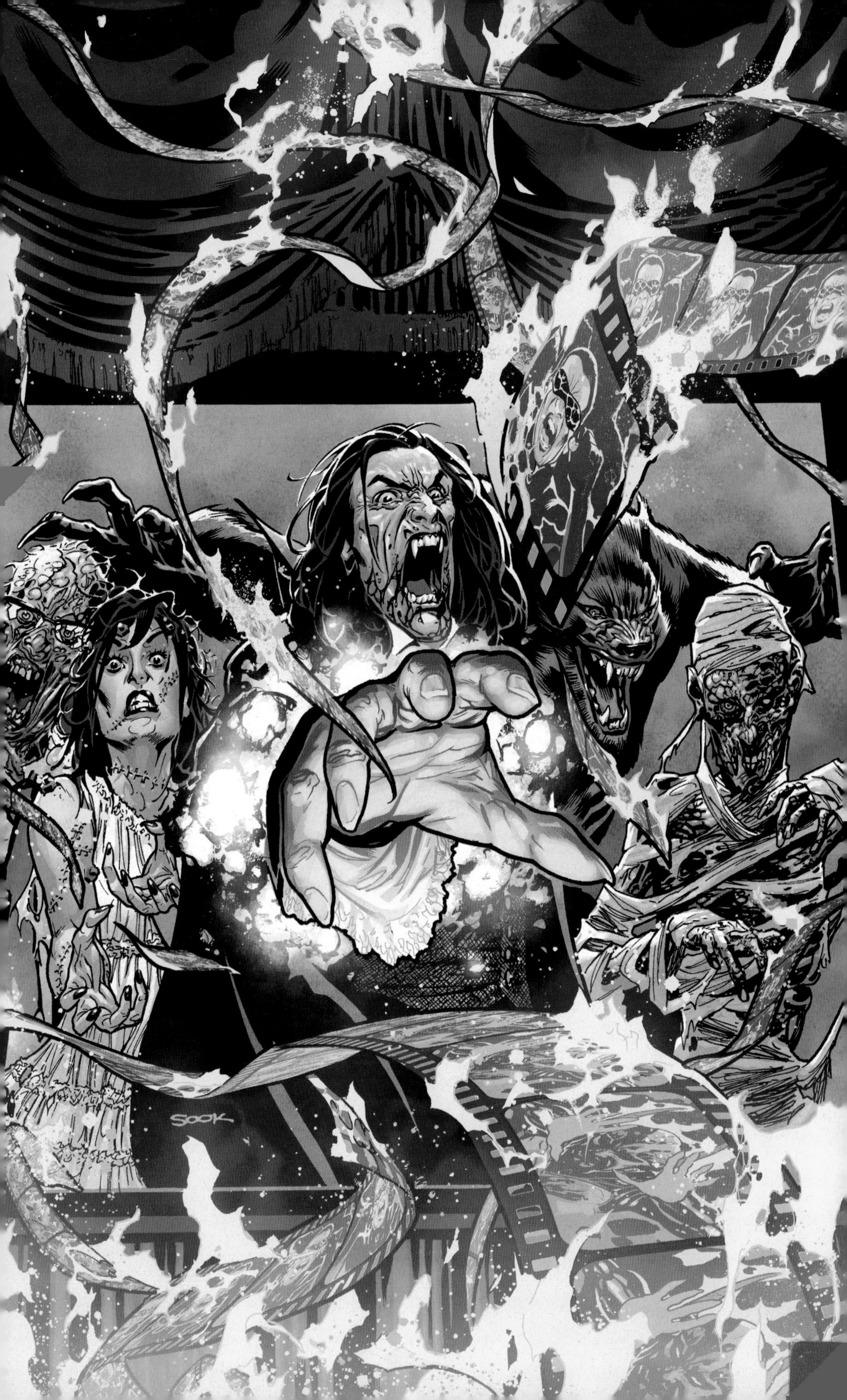
SOOK

DEVIL IN THE DETAILS

MARC ANDREYKO
writer

ROBSON ROCHA
penciller

OCLAIR ALBERT
inker

cover art by RYAN SOOK

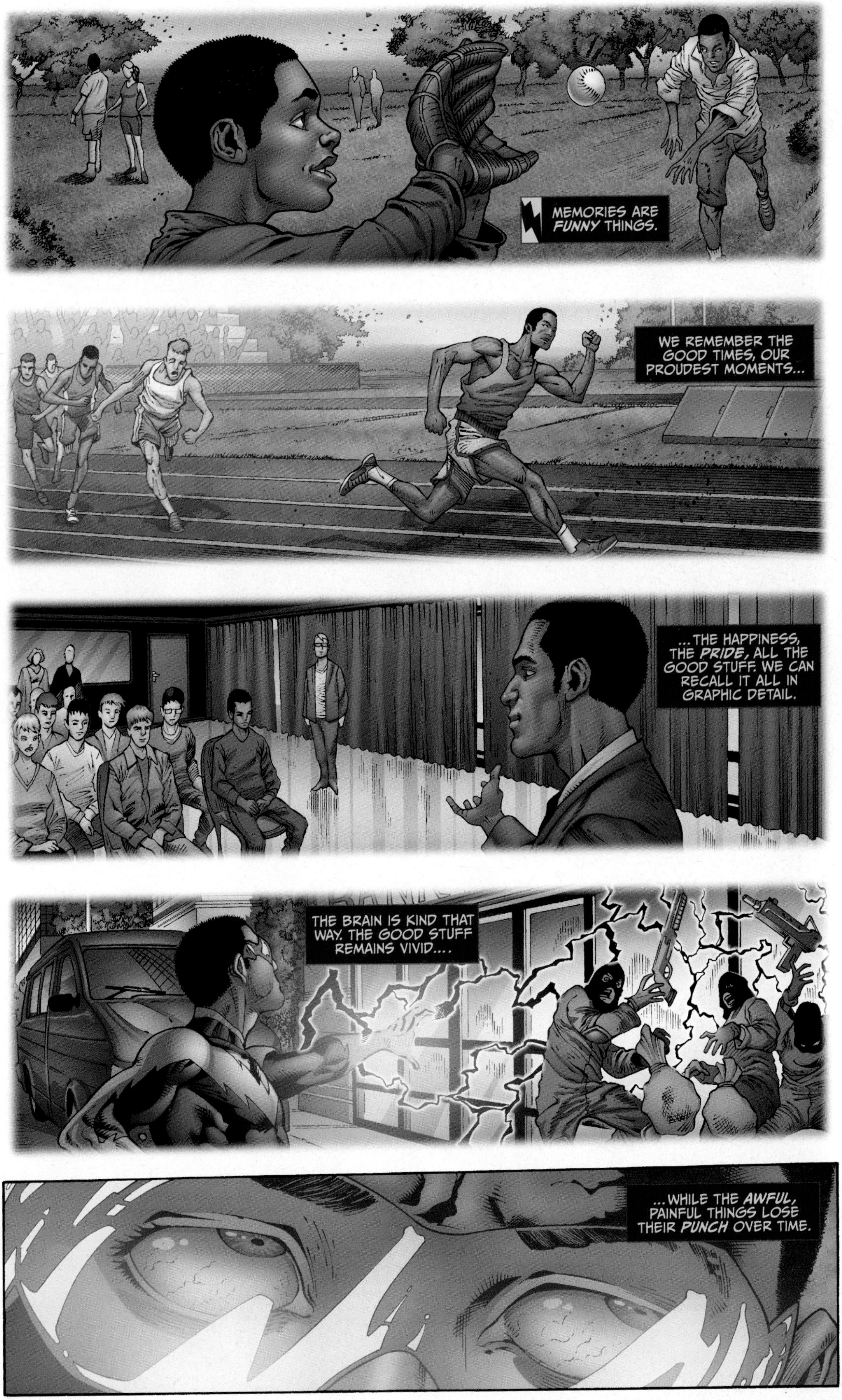
MEMORIES ARE FUNNY THINGS.
WE REMEMBER THE GOOD TIMES, OUR PROUDEST MOMENTS...
...THE HAPPINESS, THE PRIDE, ALL THE GOOD STUFF. WE CAN RECALL IT ALL IN GRAPHIC DETAIL.
THE BRAIN IS KIND THAT WAY. THE GOOD STUFF REMAINS VIVID....
...WHILE THE AWFUL, PAINFUL THINGS LOSE THEIR PUNCH OVER TIME.

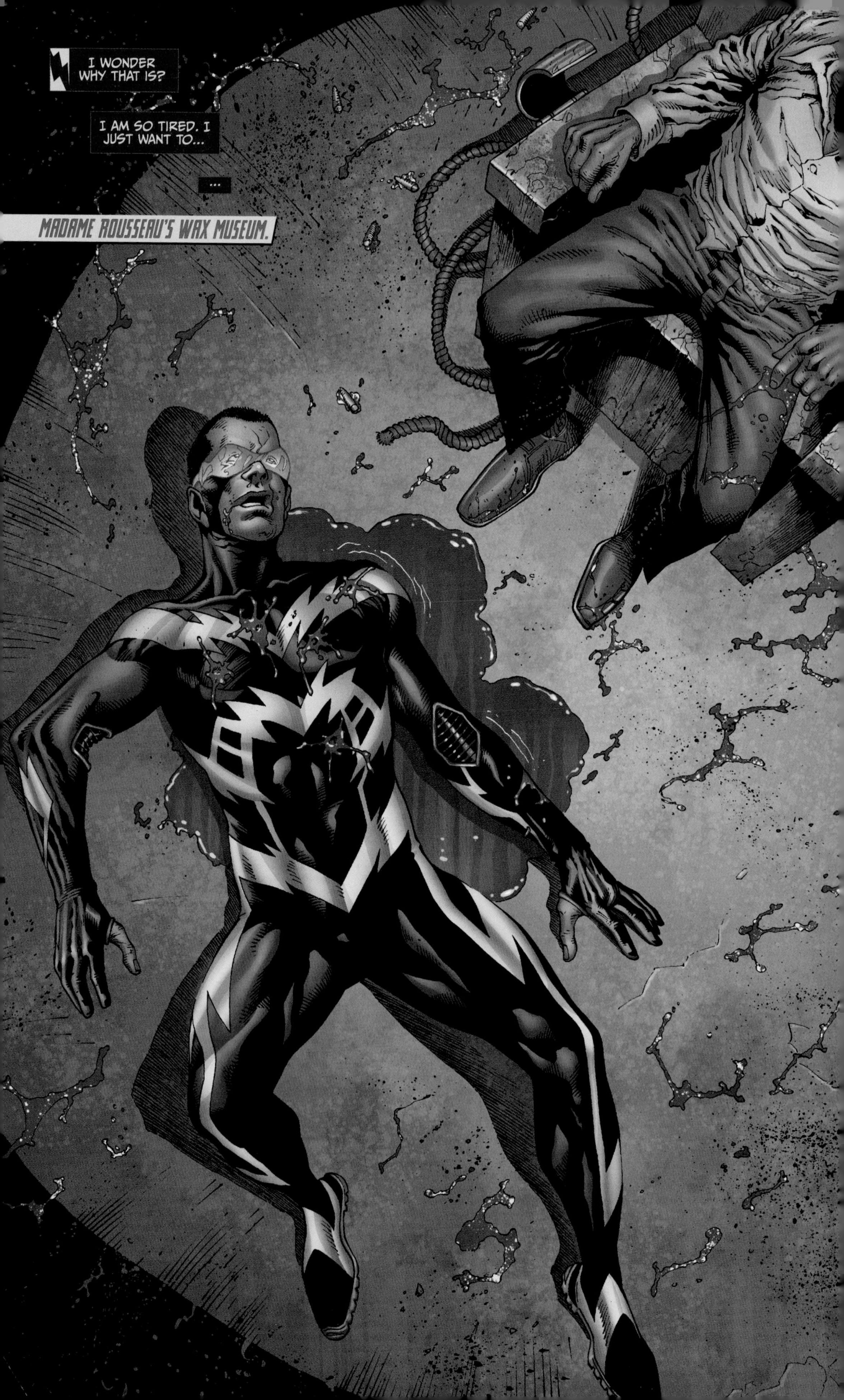
I WONDER WHY THAT IS?
I AM SO TIRED. I JUST WANT TO...
...
MADAME ROUSSEAU'S WAX MUSEUM.

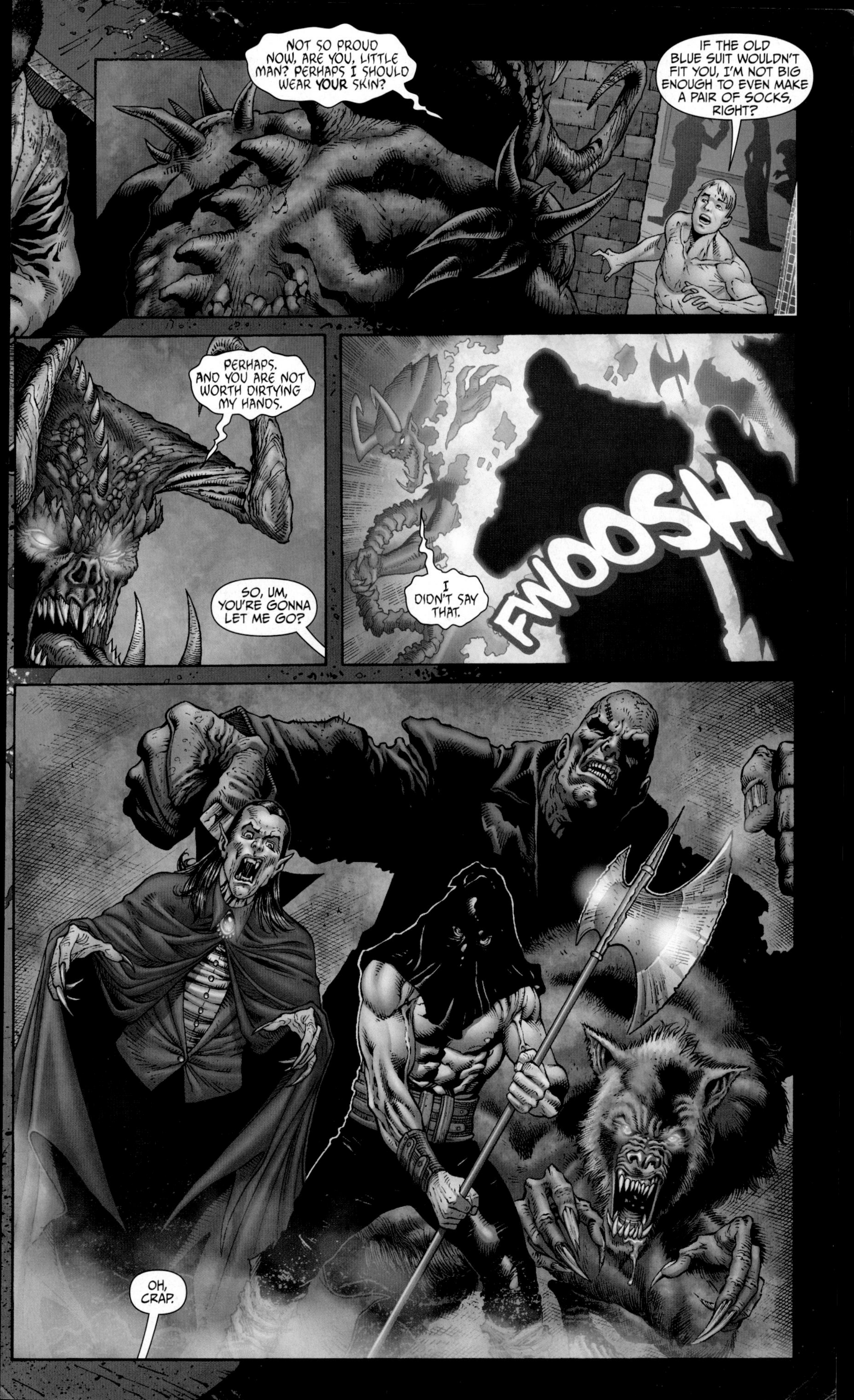
NOT SO PROUD NOW, ARE YOU, LITTLE MAN? PERHAPS I SHOULD WEAR YOUR SKIN?
IF THE OLD BLUE SUIT WOULDN'T FIT YOU, I'M NOT BIG ENOUGH TO EVEN MAKE A PAIR OF SOCKS, RIGHT?
PERHAPS. AND YOU ARE NOT WORTH DIRTYING MY HANDS.
SO, UM, YOU'RE GONNA LET ME GO?
I DIDN'T SAY THAT.
FWOOSH
OH, CRAP.

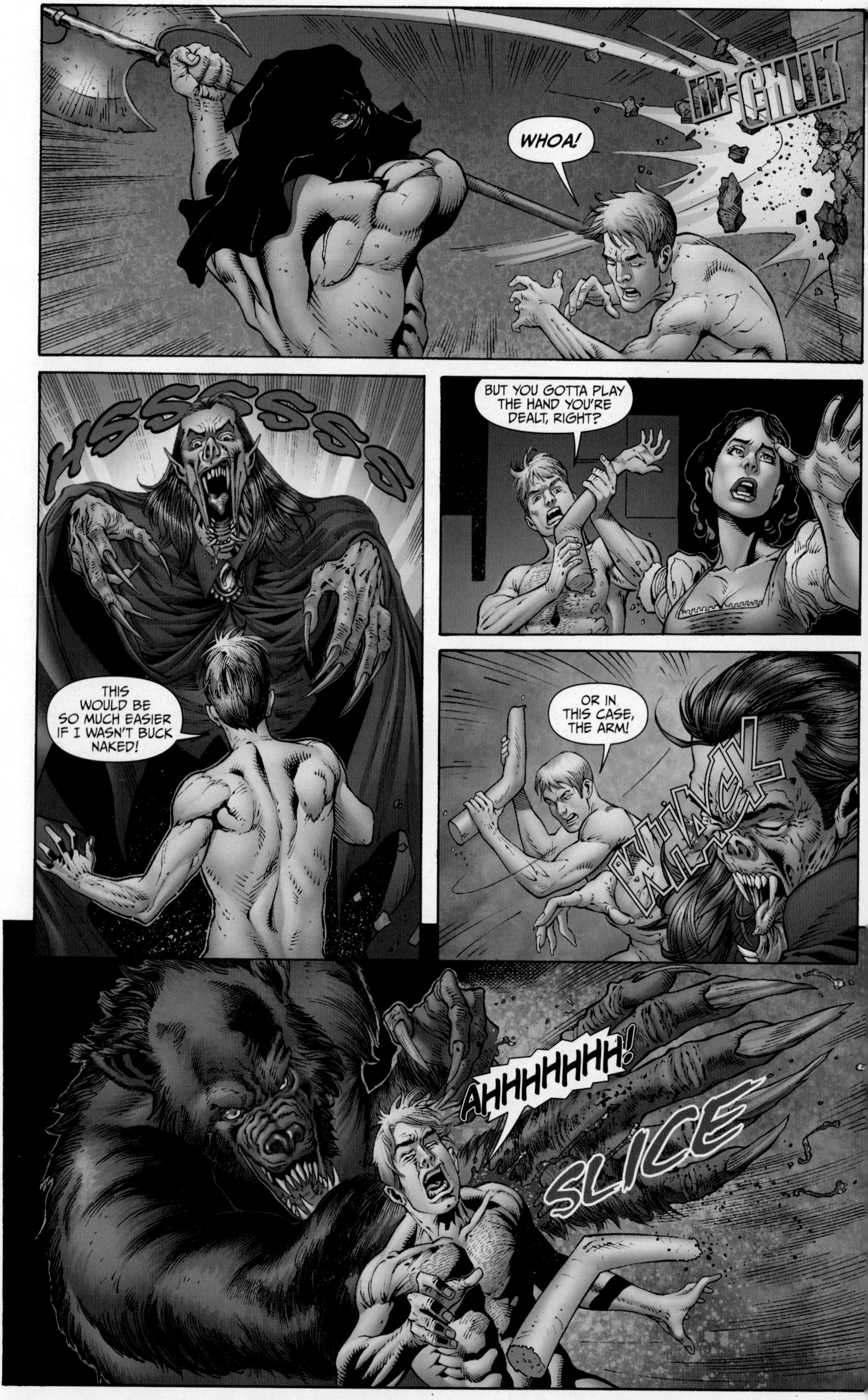
KA-CHUK
WHOA!
HSSSSSSS
THIS WOULD BE SO MUCH EASIER IF I WASN'T BUCK NAKED!
BUT YOU GOTTA PLAY THE HAND YOU'RE DEALT, RIGHT?
OR IN THIS CASE, THE ARM!
WHACK
AHHHHHHH!
SLICE

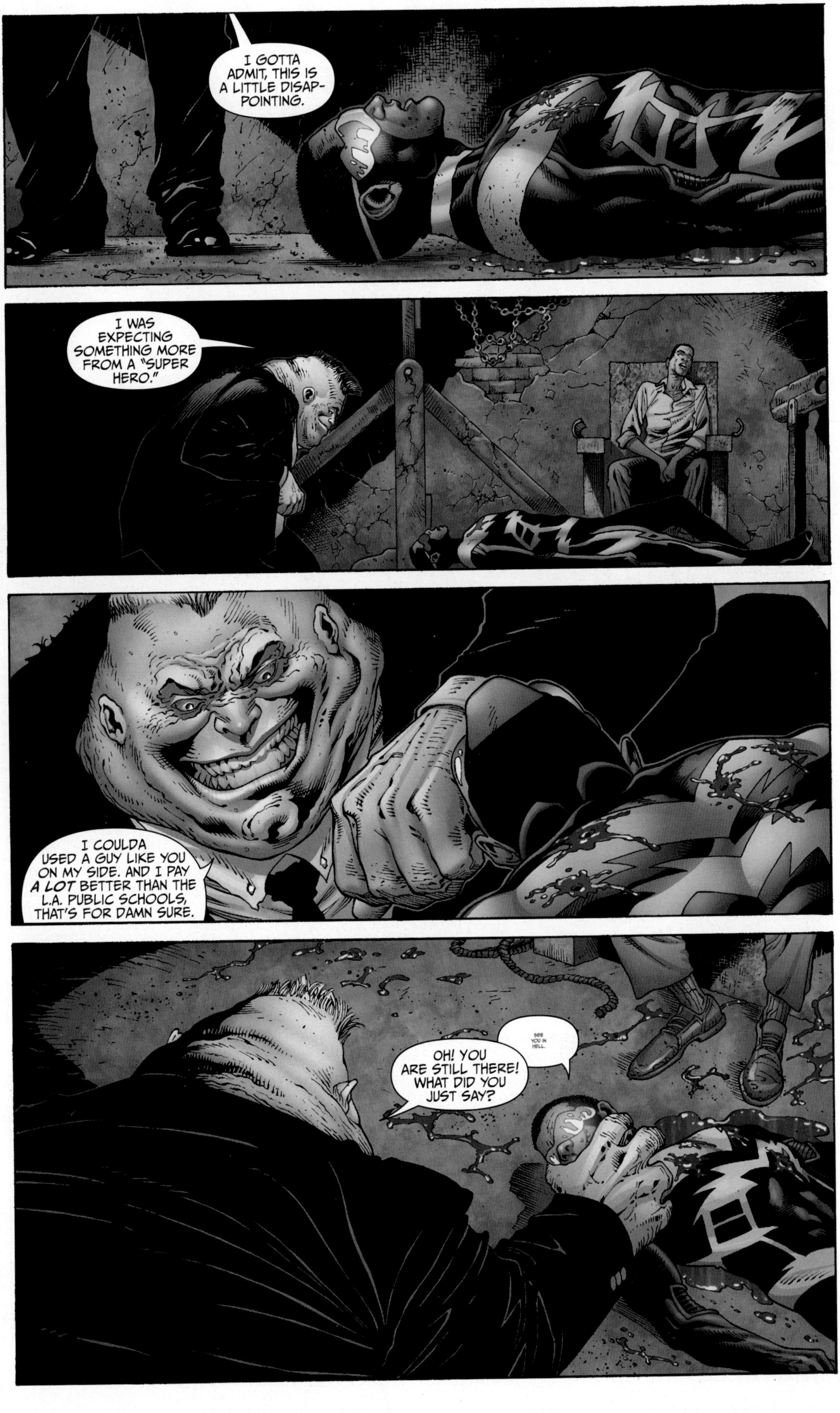
I GOTTA ADMIT, THIS IS A LITTLE DISAPPOINTING.
I WAS EXPECTING SOMETHING MORE FROM A "SUPER HERO."
I COULDA USED A GUY LIKE YOU ON MY SIDE. AND I PAY A LOT BETTER THAN THE L.A. PUBLIC SCHOOLS, THAT'S FOR DAMN SURE.
SEE YOU IN HELL.
OH! YOU ARE STILL THERE! WHAT DID YOU JUST SAY?

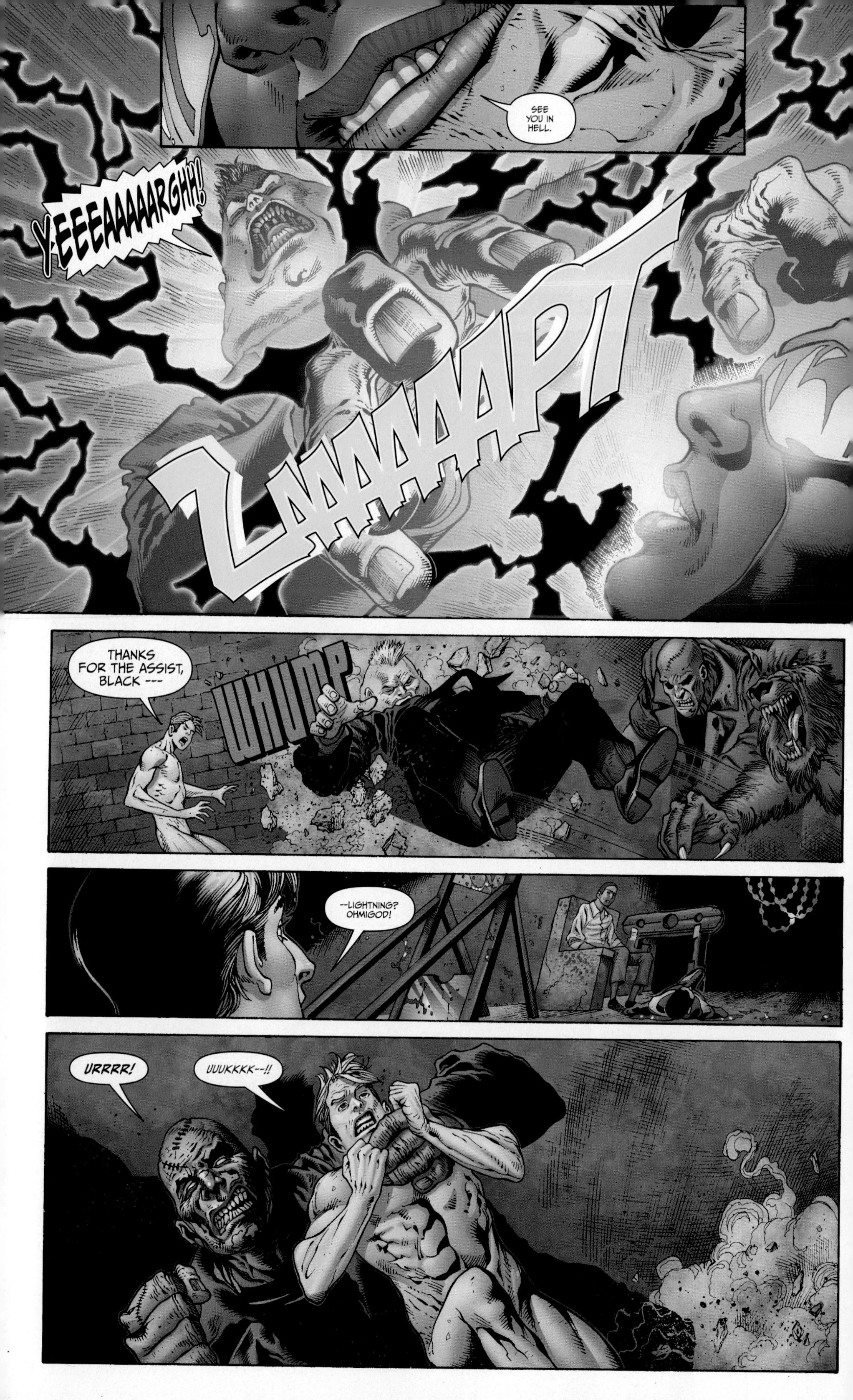
SEE YOU IN HELL.
YEEEAAAAARGHH!
ZAAAAAAPT
THANKS FOR THE ASSIST, BLACK ---
WHUMP
--LIGHTNING? OHMIGOD!
URRRR!
UUUKKKK--!!

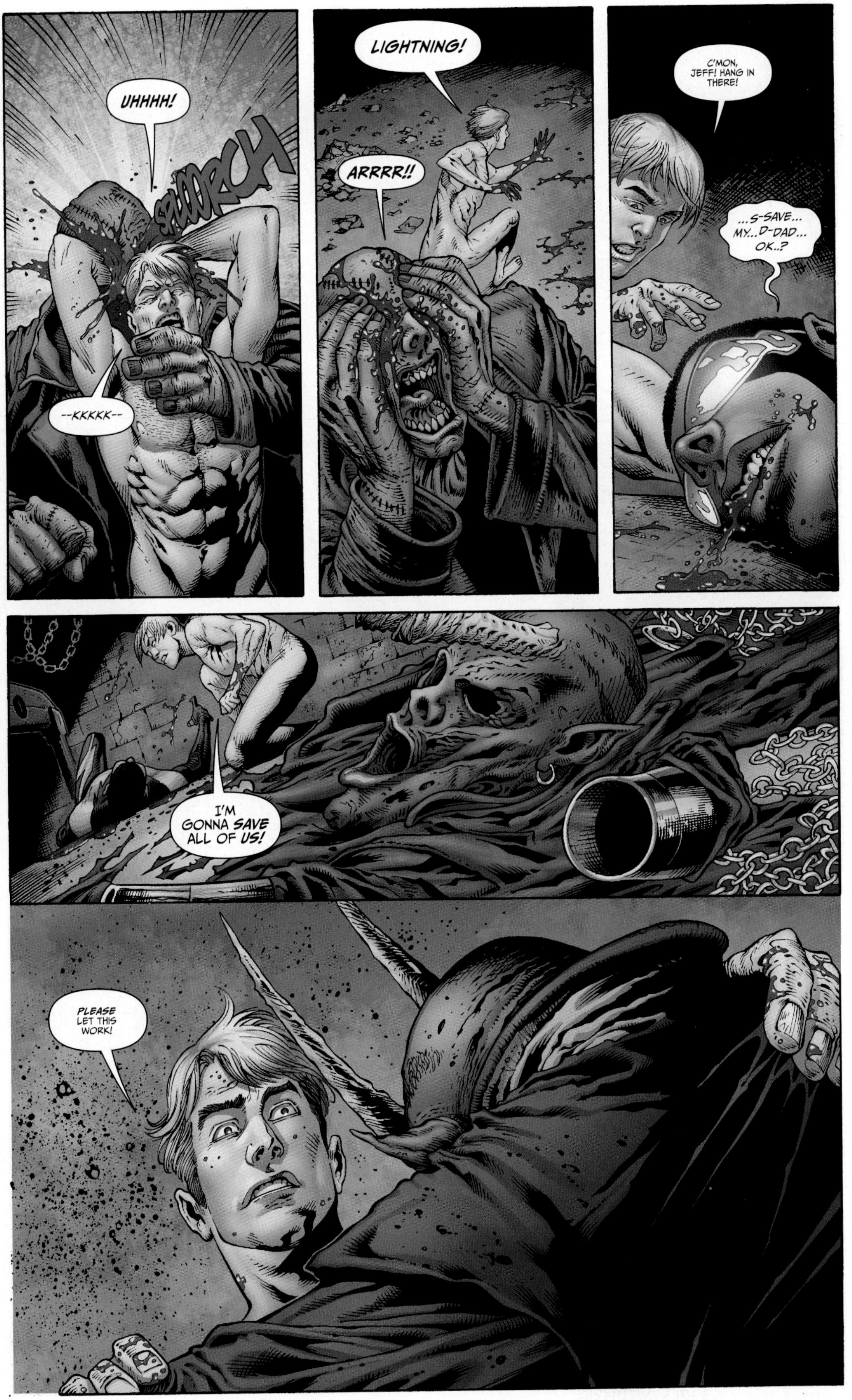
UHHHH!
SPLOORCH
--KKKKK--
LIGHTNING!
ARRRR!!
C'MON, JEFF! HANG IN THERE!
...S-SAVE... MY...D-DAD... OK..?
I'M GONNA SAVE ALL OF US!
PLEASE LET THIS WORK!

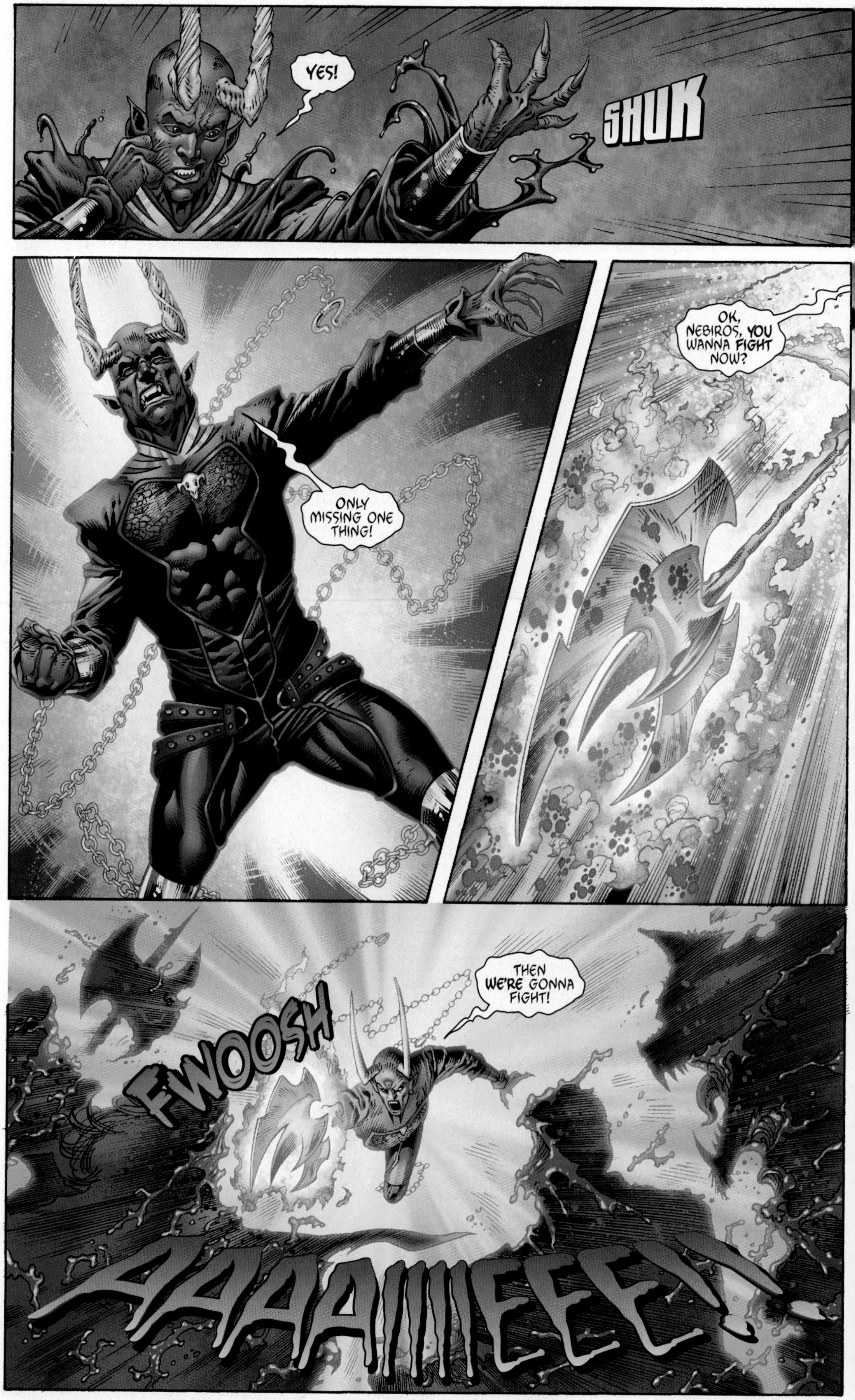
YES!
SHUK
ONLY MISSING ONE THING!
OK, NEBIROS, YOU WANNA FIGHT NOW?
FWOOSH
THEN WE'RE GONNA FIGHT!
AAAAIIIIEEE!

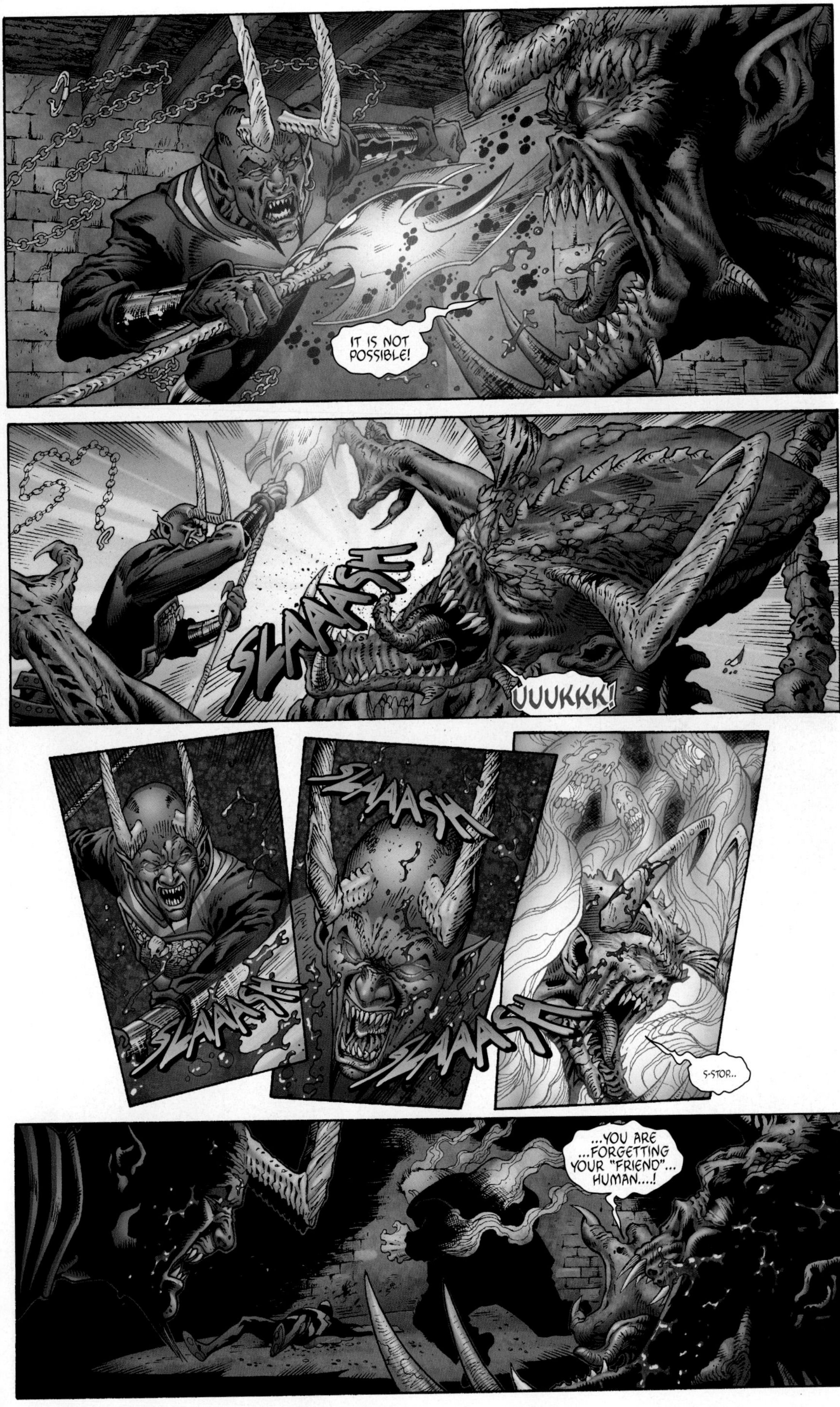
IT IS NOT POSSIBLE!
SLAAASH
UUUKKK!
SLAAASH
SLAAASH
SLAAASH
SLAAASH
S-STOP...
...YOU ARE ...FORGETTING YOUR "FRIEND"... HUMAN....!

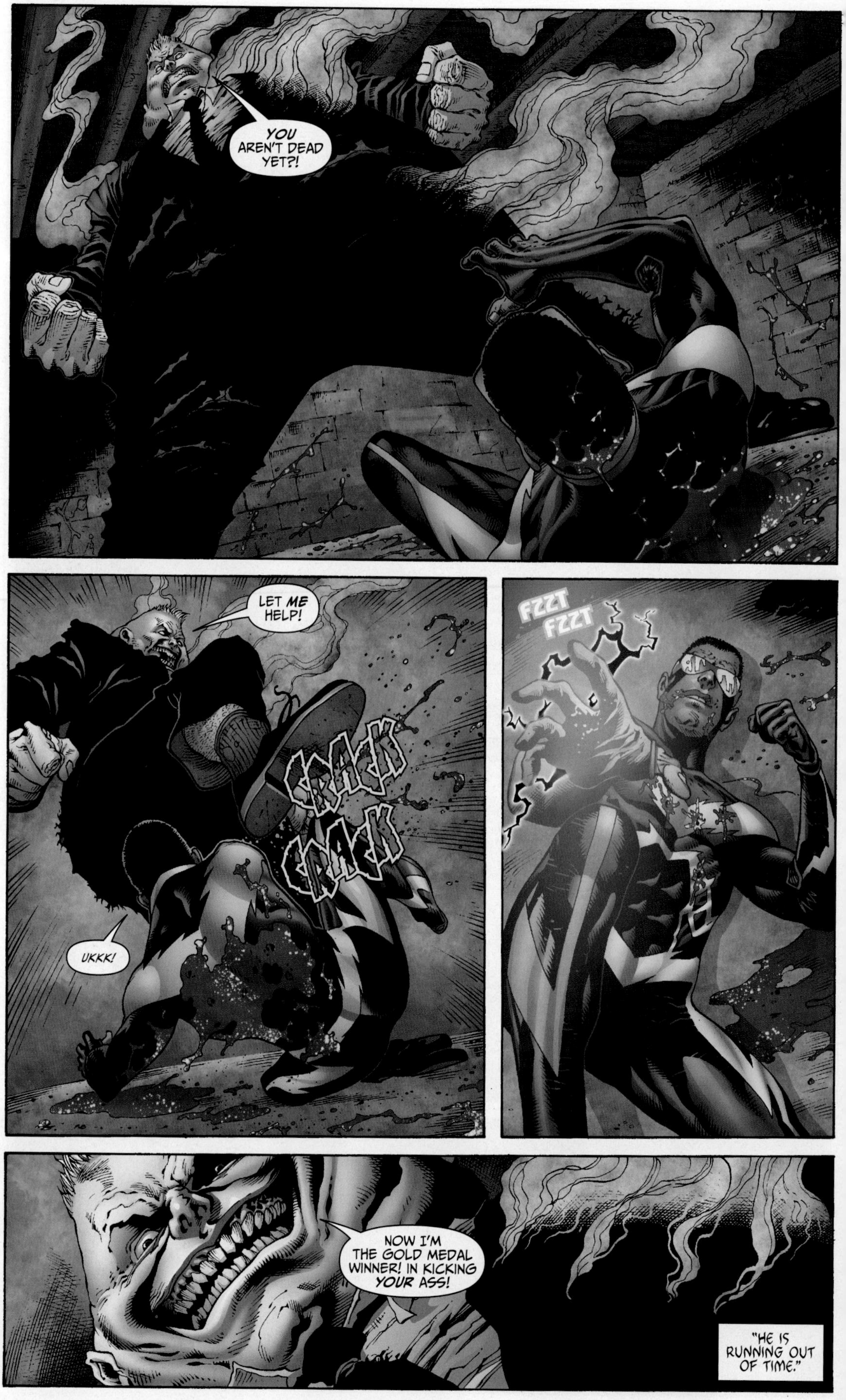
YOU AREN'T DEAD YET?!
LET ME HELP!
CRACK
CRACK
UKKK!
FZZT
FZZT
NOW I'M THE GOLD MEDAL WINNER! IN KICKING YOUR ASS!
"HE IS RUNNING OUT OF TIME."

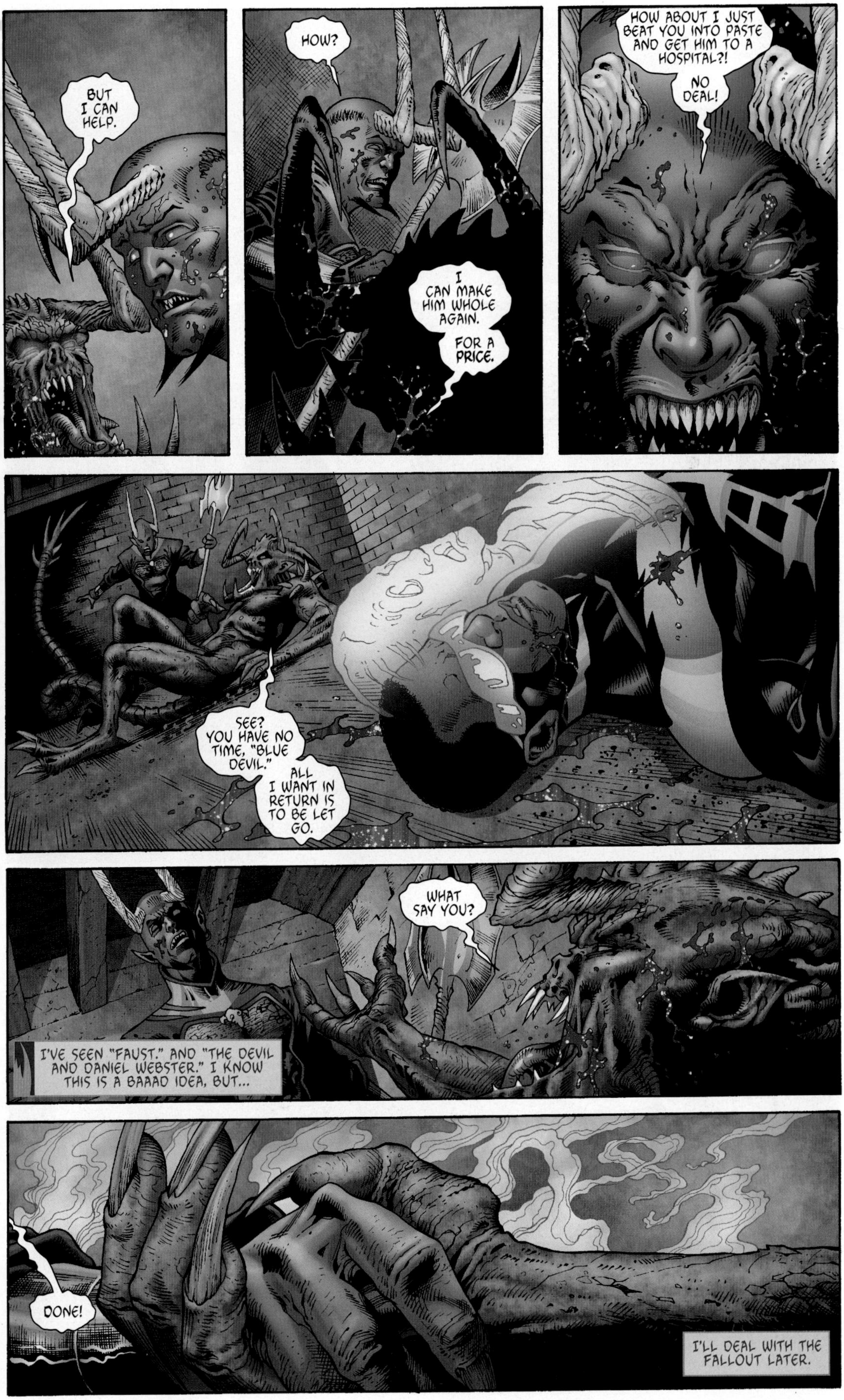
BUT I CAN HELP.
HOW?
I CAN MAKE HIM WHOLE AGAIN.
FOR A PRICE.
HOW ABOUT I JUST BEAT YOU INTO PASTE AND GET HIM TO A HOSPITAL?!
NO DEAL!
SEE? YOU HAVE NO TIME, "BLUE DEVIL."
ALL I WANT IN RETURN IS TO BE LET GO.
WHAT SAY YOU?
I'VE SEEN "FAUST." AND "THE DEVIL AND DANIEL WEBSTER." I KNOW THIS IS A BAAAD IDEA, BUT...
DONE!
I'LL DEAL WITH THE FALLOUT LATER.

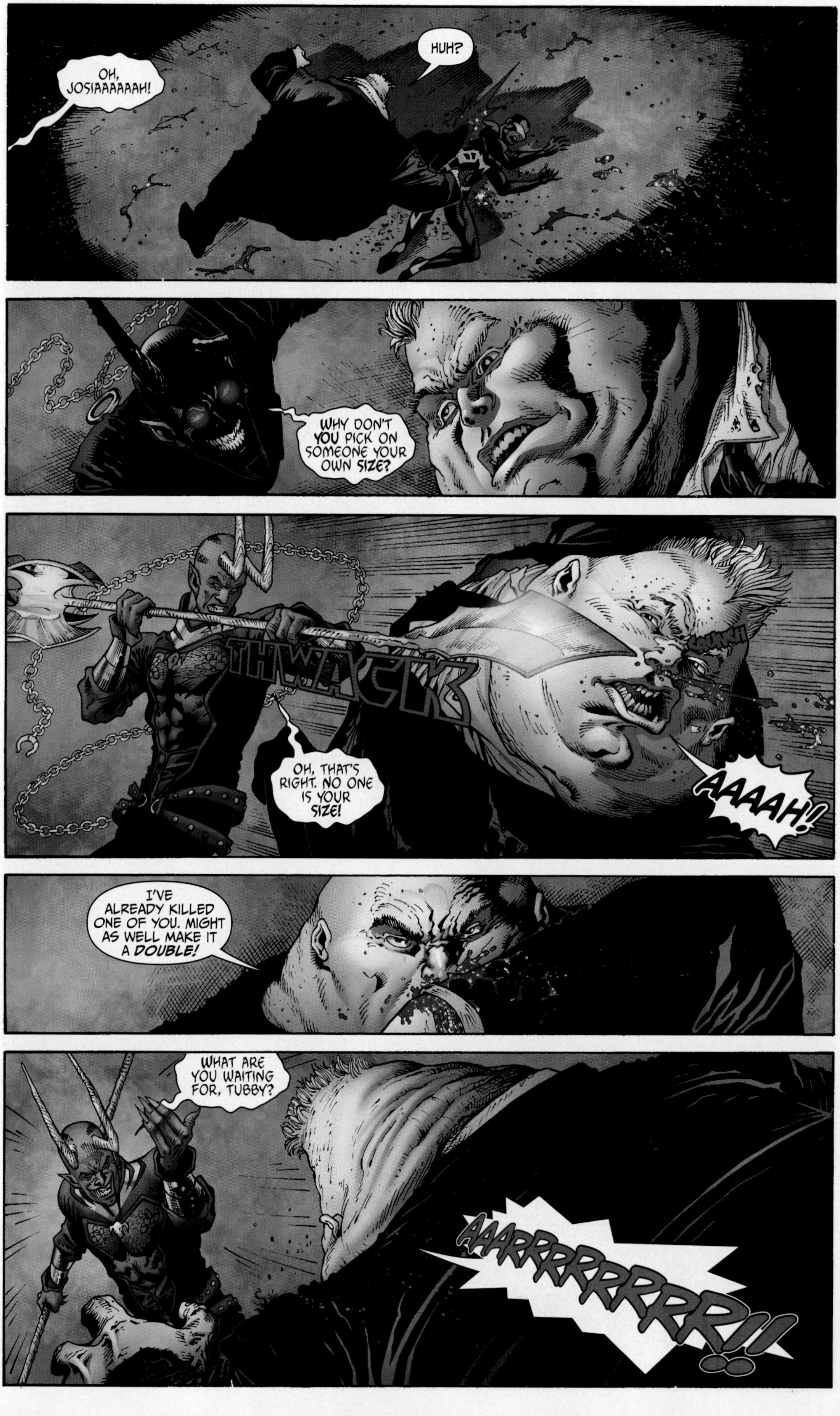
OH, JOSIAAAAAAH!
HUH?
WHY DON'T YOU PICK ON SOMEONE YOUR OWN SIZE?
THWACK
OH, THAT'S RIGHT. NO ONE IS YOUR SIZE!
AAAAH!!
I'VE ALREADY KILLED ONE OF YOU. MIGHT AS WELL MAKE IT A DOUBLE!
WHAT ARE YOU WAITING FOR, TUBBY?
AAARRRRRRRRR!!

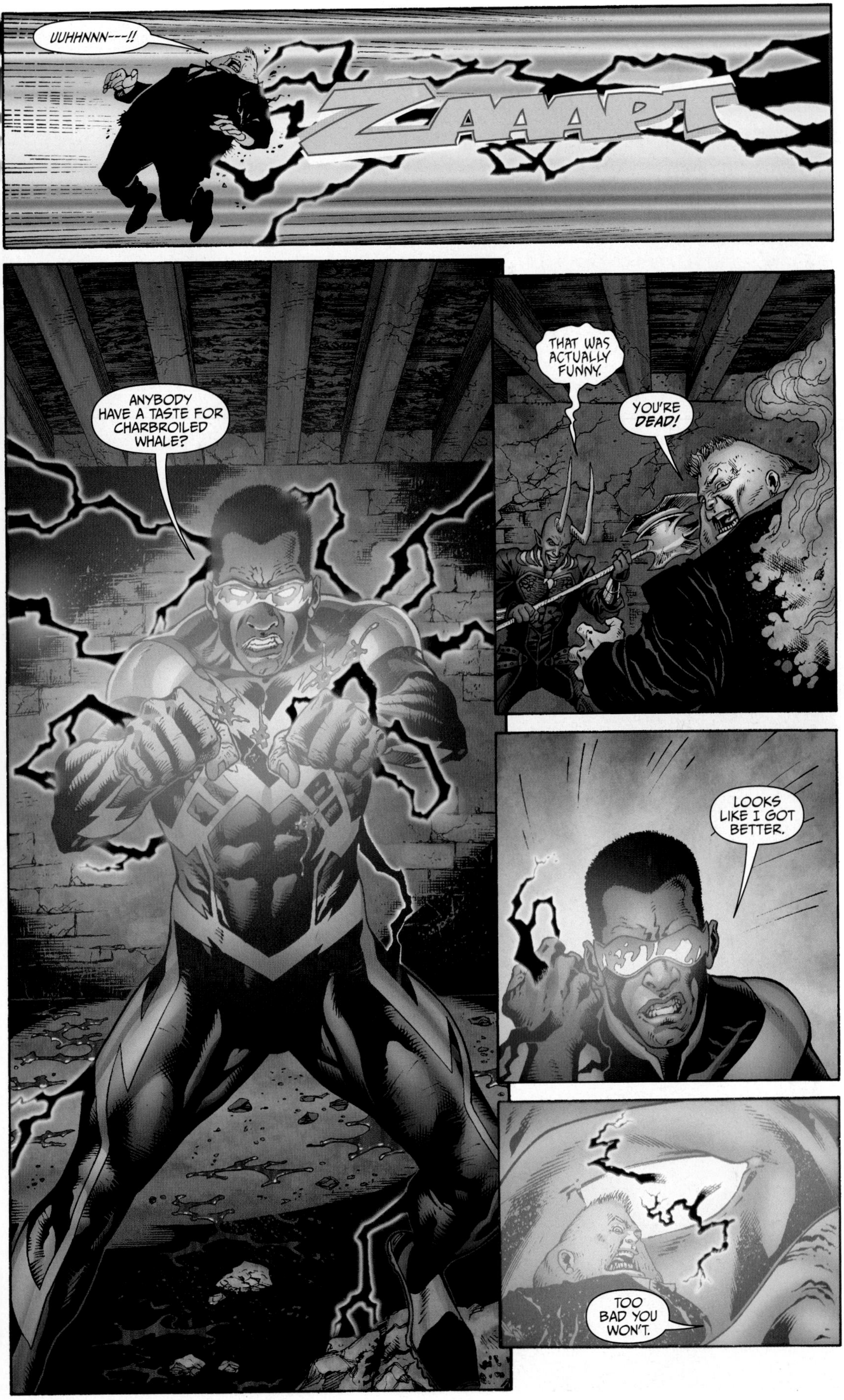
UUHHNNN---!!
ZAAAPT
ANYBODY HAVE A TASTE FOR CHARBROILED WHALE?
THAT WAS ACTUALLY FUNNY.
YOU'RE DEAD!
LOOKS LIKE I GOT BETTER.
TOO BAD YOU WON'T.

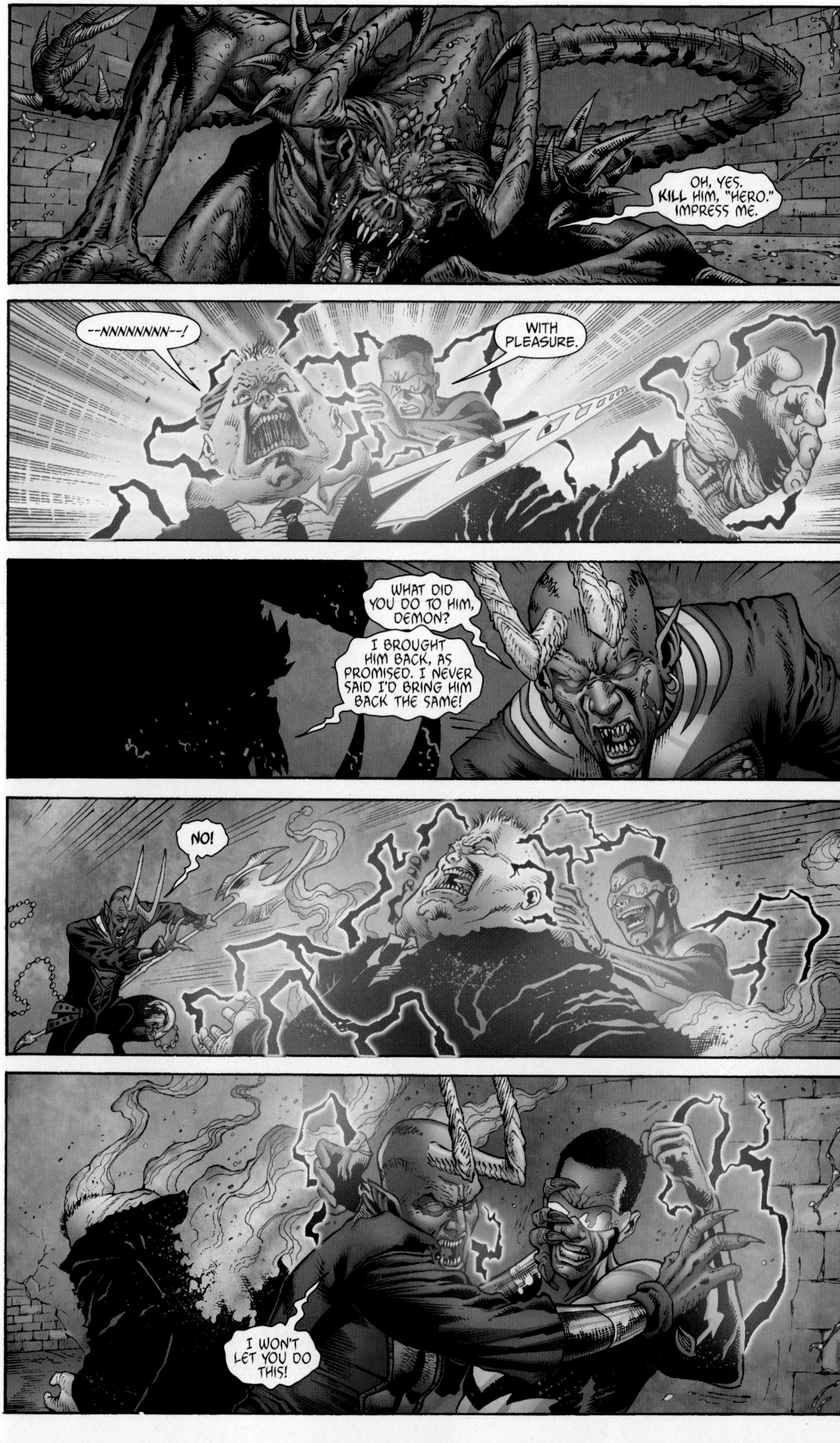
OH, YES. KILL HIM, "HERO." IMPRESS ME.
--NNNNNNNN--!
WITH PLEASURE.
WHAT DID YOU DO TO HIM, DEMON?
I BROUGHT HIM BACK, AS PROMISED. I NEVER SAID I'D BRING HIM BACK THE SAME!
NO!
I WON'T LET YOU DO THIS!

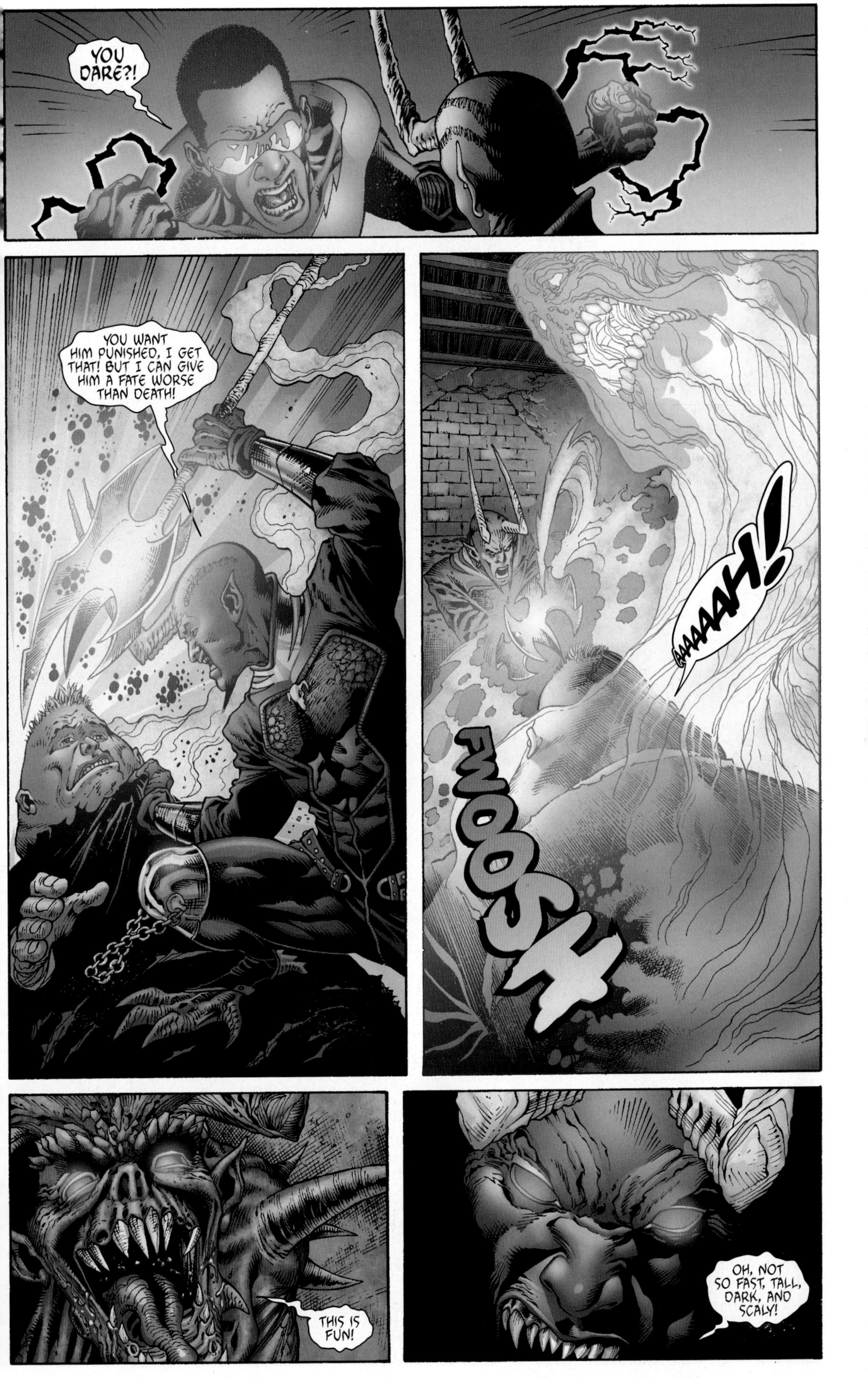
YOU DARE?!
YOU WANT HIM PUNISHED, I GET THAT! BUT I CAN GIVE HIM A FATE WORSE THAN DEATH!
AAAAAAH!
FWOOOSH
THIS IS FUN!
OH, NOT SO FAST, TALL, DARK, AND SCALY!

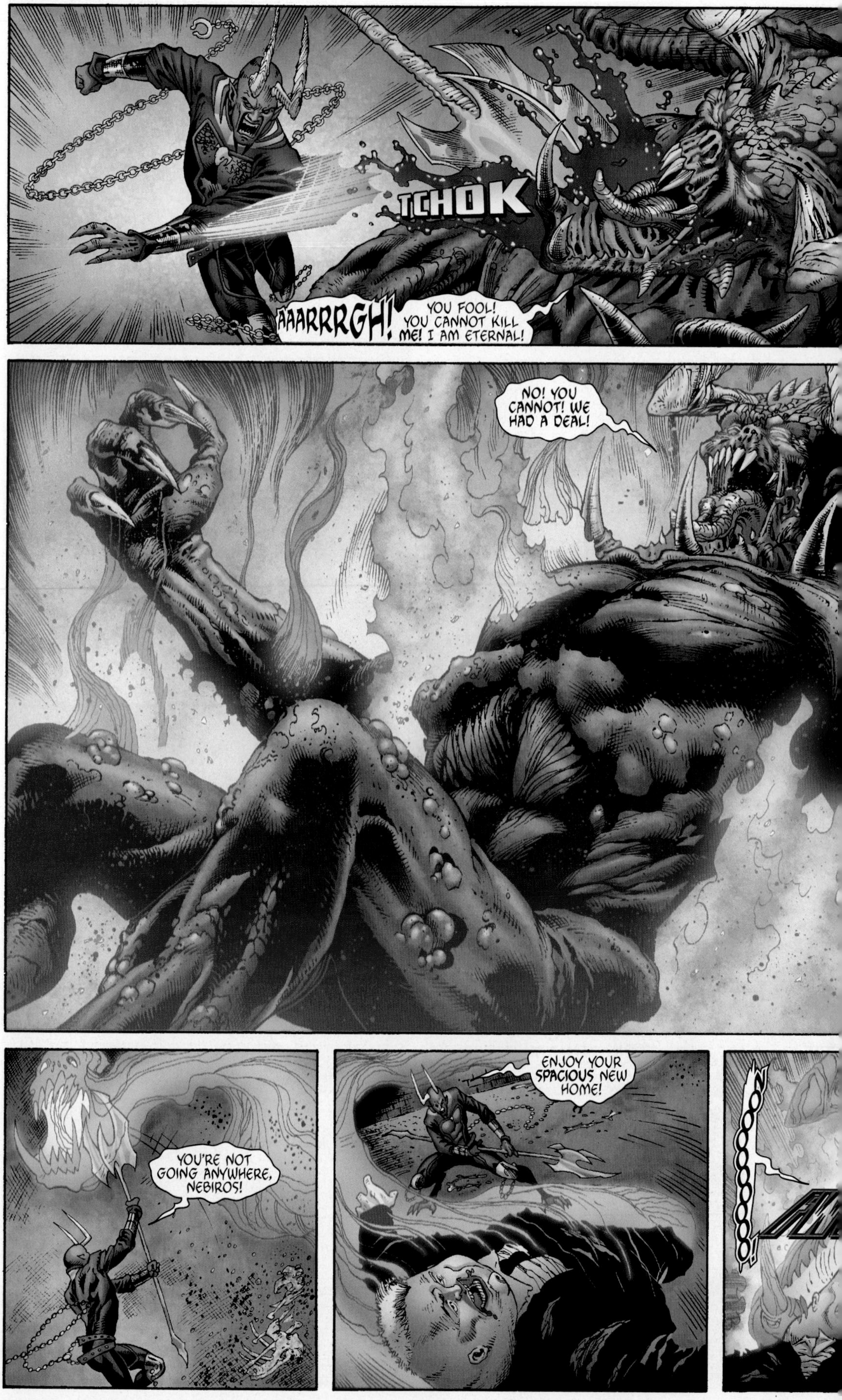
TCHOK
AAARRRGH!
YOU FOOL! YOU CANNOT KILL ME! I AM ETERNAL!
NO! YOU CANNOT! WE HAD A DEAL!
YOU'RE NOT GOING ANYWHERE, NEBIROS!
ENJOY YOUR SPACIOUS NEW HOME!
NOOOOOOOOO!

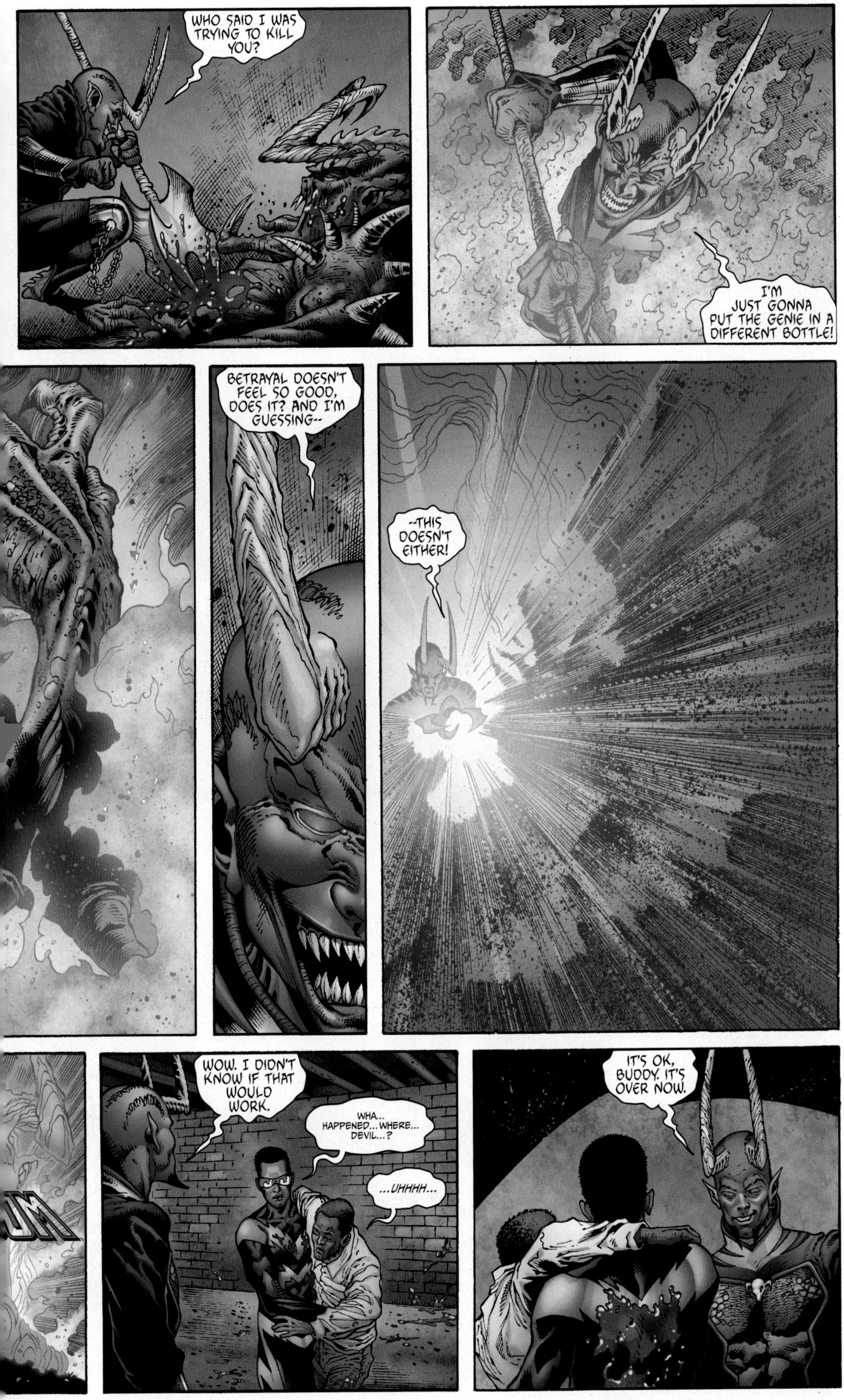
WHO SAID I WAS TRYING TO KILL YOU?
I'M JUST GONNA PUT THE GENIE IN A DIFFERENT BOTTLE!
BETRAYAL DOESN'T FEEL SO GOOD, DOES IT? AND I'M GUESSING--
--THIS DOESN'T EITHER!
WOW. I DIDN'T KNOW IF THAT WOULD WORK.
WHA... HAPPENED... WHERE... DEVIL...?
...UHHHH...
IT'S OK, BUDDY. IT'S OVER NOW.

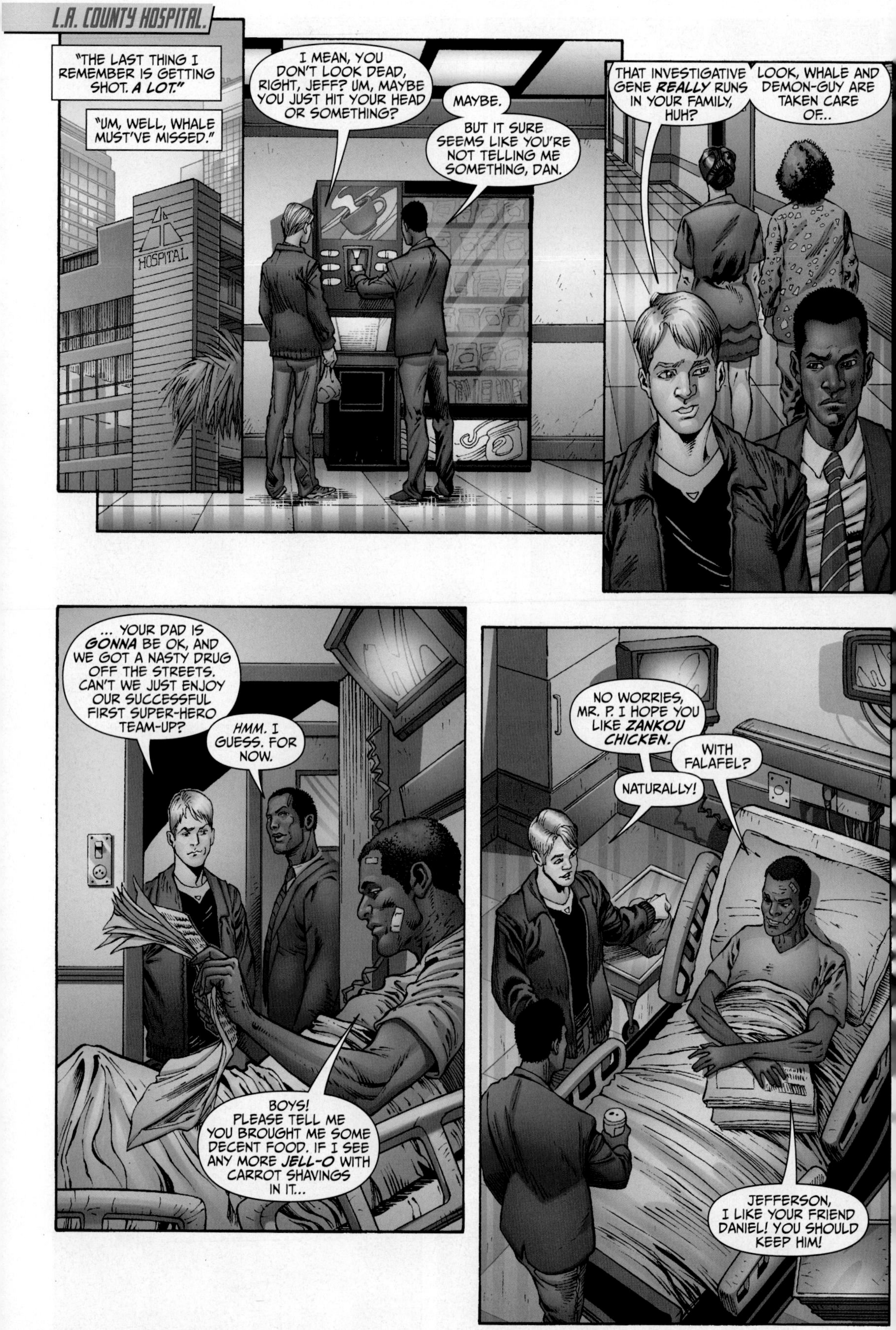
L.A. COUNTY HOSPITAL.
"THE LAST THING I REMEMBER IS GETTING SHOT. A LOT."
"UM, WELL, WHALE MUST'VE MISSED."
I MEAN, YOU DON'T LOOK DEAD, RIGHT, JEFF? UM, MAYBE YOU JUST HIT YOUR HEAD OR SOMETHING?
MAYBE.
BUT IT SURE SEEMS LIKE YOU'RE NOT TELLING ME SOMETHING, DAN.
HOSPITAL
THAT INVESTIGATIVE GENE REALLY RUNS IN YOUR FAMILY, HUH?
LOOK, WHALE AND DEMON-GUY ARE TAKEN CARE OF...
... YOUR DAD IS GONNA BE OK, AND WE GOT A NASTY DRUG OFF THE STREETS. CAN'T WE JUST ENJOY OUR SUCCESSFUL FIRST SUPER-HERO TEAM-UP?
HMM. I GUESS. FOR NOW.
BOYS! PLEASE TELL ME YOU BROUGHT ME SOME DECENT FOOD. IF I SEE ANY MORE JELL-O WITH CARROT SHAVINGS IN IT...
NO WORRIES, MR. P. I HOPE YOU LIKE ZANKOU CHICKEN.
WITH FALAFEL?
NATURALLY!
JEFFERSON, I LIKE YOUR FRIEND DANIEL! YOU SHOULD KEEP HIM!

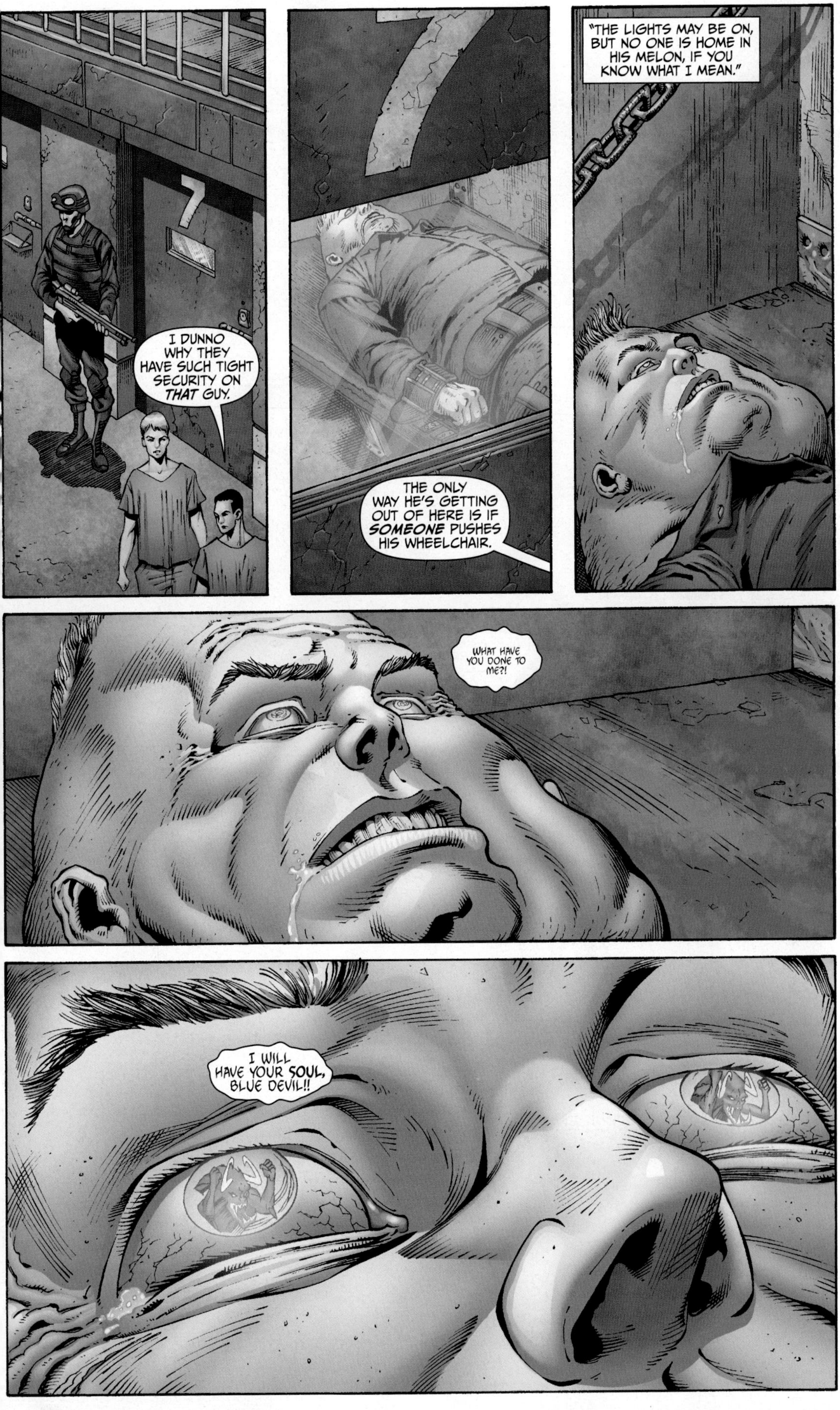
I DUNNO WHY THEY HAVE SUCH TIGHT SECURITY ON THAT GUY.
THE ONLY WAY HE'S GETTING OUT OF HERE IS IF SOMEONE PUSHES HIS WHEELCHAIR.
"THE LIGHTS MAY BE ON, BUT NO ONE IS HOME IN HIS MELON, IF YOU KNOW WHAT I MEAN."
WHAT HAVE YOU DONE TO ME?!
I WILL HAVE YOUR SOUL, BLUE DEVIL!!

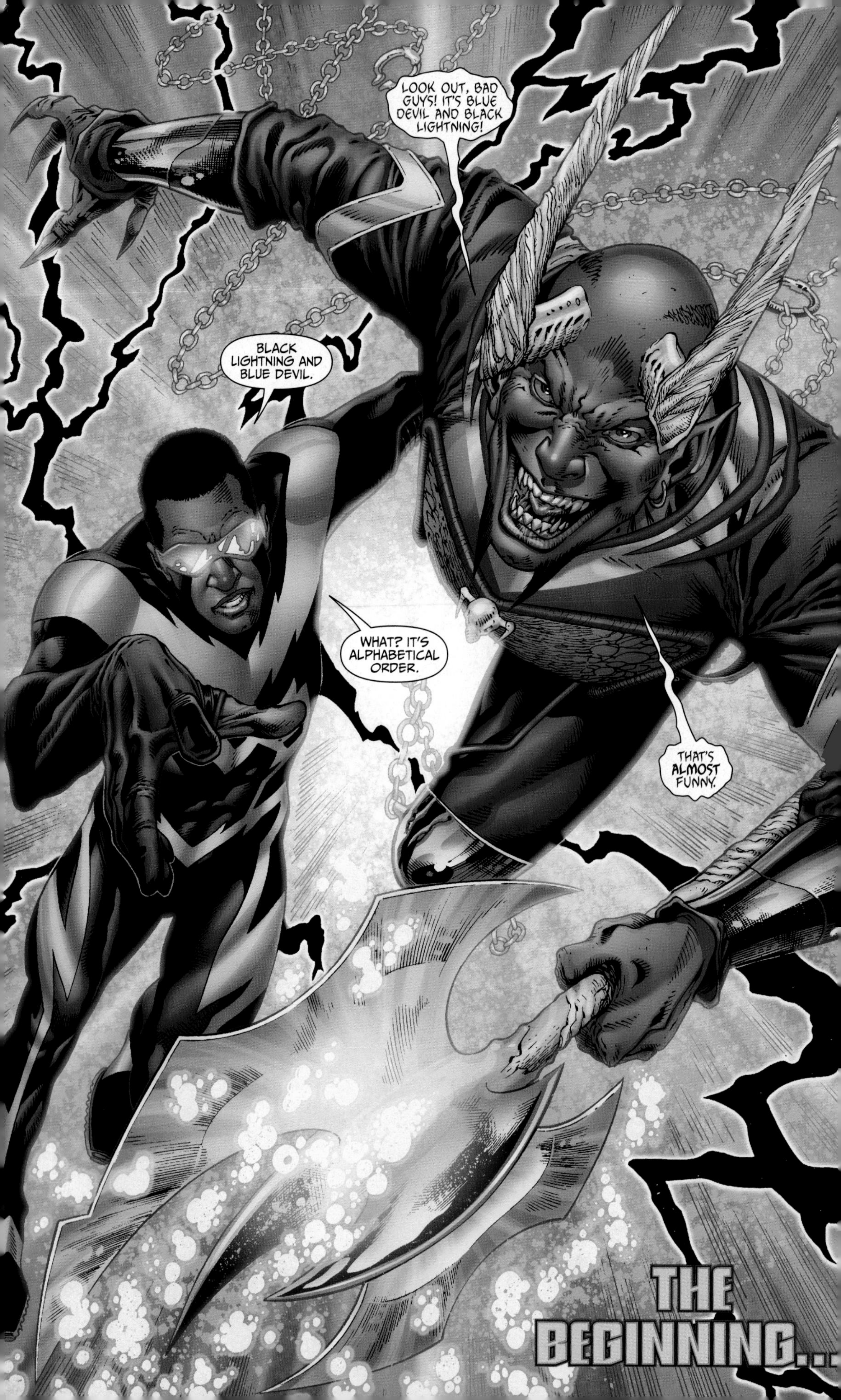

LOOK OUT, BAD GUYS! IT'S BLUE DEVIL AND BLACK LIGHTNING!
BLACK LIGHTNING AND BLUE DEVIL.
WHAT? IT'S ALPHABETICAL ORDER.
THAT'S ALMOST FUNNY.
THE BEGINNING...

ROY'S NIGHT OUT

JOE KEATINGE writer **RICKEN** artist cover art by **RYAN SOOK**

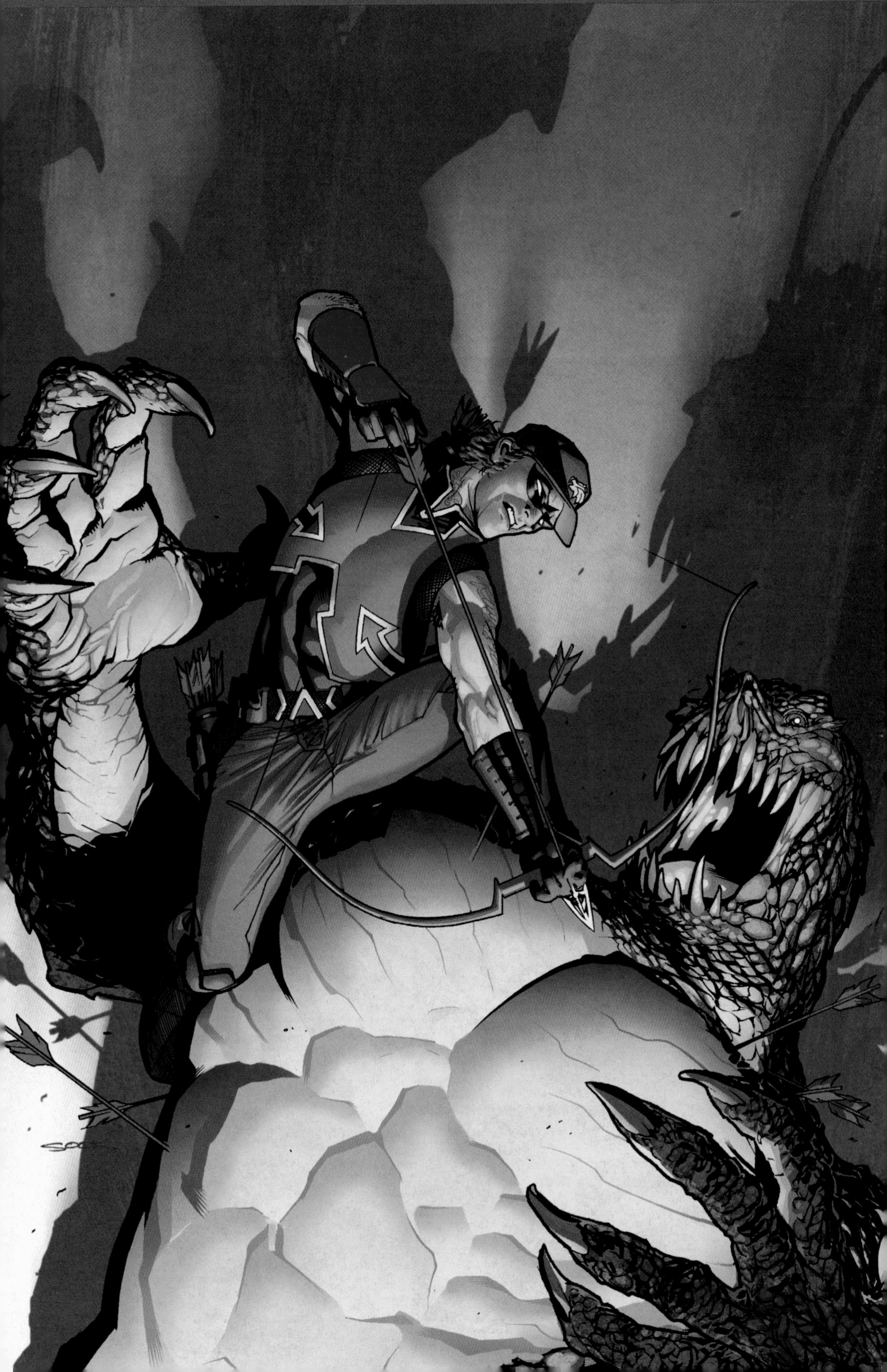

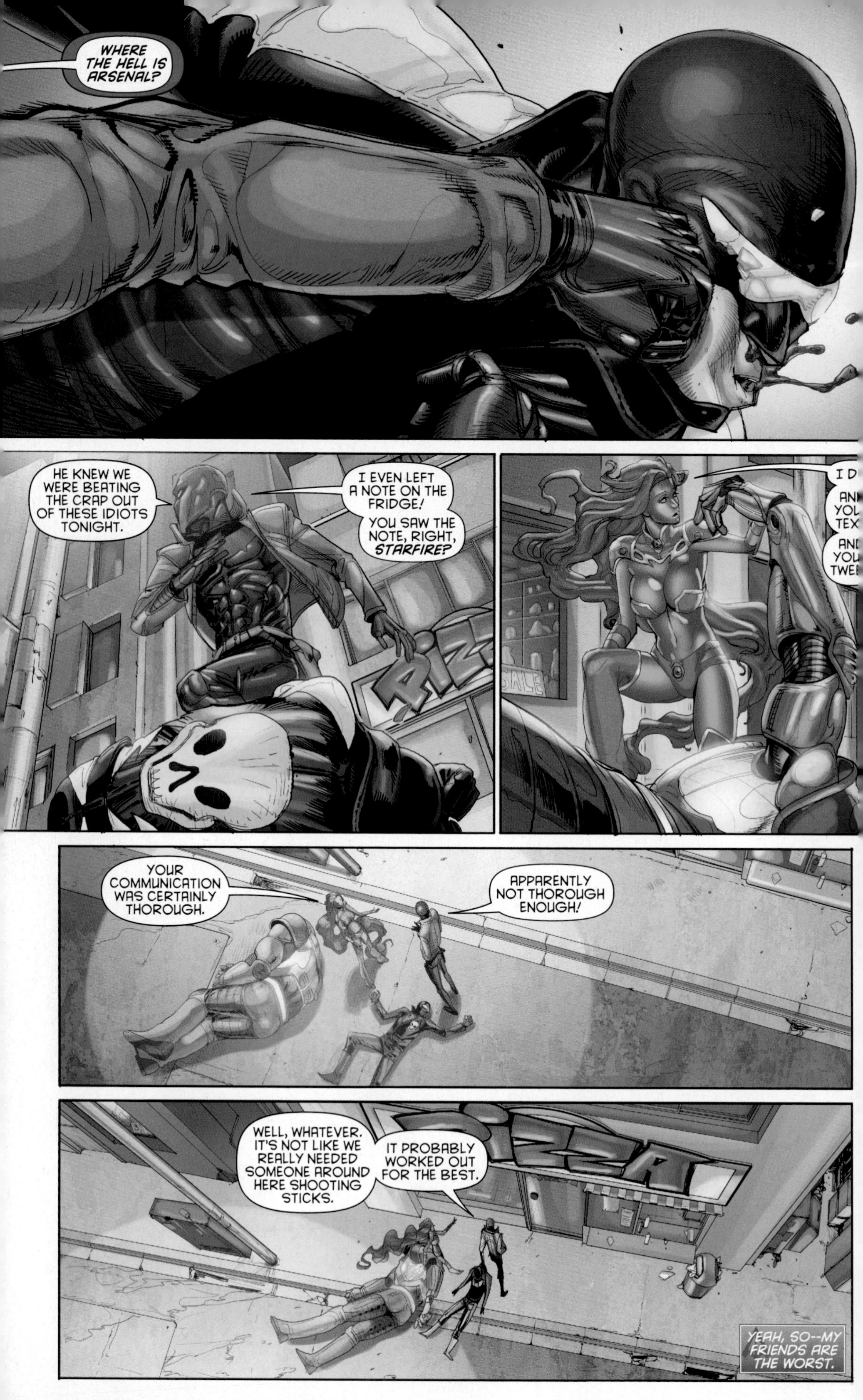
WHERE THE HELL IS ARSENAL?
HE KNEW WE WERE BEATING THE CRAP OUT OF THESE IDIOTS TONIGHT.
I EVEN LEFT A NOTE ON THE FRIDGE!
YOU SAW THE NOTE, RIGHT, STARFIRE?
YOUR COMMUNICATION WAS CERTAINLY THOROUGH.
APPARENTLY NOT THOROUGH ENOUGH!
WELL, WHATEVER. IT'S NOT LIKE WE REALLY NEEDED SOMEONE AROUND HERE SHOOTING STICKS.
IT PROBABLY WORKED OUT FOR THE BEST.
YEAH, SO--MY FRIENDS ARE THE WORST.

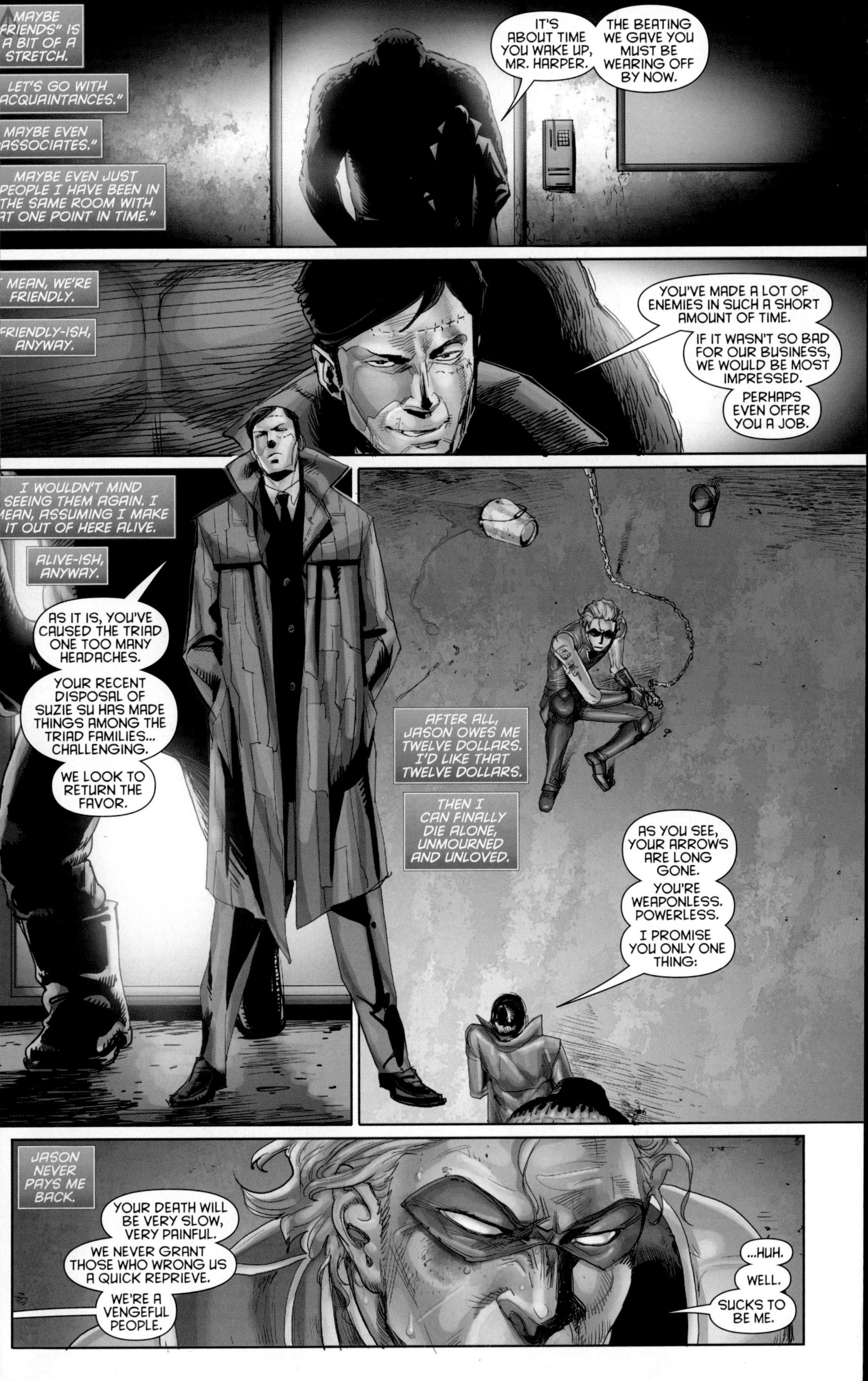
MAYBE "FRIENDS" IS A BIT OF A STRETCH.
LET'S GO WITH ACQUAINTANCES."
MAYBE EVEN ASSOCIATES."
MAYBE EVEN JUST PEOPLE I HAVE BEEN IN THE SAME ROOM WITH AT ONE POINT IN TIME."
IT'S ABOUT TIME YOU WAKE UP, MR. HARPER.
THE BEATING WE GAVE YOU MUST BE WEARING OFF BY NOW.
MEAN, WE'RE FRIENDLY.
FRIENDLY-ISH, ANYWAY.
YOU'VE MADE A LOT OF ENEMIES IN SUCH A SHORT AMOUNT OF TIME.
IF IT WASN'T SO BAD FOR OUR BUSINESS, WE WOULD BE MOST IMPRESSED.
PERHAPS EVEN OFFER YOU A JOB.
I WOULDN'T MIND SEEING THEM AGAIN. I MEAN, ASSUMING I MAKE IT OUT OF HERE ALIVE.
ALIVE-ISH, ANYWAY.
AS IT IS, YOU'VE CAUSED THE TRIAD ONE TOO MANY HEADACHES.
YOUR RECENT DISPOSAL OF SUZIE SU HAS MADE THINGS AMONG THE TRIAD FAMILIES... CHALLENGING.
WE LOOK TO RETURN THE FAVOR.
AFTER ALL, JASON OWES ME TWELVE DOLLARS. I'D LIKE THAT TWELVE DOLLARS.
THEN I CAN FINALLY DIE ALONE, UNMOURNED AND UNLOVED.
AS YOU SEE, YOUR ARROWS ARE LONG GONE.
YOU'RE WEAPONLESS. POWERLESS.
I PROMISE YOU ONLY ONE THING:
JASON NEVER PAYS ME BACK.
YOUR DEATH WILL BE VERY SLOW, VERY PAINFUL.
WE NEVER GRANT THOSE WHO WRONG US A QUICK REPRIEVE.
WE'RE A VENGEFUL PEOPLE.
...HUH.
WELL.
SUCKS TO BE ME.

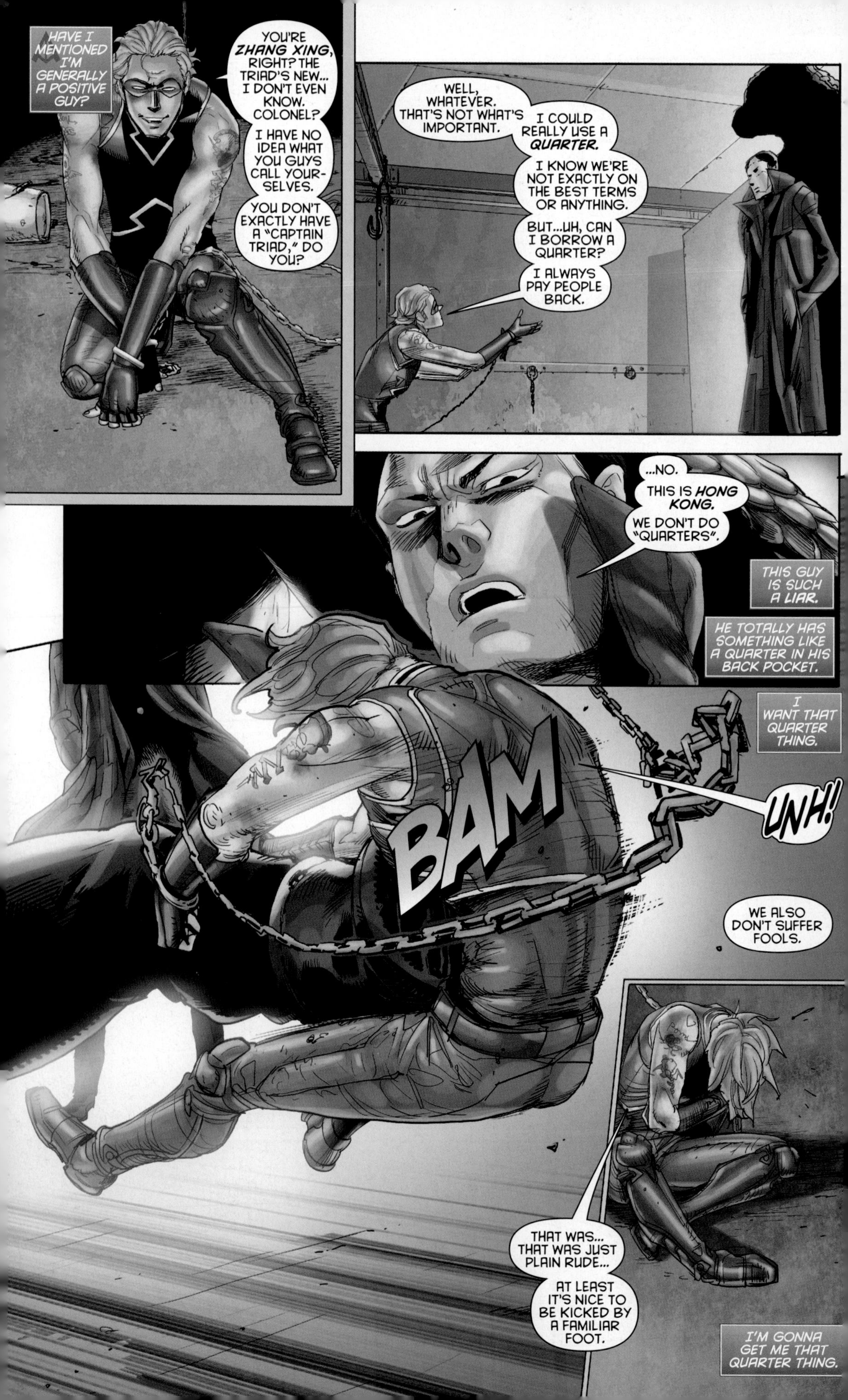
HAVE I MENTIONED I'M GENERALLY A POSITIVE GUY?
YOU'RE ZHANG XING, RIGHT? THE TRIAD'S NEW... I DON'T EVEN KNOW. COLONEL?
I HAVE NO IDEA WHAT YOU GUYS CALL YOURSELVES.
YOU DON'T EXACTLY HAVE A "CAPTAIN TRIAD," DO YOU?
WELL, WHATEVER. THAT'S NOT WHAT'S IMPORTANT.
I COULD REALLY USE A QUARTER.
I KNOW WE'RE NOT EXACTLY ON THE BEST TERMS OR ANYTHING.
BUT...UH, CAN I BORROW A QUARTER?
I ALWAYS PAY PEOPLE BACK.
...NO.
THIS IS HONG KONG.
WE DON'T DO "QUARTERS".
THIS GUY IS SUCH A LIAR.
HE TOTALLY HAS SOMETHING LIKE A QUARTER IN HIS BACK POCKET.
I WANT THAT QUARTER THING.
BAM
UNH!
WE ALSO DON'T SUFFER FOOLS.
THAT WAS... THAT WAS JUST PLAIN RUDE...
AT LEAST IT'S NICE TO BE KICKED BY A FAMILIAR FOOT.
I'M GONNA GET ME THAT QUARTER THING.

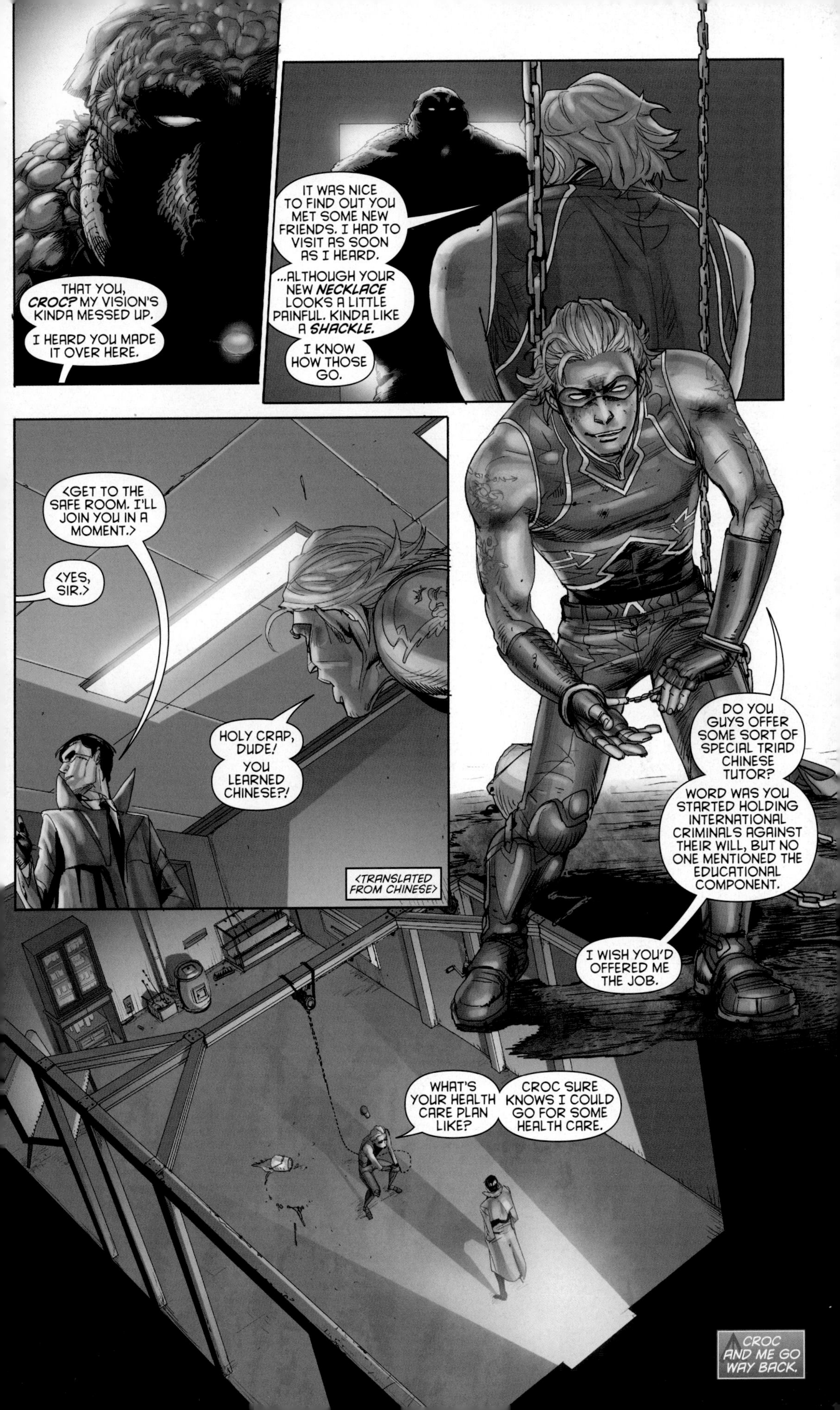

THAT YOU, CROC? MY VISION'S KINDA MESSED UP.
I HEARD YOU MADE IT OVER HERE.
IT WAS NICE TO FIND OUT YOU MET SOME NEW FRIENDS. I HAD TO VISIT AS SOON AS I HEARD.
...ALTHOUGH YOUR NEW NECKLACE LOOKS A LITTLE PAINFUL. KINDA LIKE A SHACKLE.
I KNOW HOW THOSE GO.
<GET TO THE SAFE ROOM. I'LL JOIN YOU IN A MOMENT.>
<YES, SIR.>
HOLY CRAP, DUDE!
YOU LEARNED CHINESE?!
<TRANSLATED FROM CHINESE>
DO YOU GUYS OFFER SOME SORT OF SPECIAL TRIAD CHINESE TUTOR?
WORD WAS YOU STARTED HOLDING INTERNATIONAL CRIMINALS AGAINST THEIR WILL, BUT NO ONE MENTIONED THE EDUCATIONAL COMPONENT.
I WISH YOU'D OFFERED ME THE JOB.
WHAT'S YOUR HEALTH CARE PLAN LIKE?
CROC SURE KNOWS I COULD GO FOR SOME HEALTH CARE.
CROC AND ME GO WAY BACK.

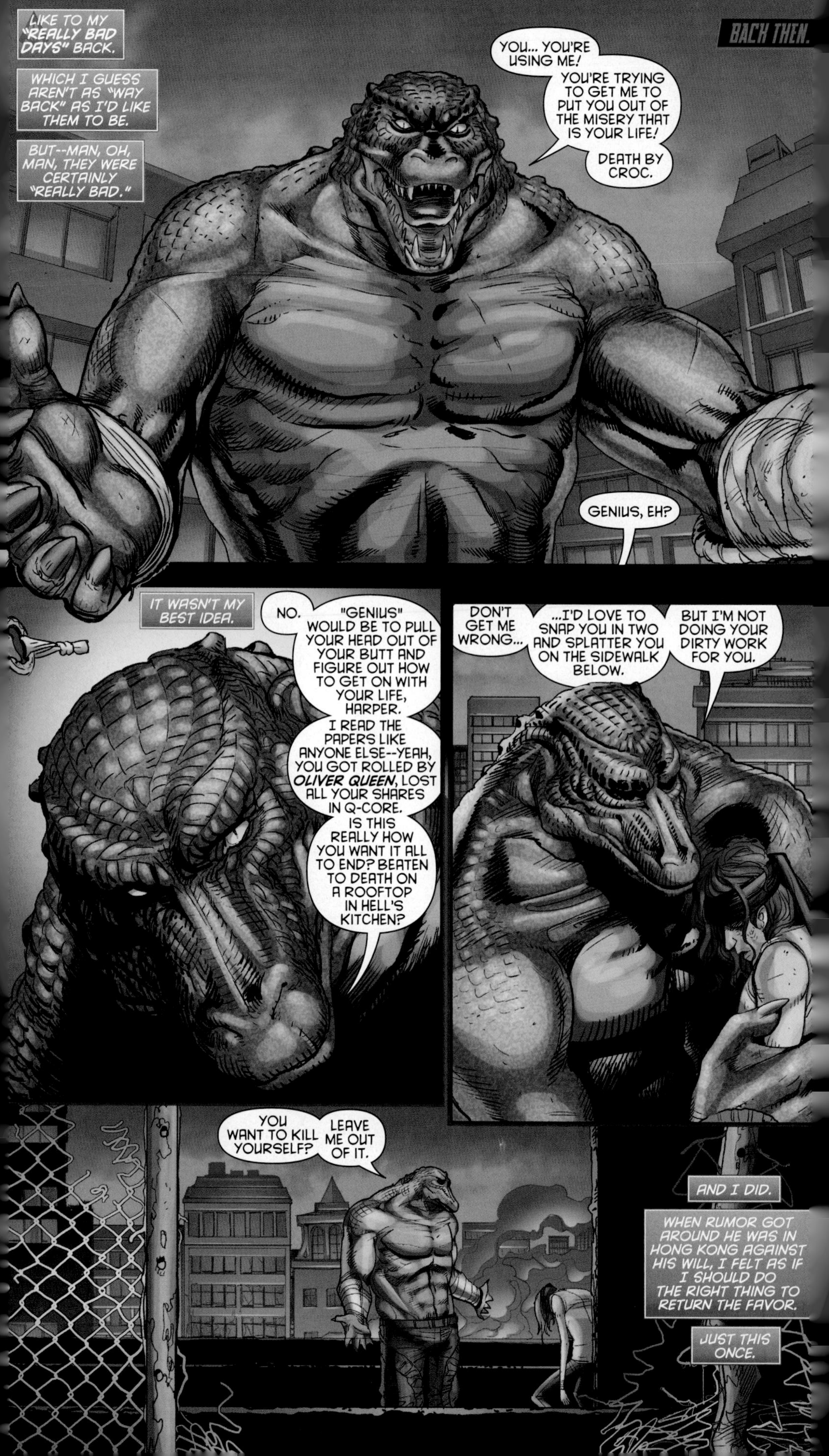
LIKE TO MY "REALLY BAD DAYS" BACK.
WHICH I GUESS AREN'T AS "WAY BACK" AS I'D LIKE THEM TO BE.
BUT--MAN, OH, MAN, THEY WERE CERTAINLY "REALLY BAD."
BACK THEN.
YOU... YOU'RE USING ME!
YOU'RE TRYING TO GET ME TO PUT YOU OUT OF THE MISERY THAT IS YOUR LIFE!
DEATH BY CROC.
GENIUS, EH?
IT WASN'T MY BEST IDEA.
NO.
"GENIUS" WOULD BE TO PULL YOUR HEAD OUT OF YOUR BUTT AND FIGURE OUT HOW TO GET ON WITH YOUR LIFE, HARPER.
I READ THE PAPERS LIKE ANYONE ELSE--YEAH, YOU GOT ROLLED BY OLIVER QUEEN, LOST ALL YOUR SHARES IN Q-CORE.
IS THIS REALLY HOW YOU WANT IT ALL TO END? BEATEN TO DEATH ON A ROOFTOP IN HELL'S KITCHEN?
DON'T GET ME WRONG...
...I'D LOVE TO SNAP YOU IN TWO AND SPLATTER YOU ON THE SIDEWALK BELOW.
BUT I'M NOT DOING YOUR DIRTY WORK FOR YOU.
YOU WANT TO KILL YOURSELF?
LEAVE ME OUT OF IT.
AND I DID.
WHEN RUMOR GOT AROUND HE WAS IN HONG KONG AGAINST HIS WILL, I FELT AS IF I SHOULD DO THE RIGHT THING TO RETURN THE FAVOR.
JUST THIS ONCE.

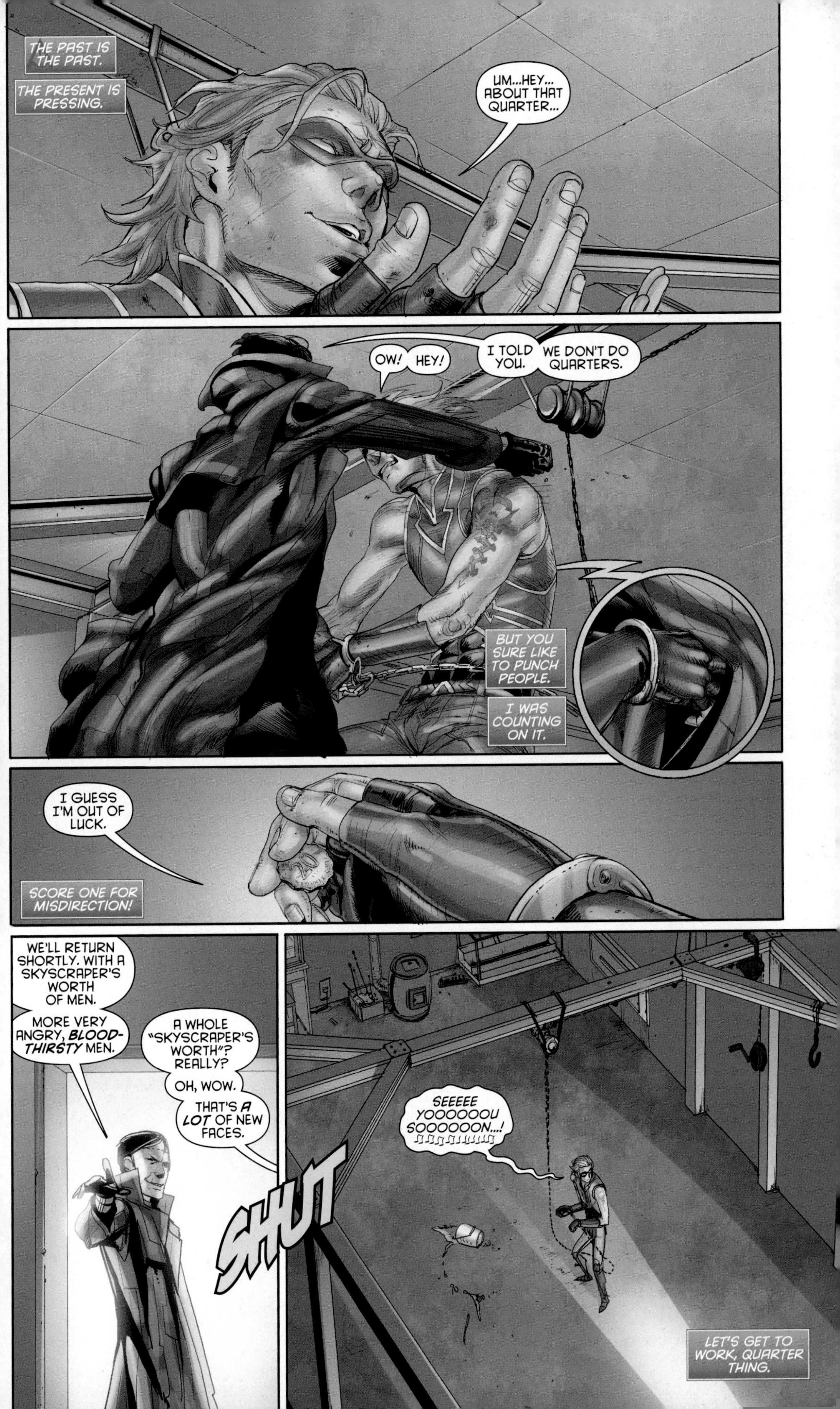

THE PAST IS THE PAST.
THE PRESENT IS PRESSING.
UM...HEY... ABOUT THAT QUARTER...
OW!
HEY!
I TOLD YOU.
WE DON'T DO QUARTERS.
BUT YOU SURE LIKE TO PUNCH PEOPLE.
I WAS COUNTING ON IT.
I GUESS I'M OUT OF LUCK.
SCORE ONE FOR MISDIRECTION!
WE'LL RETURN SHORTLY. WITH A SKYSCRAPER'S WORTH OF MEN.
MORE VERY ANGRY, BLOOD-THIRSTY MEN.
A WHOLE "SKYSCRAPER'S WORTH"? REALLY?
OH, WOW.
THAT'S A LOT OF NEW FACES.
SHUT
SEEEEE YOOOOOOU SOOOOOON...!
LET'S GET TO WORK, QUARTER THING.

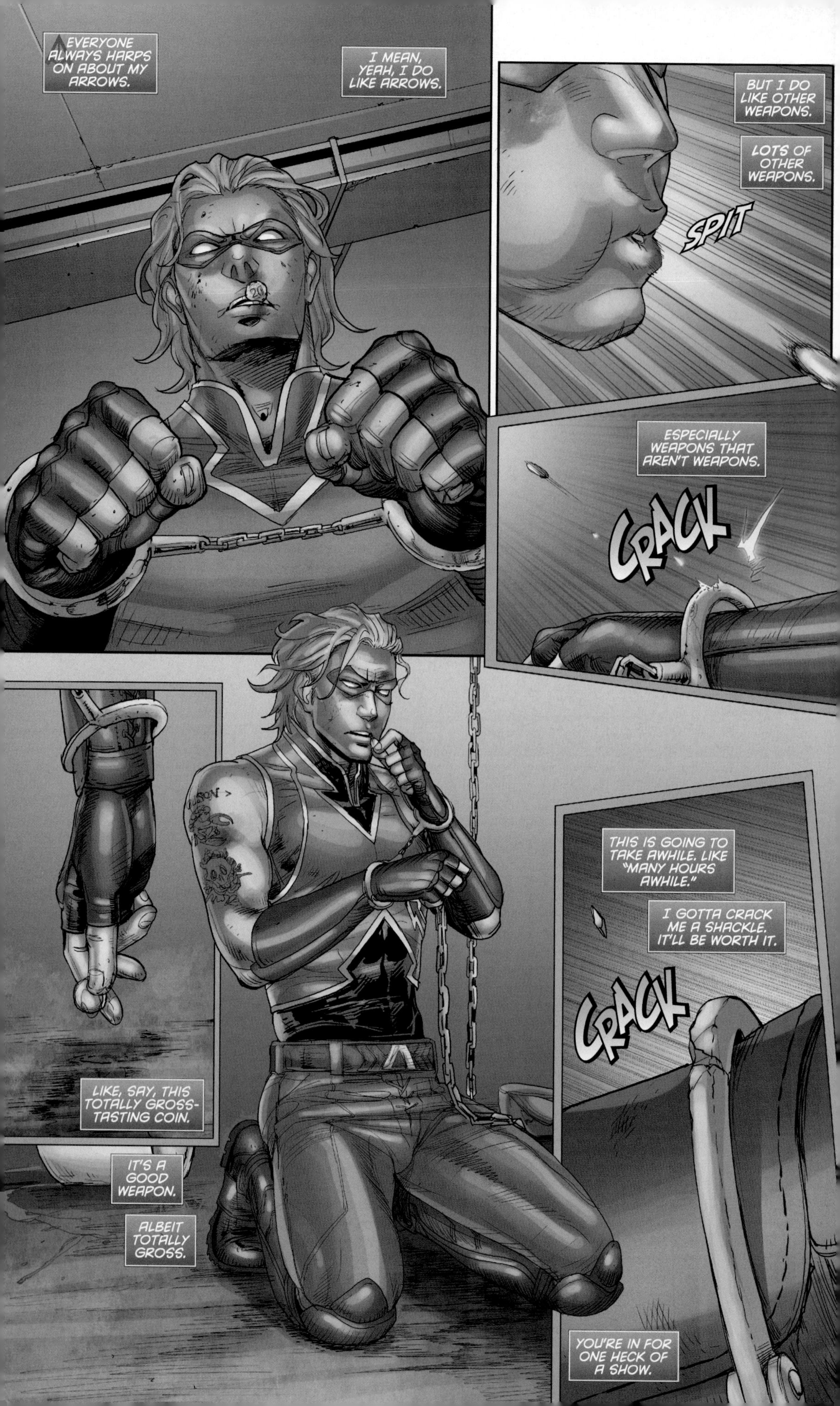
EVERYONE ALWAYS HARPS ON ABOUT MY ARROWS.
I MEAN, YEAH, I DO LIKE ARROWS.
BUT I DO LIKE OTHER WEAPONS.
LOTS OF OTHER WEAPONS.
SPIT
ESPECIALLY WEAPONS THAT AREN'T WEAPONS.
CRACK
LIKE, SAY, THIS TOTALLY GROSS-TASTING COIN.
IT'S A GOOD WEAPON.
ALBEIT TOTALLY GROSS.
THIS IS GOING TO TAKE AWHILE. LIKE "MANY HOURS AWHILE."
I GOTTA CRACK ME A SHACKLE. IT'LL BE WORTH IT.
CRACK
YOU'RE IN FOR ONE HECK OF A SHOW.

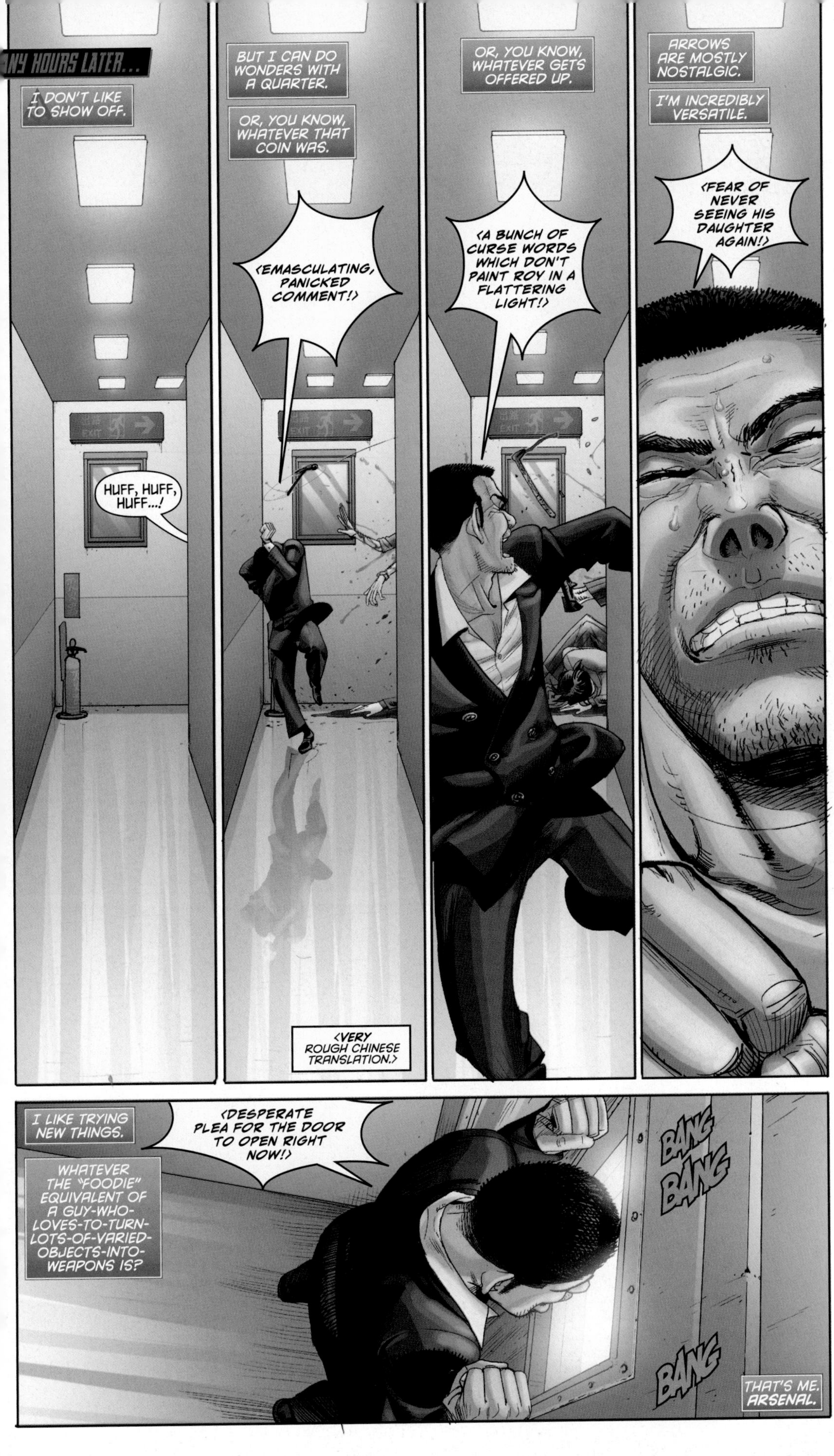
NY HOURS LATER...
I DON'T LIKE TO SHOW OFF.
HUFF, HUFF, HUFF...!
BUT I CAN DO WONDERS WITH A QUARTER.
OR, YOU KNOW, WHATEVER THAT COIN WAS.
<EMASCULATING, PANICKED COMMENT!>
<VERY ROUGH CHINESE TRANSLATION.>
OR, YOU KNOW, WHATEVER GETS OFFERED UP.
<A BUNCH OF CURSE WORDS WHICH DON'T PAINT ROY IN A FLATTERING LIGHT!>
ARROWS ARE MOSTLY NOSTALGIC.
I'M INCREDIBLY VERSATILE.
<FEAR OF NEVER SEEING HIS DAUGHTER AGAIN!>
I LIKE TRYING NEW THINGS.
WHATEVER THE "FOODIE" EQUIVALENT OF A GUY-WHO-LOVES-TO-TURN-LOTS-OF-VARIED-OBJECTS-INTO-WEAPONS IS?
<DESPERATE PLEA FOR THE DOOR TO OPEN RIGHT NOW!>
BANG
BANG
BANG
THAT'S ME. ARSENAL.

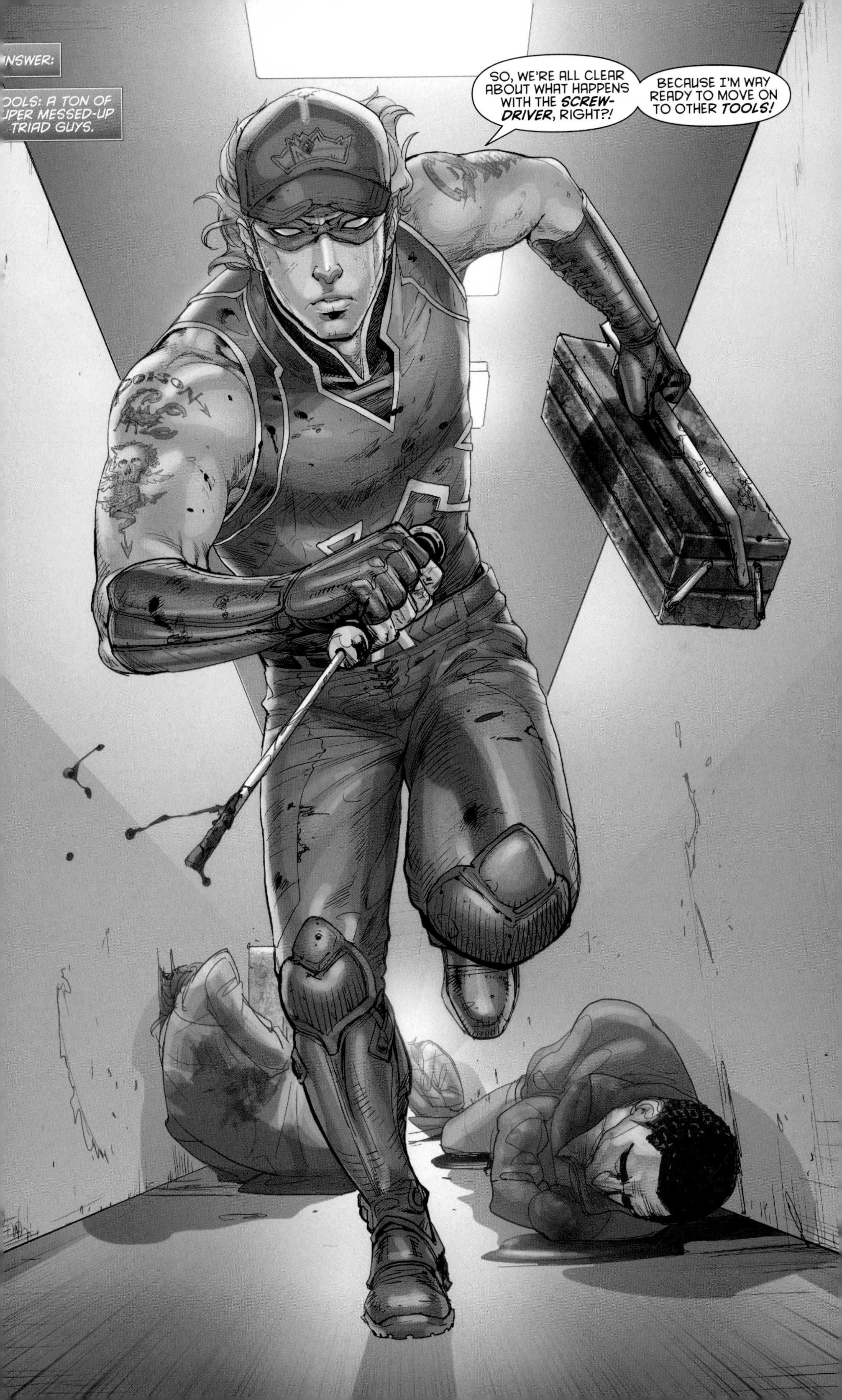

NSWER:
OOLS: A TON OF
UPER MESSED-UP
TRIAD GUYS.
SO, WE'RE ALL CLEAR ABOUT WHAT HAPPENS WITH THE SCREW-DRIVER, RIGHT?!
BECAUSE I'M WAY READY TO MOVE ON TO OTHER TOOLS!
POISON

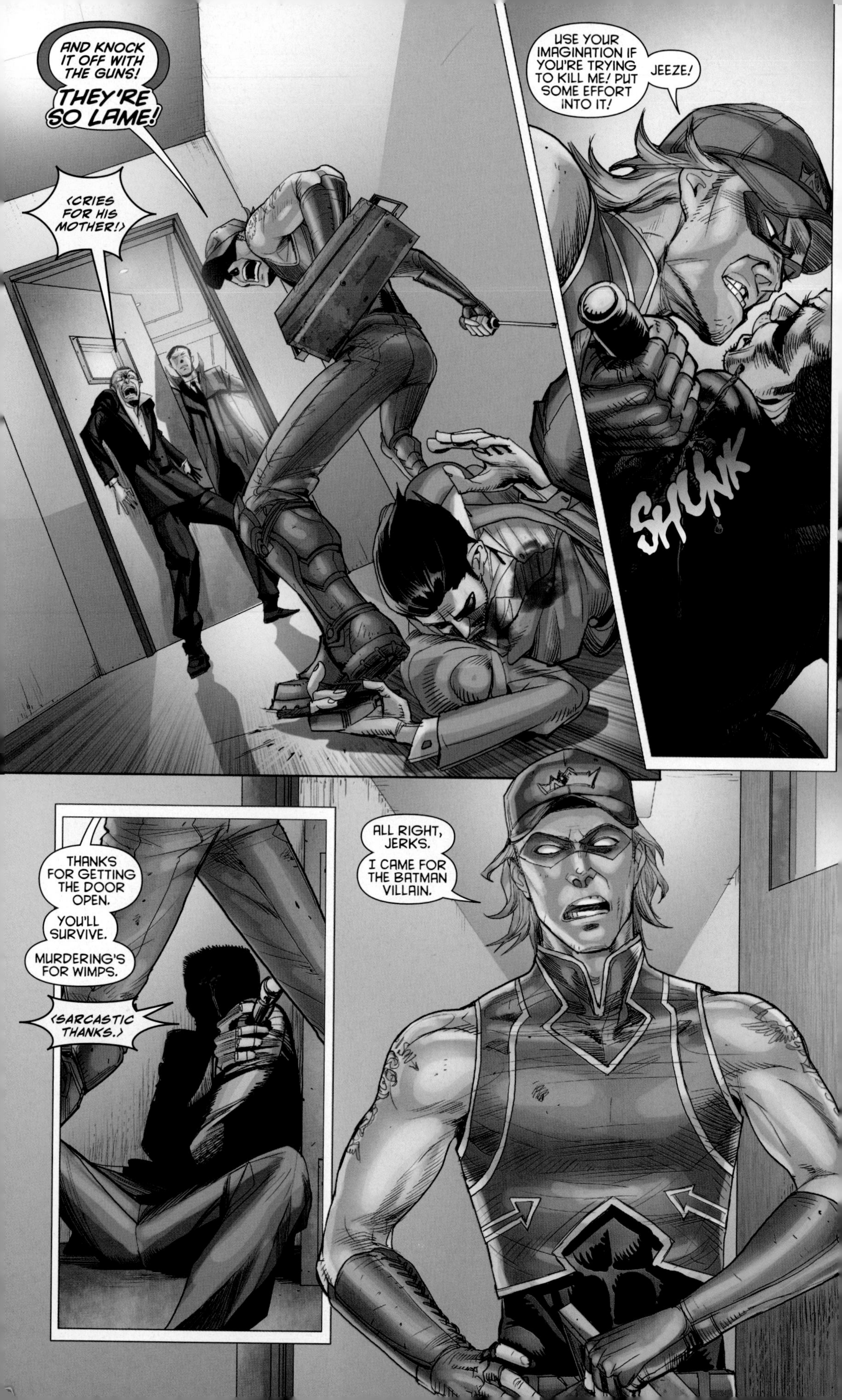

AND KNOCK IT OFF WITH THE GUNS!
THEY'RE SO LAME!
<CRIES FOR HIS MOTHER!>
USE YOUR IMAGINATION IF YOU'RE TRYING TO KILL ME! PUT SOME EFFORT INTO IT!
JEEZE!
SHUNK
THANKS FOR GETTING THE DOOR OPEN.
YOU'LL SURVIVE.
MURDERING'S FOR WIMPS.
<SARCASTIC THANKS.>
ALL RIGHT, JERKS.
I CAME FOR THE BATMAN VILLAIN.

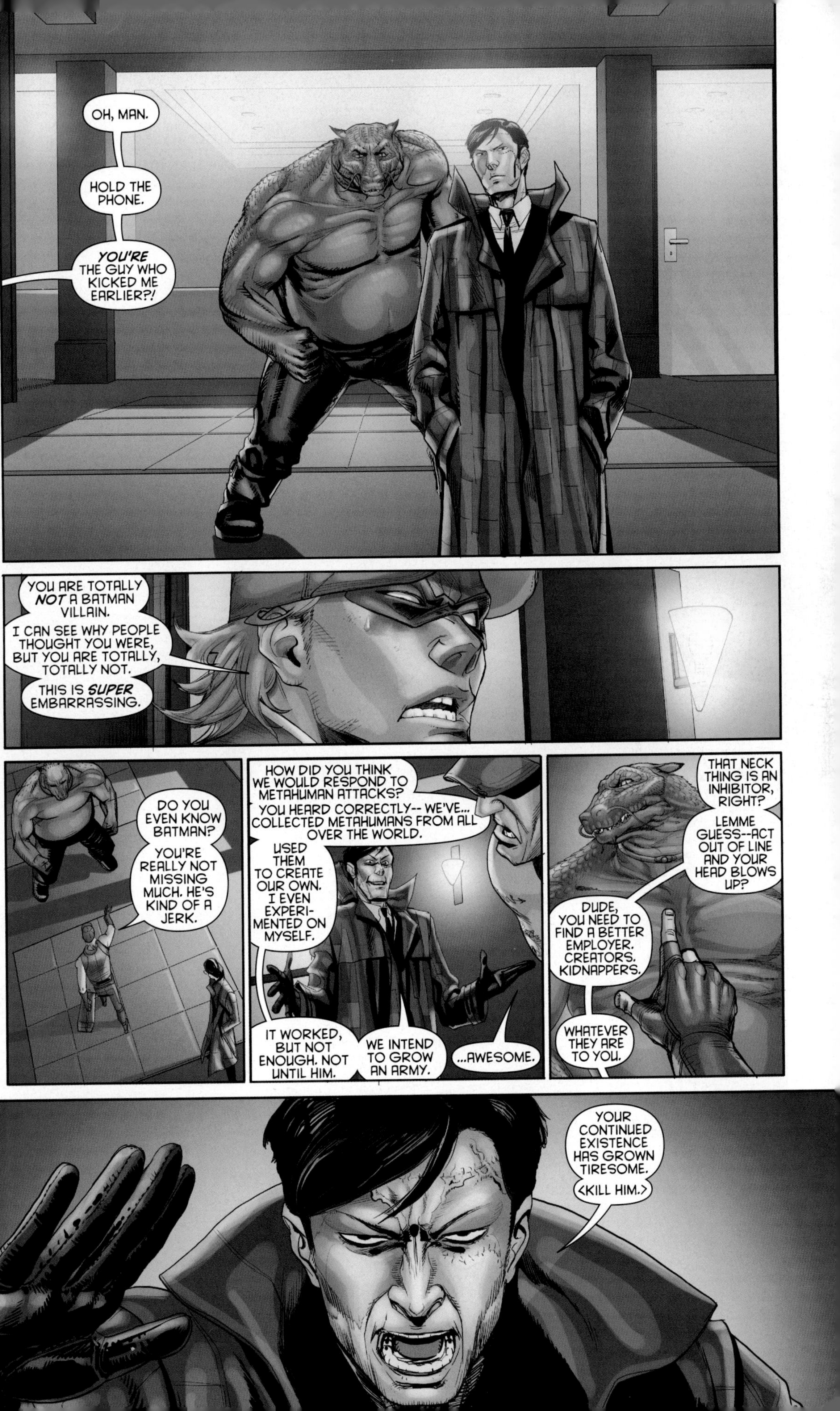
OH, MAN.
HOLD THE PHONE.
YOU'RE THE GUY WHO KICKED ME EARLIER?!
YOU ARE TOTALLY NOT A BATMAN VILLAIN.
I CAN SEE WHY PEOPLE THOUGHT YOU WERE, BUT YOU ARE TOTALLY, TOTALLY NOT.
THIS IS SUPER EMBARRASSING.
DO YOU EVEN KNOW BATMAN?
YOU'RE REALLY NOT MISSING MUCH. HE'S KIND OF A JERK.
HOW DID YOU THINK WE WOULD RESPOND TO METAHUMAN ATTACKS?
YOU HEARD CORRECTLY-- WE'VE... COLLECTED METAHUMANS FROM ALL OVER THE WORLD.
USED THEM TO CREATE OUR OWN. I EVEN EXPERI-MENTED ON MYSELF.
IT WORKED, BUT NOT ENOUGH. NOT UNTIL HIM.
WE INTEND TO GROW AN ARMY.
...AWESOME.
THAT NECK THING IS AN INHIBITOR, RIGHT?
LEMME GUESS--ACT OUT OF LINE AND YOUR HEAD BLOWS UP?
DUDE, YOU NEED TO FIND A BETTER EMPLOYER. CREATORS. KIDNAPPERS.
WHATEVER THEY ARE TO YOU.
YOUR CONTINUED EXISTENCE HAS GROWN TIRESOME.
<KILL HIM.>

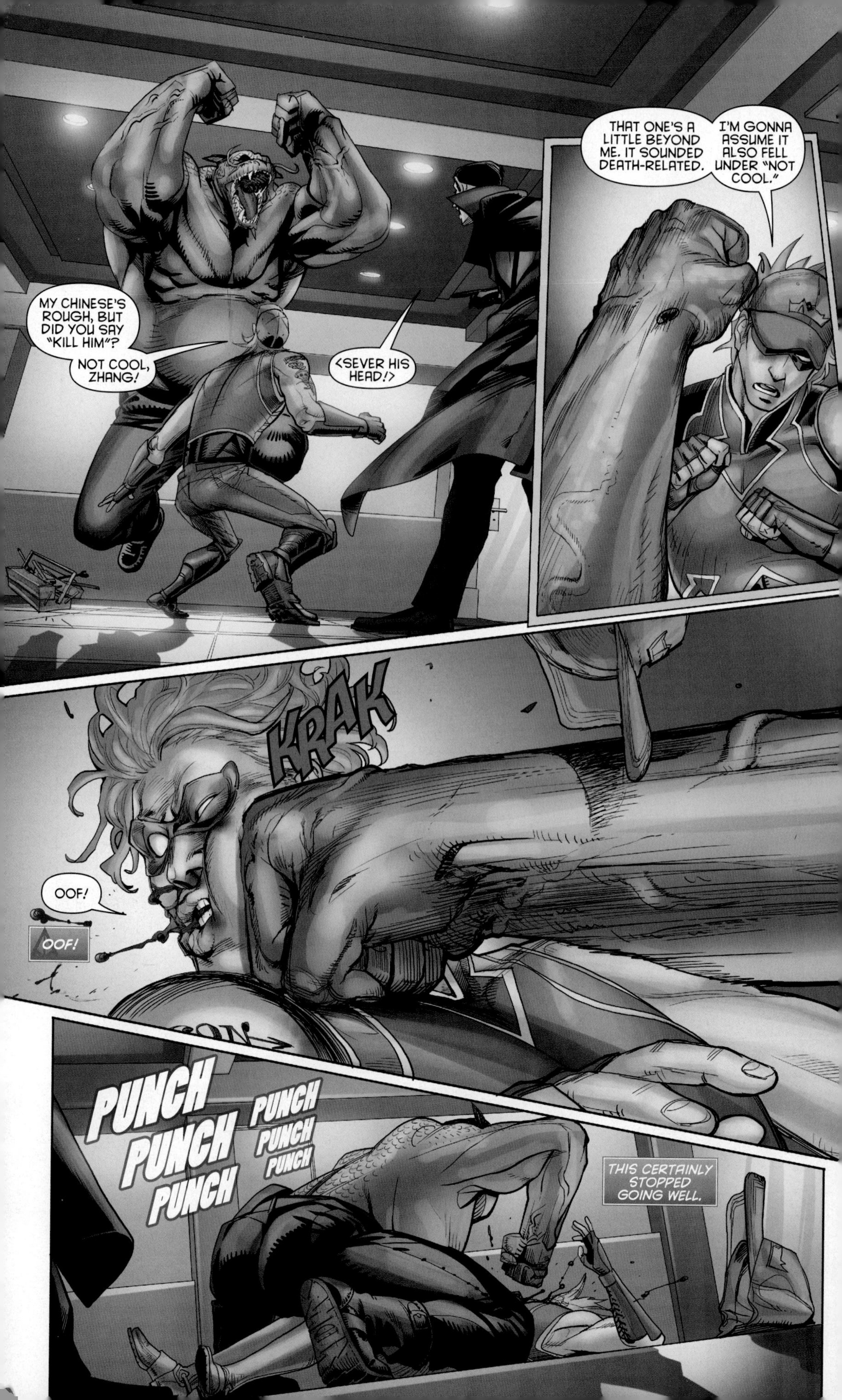
MY CHINESE'S ROUGH, BUT DID YOU SAY "KILL HIM"?
NOT COOL, ZHANG!
<SEVER HIS HEAD!>
THAT ONE'S A LITTLE BEYOND ME. IT SOUNDED DEATH-RELATED.
I'M GONNA ASSUME IT ALSO FELL UNDER "NOT COOL."
KRAK
OOF!
OOF!
PUNCH PUNCH PUNCH
PUNCH PUNCH PUNCH
THIS CERTAINLY STOPPED GOING WELL.

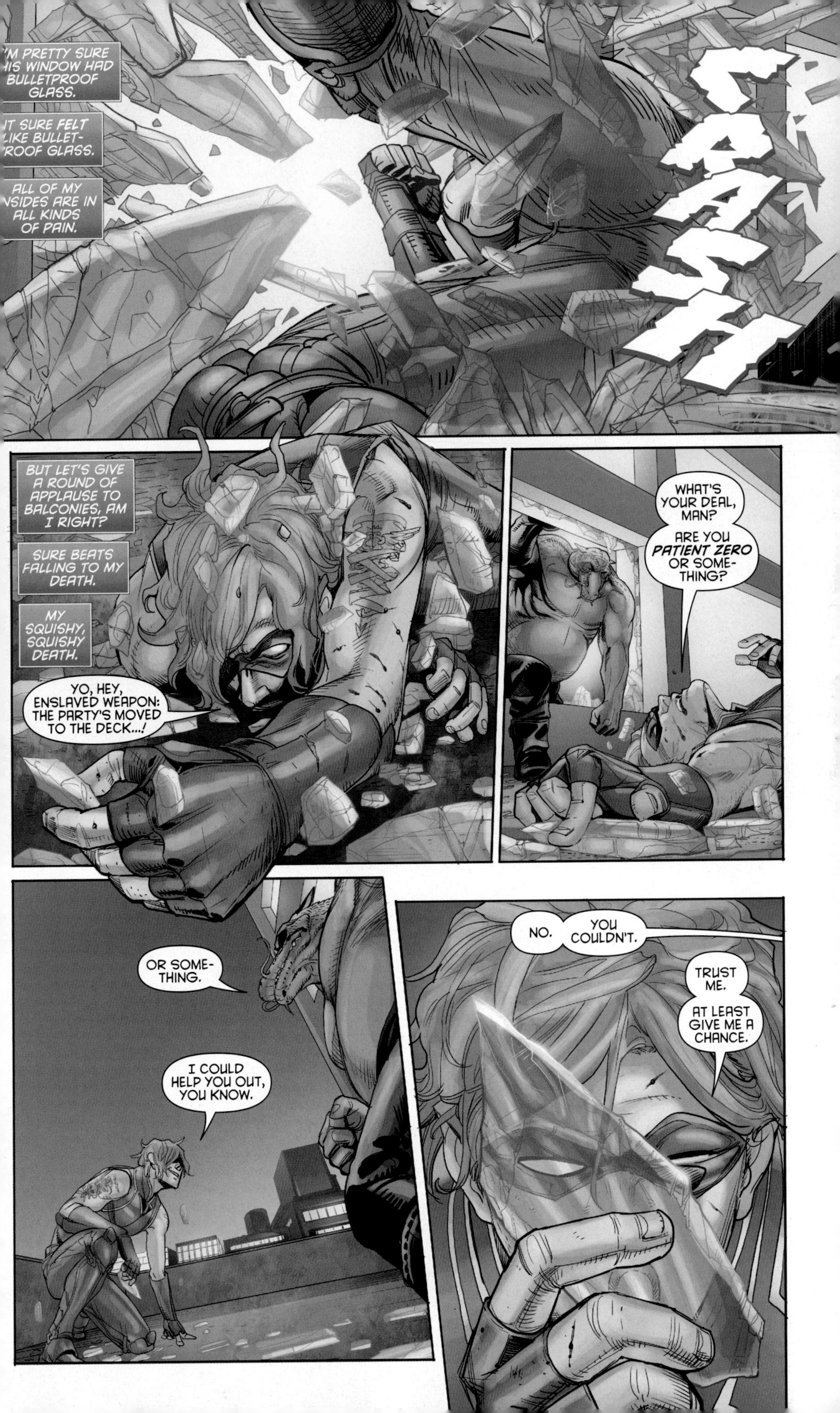

I'M PRETTY SURE THIS WINDOW HAD BULLETPROOF GLASS.
IT SURE FELT LIKE BULLET-PROOF GLASS.
ALL OF MY INSIDES ARE IN ALL KINDS OF PAIN.
CRASH
BUT LET'S GIVE A ROUND OF APPLAUSE TO BALCONIES, AM I RIGHT?
SURE BEATS FALLING TO MY DEATH.
MY SQUISHY, SQUISHY DEATH.
YO, HEY, ENSLAVED WEAPON: THE PARTY'S MOVED TO THE DECK...!
WHAT'S YOUR DEAL, MAN?
ARE YOU PATIENT ZERO OR SOME-THING?
OR SOME-THING.
I COULD HELP YOU OUT, YOU KNOW.
NO.
YOU COULDN'T.
TRUST ME.
AT LEAST GIVE ME A CHANCE.

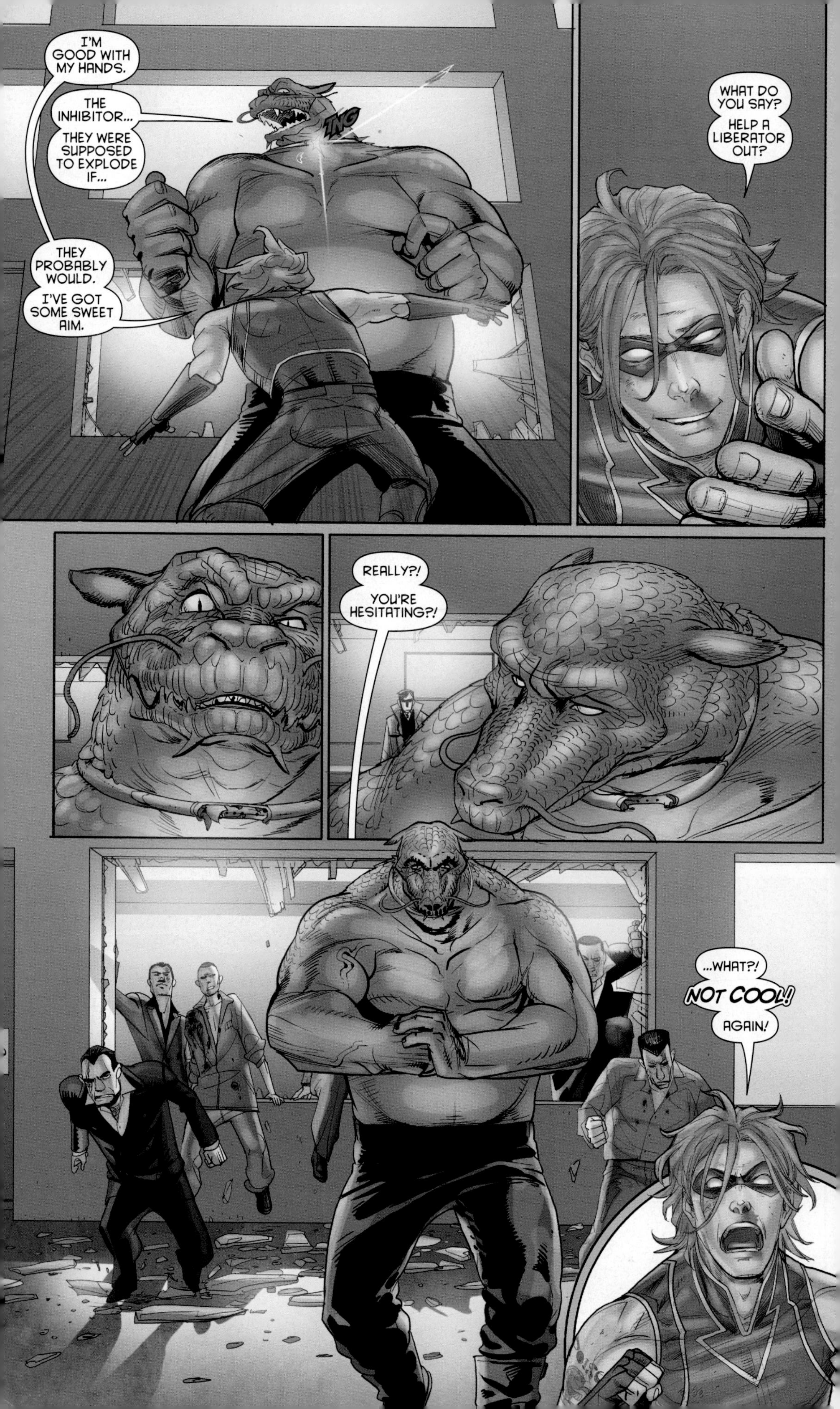
I'M GOOD WITH MY HANDS.
THE INHIBITOR...
THEY WERE SUPPOSED TO EXPLODE IF...
ZNG
THEY PROBABLY WOULD.
I'VE GOT SOME SWEET AIM.
WHAT DO YOU SAY?
HELP A LIBERATOR OUT?
REALLY?!
YOU'RE HESITATING?!
...WHAT?!
NOT COOL!
AGAIN!

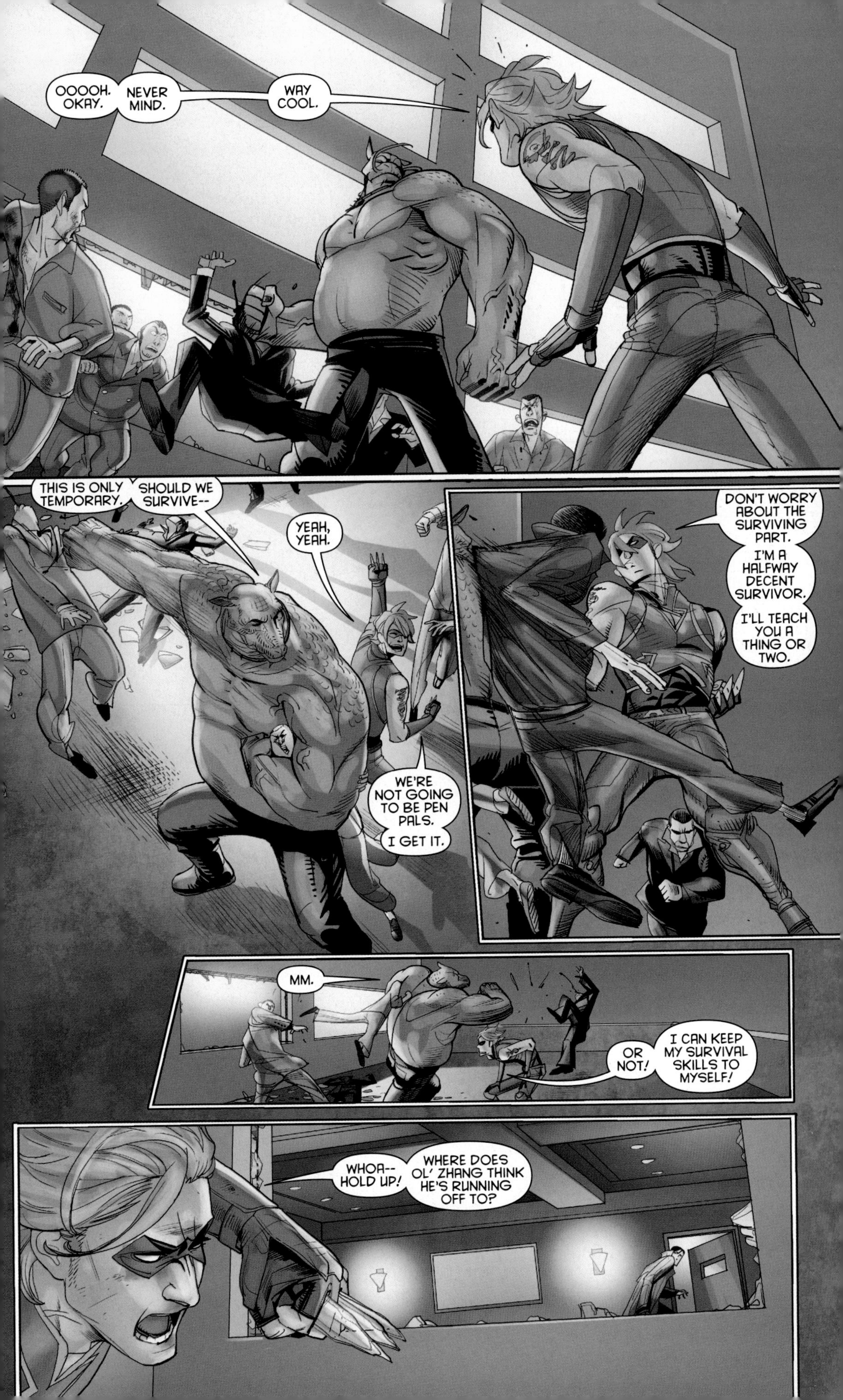
OOOOH. OKAY.
NEVER MIND.
WAY COOL.
THIS IS ONLY TEMPORARY.
SHOULD WE SURVIVE--
YEAH, YEAH.
WE'RE NOT GOING TO BE PEN PALS.
I GET IT.
DON'T WORRY ABOUT THE SURVIVING PART.
I'M A HALFWAY DECENT SURVIVOR.
I'LL TEACH YOU A THING OR TWO.
MM.
OR NOT!
I CAN KEEP MY SURVIVAL SKILLS TO MYSELF!
WHOA-- HOLD UP!
WHERE DOES OL' ZHANG THINK HE'S RUNNING OFF TO?

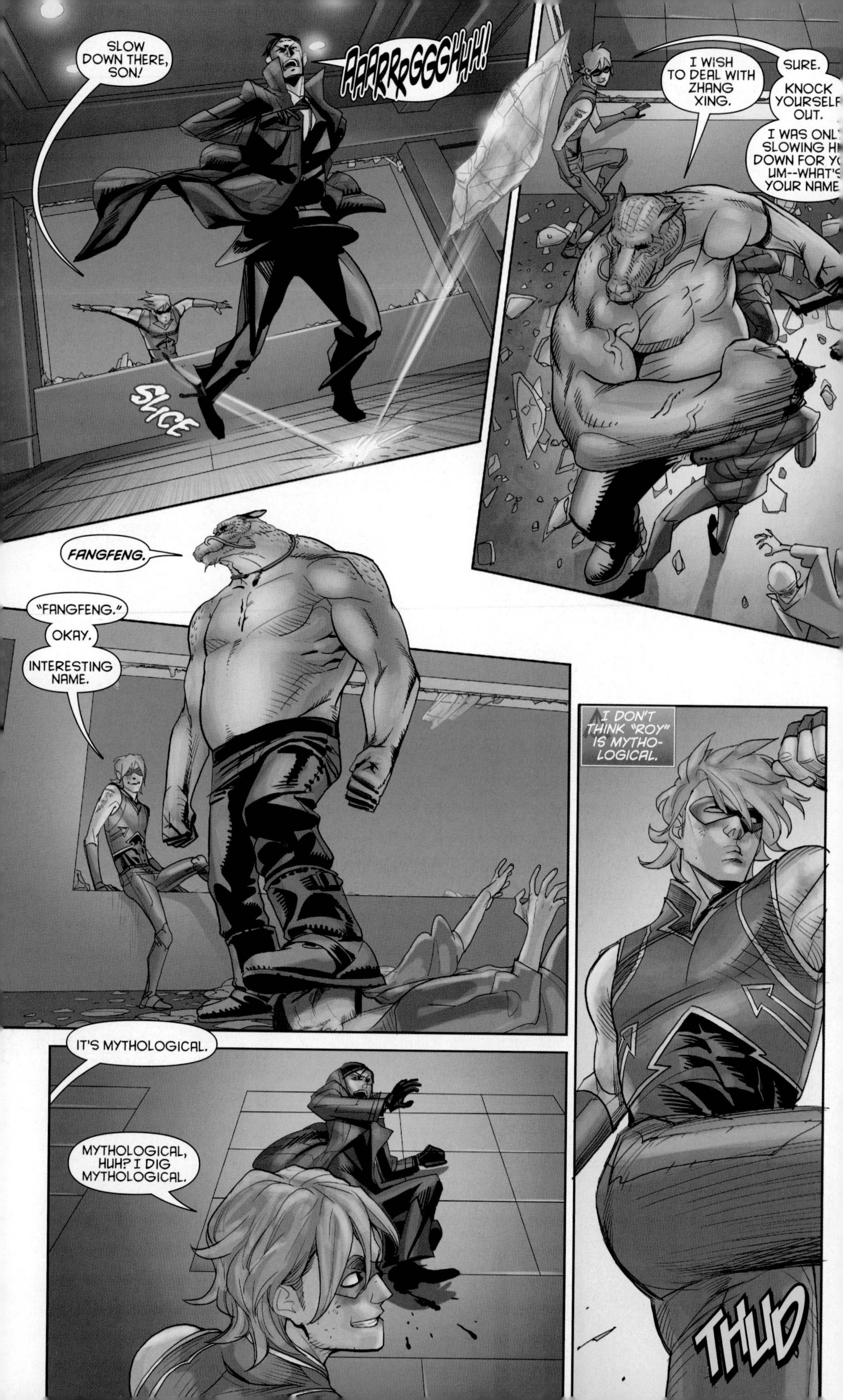
SLOW DOWN THERE, SON!
AAARRRGGGHHH!
SLICE
I WISH TO DEAL WITH ZHANG XING.
SURE.
KNOCK YOURSELF OUT.
FANGFENG.
"FANGFENG."
OKAY.
INTERESTING NAME.
IT'S MYTHOLOGICAL.
MYTHOLOGICAL, HUH? I DIG MYTHOLOGICAL.
I DON'T THINK "ROY" IS MYTHOLOGICAL.
THUD

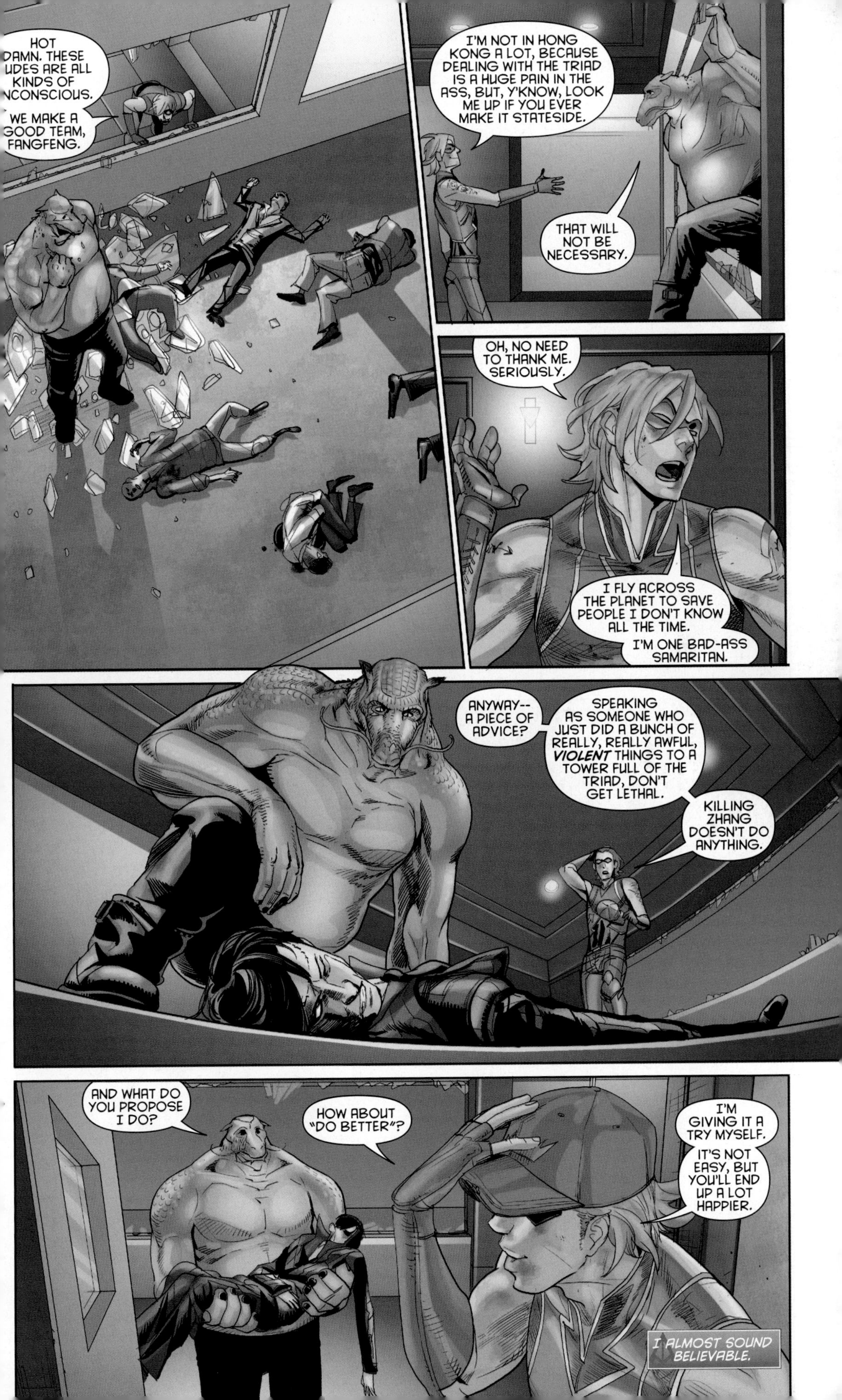
HOT DAMN. THESE DUDES ARE ALL KINDS OF UNCONSCIOUS.
WE MAKE A GOOD TEAM, FANGFENG.
I'M NOT IN HONG KONG A LOT, BECAUSE DEALING WITH THE TRIAD IS A HUGE PAIN IN THE ASS, BUT, Y'KNOW, LOOK ME UP IF YOU EVER MAKE IT STATESIDE.
THAT WILL NOT BE NECESSARY.
OH, NO NEED TO THANK ME. SERIOUSLY.
I FLY ACROSS THE PLANET TO SAVE PEOPLE I DON'T KNOW ALL THE TIME.
I'M ONE BAD-ASS SAMARITAN.
ANYWAY-- A PIECE OF ADVICE?
SPEAKING AS SOMEONE WHO JUST DID A BUNCH OF REALLY, REALLY AWFUL, VIOLENT THINGS TO A TOWER FULL OF THE TRIAD, DON'T GET LETHAL.
KILLING ZHANG DOESN'T DO ANYTHING.
AND WHAT DO YOU PROPOSE I DO?
HOW ABOUT "DO BETTER"?
I'M GIVING IT A TRY MYSELF.
IT'S NOT EASY, BUT YOU'LL END UP A LOT HAPPIER.
I ALMOST SOUND BELIEVABLE.

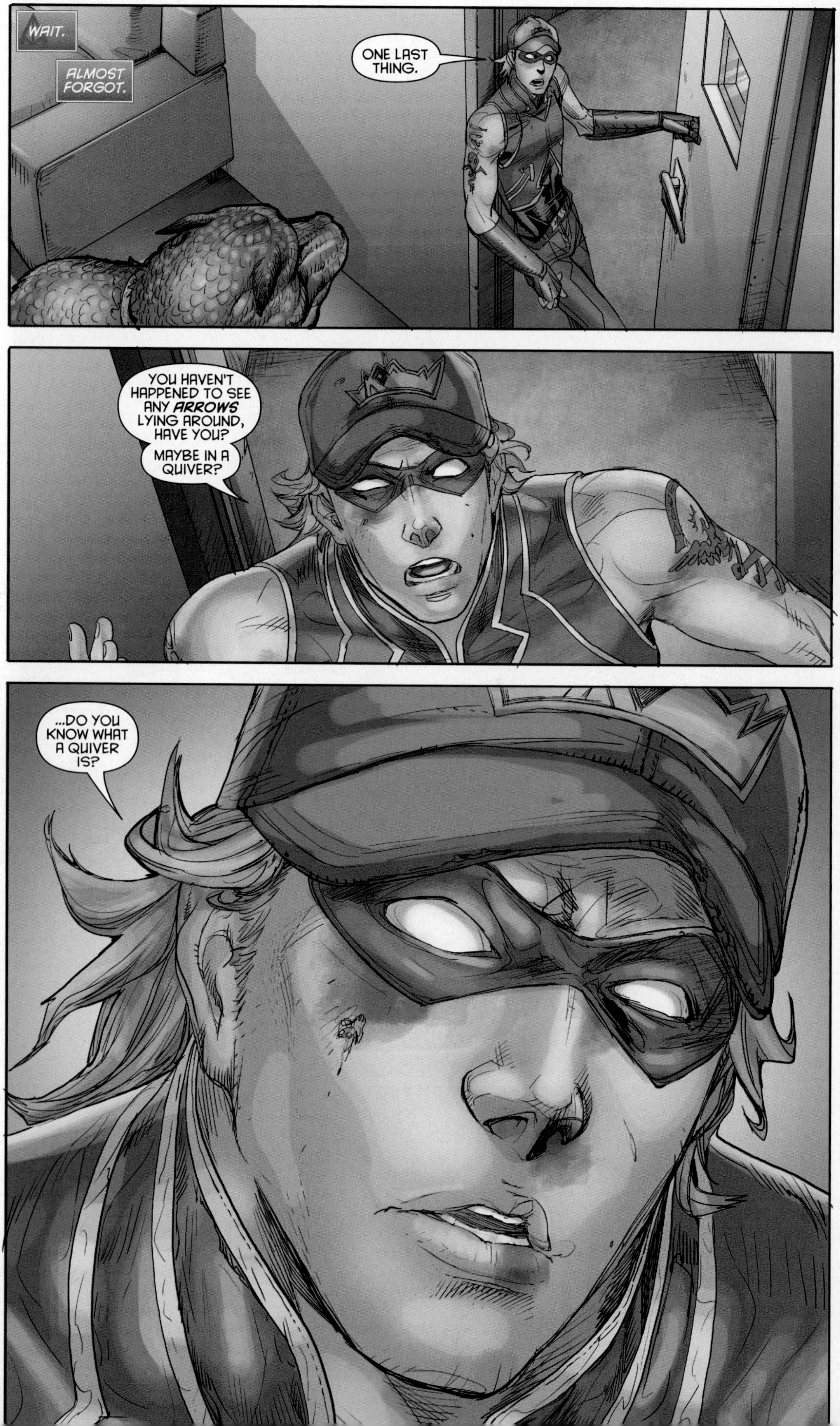
WAIT.
ALMOST FORGOT.
ONE LAST THING.
YOU HAVEN'T HAPPENED TO SEE ANY ARROWS LYING AROUND, HAVE YOU?
MAYBE IN A QUIVER?
...DO YOU KNOW WHAT A QUIVER IS?

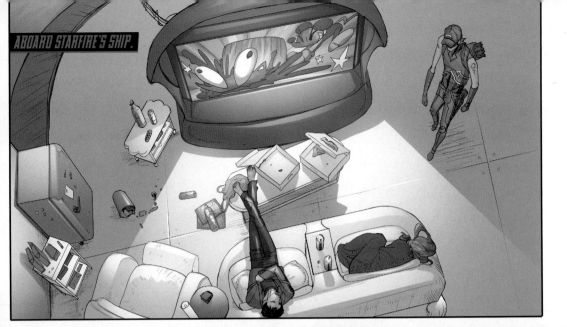

...ROY? WHERE HAVE YOU BEEN?

ME? SAME PLACE I ALWAYS GO.

MY FRIENDS MAY BE THE WORST...

NOWHERE.

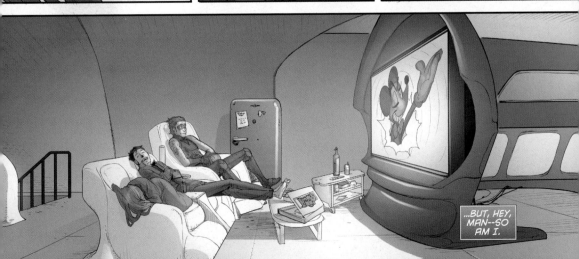

...BUT, HEY, MAN--SO AM I.

WITHOUT HONOR OR HUMANITY

JOE KEATINGE writer **FEDERICO DALLOCCHIO** artist cover art by **RYAN SOOK**

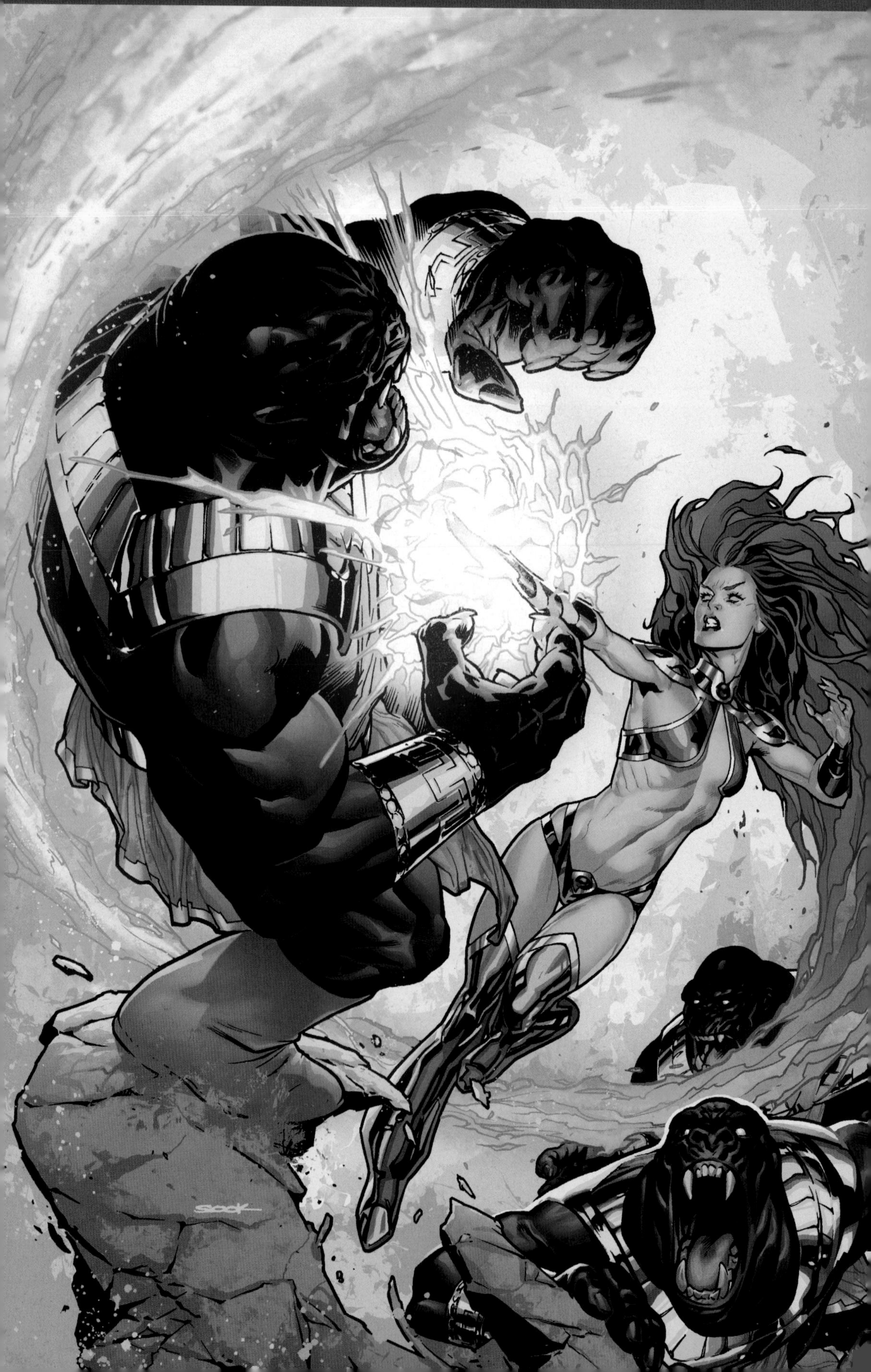

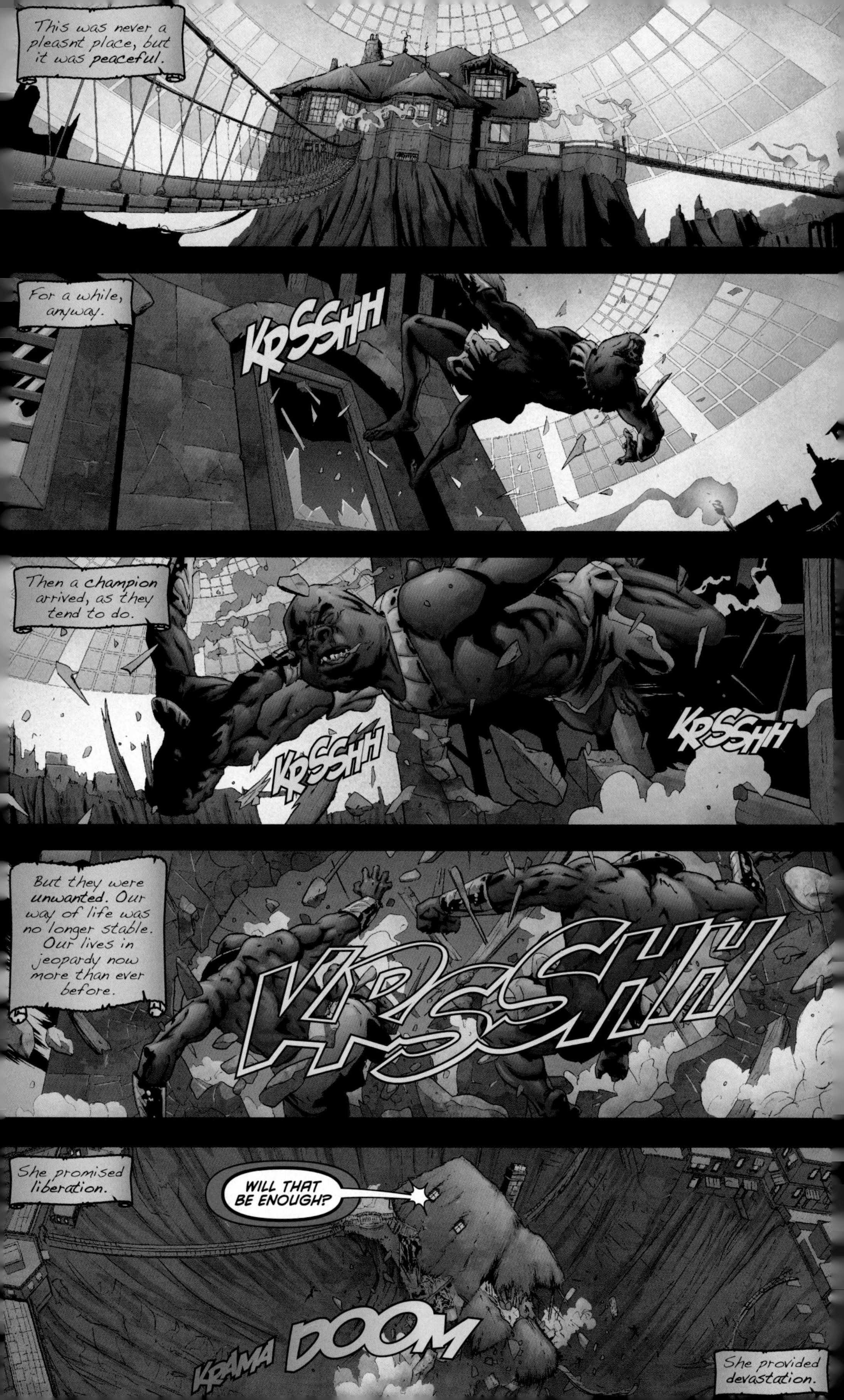

This was never a pleasnt place, but it was peaceful.
For a while, anyway.
KRSSHH
Then a champion arrived, as they tend to do.
KRSSHH
KRSSHH
But they were unwanted. Our way of life was no longer stable. Our lives in jeopardy now more than ever before.
KRSSHH
She promised liberation.
WILL THAT BE ENOUGH?
KRAMA DOOM
She provided devastation.

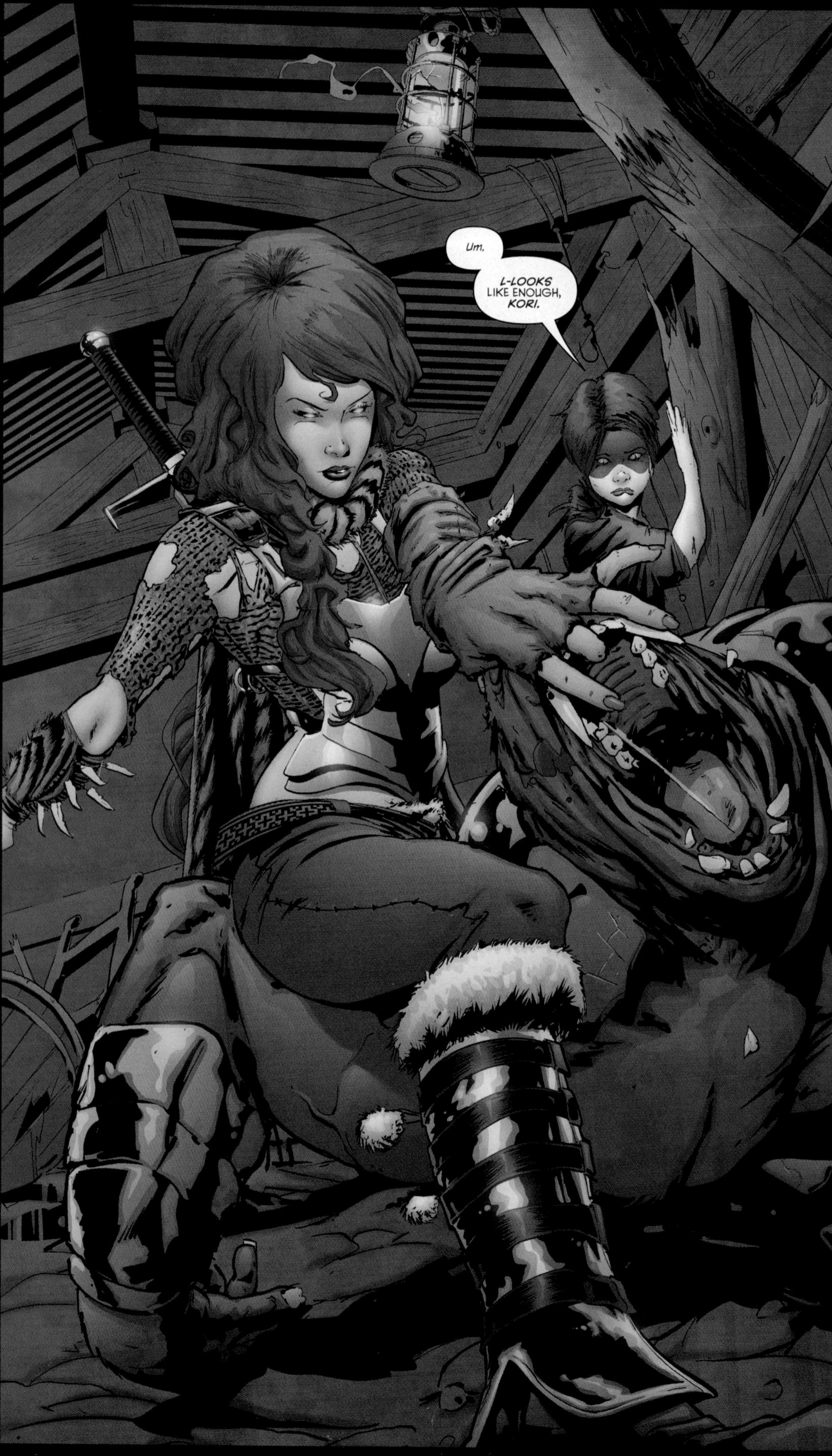
Um.
L-LOOKS LIKE ENOUGH, KORI.

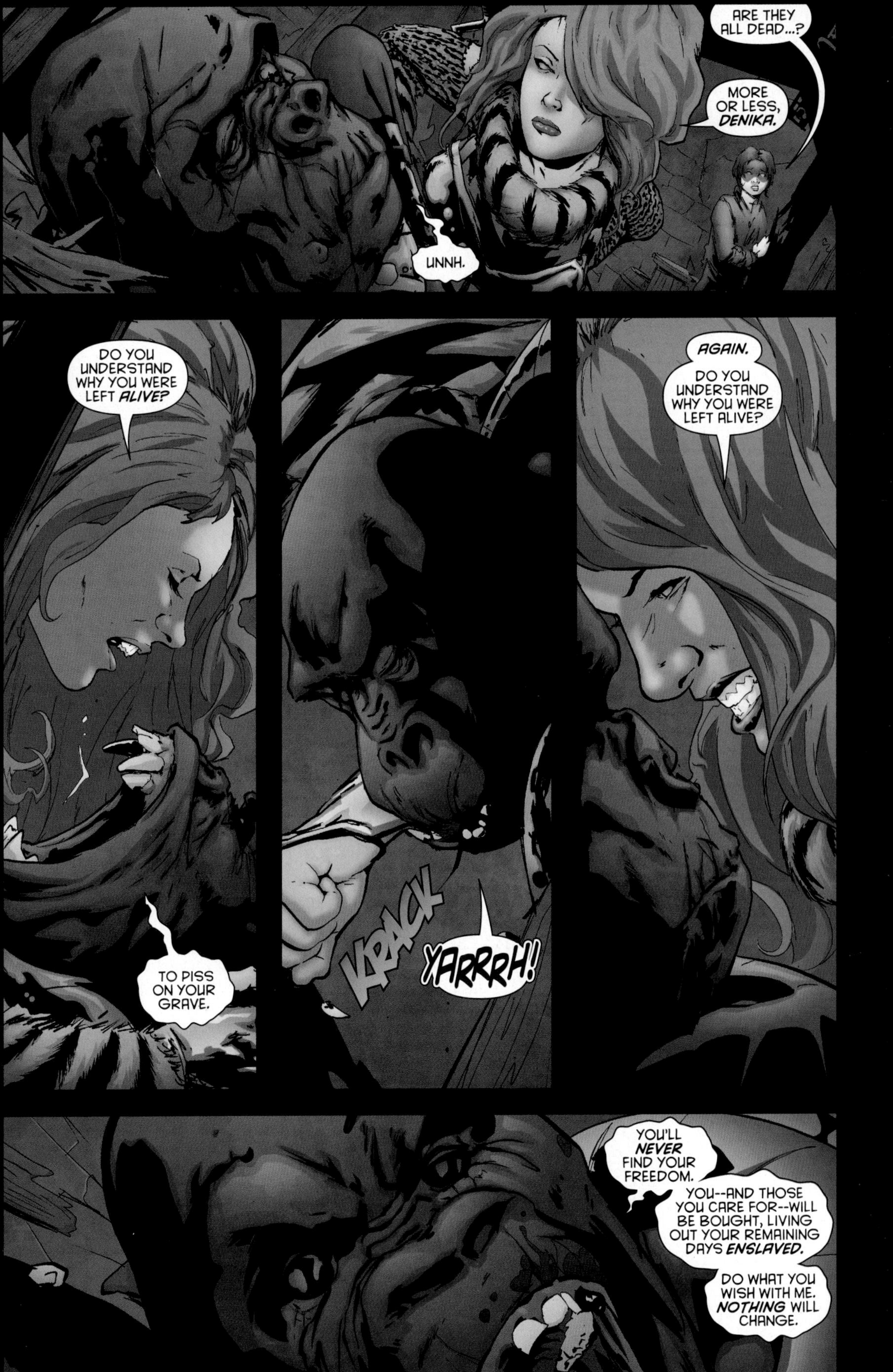

ARE THEY ALL DEAD...?
MORE OR LESS, *DENIKA.*
UNNH.
DO YOU UNDERSTAND WHY YOU WERE LEFT *ALIVE?*
TO PISS ON YOUR GRAVE.
KRACK
YARRRH!
AGAIN.
DO YOU UNDERSTAND WHY YOU WERE LEFT ALIVE?
YOU'LL *NEVER* FIND YOUR FREEDOM.
YOU--AND THOSE YOU CARE FOR--WILL BE BOUGHT, LIVING OUT YOUR REMAINING DAYS *ENSLAVED.*
DO WHAT YOU WISH WITH ME. *NOTHING* WILL CHANGE.

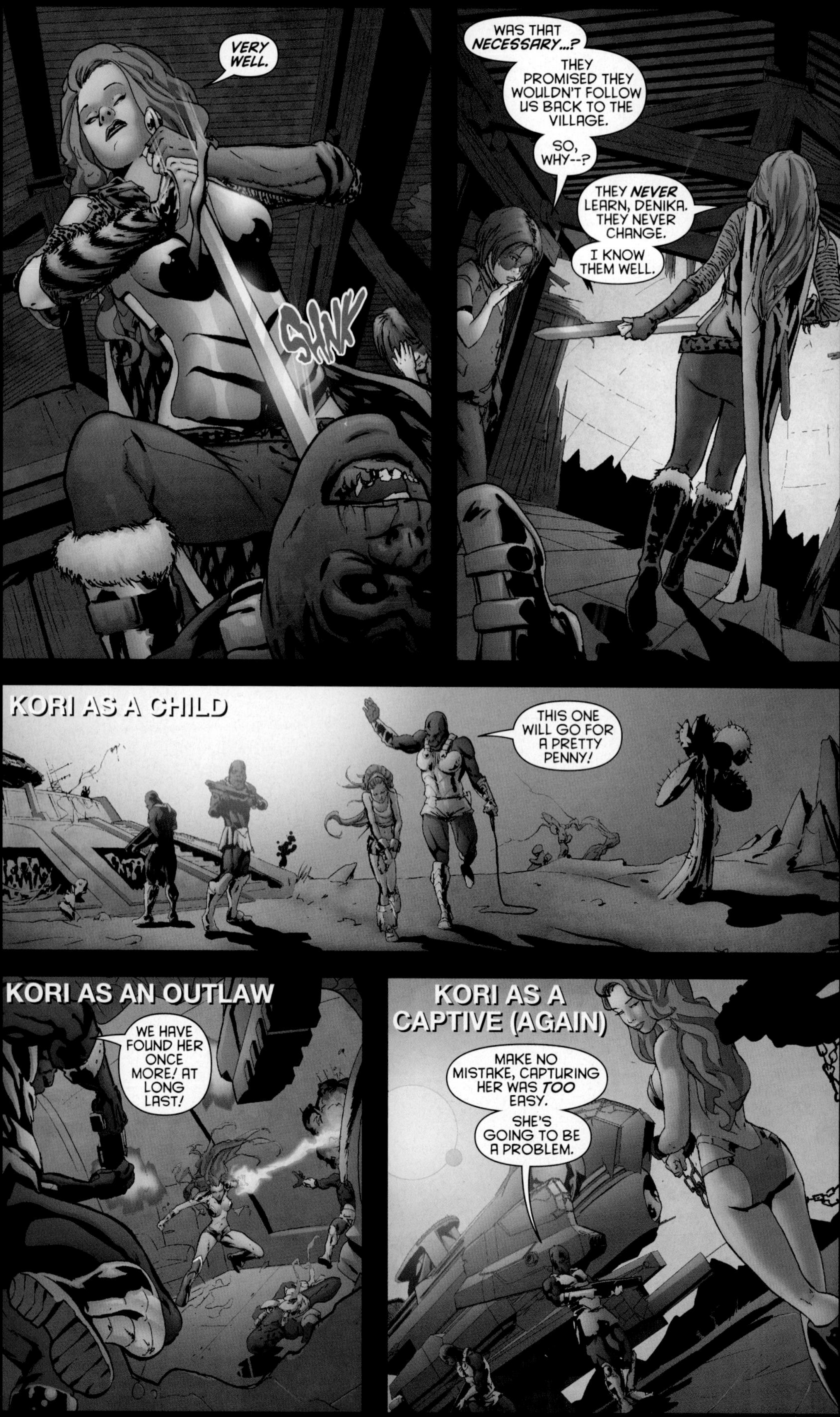
VERY WELL.
SHNK
WAS THAT NECESSARY...?
THEY PROMISED THEY WOULDN'T FOLLOW US BACK TO THE VILLAGE.
SO, WHY--?
THEY NEVER LEARN, DENIKA. THEY NEVER CHANGE.
I KNOW THEM WELL.
KORI AS A CHILD
THIS ONE WILL GO FOR A PRETTY PENNY!
KORI AS AN OUTLAW
WE HAVE FOUND HER ONCE MORE! AT LONG LAST!
KORI AS A CAPTIVE (AGAIN)
MAKE NO MISTAKE, CAPTURING HER WAS TOO EASY.
SHE'S GOING TO BE A PROBLEM.

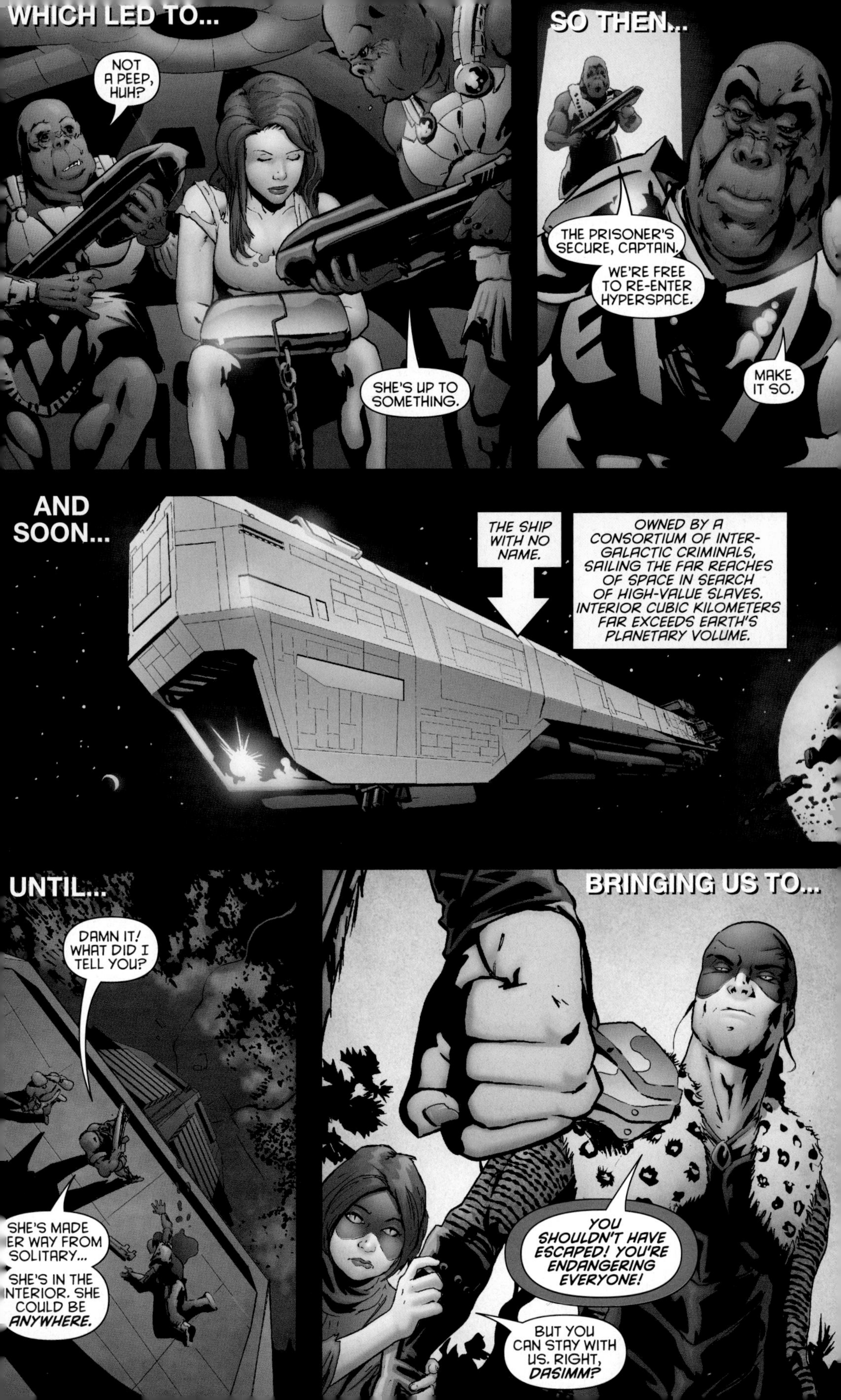

WHICH LED TO...
NOT A PEEP, HUH?
SHE'S UP TO SOMETHING.
SO THEN...
THE PRISONER'S SECURE, CAPTAIN.
WE'RE FREE TO RE-ENTER HYPERSPACE.
MAKE IT SO.
AND SOON...
THE SHIP WITH NO NAME.
OWNED BY A CONSORTIUM OF INTER-GALACTIC CRIMINALS, SAILING THE FAR REACHES OF SPACE IN SEARCH OF HIGH-VALUE SLAVES. INTERIOR CUBIC KILOMETERS FAR EXCEEDS EARTH'S PLANETARY VOLUME.
UNTIL...
DAMN IT! WHAT DID I TELL YOU?
SHE'S MADE ER WAY FROM SOLITARY...
SHE'S IN THE NTERIOR. SHE COULD BE ANYWHERE.
BRINGING US TO...
YOU SHOULDN'T HAVE ESCAPED! YOU'RE ENDANGERING EVERYONE!
BUT YOU CAN STAY WITH US. RIGHT, DASIMM?

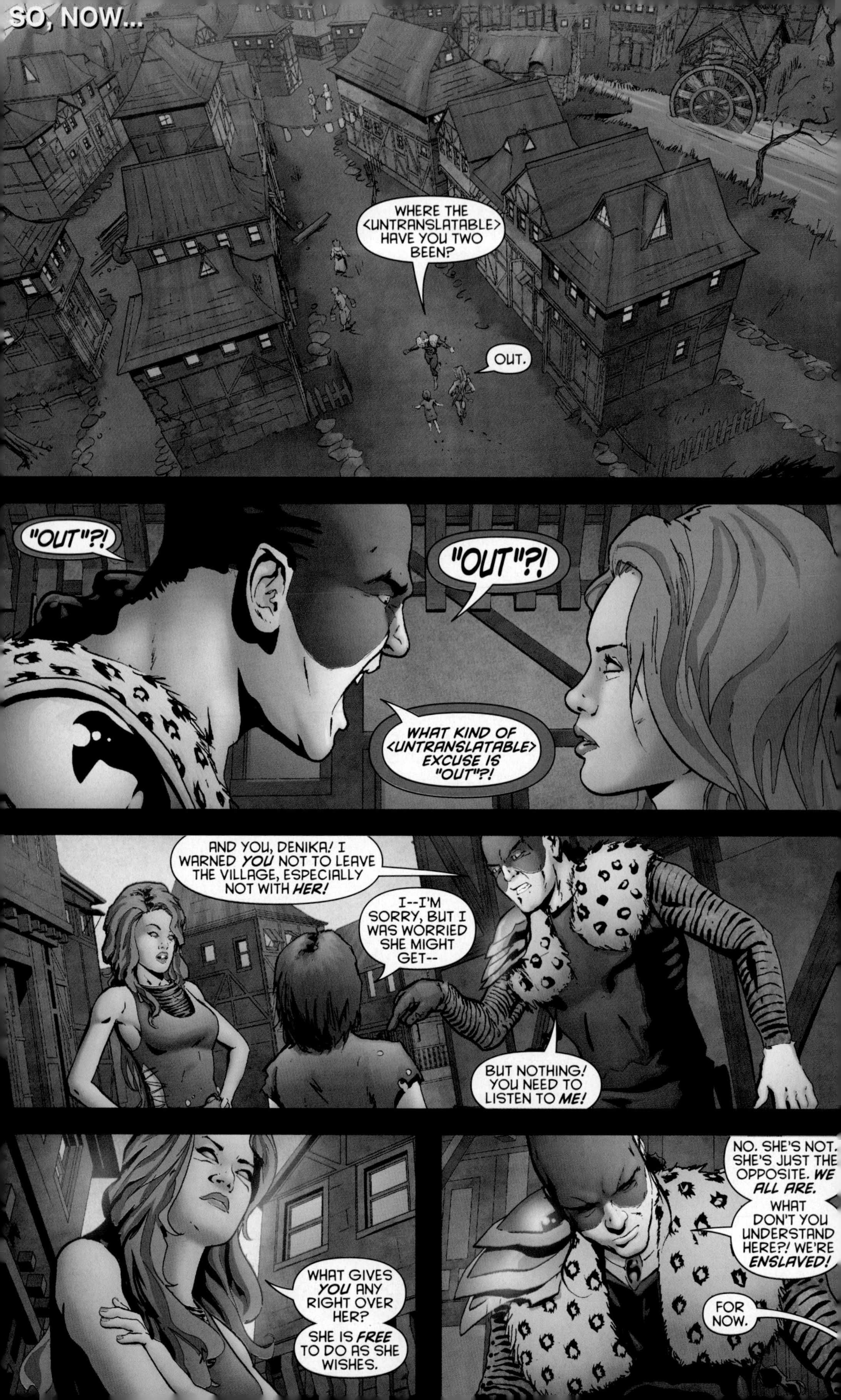

SO, NOW...
WHERE THE <UNTRANSLATABLE> HAVE YOU TWO BEEN?
OUT.
"OUT"?!
"OUT"?!
WHAT KIND OF <UNTRANSLATABLE> EXCUSE IS "OUT"?!
AND YOU, DENIKA! I WARNED *YOU* NOT TO LEAVE THE VILLAGE, ESPECIALLY NOT WITH *HER!*
I--I'M SORRY, BUT I WAS WORRIED SHE MIGHT GET--
BUT NOTHING! YOU NEED TO LISTEN TO *ME!*
WHAT GIVES *YOU* ANY RIGHT OVER HER?
SHE IS *FREE* TO DO AS SHE WISHES.
NO. SHE'S NOT. SHE'S JUST THE OPPOSITE. *WE ALL ARE.*
WHAT DON'T YOU UNDERSTAND HERE?! WE'RE *ENSLAVED!*
FOR NOW.

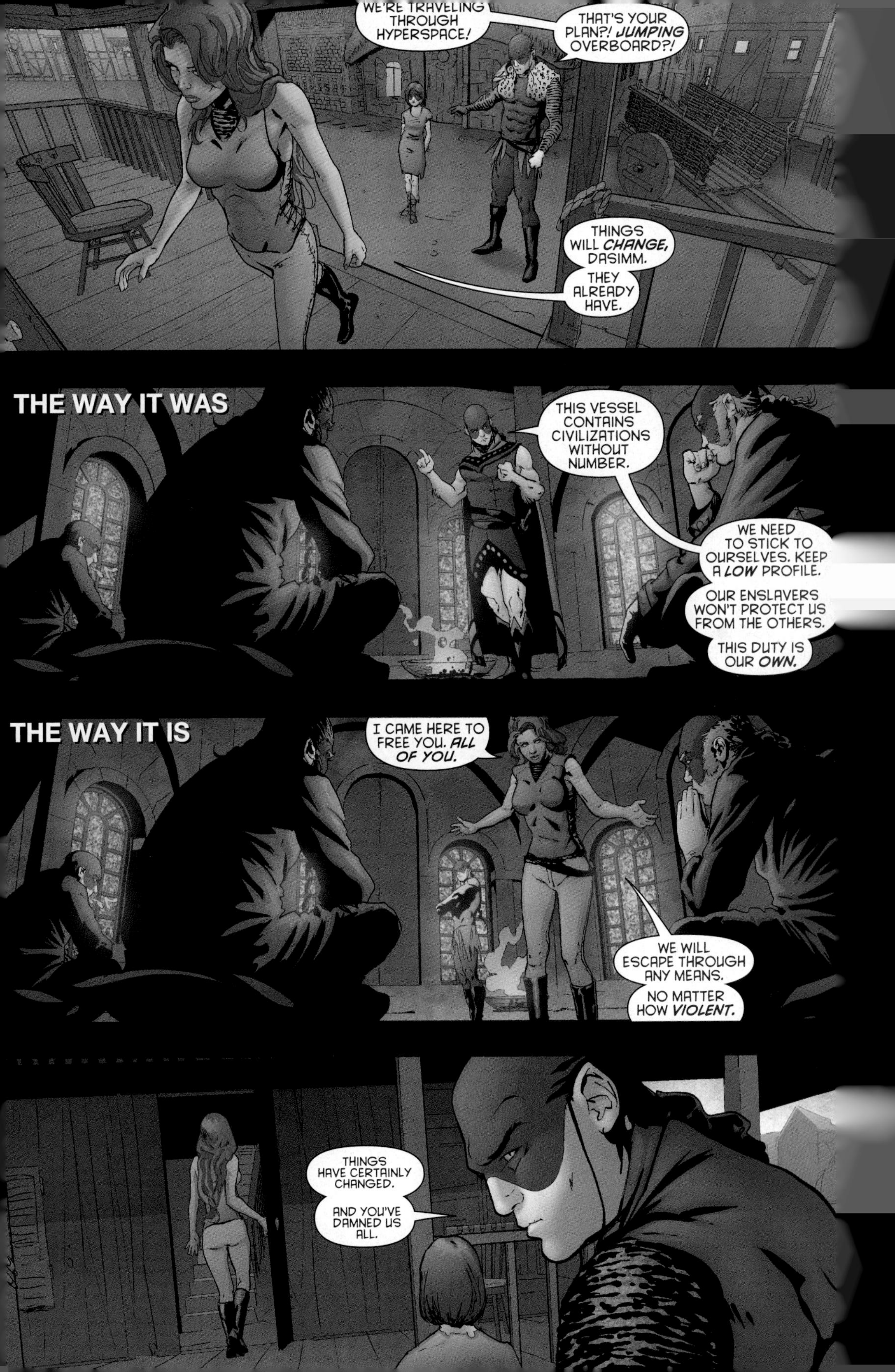
WE'RE TRAVELING THROUGH HYPERSPACE!
THAT'S YOUR PLAN?! JUMPING OVERBOARD?!
THINGS WILL CHANGE, DASIMM.
THEY ALREADY HAVE.
THE WAY IT WAS
THIS VESSEL CONTAINS CIVILIZATIONS WITHOUT NUMBER.
WE NEED TO STICK TO OURSELVES. KEEP A LOW PROFILE.
OUR ENSLAVERS WON'T PROTECT US FROM THE OTHERS.
THIS DUTY IS OUR OWN.
THE WAY IT IS
I CAME HERE TO FREE YOU. ALL OF YOU.
WE WILL ESCAPE THROUGH ANY MEANS.
NO MATTER HOW VIOLENT.
THINGS HAVE CERTAINLY CHANGED.
AND YOU'VE DAMNED US ALL.

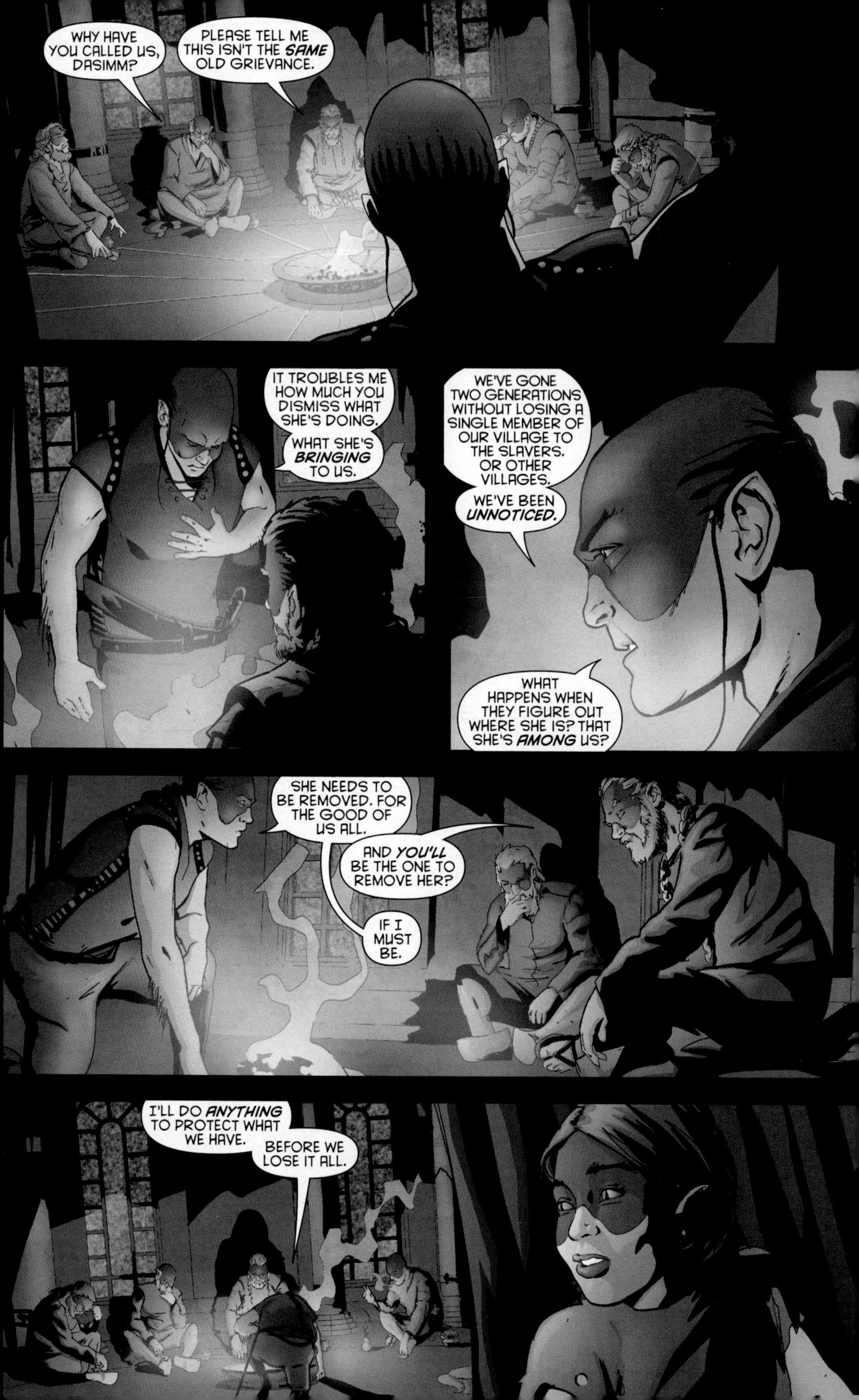
WHY HAVE YOU CALLED US, DASIMM?
PLEASE TELL ME THIS ISN'T THE *SAME* OLD GRIEVANCE.
IT TROUBLES ME HOW MUCH YOU DISMISS WHAT SHE'S DOING.
WHAT SHE'S *BRINGING* TO US.
WE'VE GONE TWO GENERATIONS WITHOUT LOSING A SINGLE MEMBER OF OUR VILLAGE TO THE SLAVERS. OR OTHER VILLAGES.
WE'VE BEEN *UNNOTICED.*
WHAT HAPPENS WHEN THEY FIGURE OUT WHERE SHE IS? THAT SHE'S *AMONG* US?
SHE NEEDS TO BE REMOVED. FOR THE GOOD OF US ALL.
AND *YOU'LL* BE THE ONE TO REMOVE HER?
IF I MUST BE.
I'LL DO *ANYTHING* TO PROTECT WHAT WE HAVE.
BEFORE WE LOSE IT ALL.

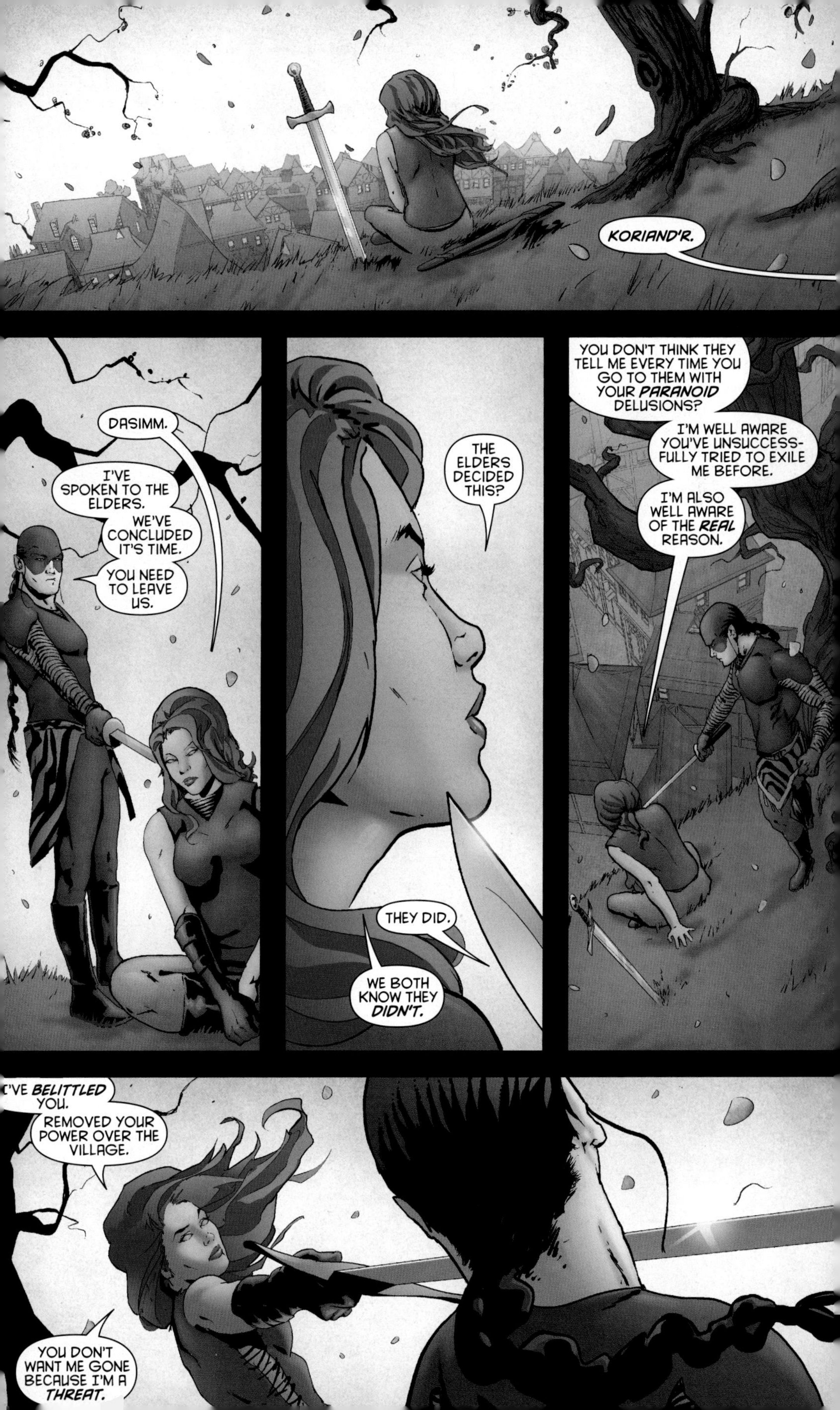
KORIAND'R.
DASIMM.
I'VE SPOKEN TO THE ELDERS.
WE'VE CONCLUDED IT'S TIME.
YOU NEED TO LEAVE US.
THE ELDERS DECIDED THIS?
THEY DID.
WE BOTH KNOW THEY *DIDN'T.*
YOU DON'T THINK THEY TELL ME EVERY TIME YOU GO TO THEM WITH YOUR *PARANOID* DELUSIONS?
I'M WELL AWARE YOU'VE UNSUCCESS-FULLY TRIED TO EXILE ME BEFORE.
I'M ALSO WELL AWARE OF THE *REAL* REASON.
I'VE *BELITTLED* YOU.
REMOVED YOUR POWER OVER THE VILLAGE.
YOU DON'T WANT ME GONE BECAUSE I'M A *THREAT.*

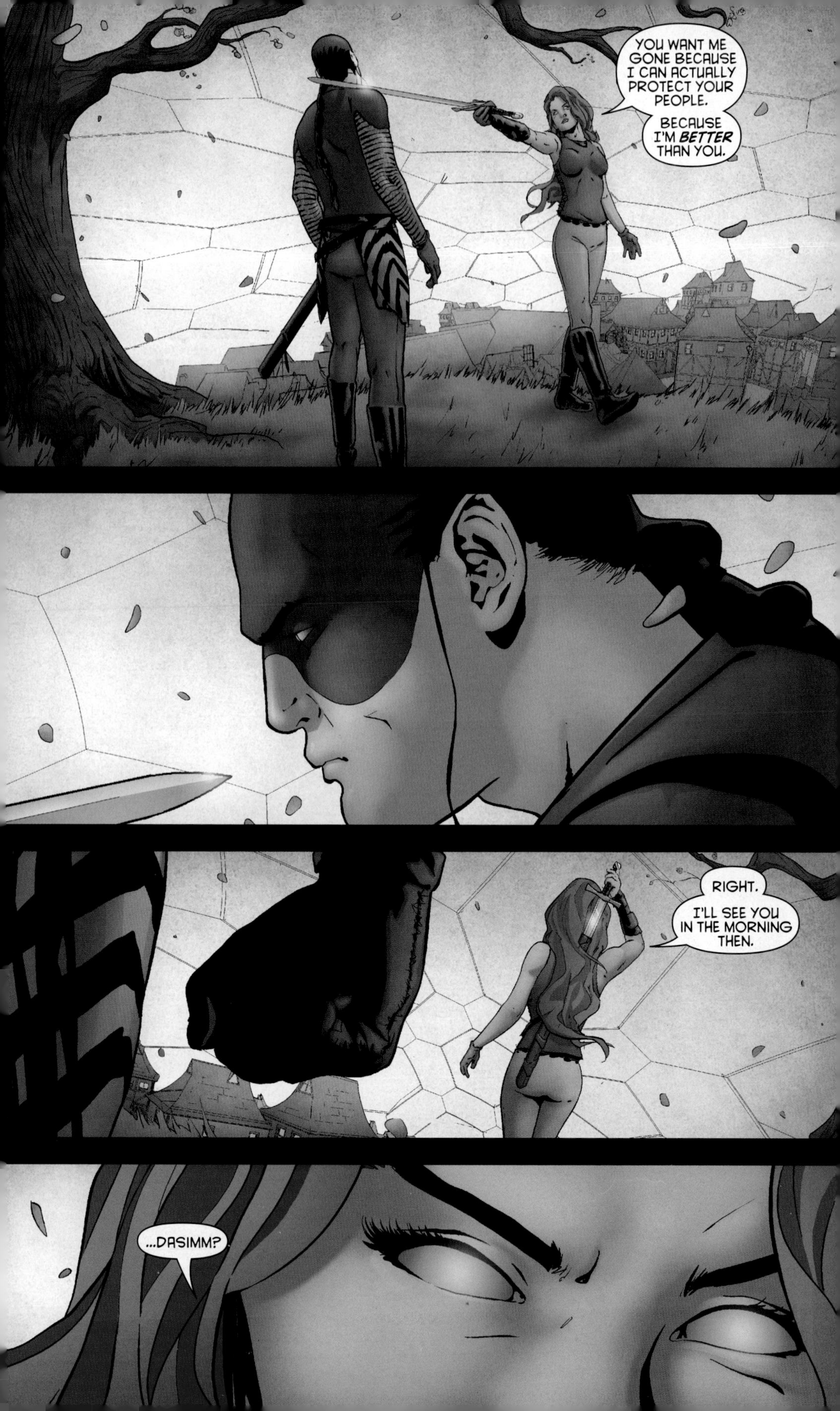
YOU WANT ME GONE BECAUSE I CAN ACTUALLY PROTECT YOUR PEOPLE.
BECAUSE I'M ***BETTER*** THAN YOU.
RIGHT.
I'LL SEE YOU IN THE MORNING THEN.
...DASIMM?

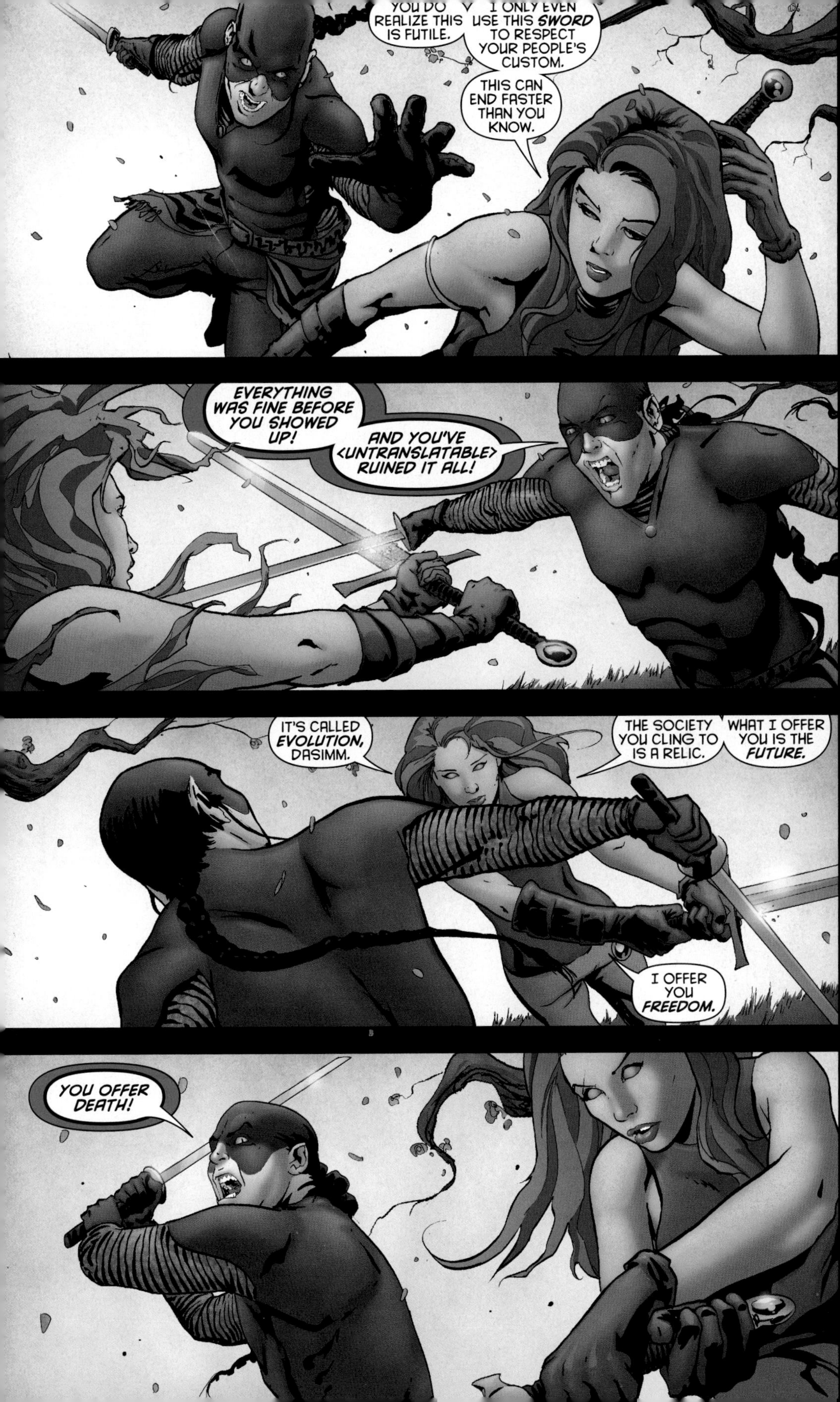
YOU DO REALIZE THIS IS FUTILE.
I ONLY EVEN USE THIS SWORD TO RESPECT YOUR PEOPLE'S CUSTOM.
THIS CAN END FASTER THAN YOU KNOW.
EVERYTHING WAS FINE BEFORE YOU SHOWED UP!
AND YOU'VE <UNTRANSLATABLE> RUINED IT ALL!
IT'S CALLED EVOLUTION, DASIMM.
THE SOCIETY YOU CLING TO IS A RELIC.
WHAT I OFFER YOU IS THE FUTURE.
I OFFER YOU FREEDOM.
YOU OFFER DEATH!

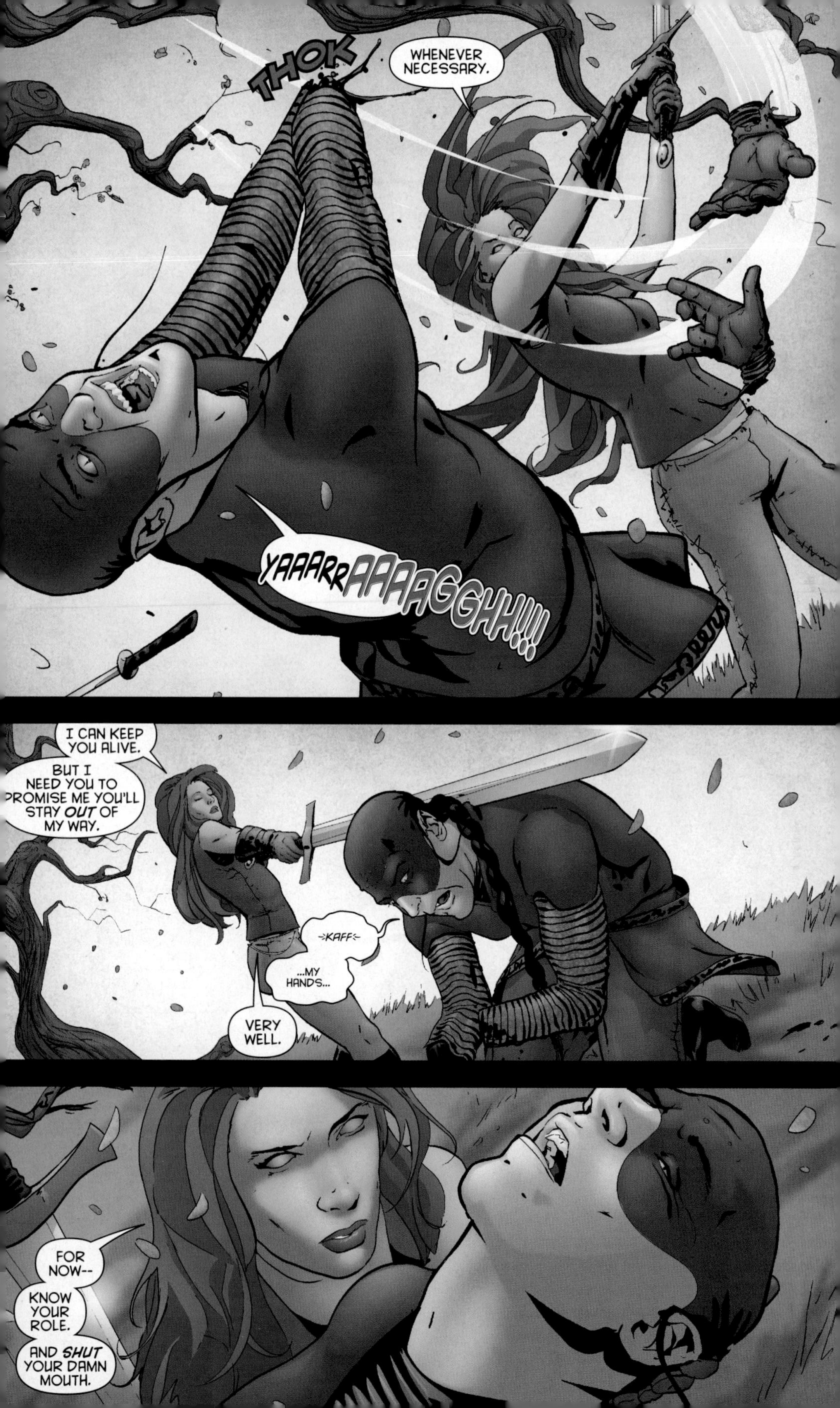
THOK
WHENEVER NECESSARY.
YAAARRAAAAGGHH!!!
I CAN KEEP YOU ALIVE.
BUT I NEED YOU TO PROMISE ME YOU'LL STAY OUT OF MY WAY.
KAFF
...MY HANDS...
VERY WELL.
FOR NOW--
KNOW YOUR ROLE.
AND SHUT YOUR DAMN MOUTH.

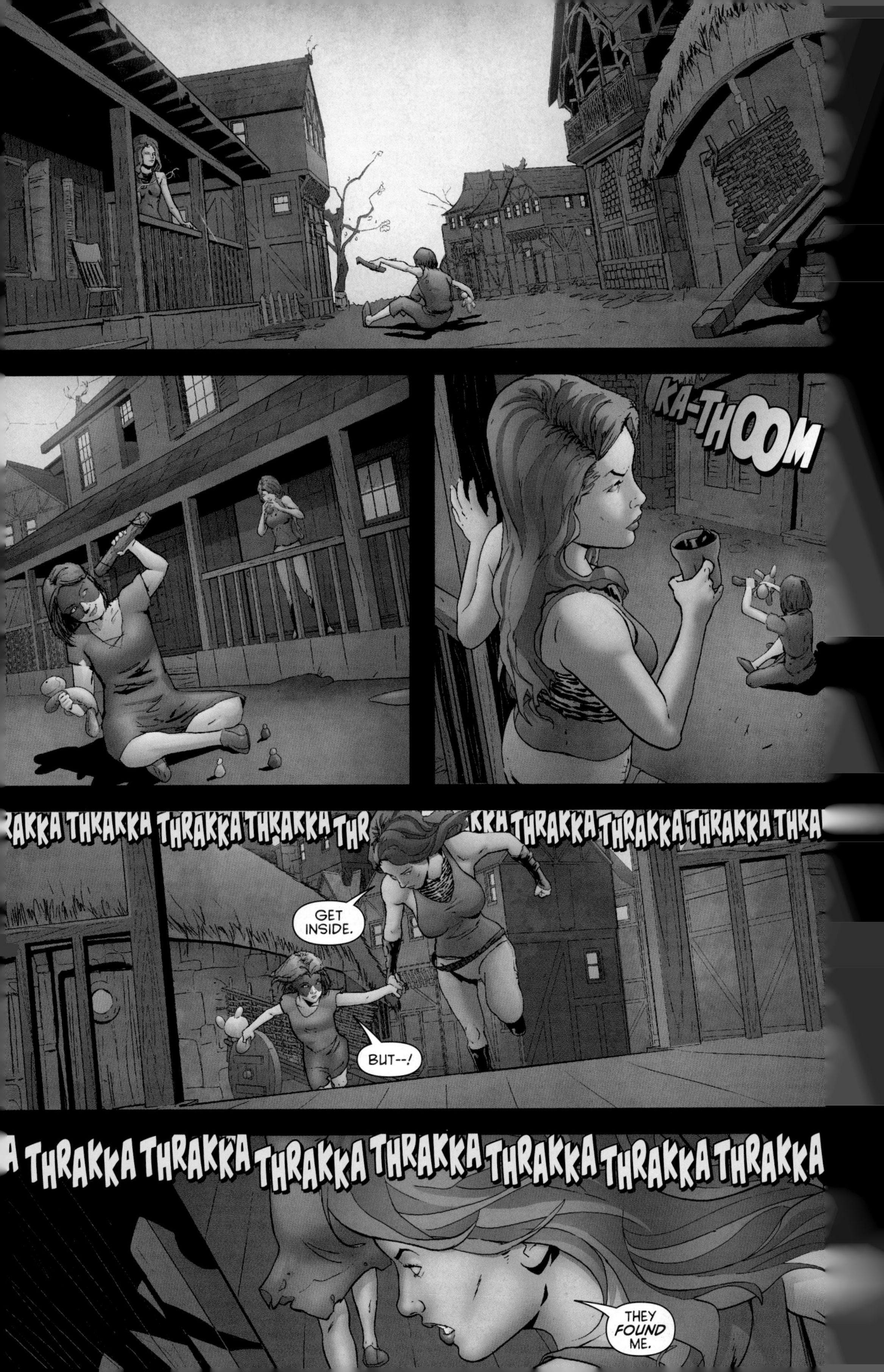

KA-THOOM
THRAKKA THRAKKA THRAKKA THRAKKA
GET INSIDE.
BUT--!
THRAKKA THRAKKA THRAKKA THRAKKA THRAKKA THRAKKA THRAKKA
THEY *FOUND* ME.

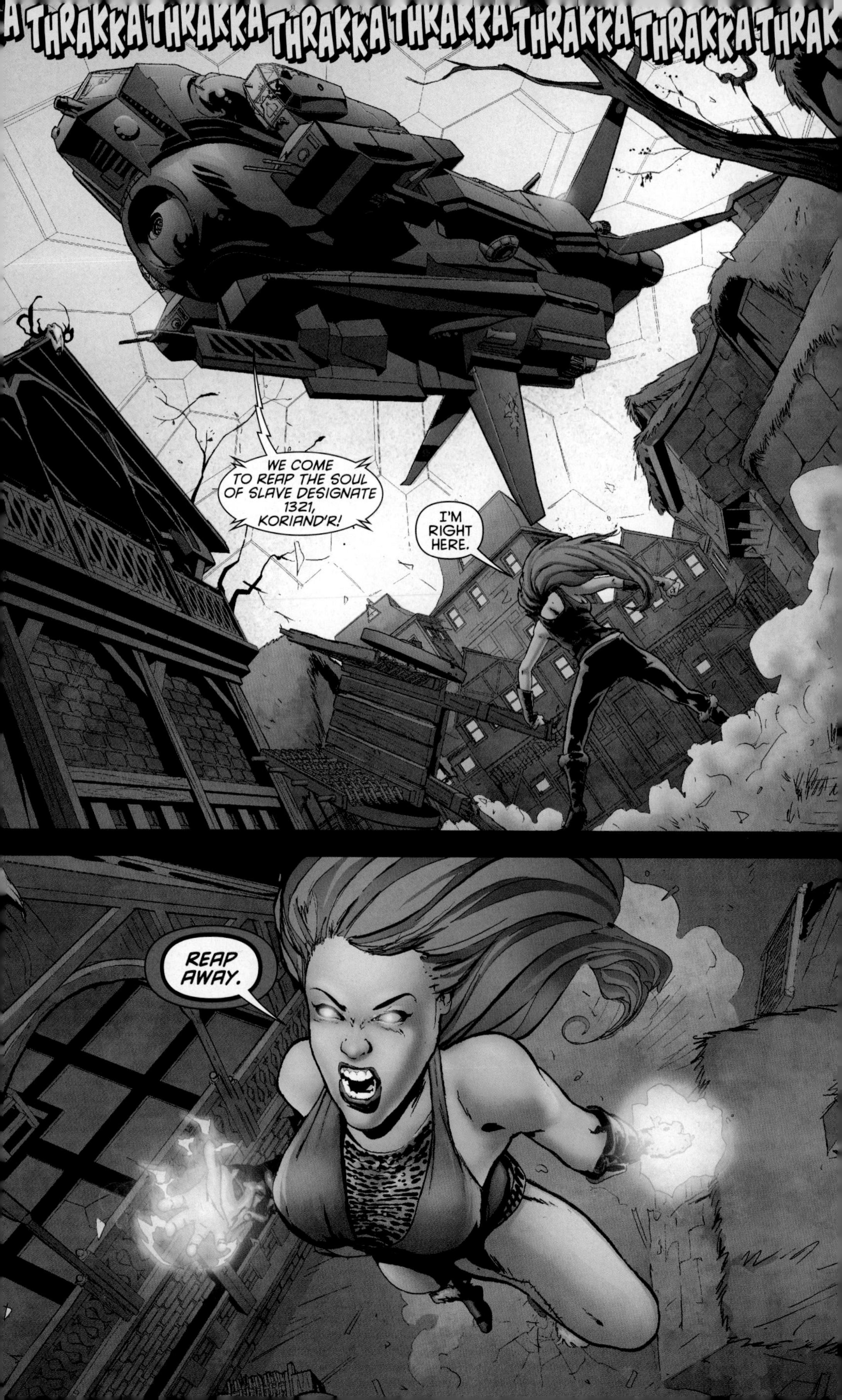
A THRAKKA THRAKKA THRAKKA THRAKKA THRAKKA THRAKKA THRAK
WE COME TO REAP THE SOUL OF SLAVE DESIGNATE 1321, KORIAND'R!
I'M RIGHT HERE.
REAP AWAY.

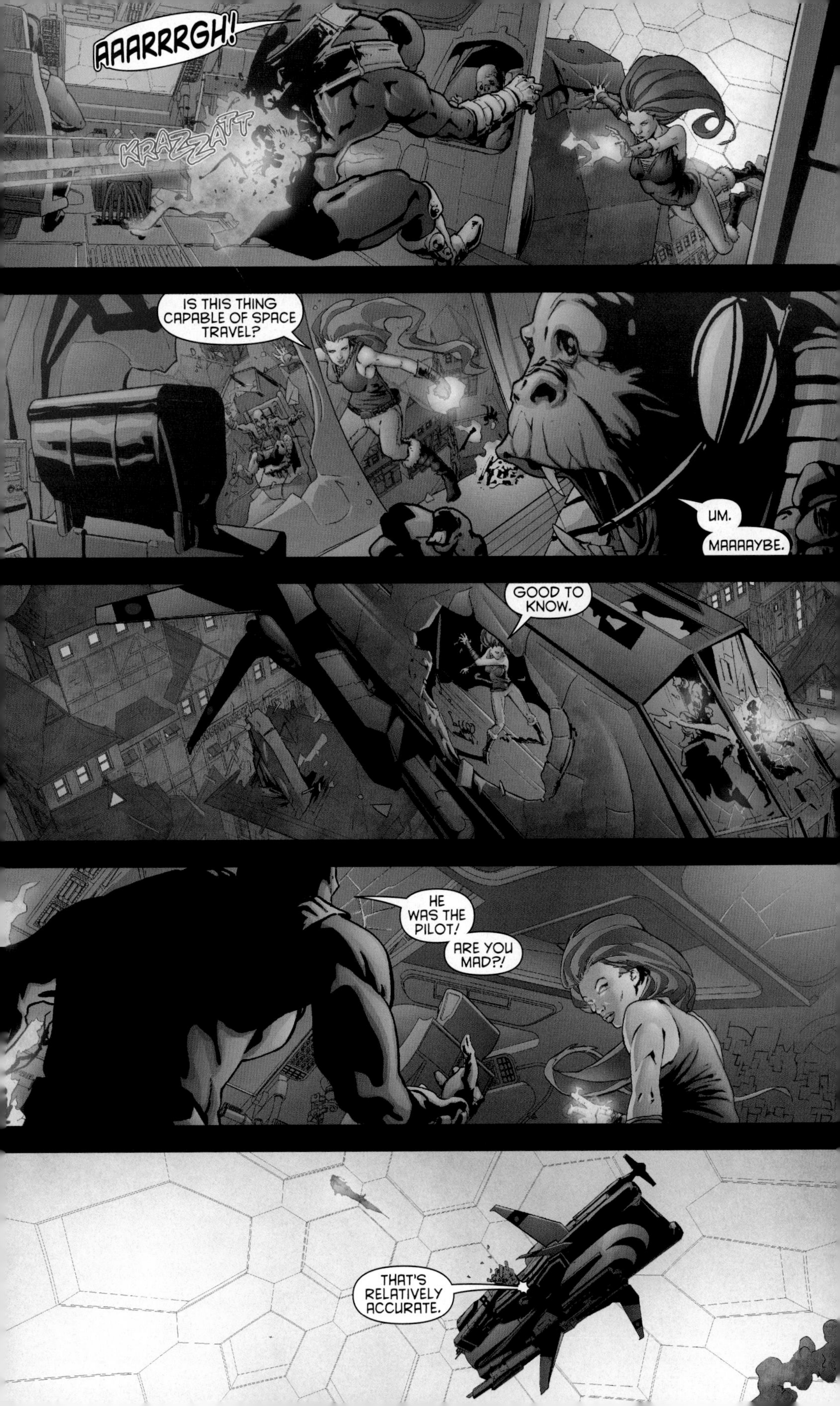
AAARRRGH!
KRAZZATT
IS THIS THING CAPABLE OF SPACE TRAVEL?
UM.
MAAAAYBE.
GOOD TO KNOW.
HE WAS THE PILOT!
ARE YOU MAD?!
THAT'S RELATIVELY ACCURATE.

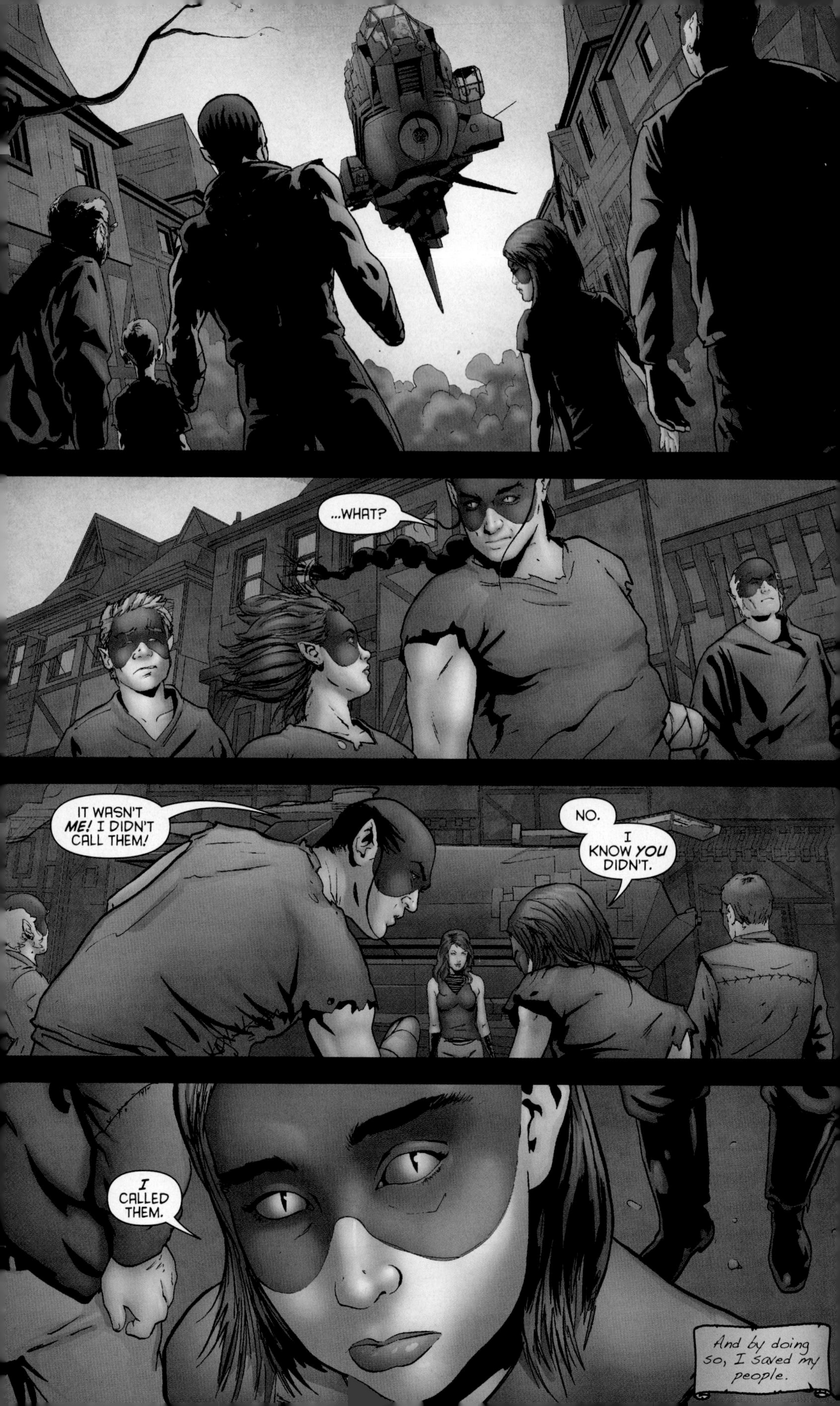
...WHAT?
IT WASN'T *ME!* I DIDN'T CALL THEM!
NO.
I KNOW *YOU* DIDN'T.
I CALLED THEM.
And by doing so, I saved my people.

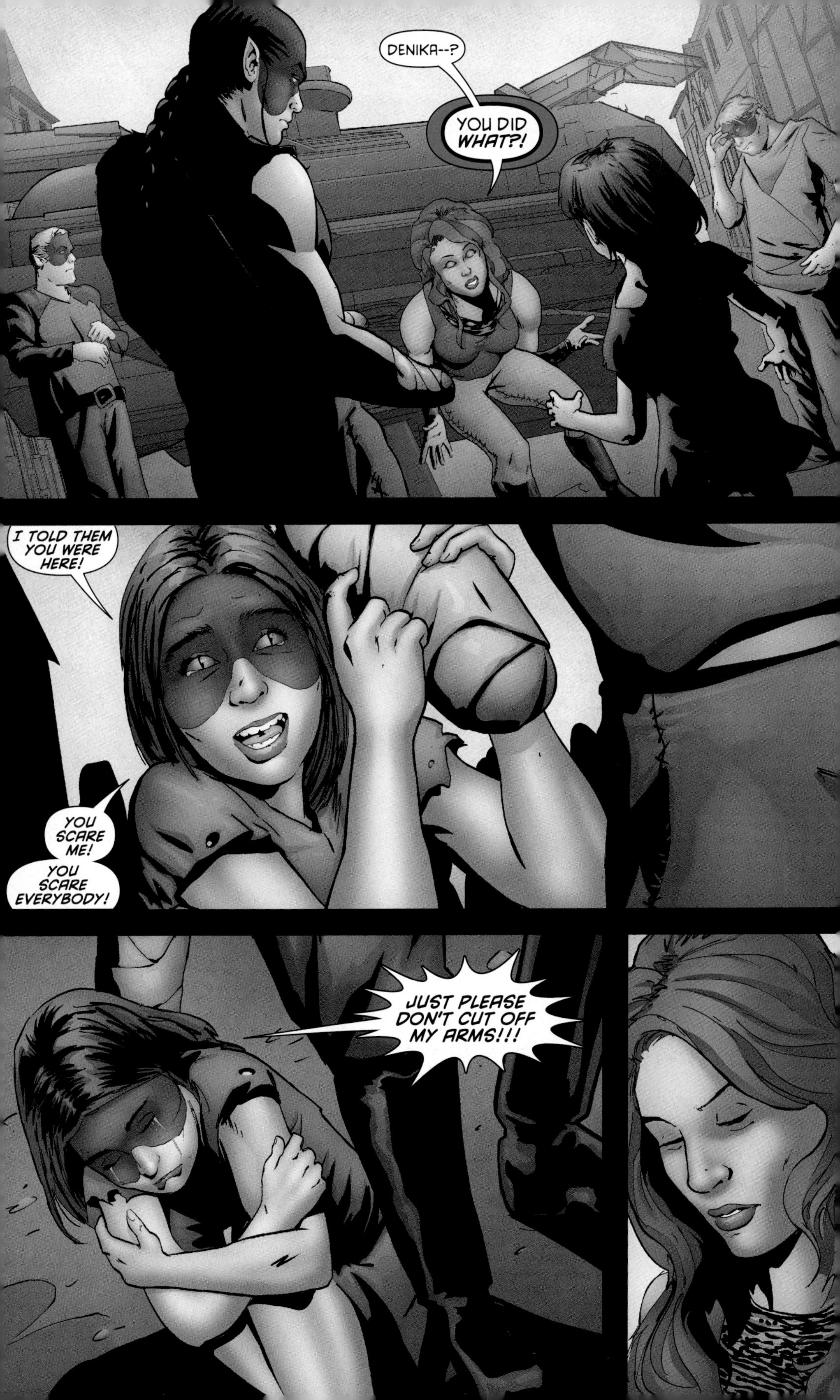
DENIKA--?
YOU DID WHAT?!
I TOLD THEM YOU WERE HERE!
YOU SCARE ME!
YOU SCARE EVERYBODY!
JUST PLEASE DON'T CUT OFF MY ARMS!!!

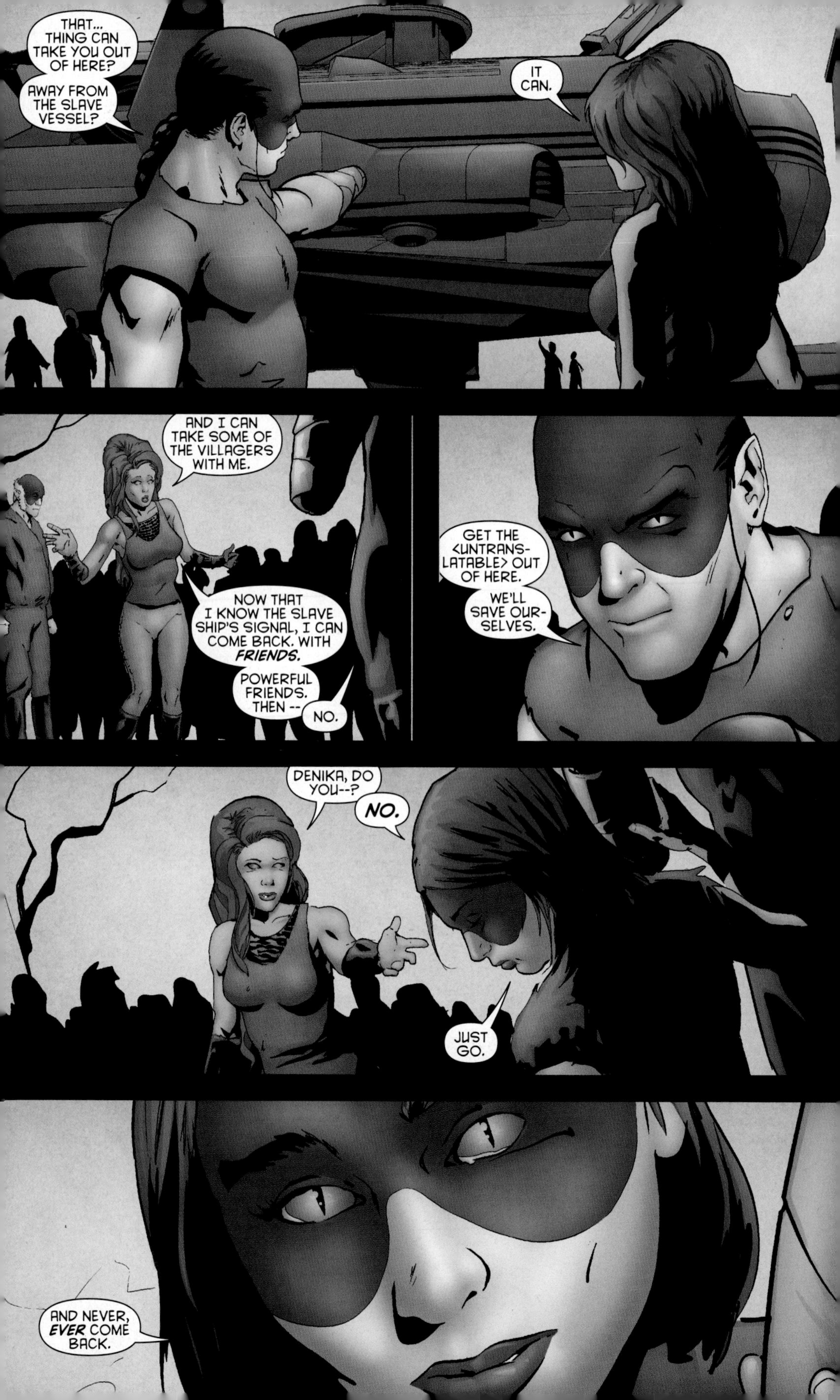
THAT... THING CAN TAKE YOU OUT OF HERE?
AWAY FROM THE SLAVE VESSEL?
IT CAN.
AND I CAN TAKE SOME OF THE VILLAGERS WITH ME.
NOW THAT I KNOW THE SLAVE SHIP'S SIGNAL, I CAN COME BACK. WITH *FRIENDS.*
POWERFUL FRIENDS. THEN --
NO.
GET THE <UNTRANSLATABLE> OUT OF HERE.
WE'LL SAVE OURSELVES.
DENIKA, DO YOU--?
NO.
JUST GO.
AND NEVER, *EVER* COME BACK.

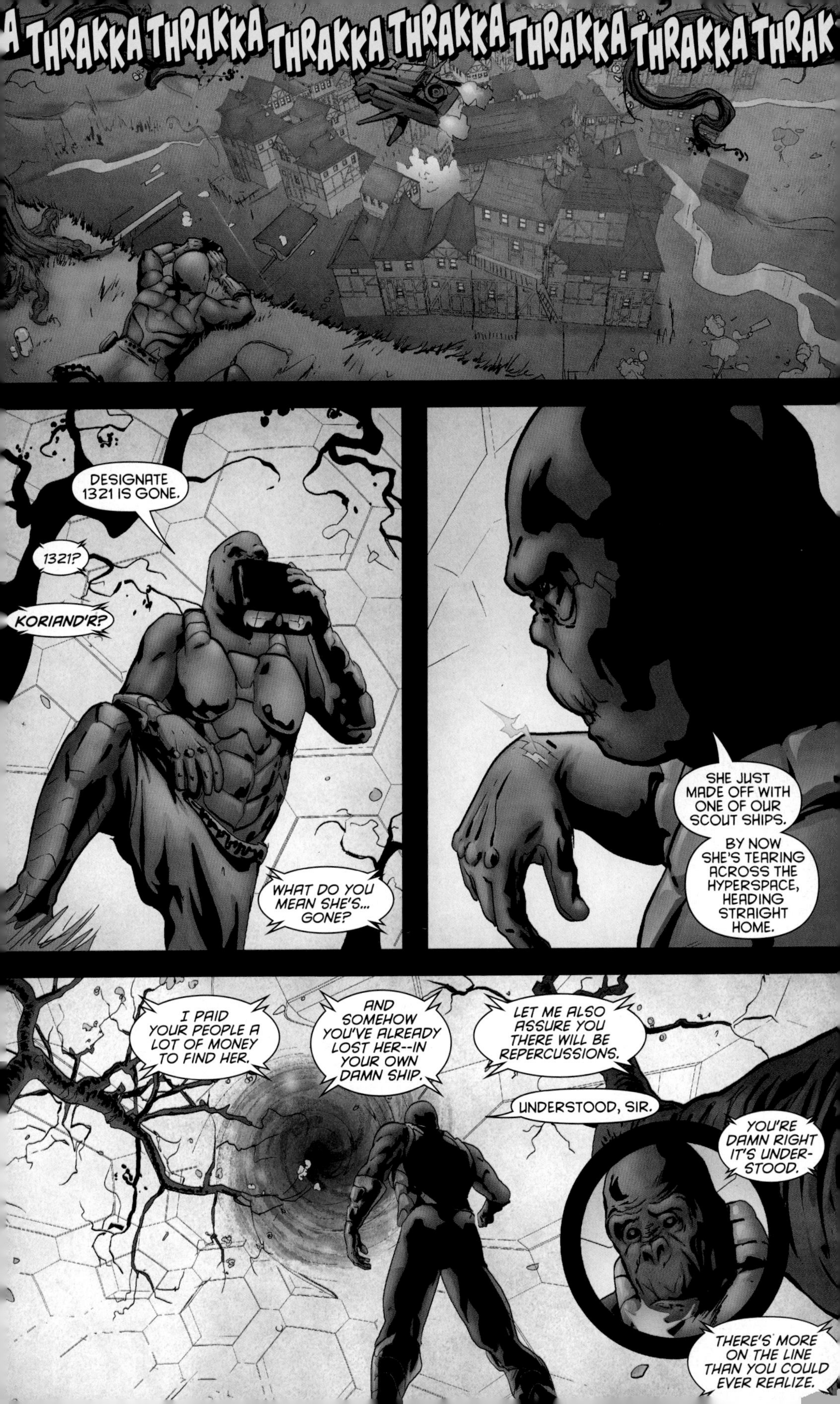
A THRAKKA THRAKKA THRAKKA THRAKKA THRAKKA THRAKKA THRAK
DESIGNATE 1321 IS GONE.
1321?
KORIAND'R?
WHAT DO YOU MEAN SHE'S... GONE?
SHE JUST MADE OFF WITH ONE OF OUR SCOUT SHIPS.
BY NOW SHE'S TEARING ACROSS THE HYPERSPACE, HEADING STRAIGHT HOME.
I PAID YOUR PEOPLE A LOT OF MONEY TO FIND HER.
AND SOMEHOW YOU'VE ALREADY LOST HER--IN YOUR OWN DAMN SHIP.
LET ME ALSO ASSURE YOU THERE WILL BE REPERCUSSIONS.
UNDERSTOOD, SIR.
YOU'RE DAMN RIGHT IT'S UNDER-STOOD.
THERE'S MORE ON THE LINE THAN YOU COULD EVER REALIZE.

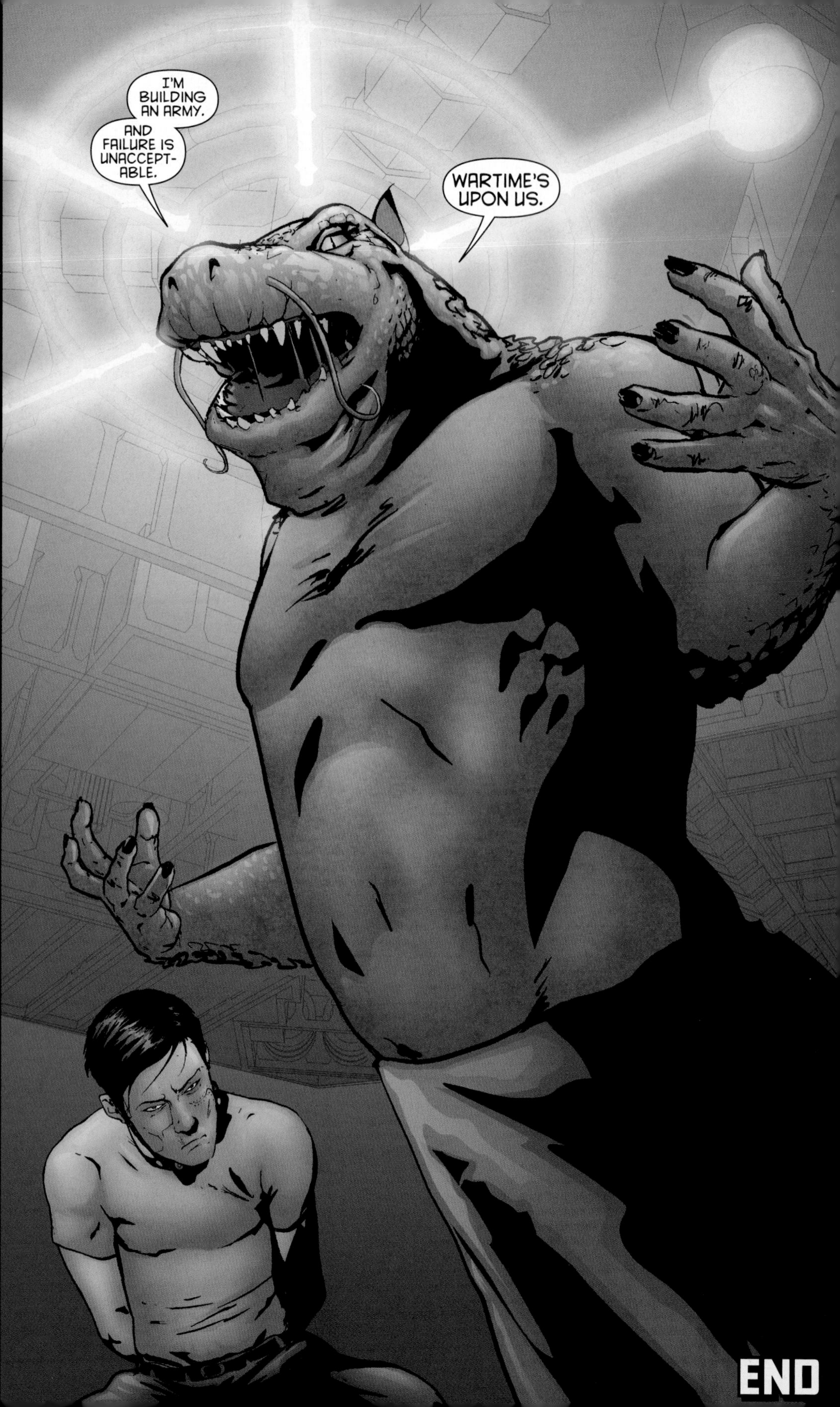
I'M BUILDING AN ARMY.
AND FAILURE IS UNACCEPT-ABLE.
WARTIME'S UPON US.
END

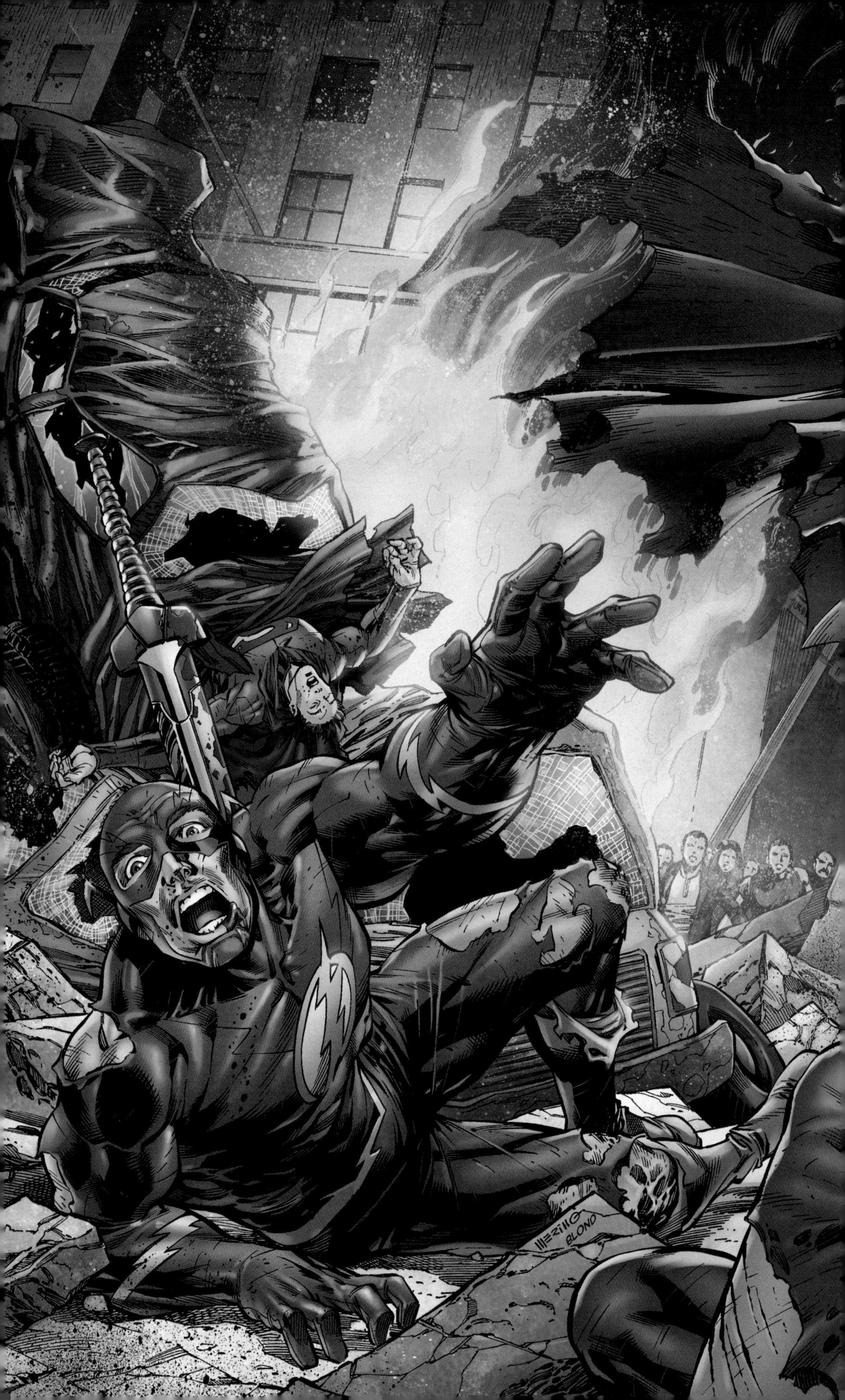

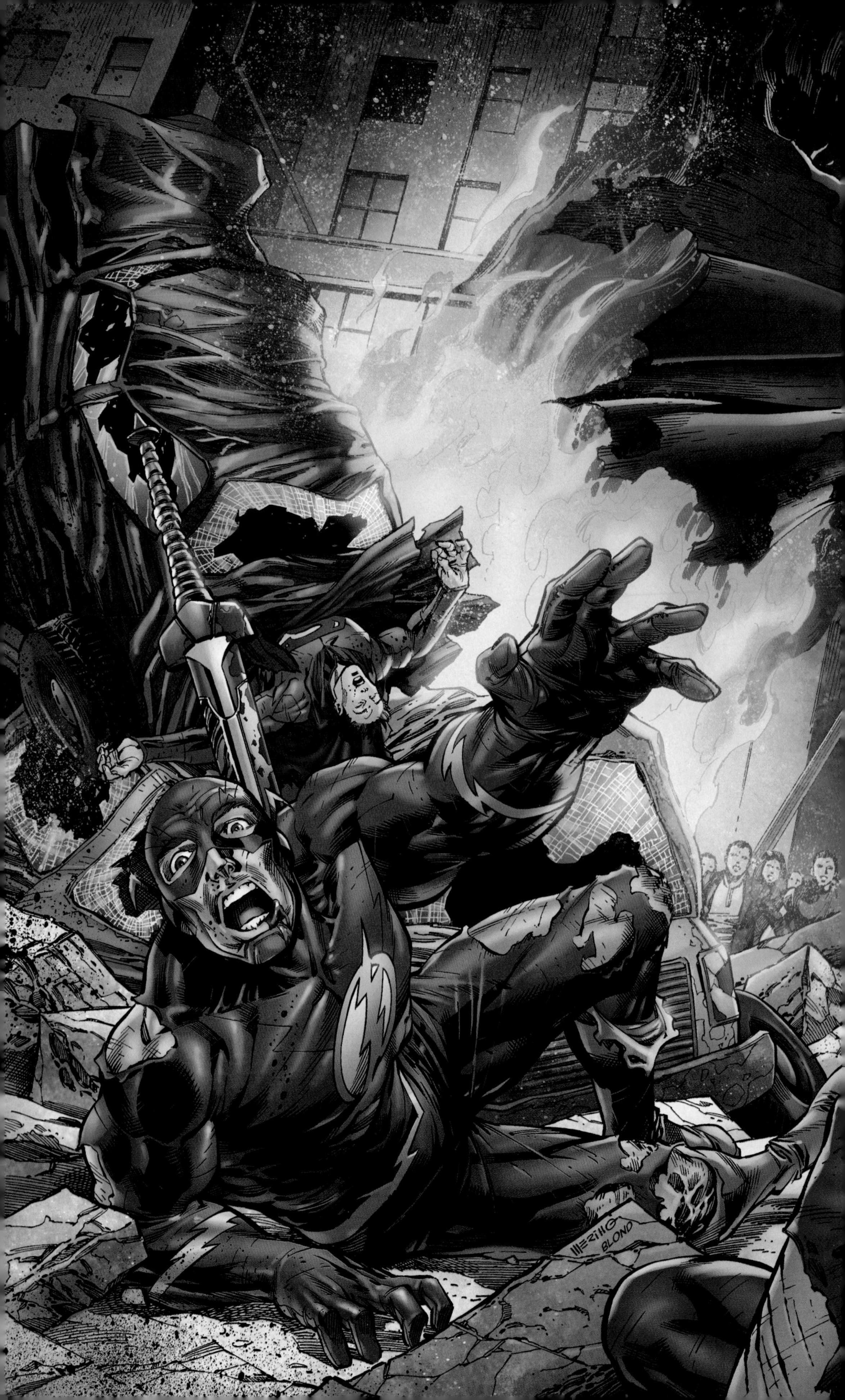
BLOND

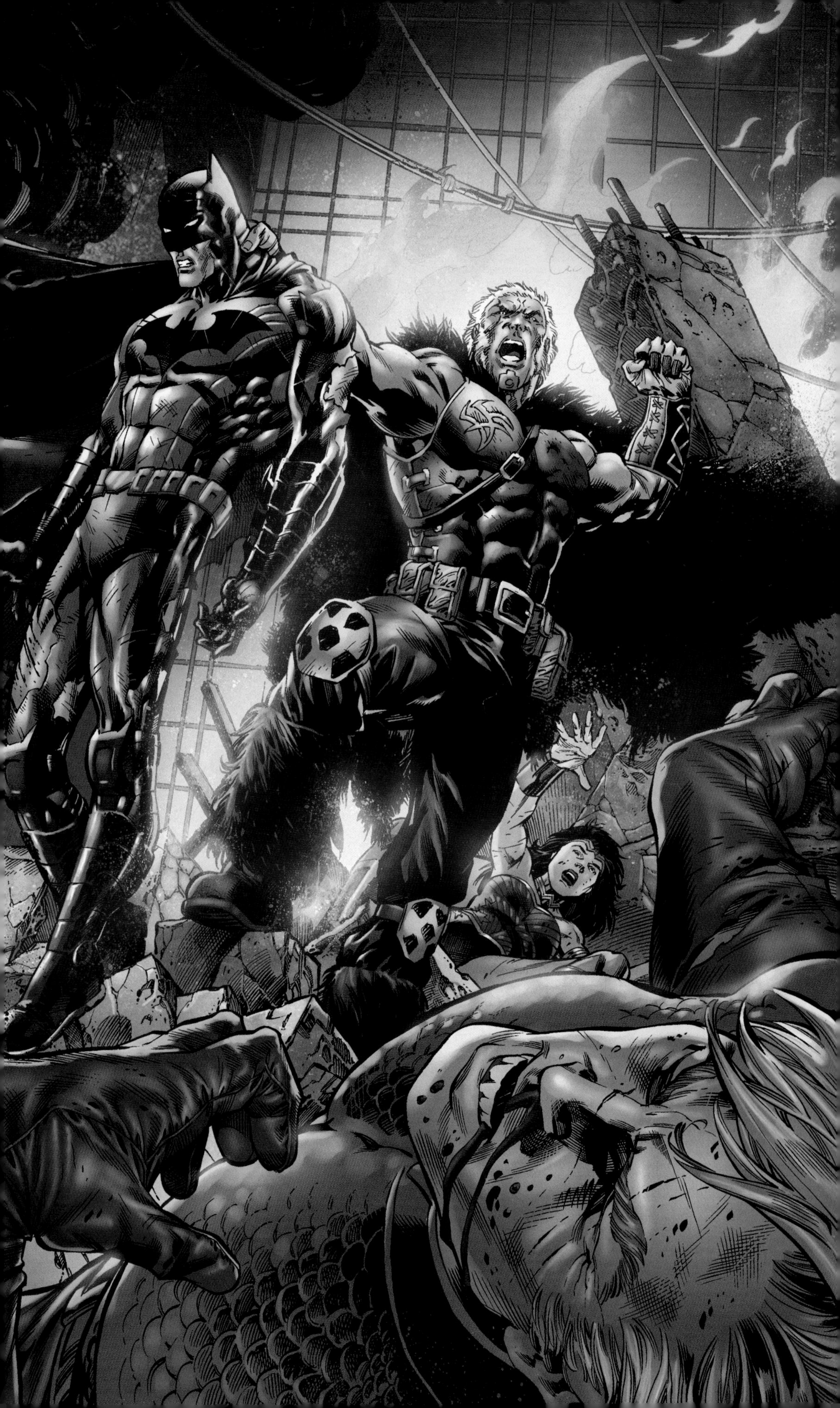

LIVING HISTORY

TONY BEDARD
writer

JAVIER PINA
artist

cover art by JESUS MERINO & BLONDE

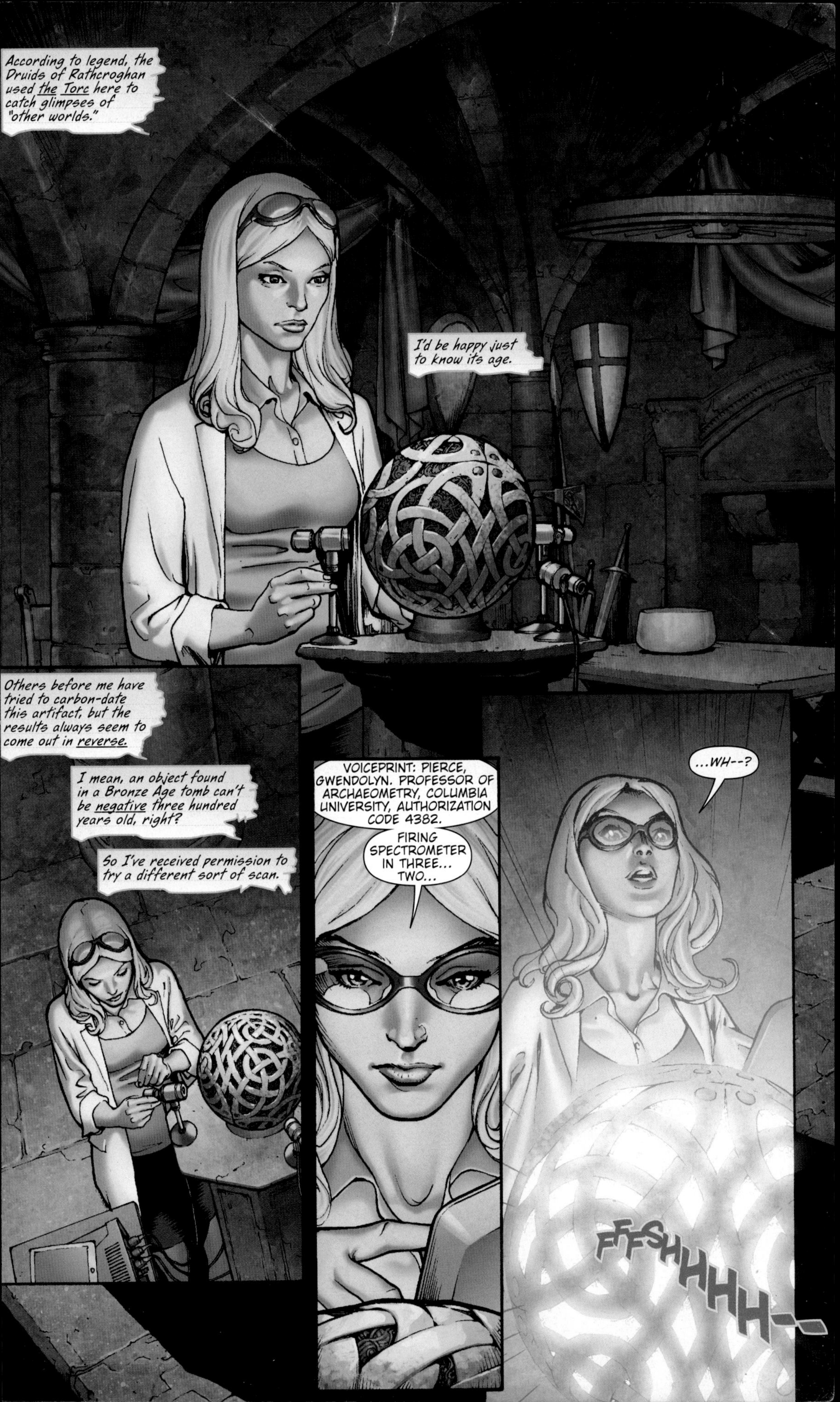

According to legend, the Druids of Rathcroghan used the Torc here to catch glimpses of "other worlds."
I'd be happy just to know it's age.
Others before me have tried to carbon-date this artifact, but the results always seem to come out in reverse.
I mean, an object found in a Bronze Age tomb can't be negative three hundred years old, right?
So I've received permission to try a different sort of scan.
VOICEPRINT: PIERCE, GWENDOLYN. PROFESSOR OF ARCHAEOMETRY, COLUMBIA UNIVERSITY, AUTHORIZATION CODE 4382.
FIRING SPECTROMETER IN THREE... TWO...
...WH--?
FFFSHHHHH--

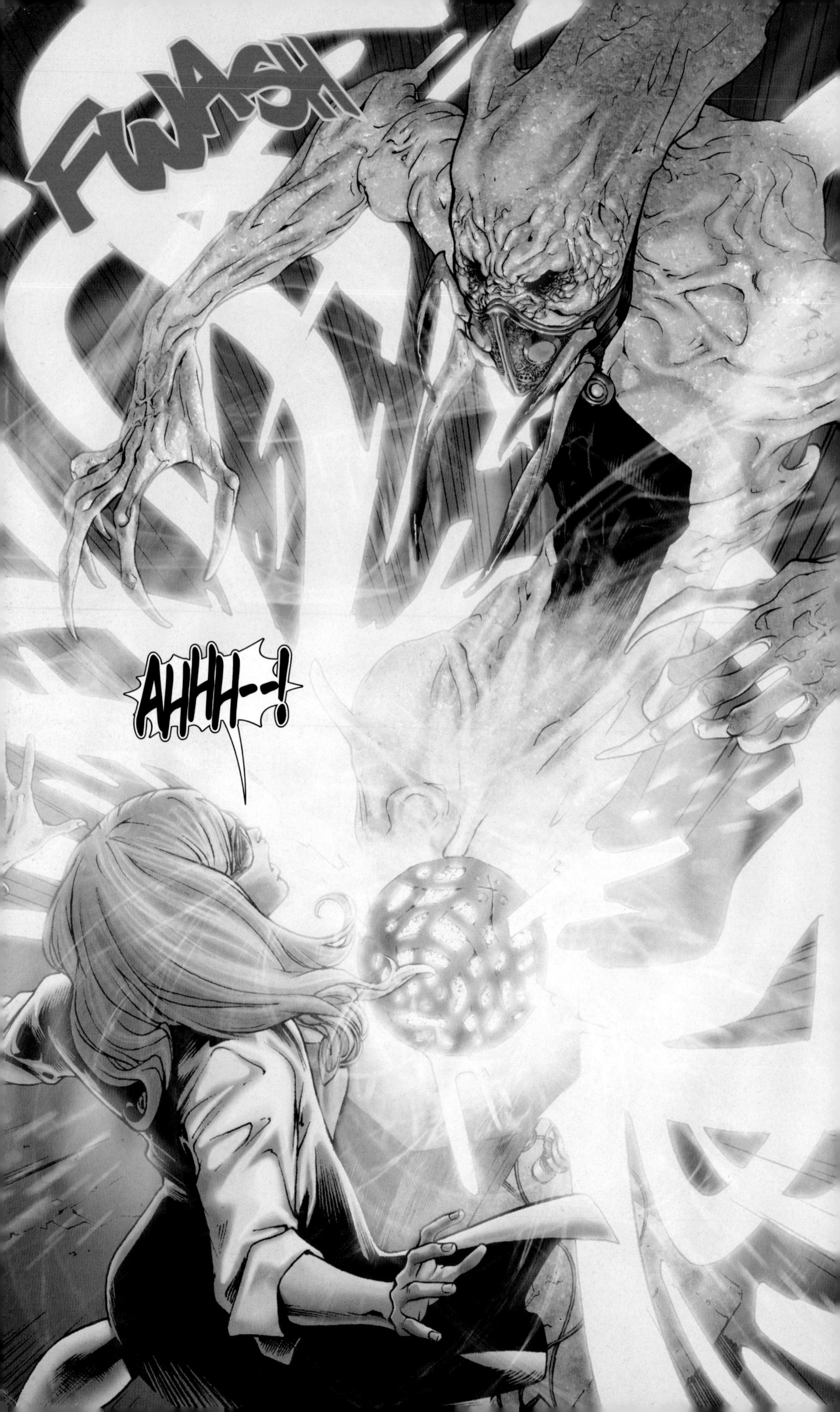
FWASH
AHHH--!

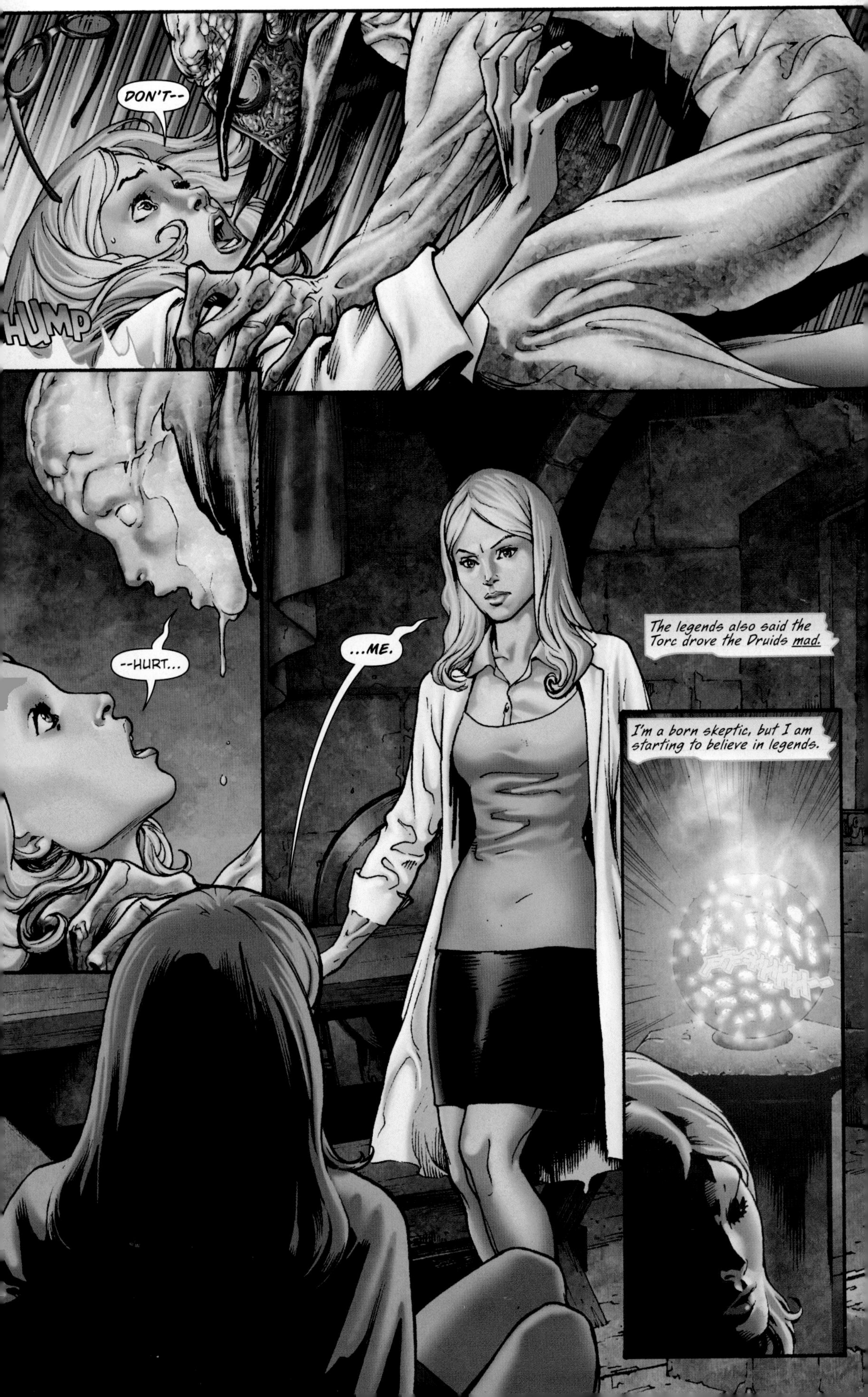
DON'T--
HUMP
--HURT...
...ME.
The legends also said the Torc drove the Druids mad.
I'm a born skeptic, but I am starting to believe in legends.

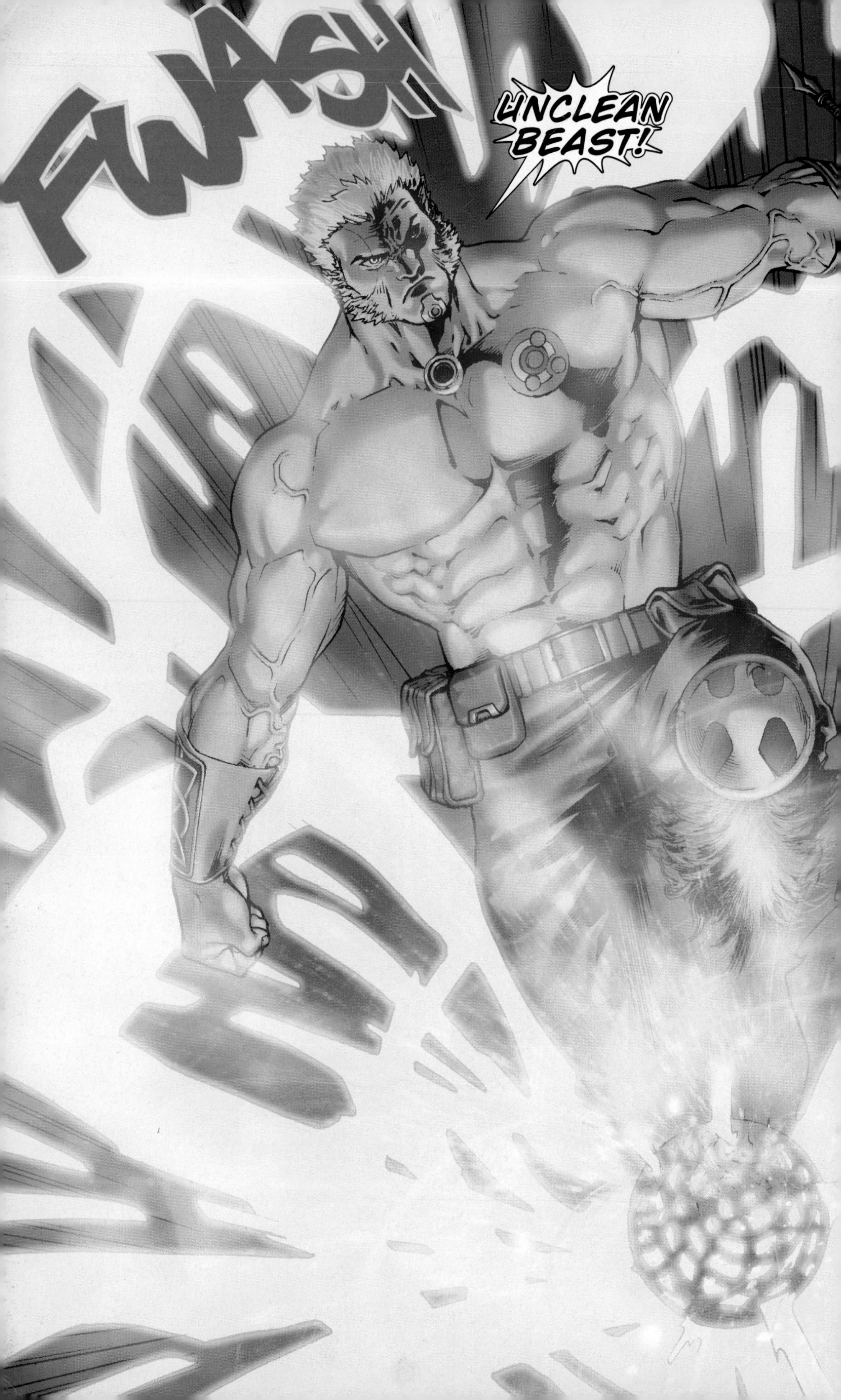
FWASH!
UNCLEAN BEAST!

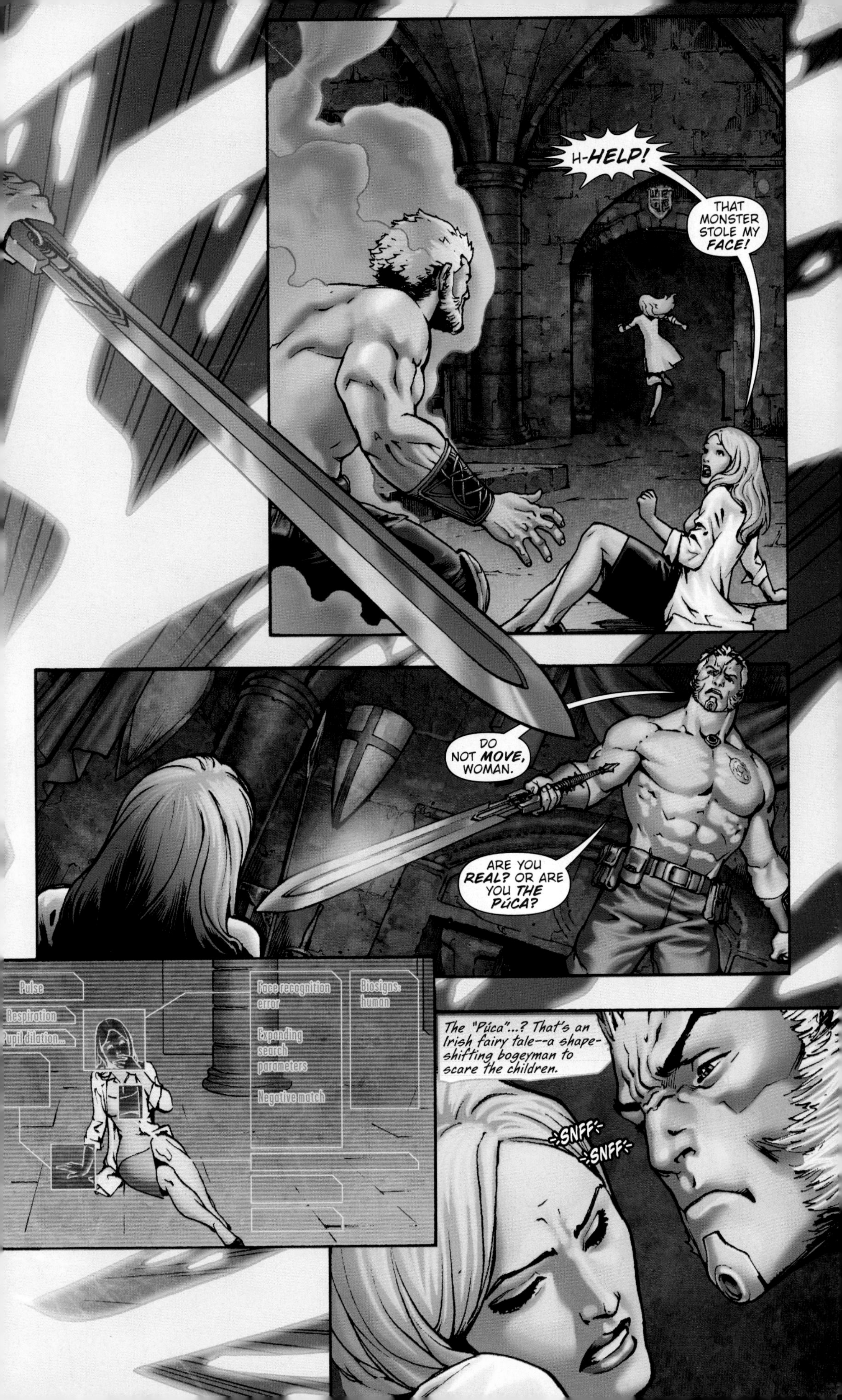
H-HELP!
THAT MONSTER STOLE MY FACE!
DO NOT MOVE, WOMAN.
ARE YOU REAL? OR ARE YOU THE PÚCA?
Pulse
Respiration
Pupil dilation...
Face recognition error
Expanding search parameters
Negative match
Biosigns: human
The "Púca"...? That's an Irish fairy tale--a shape-shifting bogeyman to scare the children.
SNFF
SNFF

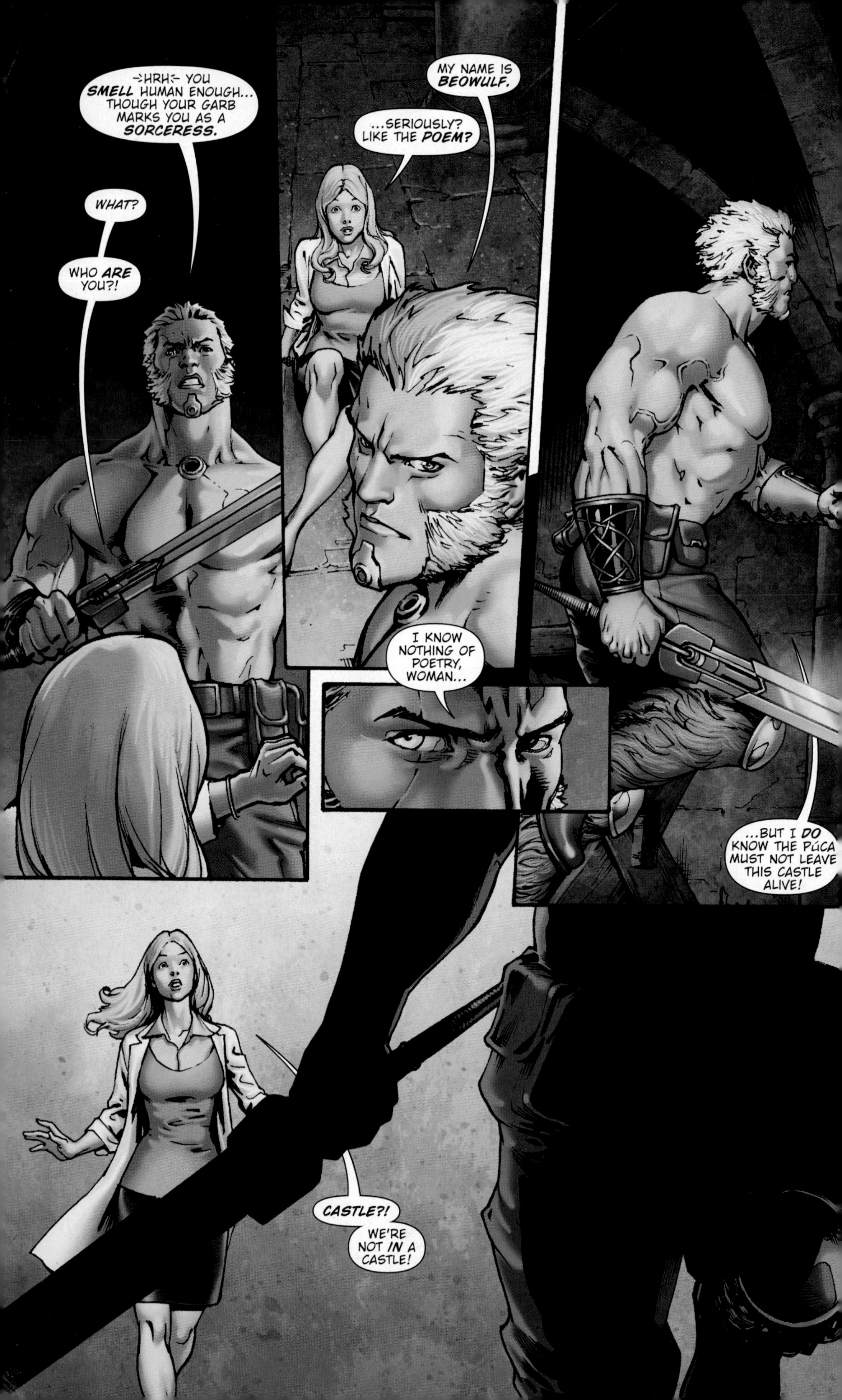

~HRH~ YOU SMELL HUMAN ENOUGH... THOUGH YOUR GARB MARKS YOU AS A SORCERESS.
WHAT?
WHO ARE YOU?!
MY NAME IS BEOWULF.
...SERIOUSLY? LIKE THE POEM?
I KNOW NOTHING OF POETRY, WOMAN...
...BUT I DO KNOW THE PÚCA MUST NOT LEAVE THIS CASTLE ALIVE!
CASTLE?!
WE'RE NOT IN A CASTLE!

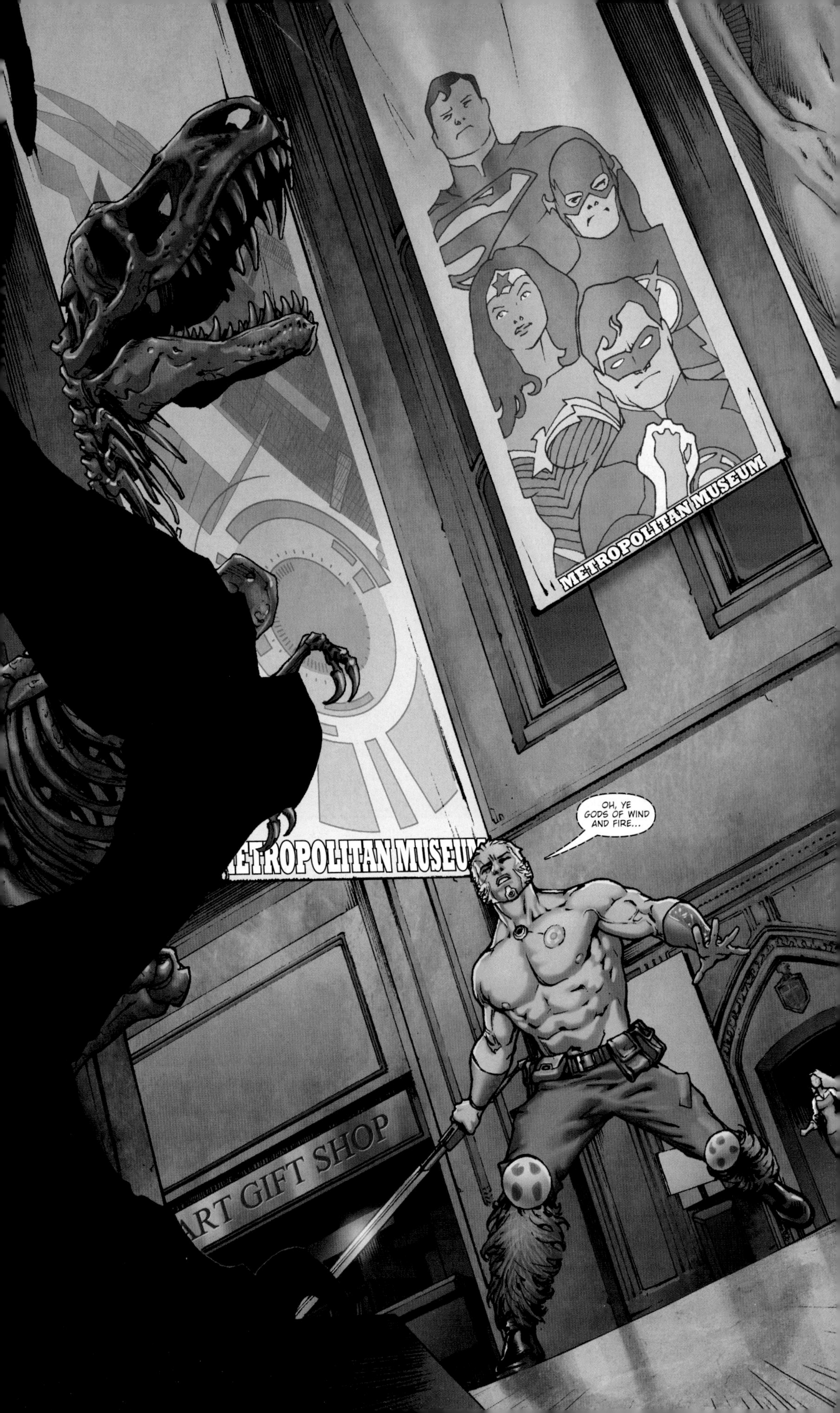
METROPOLITAN MUSEUM
METROPOLITAN MUSEUM
OH, YE GODS OF WIND AND FIRE...
ART GIFT SHOP

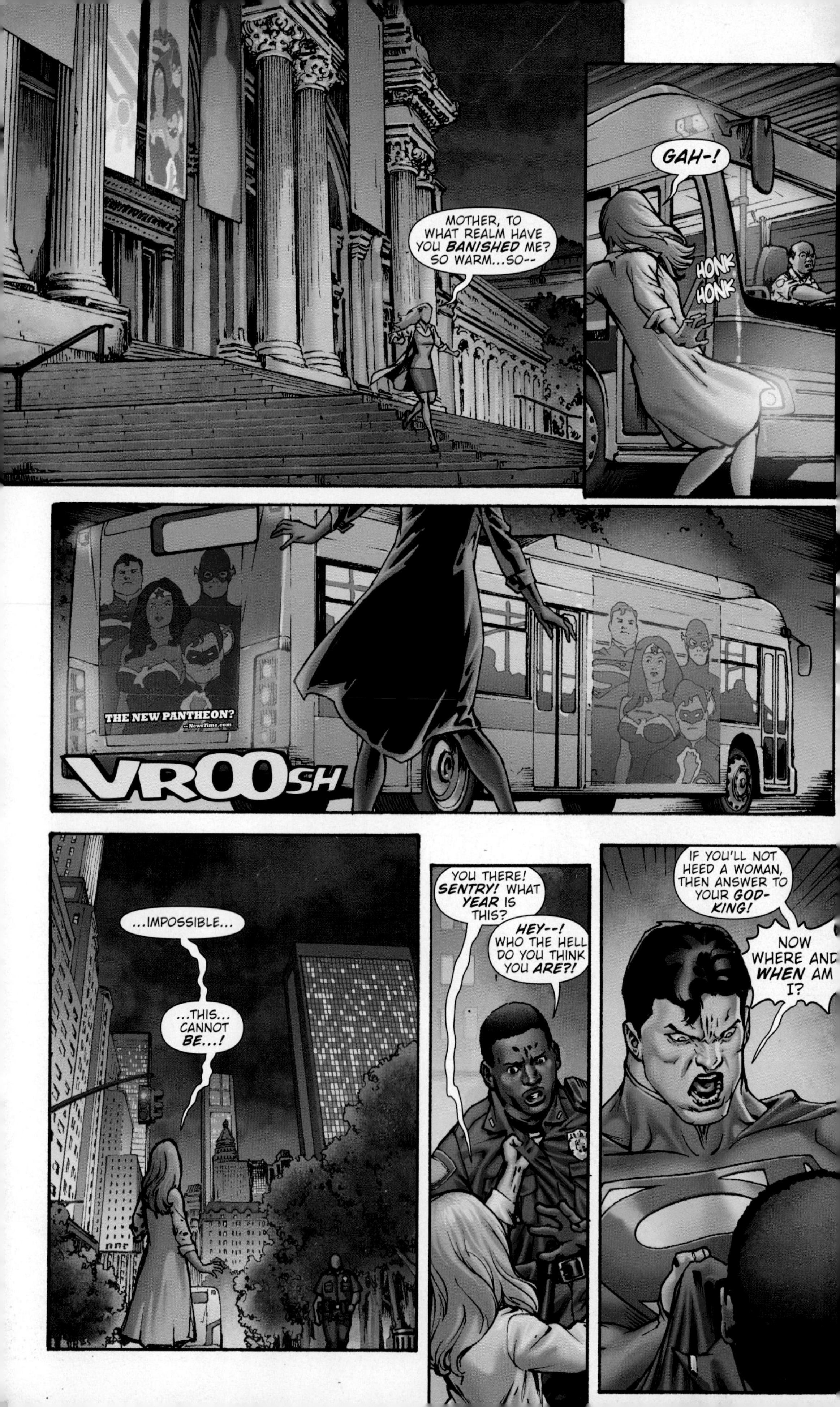

MOTHER, TO WHAT REALM HAVE YOU BANISHED ME? SO WARM...SO--
GAH-!
HONK HONK
THE NEW PANTHEON?
--NewsTime.com
VROOSH
...IMPOSSIBLE...
...THIS... CANNOT BE...!
YOU THERE! SENTRY! WHAT YEAR IS THIS?
HEY--! WHO THE HELL DO YOU THINK YOU ARE?!
IF YOU'LL NOT HEED A WOMAN, THEN ANSWER TO YOUR GOD-KING!
NOW WHERE AND WHEN AM I?

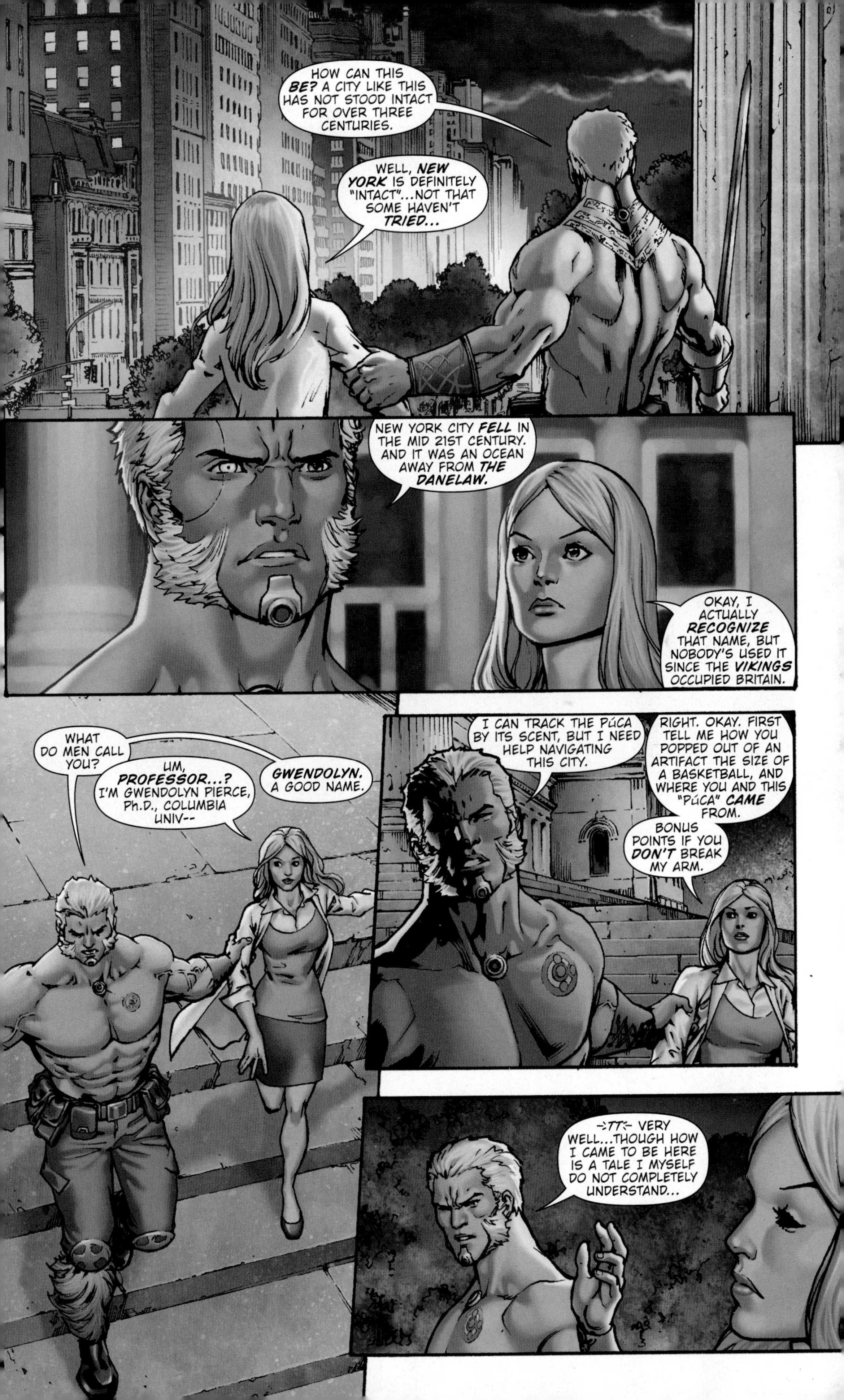
HOW CAN THIS BE? A CITY LIKE THIS HAS NOT STOOD INTACT FOR OVER THREE CENTURIES.
WELL, NEW YORK IS DEFINITELY "INTACT"...NOT THAT SOME HAVEN'T TRIED...
NEW YORK CITY FELL IN THE MID 21ST CENTURY. AND IT WAS AN OCEAN AWAY FROM THE DANELAW.
OKAY, I ACTUALLY RECOGNIZE THAT NAME, BUT NOBODY'S USED IT SINCE THE VIKINGS OCCUPIED BRITAIN.
WHAT DO MEN CALL YOU?
UM, PROFESSOR...? I'M GWENDOLYN PIERCE, Ph.D., COLUMBIA UNIV--
GWENDOLYN. A GOOD NAME.
I CAN TRACK THE PÚCA BY ITS SCENT, BUT I NEED HELP NAVIGATING THIS CITY.
RIGHT. OKAY. FIRST TELL ME HOW YOU POPPED OUT OF AN ARTIFACT THE SIZE OF A BASKETBALL, AND WHERE YOU AND THIS "PÚCA" CAME FROM.
BONUS POINTS IF YOU DON'T BREAK MY ARM.
-TT- VERY WELL...THOUGH HOW I CAME TO BE HERE IS A TALE I MYSELF DO NOT COMPLETELY UNDERSTAND...

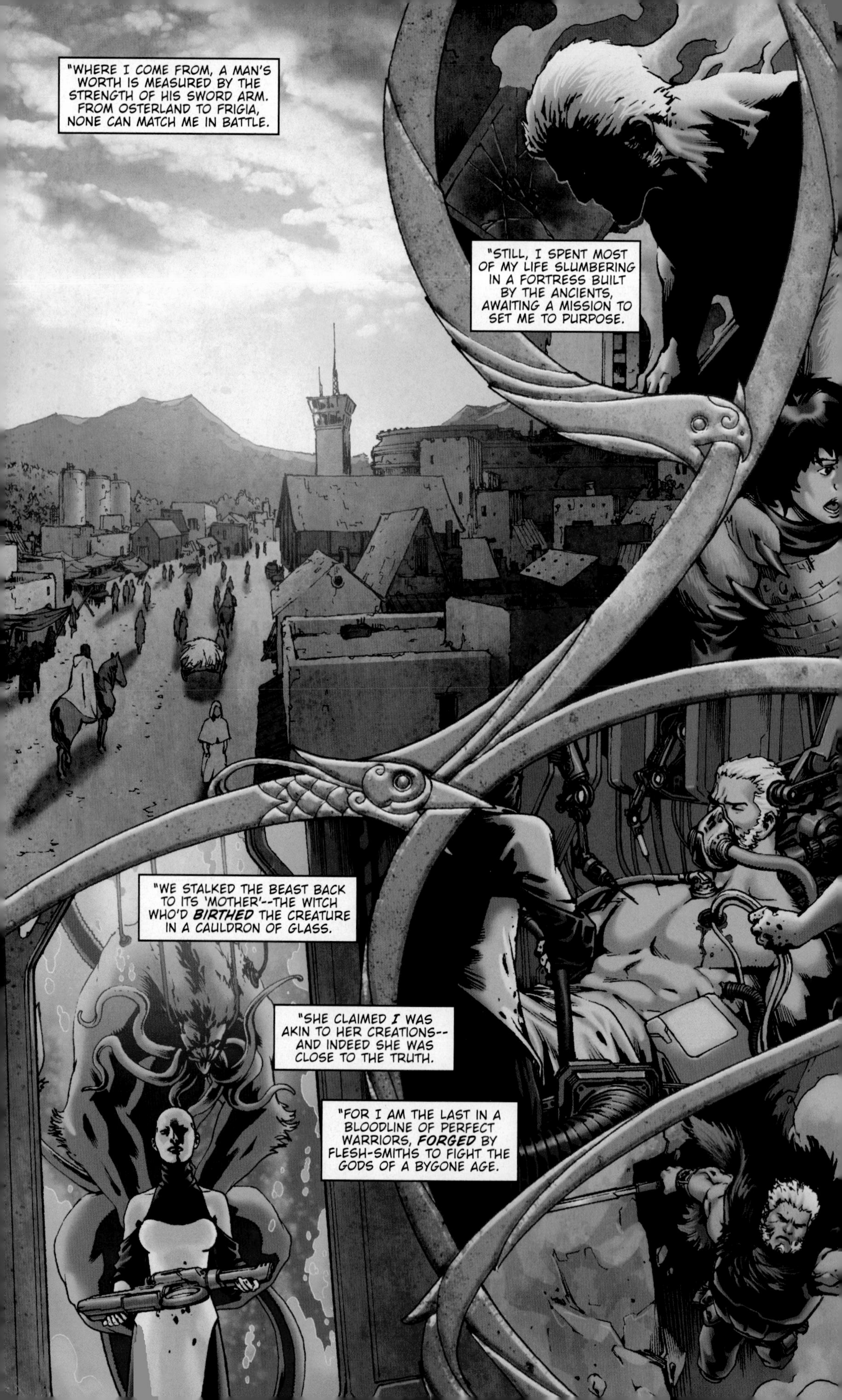
"WHERE I COME FROM, A MAN'S WORTH IS MEASURED BY THE STRENGTH OF HIS SWORD ARM. FROM OSTERLAND TO FRIGIA, NONE CAN MATCH ME IN BATTLE.
"STILL, I SPENT MOST OF MY LIFE SLUMBERING IN A FORTRESS BUILT BY THE ANCIENTS, AWAITING A MISSION TO SET ME TO PURPOSE.
"WE STALKED THE BEAST BACK TO ITS 'MOTHER'--THE WITCH WHO'D *BIRTHED* THE CREATURE IN A CAULDRON OF GLASS.
"SHE CLAIMED *I* WAS AKIN TO HER CREATIONS--AND INDEED SHE WAS CLOSE TO THE TRUTH.
"FOR I AM THE LAST IN A BLOODLINE OF PERFECT WARRIORS, *FORGED* BY FLESH-SMITHS TO FIGHT THE GODS OF A BYGONE AGE.

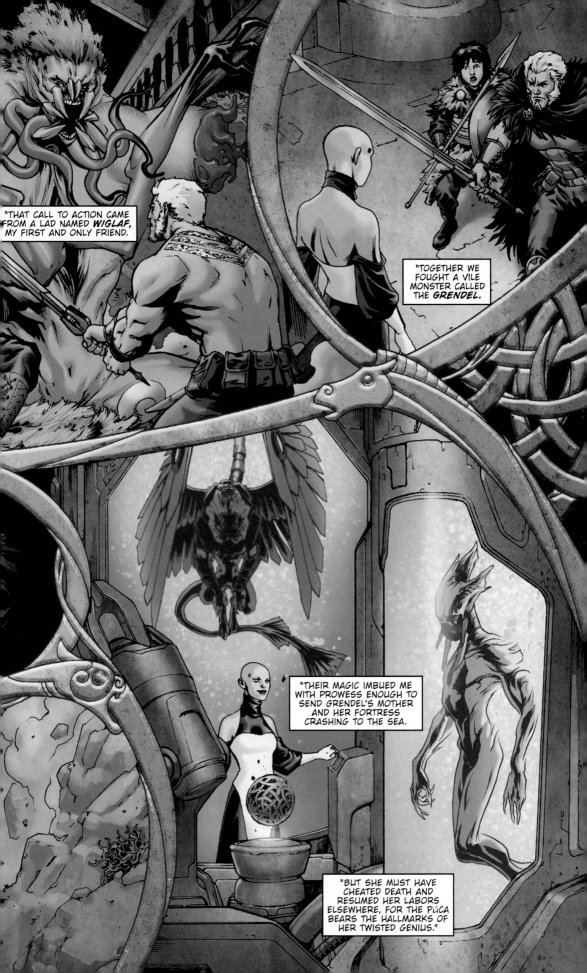

"THAT CALL TO ACTION CAME FROM A LAD NAMED *WIGLAF*, MY FIRST AND ONLY FRIEND."

"TOGETHER WE FOUGHT A VILE MONSTER CALLED THE *GRENDEL*."

"THEIR MAGIC IMBUED ME WITH PROWESS ENOUGH TO SEND GRENDEL'S MOTHER AND HER FORTRESS CRASHING TO THE SEA."

"BUT SHE MUST HAVE CHEATED DEATH AND RESUMED HER LABORS ELSEWHERE, FOR THE PÚCA BEARS THE HALLMARKS OF HER TWISTED GENIUS."

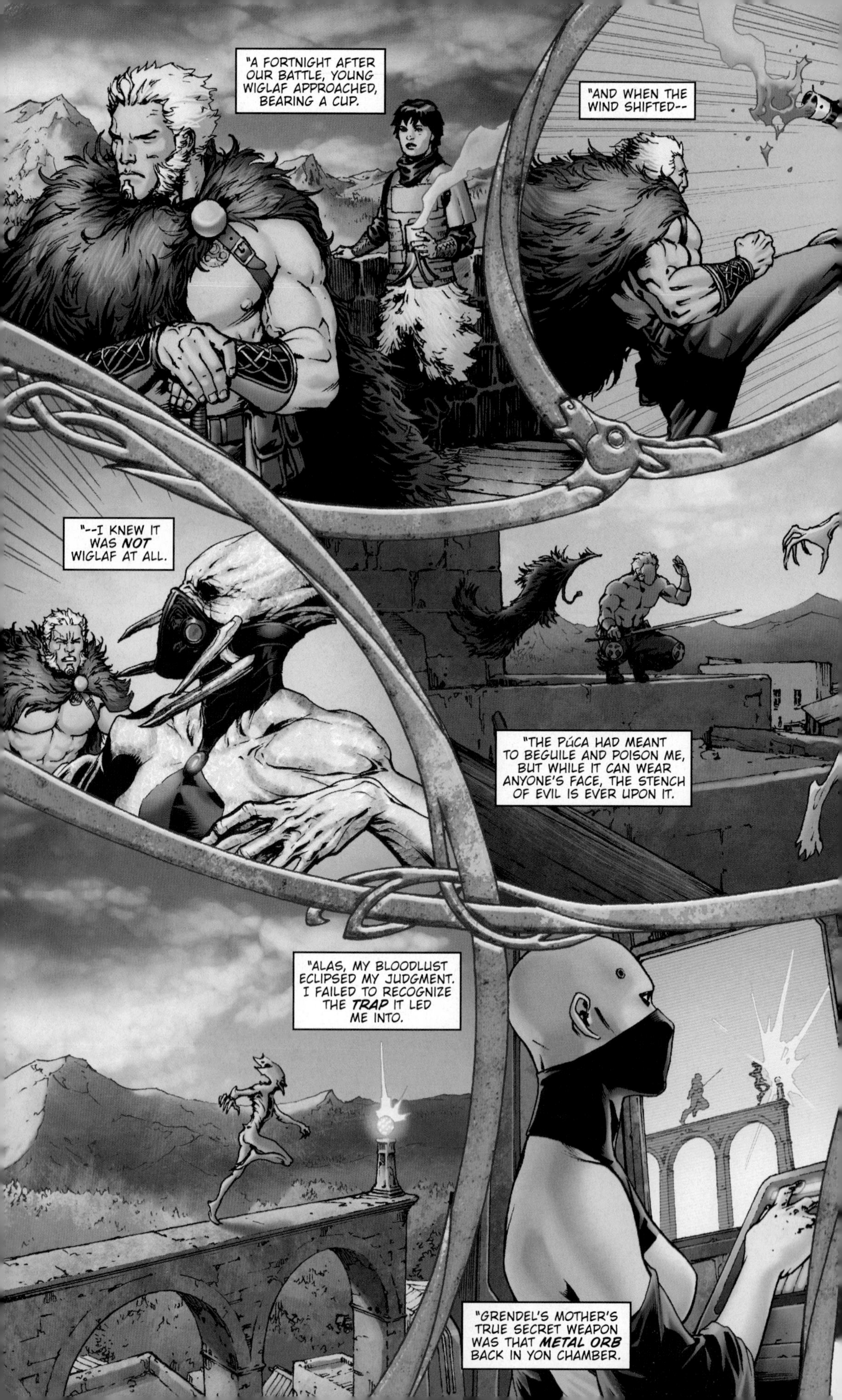
"A FORTNIGHT AFTER OUR BATTLE, YOUNG WIGLAF APPROACHED, BEARING A CUP.
"AND WHEN THE WIND SHIFTED--
"--I KNEW IT WAS NOT WIGLAF AT ALL.
"THE PÚCA HAD MEANT TO BEGUILE AND POISON ME, BUT WHILE IT CAN WEAR ANYONE'S FACE, THE STENCH OF EVIL IS EVER UPON IT.
"ALAS, MY BLOODLUST ECLIPSED MY JUDGMENT. I FAILED TO RECOGNIZE THE TRAP IT LED ME INTO.
"GRENDEL'S MOTHER'S TRUE SECRET WEAPON WAS THAT METAL ORB BACK IN YON CHAMBER.

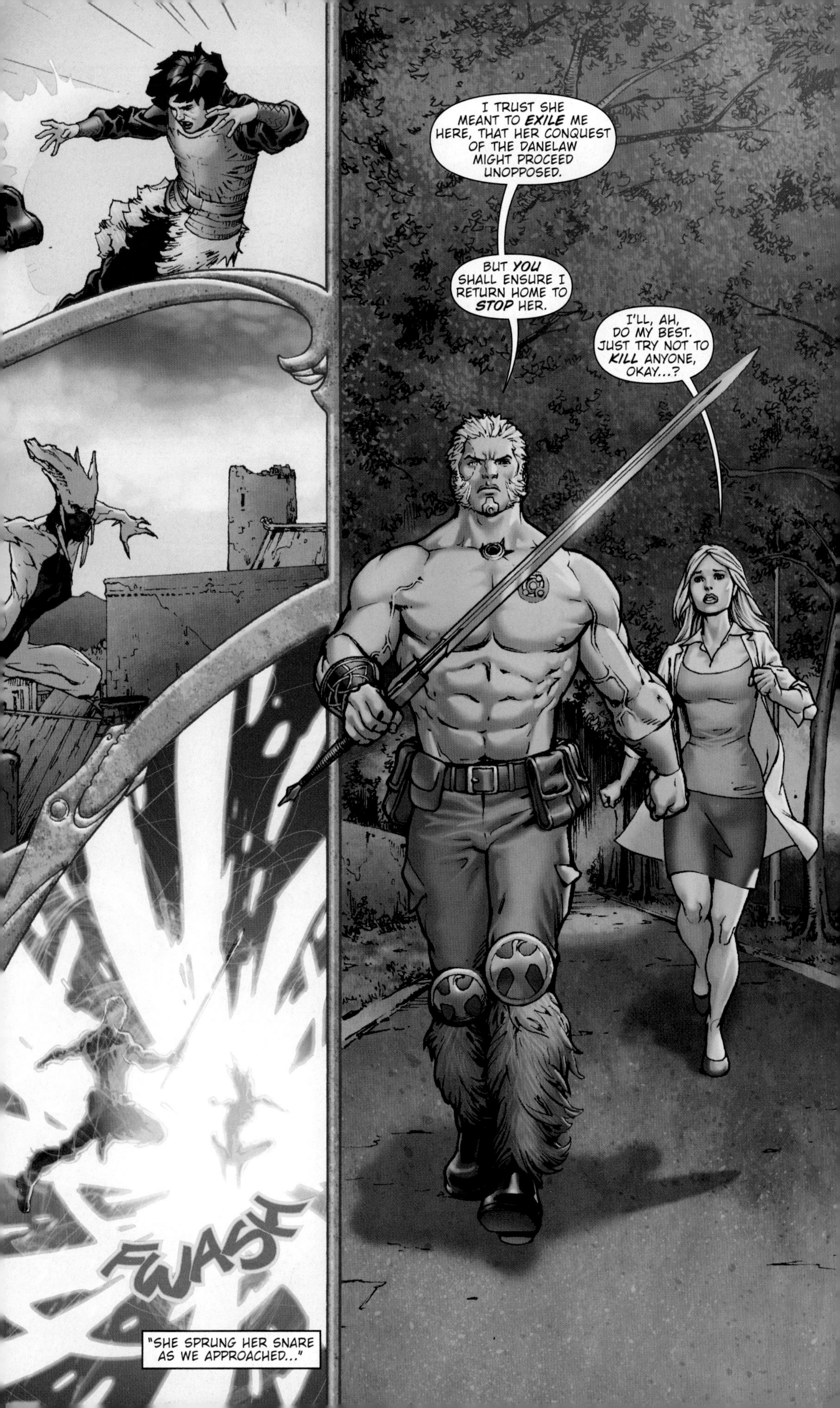

"SHE SPRUNG HER SNARE AS WE APPROACHED..."
FWASH
I TRUST SHE MEANT TO EXILE ME HERE, THAT HER CONQUEST OF THE DANELAW MIGHT PROCEED UNOPPOSED.
BUT YOU SHALL ENSURE I RETURN HOME TO STOP HER.
I'LL, AH, DO MY BEST. JUST TRY NOT TO KILL ANYONE, OKAY...?

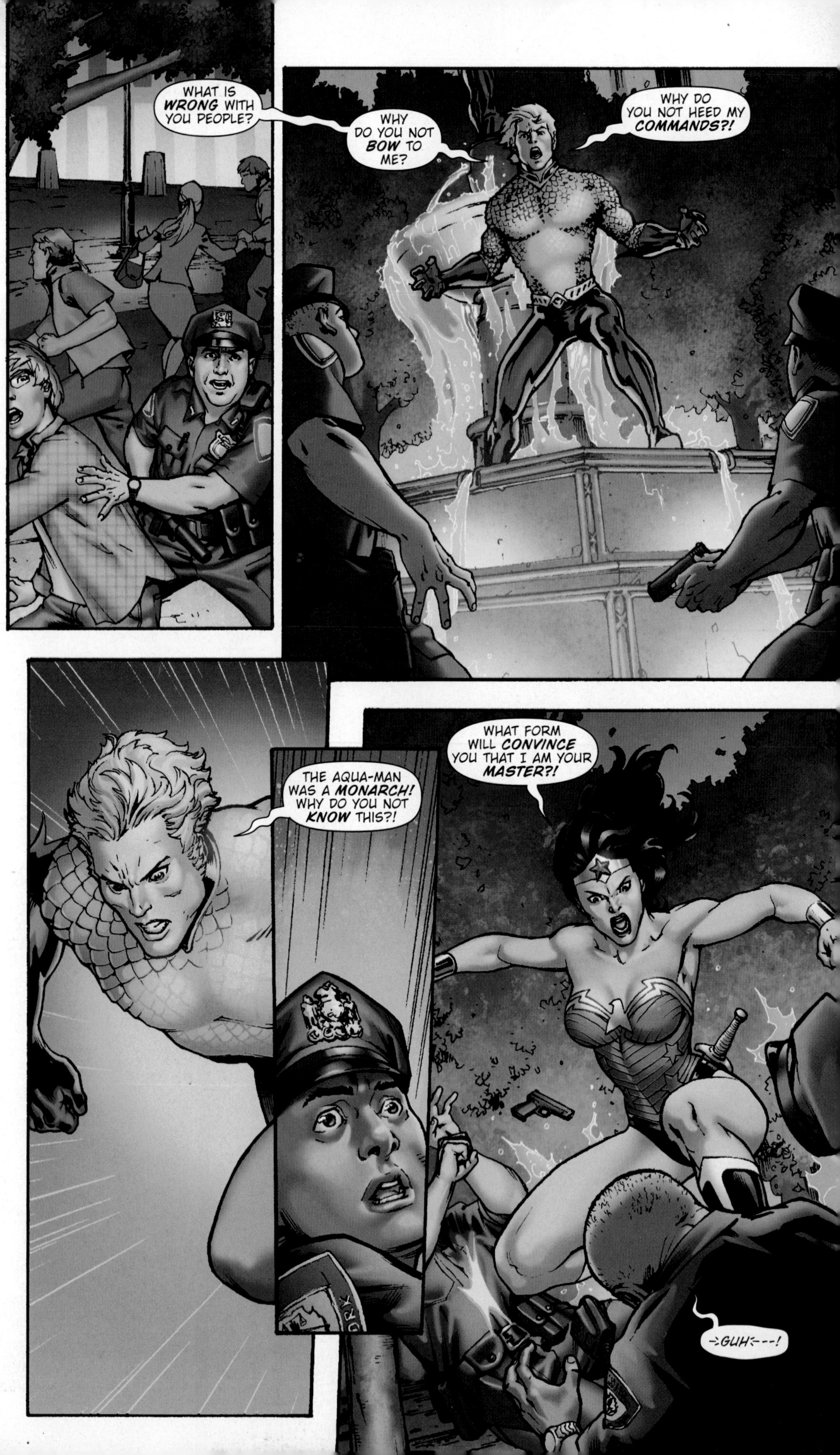

WHAT IS **WRONG** WITH YOU PEOPLE?
WHY DO YOU NOT **BOW** TO ME?
WHY DO YOU NOT HEED MY **COMMANDS?!**
THE AQUA-MAN WAS A **MONARCH!** WHY DO YOU NOT **KNOW** THIS?!
WHAT FORM WILL **CONVINCE** YOU THAT I AM YOUR **MASTER?!**
--GUH---!

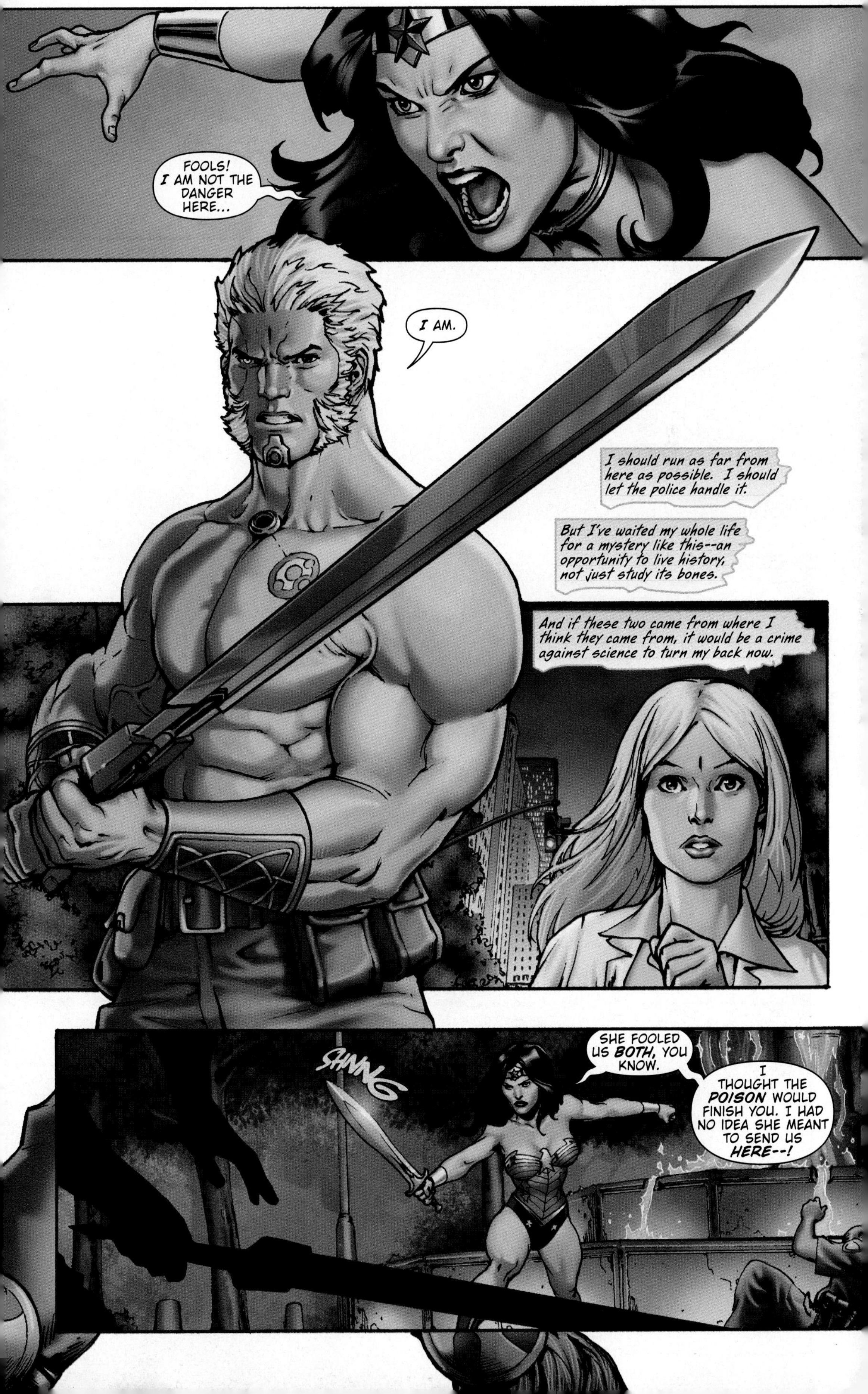

FOOLS! I AM NOT THE DANGER HERE...
I AM.
I should run as far from here as possible. I should let the police handle it.
But I've waited my whole life for a mystery like this--an opportunity to live history, not just study its bones.
And if these two came from where I think they came from, it would be a crime against science to turn my back now.
SHING
SHE FOOLED US BOTH, YOU KNOW.
I THOUGHT THE POISON WOULD FINISH YOU. I HAD NO IDEA SHE MEANT TO SEND US HERE--!

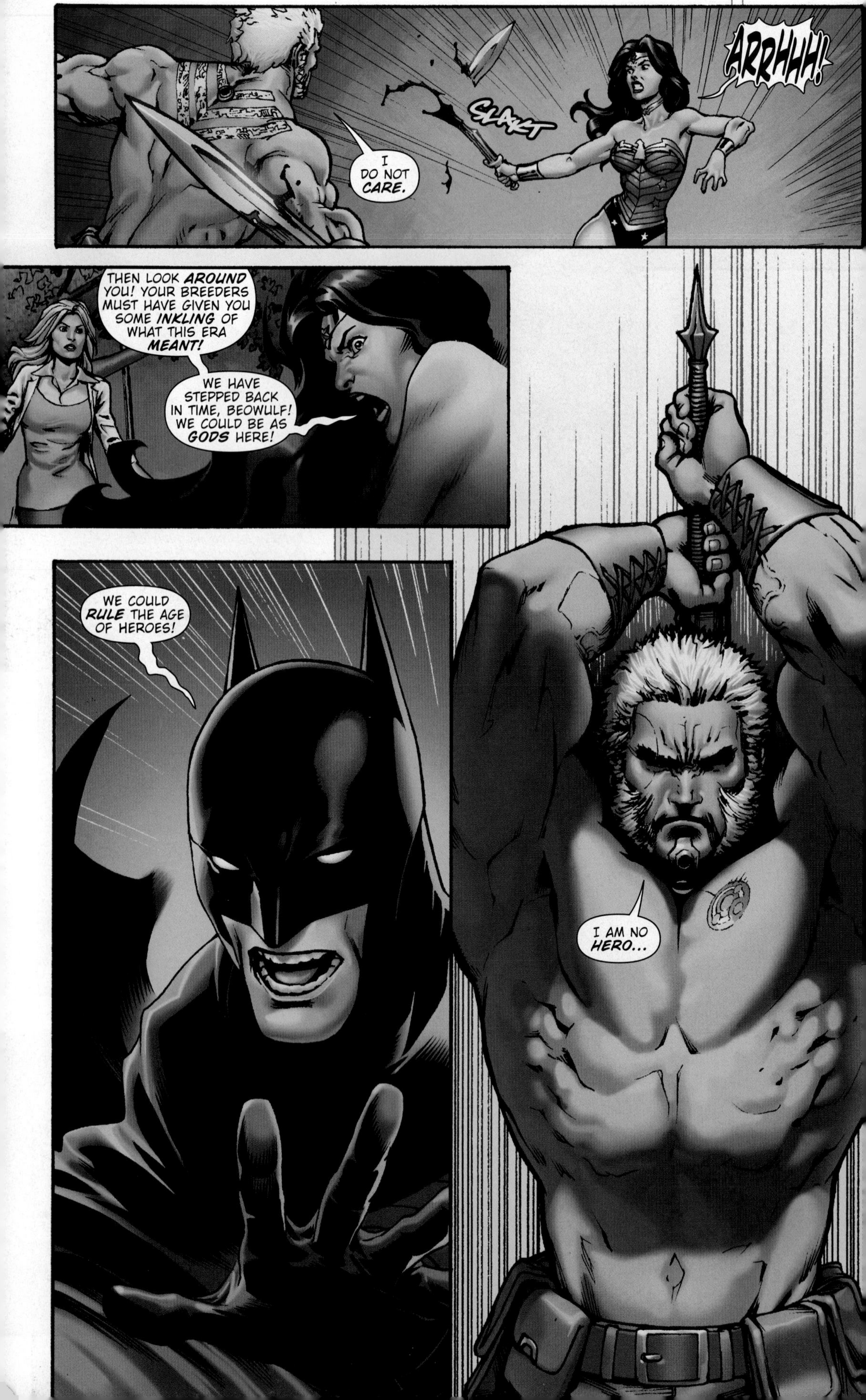
ARRHHH!
SLAKT
I DO NOT CARE.
THEN LOOK AROUND YOU! YOUR BREEDERS MUST HAVE GIVEN YOU SOME INKLING OF WHAT THIS ERA MEANT!
WE HAVE STEPPED BACK IN TIME, BEOWULF! WE COULD BE AS GODS HERE!
WE COULD RULE THE AGE OF HEROES!
I AM NO HERO...

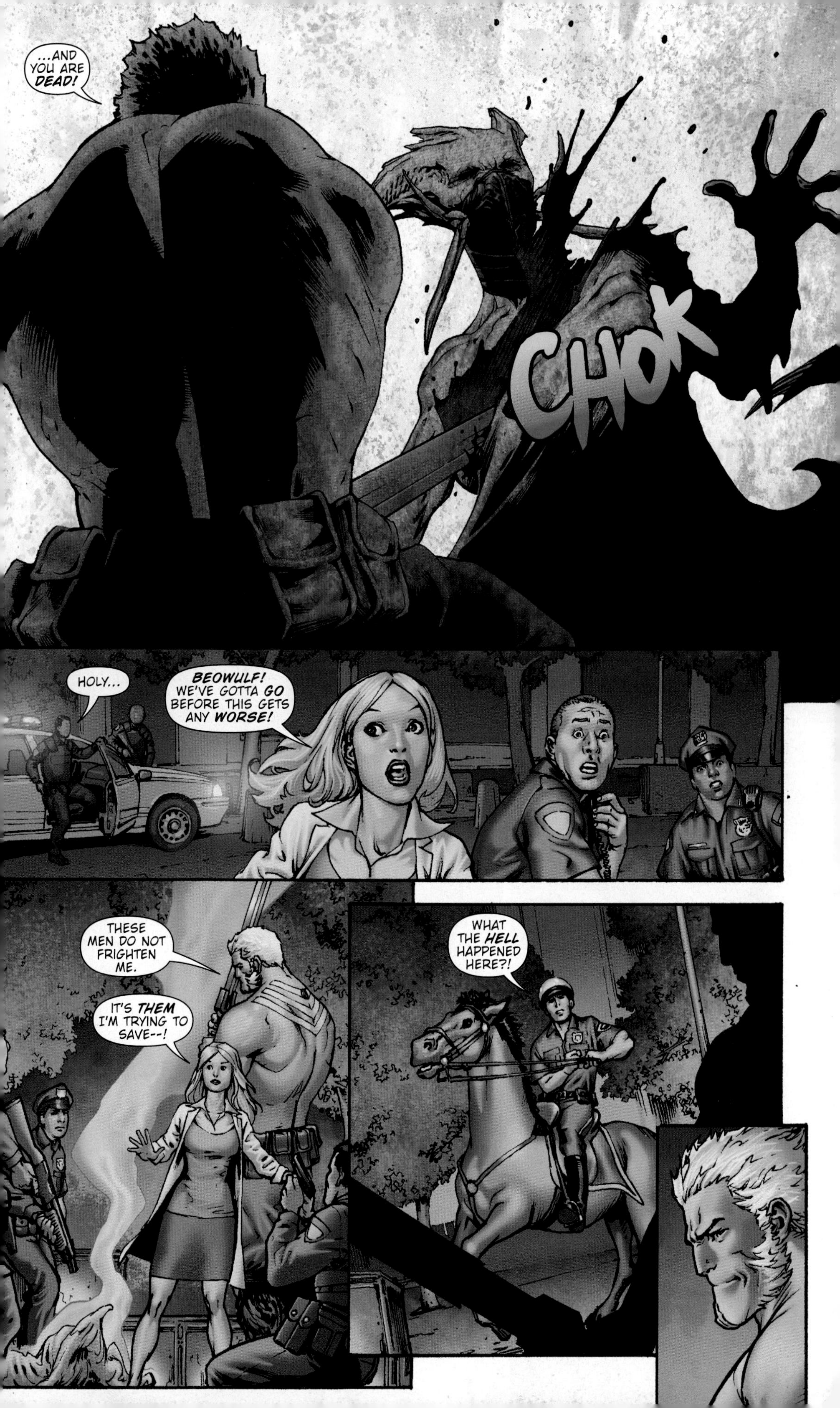
...AND YOU ARE DEAD!
CHOK
HOLY...
BEOWULF! WE'VE GOTTA GO BEFORE THIS GETS ANY WORSE!
THESE MEN DO NOT FRIGHTEN ME.
IT'S THEM I'M TRYING TO SAVE--!
WHAT THE HELL HAPPENED HERE?!

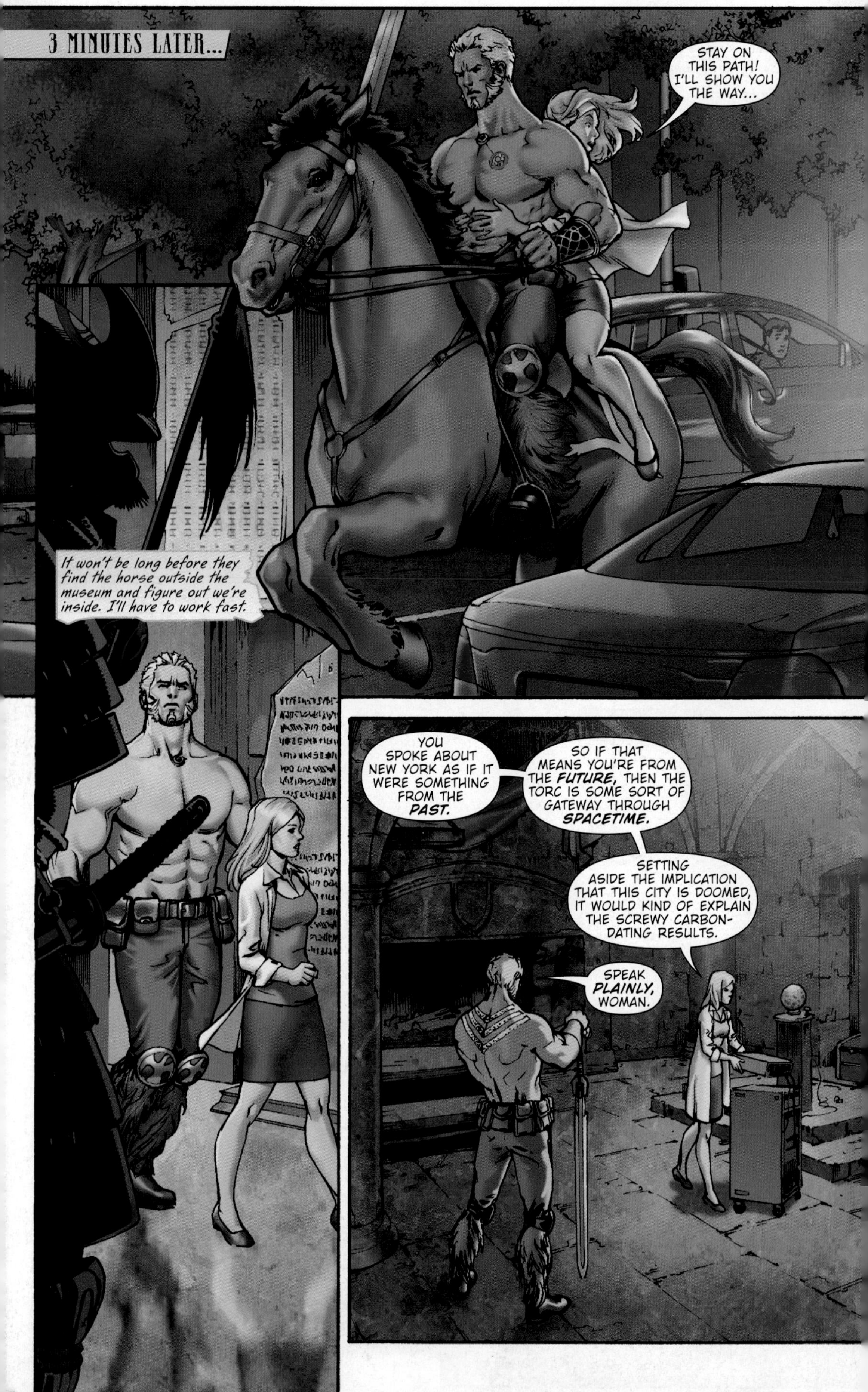
3 MINUTES LATER...
STAY ON THIS PATH! I'LL SHOW YOU THE WAY...
It won't be long before they find the horse outside the museum and figure out we're inside. I'll have to work fast.
YOU SPOKE ABOUT NEW YORK AS IF IT WERE SOMETHING FROM THE PAST.
SO IF THAT MEANS YOU'RE FROM THE FUTURE, THEN THE TORC IS SOME SORT OF GATEWAY THROUGH SPACETIME.
SETTING ASIDE THE IMPLICATION THAT THIS CITY IS DOOMED, IT WOULD KIND OF EXPLAIN THE SCREWY CARBON-DATING RESULTS.
SPEAK PLAINLY, WOMAN.

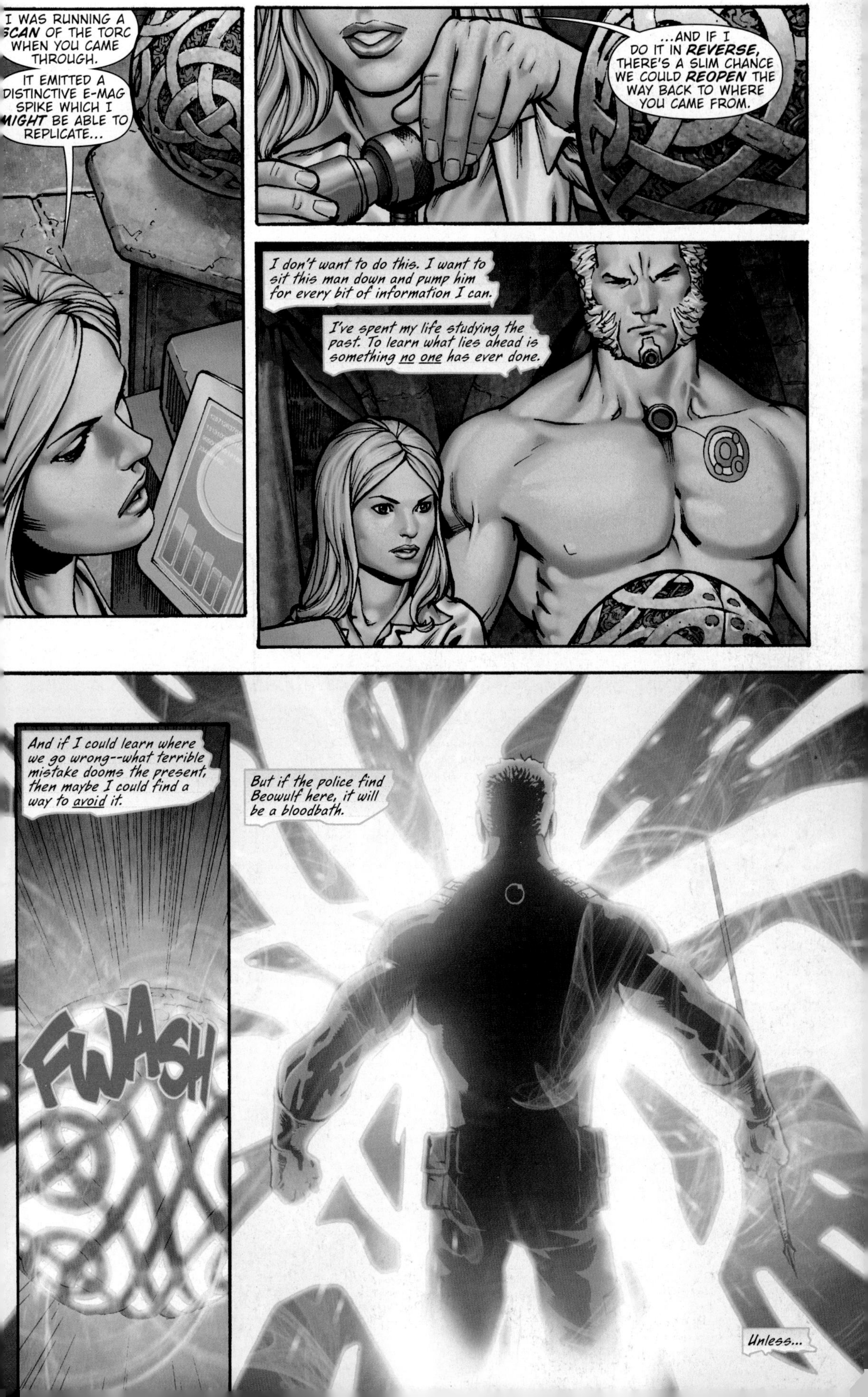
I WAS RUNNING A SCAN OF THE TORC WHEN YOU CAME THROUGH.
IT EMITTED A DISTINCTIVE E-MAG SPIKE WHICH I MIGHT BE ABLE TO REPLICATE...
...AND IF I DO IT IN REVERSE, THERE'S A SLIM CHANCE WE COULD REOPEN THE WAY BACK TO WHERE YOU CAME FROM.
I don't want to do this. I want to sit this man down and pump him for every bit of information I can.
I've spent my life studying the past. To learn what lies ahead is something no one has ever done.
And if I could learn where we go wrong--what terrible mistake dooms the present, then maybe I could find a way to avoid it.
But if the police find Beowulf here, it will be a bloodbath.
FWASH
Unless...

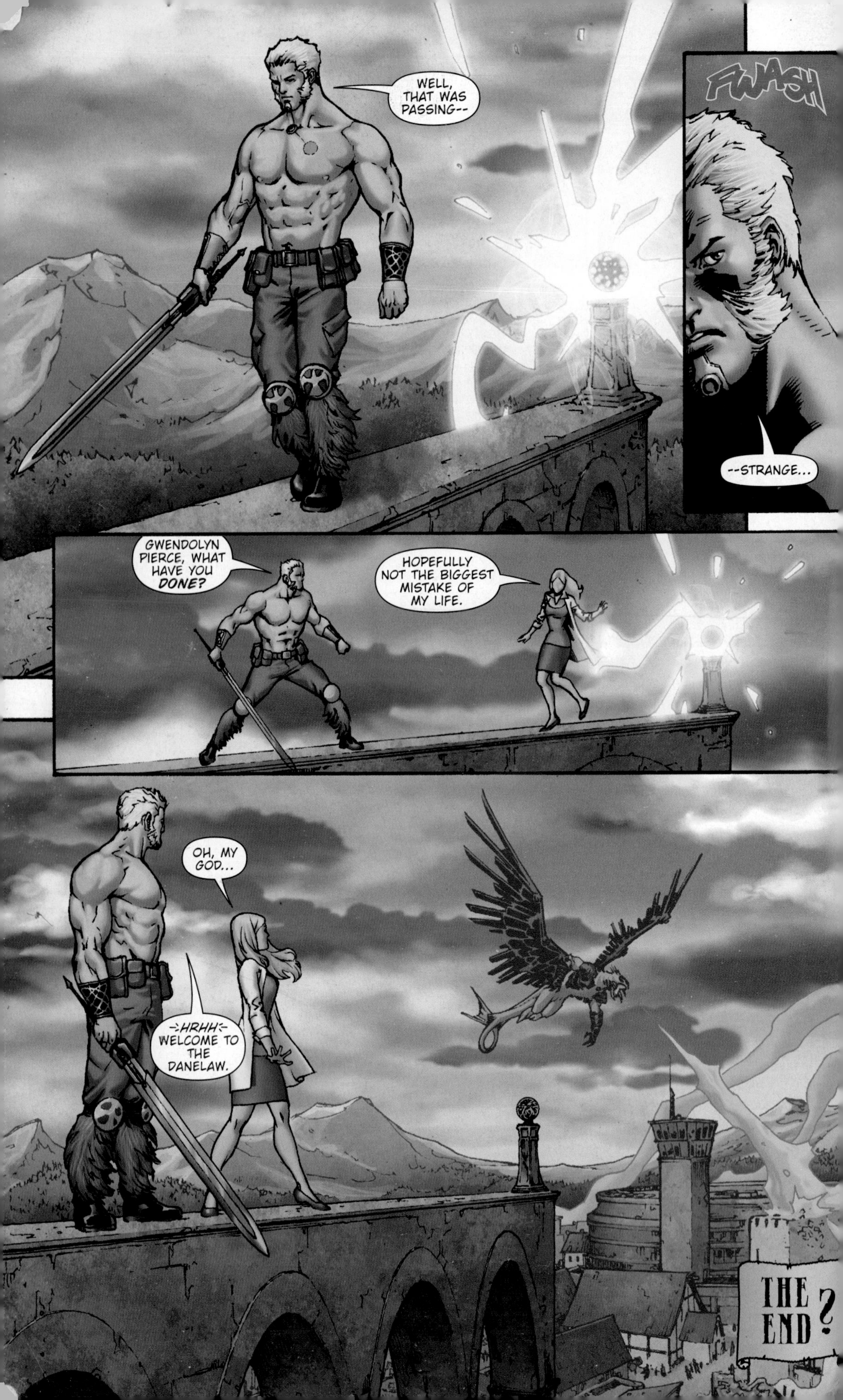

WELL, THAT WAS PASSING--
FWASH
--STRANGE...
GWENDOLYN PIERCE, WHAT HAVE YOU *DONE?*
HOPEFULLY NOT THE BIGGEST MISTAKE OF MY LIFE.
OH, MY GOD...
HRHH WELCOME TO THE DANELAW.
THE END?